Letters to Madeleine

THE FRENCH LIST

GUILLAUME APOLLINAIRE

Letters to Madeleine

Tender as Memory

EDITED BY LAURENCE CAMPA

TRANSLATED BY
DONALD NICHOLSON-SMITH

LONDON NEW YORK CALCUTTA

Seagull Books, 2018

This work has received support from the Historial de la Grande Guerre, Péronne (Somme), France. Photographic reproduction: Bibliothèque Nationale de France

Translated from *Lettres à Madeleine*: *Tendre comme le souvenir*. Augmented and revised editon, edited by Laurence Campa

First published in English by Seagull Books, 2010

ISBN   978 0 8574 2 582 9

British Library Cataloguing-in-Publication Data
A catalogue record for this book is available
from the British Library

Typeset and designed by Seagull Books, Calcutta, India
Printed at Leelabati Printers, Calcutta, India

Contents

Translator's Note   *vi*

Editor's Foreword   *viii*

Editor's Note on the New French Edition (2005)   *xxi*

Preface to the 1952 edition by Madeleine Pagès   *xxiii*

Letters to Madeleine   1

Addenda:
Four Undated Poems
and an Undated Postcard   602

Translator's Note

This translation of Apollinaire's wartime letters to Madeleine Pagès, though naturally as faithful as I can make it, has no scholarly ambitions. Translator's notes have been kept to the barest minimum (and indicated, along with Laurence Campa's editorial notes, by means of superior Arabic numerals). My aim has been a sort of English facsimile of the prose, complete with its idiosyncrasies, and a serviceable translation of the poems. In this spirit I have imitated Apollinaire's defiance of the conventions regarding commas and stops and other punctuation, and his occasional telegraphese and abbreviation, without slavishly following every instance of such transgressions and always allowing the English-language reader's need for clarity to guide me.

In the same spirit of mimicry I have done nothing to soften the repetitious and perhaps even tiresome effect of Apollinaire's endless declarations of love for Madeleine. One might do worse, in the poet's defence, than recall Francis Bacon's remark that 'speaking in a perpetual hyperbole is comely in nothing but in love'.

Inasmuch as I felt I must choose one particular form of English, I tried my best to have Apollinaire 'express himself' in the idiom being used at the time by his British opposite numbers never far distant from him on the Western Front.

As for the poems sent to Madeleine, I have kept the French and followed it in each case with a plain translation. I would urge anyone interested in an English-language commentary on the majority of the poems sent to Madeleine, which were eventually incorporated in their final versions into Apollinaire's collection *Calligrammes* (1918), to consult Anne Hyde Greet and S. I. Lockerbie's magisterial annotated translation: *Calligrammes*: *Poems of Peace and War* (*1913–1916*) (Berkeley: University of California Press, 1980).

I am most grateful to Fabrice Rozié of the Cultural Services of the French Embassy in New York and Guy Walter of the Villa Gillet in Lyons for offering me a translator's residency under the auspices of the Villa. During my two sojourns by the Saône everyone concerned showed me unstinting hospitality and kindness—and friendship.

The present translation benefited in 2008 from a grant (*bourse de séjour*) from the French Centre National du Livre to facilitate library research in Paris, and for that I am very much obliged.

I wish to thank all who those who have so generously offered help on issues of fact or translation or literary judgement, among them Marie-France Albert, Robert and Evelyne Chasse, Hélène Fleury, Claire Labarbe, Cathy Pozzo di Borgo, and Alyson Waters.

Mia Nadezhda Rublowska has applied her critical eye to every word of this work and there is no way for me to thank her adequately for her contribution. She was present at the birth of the project, indeed before it was even a gleam in the translator's eye. This translation is dedicated with love to Mia.

D. N.-S

TRANSLATOR'S NOTE

Editor's Foreword

'You should know that this region is now full of enchantment for me because of the letters I have received from you here, and because of the great secret, our secret, that you have entrusted to me.' When he wrote this sentence to Madeleine Pagès on 17 July 1915, Guillaume Apollinaire found himself 'amid the horrible horror of millions of fat bluebottles' in the sector of Les Hurlus, 'a sinister place where, to all the horrors of war, to the horror of the site itself, and to the terrifying proximity of so many cemeteries, is added the dearth of trees, of water, even of any real earth' (letter of 1 July 1915). The loving couple had declared their feelings for each other a few days earlier. Love became their secret and their most precious possession: 'You are right,' the poet reiterated on 13 August 1915. 'We shall keep our love a secret; it will be ours alone.' From then on, the two undertook to nourish their secret by means of letters and poetry. Apollinaire even devised a new form, the 'secret poem'—pure sensual celebration, an act of love in words offered to the beloved as an authentic gift of the self.

Many years later, in 1952, the first edition of Apollinaire's letters to Madeleine was published as *Tendre comme le souvenir* (Paris: Gallimard). Mademoiselle Pagès, who had hitherto modestly declined to make her personal history public, now consented to the publication of the letters. The poems that Apollinaire had sent her from the Front fell, in fact, into two categories: those, whether love poems or not, such as 'Thunder Palace' or 'Song of the Horizon in Champagne', which were entrusted to Madeleine for protection from the hazards of the war, and which she was to copy with a view to later publication; and those, described as 'secret,' love poems for the most part, which were specifically addressed to her. During the New Year's leave that Apollinaire spent with Madeleine in Oran from 26 December 1915 to 9 January 1916, he asked his fiancée to copy everything that he had sent her. And he informed her that he planned to publish, with all appropriate precautions, several of the 'secret poems' once they were married. This intent, which was a continual worry to Madeleine (see Apollinaire's letter to her of 25 January 1916), was in fact never realized. On the other hand, those poems which Apollinaire eventually included in his *Calligrammes* (1918) lost a good deal of their intimate feeling. Copies made by the young woman and sent back to the poet in the early months of 1916 began to circulate, however, during the interwar years. Some 'secret poems' were even published in a pirate edition in 1949. In these circumstances, wearied by the intrusiveness and pirating, Madeleine Pagès decided that, with the help of Marcel Adéma, she would publish the letters from Apollinaire in her possession.

In compliance with Pagès's wishes, however, the first edition of *Tendre comme le souvenir*, whose title is borrowed from a line of the poem 'À Madeleine,' sent to her by Apollinaire on 11 August 1915, was a book full of obscurities. The surname 'Pagès' did not appear in its pages; many passages were excised; and several 'secret poems' disappeared in whole or in part. These cuts were directed in the main at the most erotic sections, but they also included references to Madeleine's own letters that were deemed too specific, and realistic allusions to her body. That first edition also occasionally eliminated references to various figures—relatives, friends or acquaintances of the lovers. For instance, in his letter of 30 July 1915, where he recounts the incident of the Iberian statuettes stolen from the Louvre, which occasioned his brief imprisonment in the prison of La Santé in 1911, Apollinaire implicated Picasso, but the painter's name was replaced by an 'X' in *Tendre comme le souvenir*, even though research had long since established Picasso's involvement.

Some omissions were clearly designed to protect Apollinaire's own military honour: at the end of his long letter of 30 July 1915, for instance, he wished himself and Madeleine far away 'from this war which goes on forever and on which as a good soldier I shall refrain from stating an opinion even though I do have one in my heart of hearts that is henceforward irreversible.' And on 9 December, sorely tested by having been kept on the front line since 28 November, he wrote to his fiancée that 'a lucky wound could end this war for me and get me to safety'. Thousands of servicemen must surely have made the same wish after a few weeks of combat. Today such sentiments, so far from diminishing Apollinaire's dignity and courage, reveal a touching fragility in him, along with an absence of either bellicosity or irresolution.

There were a few other excisions too, seemingly insignificant but no doubt meaningful to Madeleine Pagès.

In 1966 Pierre-Marcel Adéma and Michel Décaudin prepared a revised version of *Tendre comme le souvenir* for inclusion in Apollinaire's complete works.[1] Conformity to the text of the original letters was enhanced, and a certain number of additions were made, but many gaps remained; it was still too early to reveal all the secrets of the correspondence.

1 *Oeuvres complètes*, VOL. 4 (Paris: Balland-Lecat, 1966).

Today all such obstacles have been removed. This new edition of Apollinaire's letters to Madeleine Pagès presents all the extant texts in unabridged form. Complete exhaustiveness is impossible to achieve, however, for though almost all the poet's letters are preserved in the manuscripts department of the Bibliothèque Nationale de France, there are a few lacunae. Some of these it has been possible to fill by reference to other sources, but in some cases all traces have been lost, notably in that of Apollinaire's very last letters to Madeleine in the winter of 1916. Madeleine's own letters, too, are inaccessible, scattered in private collections. But now at least we have a much clearer and more coherent version of the correspondence. Even as relayed via the responses of 'Gui', Madeleine's voice is clearly discernible: it is plain, for example, that she participated actively in the amorous exchange with encouragement, initiative and suggestion. The original title, *Tendre comme le souvenir*, by lending a somewhat sentimental, almost elegiac tone to the letters to Madeleine, effectively attenuated their flamboyant eroticism. The present restoration of the text in its entirety points up the sensual and lyrical crescendo that it embodies; and the radical shift in tone that occurs after Apollinaire's leave in Oran appears by extension even more brutal and distressing. This gripping love story nevertheless retains all the mystery that likens it to life itself.

* * *

On 2 January 1915, Apollinaire bade farewell to his mistress Lou de Coligny-Châtillon at the Nice station after a forty-eight-hour leave spent with her. He was returning to the 38th Field Artillery Regiment in Nîmes, where he was in training. In his compartment he met a young schoolteacher, Madeleine Pagès, travelling to Marseilles to catch a boat: after spending the holidays at her sister-in-law's house in

Nice, she was heading home to Lamur, near Oran in Algeria. The two passengers took a liking to each other, spoke of poetry, and exchanged addresses.

Three months later, on 28 March, after a final meeting in Marseilles, Apollinaire and Lou separated definitively while vowing to write to one another and remain friends. On 4 April, which was Easter Sunday, Apollinaire left Nîmes by military train for the Champagne front, arriving at Mourmelon-le-Grand two days later. He took up his duties as liaison agent on 10 April in the wooded and boggy sector of Beaumont-sur-Vesles, some twelve kilometres behind the firing line. More shaken by the break-up with Lou than he was ready to admit, the poet stoked the dying embers of their love by addressing poems to her that alternated between the melancholic and the playful.[2] Beginning in the early summer, his letters to his former lover grew less and less frequent, eliciting not a little irritation on Lou's part. The fact was that, as early as 16 April, he had sent his first missive, a postcard, to Mademoiselle Pagès. Very soon his letters, with Madeleine's complicity, took on first a bantering and then a distinctly tender tone. For several weeks he begged his 'petite fée', his little fairy, to make him a declaration of love: on 2 July, he implored her to 'write those words that make one live'. Once such vows had been exchanged, the two of them developed an epistolary relationship founded on the notions of love at first sight and of the perfect love. Their correspondence transcended the distance between them. By means of letters they got to know each other and learnt how to love and desire each other. A teacher of French at a girls' lycée in Oran, Madeleine was twenty-two, having been born on 14 November 1892 in La Roche-sur-Yon (Vendée). Her father, a philosophy teacher, was now dead. As the eldest daughter of a large family, she lived with her mother and helped take care of five younger siblings. Her older brother Jean, married and a resident of Nice, was on active duty in the artillery. The partic-

2 See Guillaume Apollinaire, *Lettres à Lou* (Michel Décaudin ed.) (Paris: Gallimard, 1969).

xii

ulars of her personal life were of scant interest to Apollinaire, how-ever. Deeply preoccupied by his love for her, and forever scrutinizing his photographs of her, his main concern was to solidify his evanescent image of this untouchable young woman with her grey-green eyes and long dark hair. He continually urged her to describe herself in the most intimate detail. Though no dragon of virtue, his virginal corre-spondent was naturally not prepared to comply without protest. For letter after letter, the poet strove mightily to persuade her of his sin-cerity. He even bared his own soul, as it were, by offering a detailed account of his past love life (30 July 1915). Replacing the military topography that surrounded him by an emotional one, a *Carte du Ten-dre* of his own, Apollinaire sought, so as not to alarm the object of his affections, to advance one step at a time through the initial thrill of discovery, the pleasure of intimacy, and the fluster of emotional fusion. He sounded out misunderstandings and strove to outflank the obstacles set up by modesty. He was by turns seductive and courtly, authoritarian and easygoing, suggestive and straighforward, whimsi-cal and passionate. How could Madeleine have failed in the end to succumb to so extraordinarily liberal-minded a suitor, as impatient with convention as he was with credibility, who passed so easily from outrageousness to subtlety and used pious lies to expresss his true feel-ings? The poet pressed all the powers of his pen into the service of love, producing a steady stream of long discourses, dazzling insights, poems with multiple meanings, and elegant 'calligrammes'.

On 10 August 1915, Apollinaire asked Madame Pagès for her daughter's hand in marriage. His request was favourably received. Once officially engaged, the couple were able to give free rein to their sensual exchange. Apollinaire's letters became ever more passionate. His love poems, hitherto sentimental and delicate, now burnt with an extraordinary intensity and combined the influences of Greek mythol-ogy and the Song of Songs with the daily reality of war. Neither his duties as a chief of piece as of 1 September, nor the major offensive that began in Champagne on the twenty-fifth of that month, nor even his transfer to the front line as an infantry officer at the end of November could stanch the flow of Apollinaire's letters to Madeleine.

At the end of December, the long-awaited leave of Second Lieutenant Guillaume Apollinaire de Kostrowitzky arrived at last. He spent fifteen days in Oran. Upon his return, he still seemed deeply affected by the sweetness of his fiancée and aglow from the Algerian sunshine. Yet of his earlier erotic élan no trace remained. His letters, still affectionate, tended to get shorter. Apollinaire evoked the possibility of a marriage by proxy without much apparent conviction. Before long, it became clear that his heart was no longer in it; the poet was sending his fiancée little more than platitudes, forgetting many a time to add a tender word, or even to sign his letter. Understandably enough, Madeleine was alarmed; Apollinaire blamed his living conditions for his lack of demonstrativeness: at this time he was on a rest period in Damery, an exhausting period during which as a field officer he was obliged to attend lectures, go on endless manoeuvres and suffer all the agonies of barracks life.

This change of heart is nevertheless mysterious. We know nothing of Apollinaire's stay in Oran. Was he disappointed in this fiancée whose image his wishes and imagination had so passionately constructed? Did the large Pagès family intrude too much on the lovers' intimacy? Or did the poet experience the same distress as so many other soldiers on leave driven into deep depression by the contrast between life at the Front and life behind the lines? What is certain is that Apollinaire's return to active duty compromised an equilibrium that the power of love was soon no longer able to buttress. Despite his familiarity with combat, despite his grit and force of character, there can be no doubt that, like his friend Gabriel Boissy whom he met again at Damery and who seemed to him prematurely aged (letter of 19

January 1916), and indeed like most participants in this apocalypse, Apollinaire fell victim to the trauma of war. All the same, his letters to Madeleine were now markedly gloomier than those he sent to other correspondents. The wound he sustained on 17 March 1916 worsened his detachment. True, he scribbled a few words to Madeleine from the ambulance unit in the Aisne where he was immediately taken, and again from the Hôtel-Dieu in Château-Thierry where he received first aid; later he sent her news of his progress from the Val-de-Grâce and Italian hospitals in Paris, but he dissuaded her from coming to see him. The complications ensuing from his injury tested him sorely. After his trepanning on 9 May, devastated by the death of several comrades-in-arms and 'disgusted' by the attitude of Paris society to the war, the convalescent Apollinaire, without saying it in so many words, effectively abandoned his fiancée. By the end of 1916, everything was over between them.

* * *

These letters to Madeleine Pagès have great biographical and historical value. They constitute a unique document on the life of the fighting forces during the Great War. At the same time they bear witness to the characteristic yet deeply idiosyncratic experience of the author of *Calligrammes* at an especially crucial moment of his existence as man and artist. The young woman to whom he writes is straightforward, sensitive and cultured. Apollinaire can share with her his thoughts on art and literature, on Racine and Romain Rolland, Paul Fort and Perrault, Tolstoy and Dostoevsky. He tells her about his childhood and his tastes, offering the smallest details of his daily life at the Front and his grandest aesthetic ideas. He puts much more of himself into these letters than he had in his mostly earlier correspondence with Lou. In his very first letters to Madeleine, he sketches a not unhumorous self-portrait. His personality as a poet is the aspect of himself that he is most concerned to convey, reassuring the young woman while at the same time pointing up the appeal of his circumstances: 'My poet's life is assuredly of the oddest, but fate has always beset me with so many troubles, which despite all I find utterly delightful, that I am one of humanity's greatest joys' (30 July 1915).

For Apollinaire, who never kept a war diary in any ordinary sense, his letters served as a kind of journal in which he could record impressions that he intended to make use of once peace came. Events and personal choices had thrust this man, so accustomed to Parisian comforts, the pleasures of feminine company and the effervescence of a cosmopolitan artistic milieu, into the chaos of a rough, masculine and precarious world. As an N.C.O. in the artillery, he lived at first in a hut in the woods, then in a 'hypogeum' or dugout in a cemetery. Later, as an infantry officer, he found himself in a trench where, 'down below ground' (2 December 1915), exposed to the most fearsome machinery of war, he slept on the bare earth, waded through the mud—and led a wandering and unblinkered life not unlike that of the itinerant circus performers who had peopled his poems of an earlier day. A loyal friend, he mourned his dead comrades; a caring officer, he strove to ameliorate the wretched living conditions of the thirty-odd men in his section, men whose fate he shared.

How was it possible to hold on? To avoid falling prey to alienation and brutalization? As a volunteer, Apollinaire chose the ascetic path, which he evokes in the poem 'Exercise' (sent on 22 November 1915). But above all he had a fierce faith in his own imaginative and creative powers, and counted on them to transfigure the realities of war. He made an art of the craft activity in which some of his comrades engaged with a view to commerce or barter, turning aluminium from a German plane that had crashed between the lines into engagement rings 'fallen from the heavens' that he sent to his fiancée (20 October 1915).

His chief preoccupation and his salvation was loving Madeleine and telling her so in writing. No matter how frequently he was interrupted, he would always take up a letter where he had left off, disregarding disjointedness or repetition. No matter if he was called upon to give the order to fire: let the dust dry the ink on his missive. The more dangerous his circumstances grew, the more he crammed onto each page, leaving not a single blank space, taking possession of Madeleine, writing to feel alive, penning every letter as though it were the last. The whole sheaf of this correspondence bears traces of the conditions under which Apollinaire wrote: he used military postcards, stray pieces of paper inscribed in pencil, wrapping paper, magazine covers, whatever was to hand. On 30 August 1915, recently assigned the task of 'fire observer', completely alone at night on 'a desolate hilltop subjected to continual bombardment', Apollinaire wrote to Madeleine on a tiny rectangle of paper that he darkened over its entire surface with a microscopic script suggesting the tenuousness of the poet's life itself.

For Apollinaire writing was the last refuge of beauty: the second poem sent to Madeleine was a calligrammatic composition written on a piece of birch bark, birch being a common tree in the vicinity; and the poem 'To Madeleine' was inscribed on the back of a picture of General Joffre cut out in the shape of an artillery shell—the plastic expression of an oft-recurring Apollinairian poetic and erotic image. The creator is always at work, shifting the tone, alternating between free verse and rhyme, calligrammes and drawings, habitually cannibalizing several old poems to construct new ones. Amorous lyricism is not confined to love poetry: at times it animates the prose of the letters, lending it a rhythm of its own, a poetic quality.

What becomes of someone who thus entrusts his fate to the vicissitudes of love and poetry? Once enlisted, how well can creativity with its limited means defend life? War put Apollinaire's poetic powers, fierce will and vitality to the severest of tests. 'La Tranchée', a poem written shortly after his transfer to the infantry and discovery of the farthest limits of the conflict's atrocity, and sent to Madeleine on 7 December 1915, shows just how hard it is for poetry to encapsulate horror. The sheer scale of the war's devastation, and before long the waning of love worked overtime to stem the flow of inspiration of a poet who just a few months earlier (11 August 1915) had asserted that 'Life is painful only for those who keep their distance from poetry, thanks to which it is true that we are made in God's image.' The story of Gui and Madeleine is indeed a sad one. Its end signals the retreat, albeit temporary, of poetry and love in face of war triumphant.

* * *

Living, loving and creating were one and the same for Apollinaire. Of the fact that the poet needed to be in love in order to tolerate war, to protect and preserve himself, there can be no doubt. But nor should doubt be cast on the sincerity of his feelings towards Madeleine, or towards Lou. The apparent similarity between the two sets of letters, however, turns out on closer inspection to go no deeper than the sweet nothings of all amorous exchange.

With Madeleine, Apollinaire opted for secrecy. But the fertile and inventive mind of this master of the paradox turned the constraints of the military censorship into a means for refining the art of letter-writing, so that discretion itself nourished love and sparked creativity. 'Adding to the secrecy' meant enlarging the place of love and poetry in the life of the combatant, reducing the distance between him and Madeleine by widening the gap between the two of them and the rest of the world: secrecy became a bulwark against promiscuity, vulgarity, horror. Readers who relish the extreme freedom of Apollinaire's letters to Lou will find, to their surprise or even disappointment, that those to Madeleine, while no less intense, are informed by the poet's rather conventional ideal of marriage. The conjugal arrangement that he calls 'Duty' does not correspond merely to a deep aspiration of his own, and to the wishes of Madeleine, but also in its way to a basic ambition of Apollinaire's poetics, namely the fusion of order and adventure. Within the privacy of the marriage relationship, the madness of the erotic could be unleashed without disturbing Madeleine's modesty. In this way love became a cult, a mystery after the fashion of the ancient Eleusinian festivities, and called for 'a special language' (18 September 1915) embodying the rhythms of intimate discovery: little by little, in parallel with the progression towards carnal union, the language of love found its own words. What finer mission could a poet undertake? 'Adding to the secrecy' thus entailed an enrichment of language—its mining and reinvention for the sake of penetrating the mystery of Madeleine'a body, glimpsed on the train to Nice, unknown, inviolate, violently desired. For Apollinaire the sex of the woman loved became the forecourt (*parvis*) of a holy temple reserved for a solitary initiate. In 'The 6th Secret Poem', set down beneath a pen-and-ink drawing of a panther,[3] Madeleine takes the form of a luxuriant realm, a deep jungle filled by the sounds of fabulous beasts. In the frigid moonscape of the Champagne front, where every minute might be the last, the poet's imagination and words explored a dark virgin forest, exorcising the disasters of History by evoking the *illud tempus* of myth. This was assuredly a kind of madness, but Apollinaire entertained a clear-eyed hope that he might yet escape the fatal destiny of Ixion coupling with a mere 'cloud image' of his beloved Juno, and that his own inspiration, his 'dearest handiwork' might become flesh.

3 See p. 284.

With respect to war and love alike, these letters push the clash between the violence of reality and the powers of language as far as it will go.

* * *

In the interwar years, Madeleine, who never married, taught first at the girls' lycée of Saint-Cloud and then at a lycée in Nice. She left all her pupils with glowing memories of her. In Nice she lived in the same street where Apollinaire had enlisted in December 1914. She died at Antibes in 1965.

The Great War tested Apollinaire's resources to the limit, but he was ready to defend life, creativity and love to his last breath. Madeleine was undoubtedly something of a cloud image, yet it was she who allowed Apollinaire to live, to write, to know happiness 'despite the sadness of the chalk and the never-ending brutality of the cannon fire' ('Plainte', sent on 8 October 1915). Perhaps, after the fashion of the purloined letter, the secret of this correspondence lies in plain sight, in the simple beauty of this line from the poem 'Hill 146' sent to Madeleine on 2 July 1915):

Madeleine whatever does not belong to love is so much lost

Laurence Campa

xx

Editor's Note on the New French Edition (2005)

xxi

The present edition seeks to follow Apollinaire's manuscripts as closely as possible, restoring passages previously modified or omitted and so far as possible rectifying all earlier misreadings.[1] Every effort has been made to preserve Apollinaire's punctuation, even though that punctuation, as was the poet's wont, is extremely erratic, and even in many places frankly indecipherable. Once they recover from their initial surprise, readers, especially those familiar with Apollinaire, should have no difficulty following the poet's rhythm. On the other hand, spelling has been corrected or harmonized, and missing letters and syllables supplied. A very few passages have been repunctuated to facilitate comprehension. Did not Apollinaire himself write to Madeleine, 'my little fairy will no doubt supply the words left out and repair awkward sentences and other shortcomings' (30 July 1915)? The compact feeling of certain pages, startling changes of subject, syntactical wanderings and oversights of various kinds are all apt to disconcert at first. Yet the unaffected spontaneity and poignantly precarious feeling make us ever more aware that these are both love and war letters.

1 The editors of the first edition (1952) did not only eliminate many passages in accordance with the wishes of Madeleine Pagès, they also repunctuated and reparagraphed the letters, doubtless out of concern for readability. Pierre-Marcel Adéma was furthermore obliged to transcribe the manuscript letters in very short order, with the result that many errors inevitably crept in. The expanded version of the Balland-Lecat edition of 1996 was much improved in all these respects. [A few minor corrections to the 2005 edition were made for the cheaper 'Folio' reprint of 2006 (Paris: Gallimard).—Tr.]

The diagrams, drawings and calligrammatic poems that enrich this correspondence have been reproduced in facsimile.[2] The texts of calligrammes have also been given in the body of the text, although it should be borne in mind that Apollinaire's calligrammes are forms whose meaning depends on the interaction of all their component elements—visual, written or audible—and on a spatial reading, an overall apprehension, of the 'text'. Linear transcription can thus amount to no more than a kind of aid to decipherment, and it is offered here merely to enhance the reader's appreciation of the surprising beauty of these poems and the new aesthetic principle to which they answer.

Nota bene: Editorial notes are indicated by superior Arabic numerals; asterisks refer the reader to Apollinaire's notes in the margins of his letters.

L. C.

[2] Some rudimentary and anecdotal diagrams accompanying Apollinaire's letters of 14 September 1915 and 23 February 1916 have been omitted.

Preface to the 1952 Edition by Madeleine Pagès

I first met Guillaume Apollinaire on the train taking me back from Nice to Marseilles on 1 January 1915. I had been spending my Christmas holidays in Nice with the family of my elder brother, a second lieutenant in the artillery, and was now returning to Oran on the boat sailing from Marseilles that evening, the *Sidi-Brahim* I think it was.

I was happy. I had enjoyed my holiday. My suitcase was full of presents for my mother, sisters and little brothers waiting for me at home. I was wearing a pretty hat that I was very proud of, and the morning was glorious.

Getting my ticket for this eight o'clock train and picking a second-class compartment right in the middle of the carriage had all seemed easy and pleasant. So it was with confidence that I climbed in, lifted my case onto the netting and set a book, a newspaper and some sandwiches near to hand.

The station seemed deserted except for the few employees on duty. Cosy in my corner, I was getting ready to relish the joy of solitude all the way to Marseilles when a soldier came into the compartment and murmured an apology as he slipped in front of me and leant out of the window to speak to a lady who was seeing him off. Was he a private or an officer, I wondered. But I have never known how to tell ranks apart. All I knew was that he was tall, or tallish, but rather short in the legs and barrel-chested. He wore a képi that was too small for him, pushed back on his head.

So much for my solitude. I was tempted to move to the next compartment, but how to do so without its being obvious? But now the soldier was speaking softly to the lady: 'Poetry? You say you would like to read some poetry? Read Baudelaire's *Fleurs du Mal*.'

Had he really said 'Baudelaire's *Fleurs du Mal*'? That did it: I would stay put.

The lady came into the compartment for a moment to say her goodbyes to the soldier. She was tall and thin, and seemed tired. I slipped out into the corridor so as not to seem indiscreet.

When the lady got off I returned to my seat, and once again I heard the soldier's voice as he leant out of the window: 'Don't stay there on the platform—you'll catch cold. Go back to the hotel, the room is paid for until noon.'

The train pulled out. The morning was now finer than ever. The carriage was well heated. I smiled to myself as I thought of the knick-knacks in my suitcase and how happy my sisters would be when they got them. I wanted to tell someone about them.

There it was!—the little beach with its pink sand and its pines where I had gone with my brother at the time of his wedding the year before. And there was the sea, so beautiful! I must have reacted audibly at the sight of it, for the soldier left his own corner and stood by me, and we both gazed at it, suddenly united in our admiration for its marvellous blueness.

We spoke then of Nice, which we were leaving behind and which he knew better than I. I listened wide-eyed as he began to tell me about the Old City with its Italian houses and laundry strung up in raggedy banners across the streets; as he spoke of the market, of Paillon and of Les Collinettes, I took a liking to his slightly husky voice, his profile, and the indolent movements of his hands, which bore no ring. His quick glances in my direction put me completely at ease.

We passed the roadstead of Golfe Juan, where that morning ships of the Mediterranean Fleet lay at anchor; we saw the little sails of fishing boats that had put out despite the holiday; and the cactuses clinging to the shoreline put me in mind of Oran, Algiers and Bône—all those towns where I had lived and that I found lovelier and livelier than those we were leaving behind. Whenever I spoke to my travelling companion I smiled unabashedly now, and each time I looked up I found his gaze fixed on me. His eyes were brown, like his hair; his features were truly striking—he was distinctly more handsome without his képi. But it was ten o'clock! Not without a deep blush, I offered him one of my extra sandwiches, and he accepted it amiably. As the train picked up speed, the two of us chewed in unselfconscious contentment to its rhythm, and somehow or other we got to talking of the poets: I fancy he asked me, as he made short work of a slice of ham, whether I liked poetry, and I replied that I held it as dear as life itself, and indeed could not separate the two. So delighted was he with this response that I thought he was going to kiss me; I felt there was something he wanted to tell me, but he bethought himself and began bringing up various poets. He asked me which ones I knew, and who my favourites were, and after a moment we were vying with one another uproariously as we named poets and recited lines[1]:

Voici des fruits, des fleurs, des feuilles et des branches
Here are fruits, flowers, leaves and branches

[1] The verses quoted are from Verlaine, Baudelaire, Clément Marot and Villon respectively.—Tr.

* * *

Sois sage ô ma douleur et tiens-toi plus tranquille

Be good, my sorrow, and quiet yourself down

And the following verses we recited together, suddenly standing at the window, looking out at the coast, itself so young, and the shimmering sea:

Sur le printemps de ma jeunesse folle
Je ressemblais l'arondelle qui vole . . .

In the springtime of my wild youth
I was like a swallow on the wing

'Do you know Villon, Mademoiselle? He is so dear to my heart.' To this I delightedly responded:

Femme je suis, povrette et ancienne,
Qui rien ne scay: oncques lettre ne leuz

A woman am I, a poor old woman
Who knows nothing, and cannot read a single letter

* * *

But before long the poetry itself made us more serious and more distant and dreamy, and I sank back into my corner and closed my eyes.

The verses he had been reciting continued to run through my head. Never before had I prized them so highly. It was as though he had held them in his hands and enjoyed their feel as much as their sound, yet he had pronounced them, or rather murmured them, with a simplicity that I could never rival: amazed, disarmed, I had let him complete even the lines begun by me.

When the train stopped at Fréjus a new passenger entered our compartment. What a shame! But truth to tell I had no wish to go on talking, and I folded my hands demurely over my closed book.

The newcomer sat across from us—the soldier moved not at all, as though to convey the impression that he and I were travelling together. I was slightly embarrassed to be caught on such friendly terms with someone who was after all a stranger.

The soldier himself was not happy, as I could tell from the sighing and fidgetiness to my left, where he was sitting. My embarrassment notwithstanding, I was concerned about the little disappointment that he had suffered on my account, and after a moment I turned towards him with a smile. His response was so shy and his answering smile so wide that I was quite flustered. Never before in my life had I been enveloped by such a rush of tender feelings. Just then, however, the stranger started to talk to the soldier, asking him about his company and his depot and other military matters that held no interest for me. Before long the topic shifted to business, trade problems, transportation bottlenecks and who knows what. The soldier always had precise answers. The two men soon discovered that they had acquaintances in common. When Monaco came up, the soldier mentioned having attended a Catholic school there, upon which his interlocutor exclaimed 'So did I!' When they introduced themselves, I heard the soldier give a foreign surname that I could not catch and the given name Guillaume. As dates were compared, it transpired that the soldier's brother Albert had been a classmate of the other man's. At which juncture my soldier turned to me and, by way of including me in the conversation, began telling funny stories about a particular teacher who, if the tales were to be believed, must have had a terrible time with young men given to releasing cockchafers in the classroom, sticking papier-mâché pellets to the ceiling, and tormenting him with all manner of charming tricks of that kind. I laughed, but sensed that there was more than a little rodomontade in these anecdotes, and that my soldier, at the age of twelve, must surely have been a good-natured lad, chubby and placid and a dreamer quite incapable, whatever he might now claim, of harming a fly.

The other man got off at the next station, and we were alone once again, our mood a little more serious. The soldier reached for my book and toyed with it for a moment. In a slow voice he began speaking of poetry again, of how much it could express and how it could bring things to life. Then he started trying in a playful spirit to encapsulate each of the towns we had passed through in a single image. Nice he saw as a rearing horse, a thoroughbred on its hind legs amidst the cheering and the tossed flowers of Carnival.

For my part I envisioned Villefranche as a great conch shell open to sea and sky.

Very softly, as if picking up the thread of our earlier conversation, he murmured, 'I too am a poet, Mademoiselle. My pen name is Guillaume Apollinaire. Have you ever heard of me?'

A poet! He was a poet! I could hardly wait to tell my family at home. I was almost choking with excitement, yet I could only reply, in weak and uncertain tones, that no, I had never heard of him.

He was surprised by my answer. 'You seem so well informed in Algeria about the poets that I supposed . . .'

'I'm ashamed to tell you,' I replied, 'that my knowledge of modern poets is derived solely from a little anthology that costs all of fifteen sous and is called *The Hundred Best French Poems*. There is nothing of yours in there yet, at least not in my edition!'

He assured me that the selection must nonetheless be very good, judging by all that I had learned by heart. 'But I would so like you to be acquainted with my verse. With your permission, I'll send you a volume, *Alcools*, that appeared in 1913, and I hope you will tell me what you think of it.' I thanked him with a nod and a smile.

His name now began to seem so familiar to me that I doubted my own memory: Guillaume Apollinaire! How could I have told him that his name was unknown to me?

Had that name not jumped out at me one morning from the newspaper? Had I not found it to be a fine name? And had I not been amused by the bold allusion to Apollo?

All the same, I was so uncertain of this recollection that I did not mention it, and we both fell silent, lost in our thoughts.

I wondered whether the lady in Nice was reading *Les Fleurs du Mal* by now, if she had been able to find it at the station bookstall.

I checked to see whether my railway ticket was safely in my bag. I had to find my steamer ticket too.

I must think as well about how I could get rid of this soldier—in a nice way, of course, but firmly: I could hardly go walking in Marseilles with him!

I began to have doubts about the little presents I was taking home: miniature Copenhagen china no bigger than one's thumb—a small vase decorated with a blue flower pattern on a white ground, and a miniature coffee service on a tray which I had earlier found quite delightful. Would my soldier not perhaps have looked more favourably on the Nabeul glazed earthenware that I used to take home from Bône—little objects of a far simpler and more authentic kind?

He had leant his head back against the upholstery, closed his eyes and seemed suddenly sad and weary. I was overwhelmed by an expressiveness that I would never have thought possible for a face in repose.

Opening his eyes, he drew a tiny notebook from his pocket and held it out to me. 'Would you be so kind as to write your address here?' I used his pencil, writing with great care. I omitted 'Mademoiselle', a gesture I felt was relaxed and—well, charming; but then I decided that my bare name on the paper was in distinctly bad taste.

The tenderest of smiles from the soldier made life feel sweet and simple again.

We were coming into Marseilles, and it was time to put my hat back on. The soldier passed it to me. Before the mirror I fluffed up my hair and with astonishment contemplated the changed face I saw there, rather pale and with eyes that were too large. Then, behind my reflection, I saw that of the poet, observing my movements with amusement, and was able to look at him for longer than at any time since the beginning of our journey.

xxx

As I lowered my veil over my face our eyes met in the mirror and I smiled at him, overjoyed at his attentive and tender gaze but disturbed by feelings all trace of which must be banished from my eyes before I left the mirror and turned round.

The little veil that with upraised fingers I tightened around my throat and secured at the nape of my neck with a little pin nevertheless distanced me somewhat from him. He realized this, and his eyes, which I scrutinized apprehensively, became sad; so did his mouth, and the whole of that face which, now that I had turned towards him, I no longer wished to look at.

The time came to get my suitcase down: the train was pulling into the station. Saying goodbye would be difficult, and I was eager for it to be over.

I could no longer bear his tender glances, his sweet voice, and the idea of touching his hand was intolerable; I felt I might take to my heels the instant we were out of the carriage.

I could not wait to be on the platform, on the boat—indeed I wished I were already back at home.

I needed him to be gone—so that I could think about him.

The train had come to a halt. The soldier got out first, with my suitcase, then turned and helped me out, like a lady, holding my hand in his for a moment and kissing it. I don't know whether we bade each other farewell, but I began to run, my heart pounding. Before reaching the barrier, however, I turned and saw him standing in front of our carriage door, arms dangling, watching me run.

Had he seen me look back? He must have, for he started running after me, and just as I was handing my ticket to the collector in frantic haste I felt his breath on the back of my neck and heard him murmur 'Au revoir, Mademoiselle'.

This time I did not turn, but leapt into a cab at the front of the station, crying 'To the dock, please, driver, to the Compagnie des Transports Maritimes, for the *Sidi-Brahim*!'

It was only once I was safe in my cabin, which the chief steward kindly opened for me two hours in advance, did I begin to regret my mad flight, and to find the words of farewell that I should have spoken.

Here I was, the would-be seasoned traveller, quick-witted and distinguished, emancipated in speech and style, reduced to an ill-mannered young girl—or, even more horrifying, to an unworldly *provincial*. Yes, that was it: an unworldly provincial! Whatever must he think of me?

Why, he must think just that!

What was more, I had omitted to have lunch in Marseilles. So much for the bouillabaisse at Basso's meant to add a colourful detail to the family chronicle, to which I added a chapter each time I went travelling.

Would they all be at dockside to greet me?

I should not mention the poet too soon: I must plan my effects carefully. A few oratorical precautions would need to be taken to make sure that my story was perfectly conveyed, but I felt that in that respect I could rely on the inspiration of the moment.

Stretched out on my bunk, I was aware as in a dream of the sounds of the ship being prepared for departure; in any case I knew these sounds so well that I had no need to listen to them. The chief steward had assured me that I would be alone in the cabin since there were so few passengers at this season, and I was delighted to hear it.

Three strident blasts on the siren, and we were on our way. But the sea I had found so beautiful that morning was getting rough, and on the crossing I was treated to a full-blown storm.

And a private storm too: my first.

Letters to Madeleine

1 Picture postcard: 'Glannes (Meuse): The remains of the village after the passage of the barbarians.'

16 April 1915[1]

Mademoiselle,

I was unable to send my book of poems because my publisher is in the army like me and his firm is closed. I shall send it to you as soon as I can. Do you remember me, between Nice and Marseilles on 1 January?

With my most respectful greetings

I kiss your hand

Guillaume Apollinaire

Sender: Corporal Gui de Kostrowitzky
38th Field Artillery
45th Battery
Postal Sector 59

3

5 May 1914[1]   **1** 1915.

Mademoiselle,

What a terrific surprise I had last night about ten o'clock during an incredibly heavy bombardment accompanied by rifle fire and the continual rattle of machine guns. I was still on horseback, in the dark night of the forest where we live in our huts, when I heard the post orderly shout:

4

'A package from Algeria for you!'

And there sure enough was a lovely parcel from Oran as the Austrian 120s and 88s and the Boche 77s continued to rain down. A miniature ammunition crate loaded with delightful shells of peace! I cannot thank you in person, but until the opportunity to do so presents itself, and since I am not alone in having enjoyed your gracious gift, let me send you the thanks of our battery's N.C.O.'s, all of whom sampled the cigars and like me found them exquisite.

And now, sitting on a sack of oats with a tree trunk for a writing-table, I see you once more, the talkative little traveller with such long eyelashes and such an expressive face. A few short hours on the train! But what a marvellous memory to set against the background of war, as the rain falls and as the thunder over towards Perthes is dealing desperation and death. Around here it is calmer than last night, just the odd shell whining over my hut.

. . . I resume my letter to my discreet and far-off messenger from beautiful sunny Africa; the wind and rain here have completely subsided. The forest with its dark recesses is all around me. Glimpsed between the branches, the sky gives me the gentle impression of a dark blue eye, immense and ever-faithful.

We are at the very forefront of France-in-arms. The artillery is very close to the infantry, whose trenches are just sixty metres from those of the Germans. Every single tree is scarred by shellfire; the trunks are smashed—chewed up like the ends of the pen-holders of my schooldays . . .

> *Voici quelques pauvres fleurettes*
> *De merisier et de lilas . . .*
> *Si Mai, chez vous, a plus de fêtes*
> *Chez nous il a bien plus d'*éclats
> *Mais ce sont nos seules fleurettes*:
> *Brins de merise et de lilas . . .*

> Here are a few poor little flowers
> Cherry blossom and lilac . . .
> If your May has more festivals than ours
> At least we have far more *flashes*[2]
> But these are our only little flowers:
> These sprigs of cherry and lilac

2 Or *shrapnel*.—Tr.

I resume my letter for a 3rd time, by candlelight. Meanwhile the post orderly has brought me my very own sprig of lilac, your charming letter, and first of all I must reply to your postscript. I know nothing of the village you enquire about. I am not even in that sector. It is strictly prohibited for us to send postcards with views of the regions where we are; I am nearer to the Cathedral, the earth here is marly.

I did not dare write you earlier, considering that I was unable to keep my promise to send you *Alcools*, my book of poems. All the

5

GUILLAUME APOLLINAIRE

same, and let me be quite candid about this, I have often, very often thought of you. I am so far away that I feel that I may say as much without shocking you.

Your letter took ten days to reach me, and even though I now have your kind promise, I shall have to wait twenty days or a month for your reply! So write me a little more often, and I for my part will also write as often as I can, if that is agreeable to you, and in my next letter will tell you about my life, the trenches, my horse Loulou and even, if there is room, about poetry.

Unless, of course, too long a silence should give you more than enough news—Mademoiselle, I lay at your feet the very sincerest respects of your

Guillaume Apollinaire

6

Little fairy, we had the same notion, we both felt the same concern: neither of us must let too much time pass before sending news. Your sweet card of today—sent on the 3rd—was an even more marvellous surprise (if possible) than your first letter, for I was expecting nothing before twenty days or so had gone by.

I wanted to write you these last few days but I haven't had a moment to myself—

I promised you details about life here, and this new card of yours asks for such details.

Today let me tell you about the infantrymen's trenches, where I go from time to time. Here is what happened on my last visit to these trenches whose task it is to defend France. I set off with a driver and a gunner. We stopped to look at several unexploded Boche or Austrian shells, then continued on our way until we came upon a battery belonging to another regiment that was then taking up position. Zoom! Bang! An Austrian 88 exploded four steps away from us and the gunners of the other regiment shouted to us to take refuge with them in their barely completed underground shelters, but the bombardment continued. We were flat on our stomachs, crawling. A revolver-cannon shell, a very little shell, buried itself without exploding at the very spot from which we had just crawled away. No sooner did we get into a shelter than a shell went off at the entrance, throwing leaves and earth all over us. We waited the storm out, then

GUILLAUME APOLLINAIRE

off we went again. We reached the infantry trenches without further difficulty. These trenches are white, dug through the chalk, and incredibly clean and silent. As I have written to someone else, I thought that the Great Wall of China must be like this, but this is a ditch, or rather ditches, for all these communication trenches are linked together ad infinitum. They have names. One of them even has your name: Madeleine Alley. I followed its path filled with feelings that I doubt you could take seriously. In each trench, every five or six metres, is a recess you get into so as to let those coming the other way pass, and opposite each such recess is a hole to drain water out. Most of the communication trenches are head height, but there is one through which you have to crawl—a second-line trench. In the front-line trenches we were just 80 metres from the Boche trenches, you could see them easily from the loopholes and bays. There are bays all along the front line, and at some advanced positions instead of bays there are loopholes: wooden crates with no top or bottom set into the parapet with small sandbags above and around them. That is where the sentries are posted. You don't see many soldiers. They are in their dugouts. You may see the feet of those who are sleeping, or sometimes at the entrance to one of these holes someone may be reading. During an earlier visit I came upon a sergeant reading a novel by Walter Scott. This time I found a warrant officer reading Gérard de Nerval's translation of Goethe's *Faust*, a corporal engrossed in Louis Noir's *Les Millions du Trappeur* (The Trapper's Millions), and a second lieutenant with, open upon his knees, that relentlessly depraved book *Dangerous Liaisons*, whose author, Laclos, the undoubted inventor of true vice, Vice with a capital V, was if memory serves an artillery officer. The front-line trenches with their listening posts seemed fragile, light-weight, nothing but a veil over the face of a France that they nevertheless protect from the stings of awful insects.

Bullets whistled over our heads—harmlessly, of course. They whistled through the silence, or rather they lashed that great silence. Here and there a few *poilus* were polishing the rings they make out of aluminium from the fuses of the Boche 77s, but our visit was over and we made our way back to the rear through communication trenches where young soldiers were washing (or delousing) themselves.

Apropos of the rings, if you would be so kind as to send me the measurement of your ring finger, in two or three days I shall make you one like those the others make—that is, if you would like me to. These are not fine jewellery of course, but they are rather nice, rather poignant, and they make amusing war souvenirs. That's all for today—next time I'll tell you about the artillery, which as you know is positioned not far behind the infantry.

I must admit we get a little bored at times in the forest.

Write me at length, my charming little vision. I dare not ask you for a photograph, but if you only knew how much pleasure it would give me to have one, you would perhaps be persuaded to overlook a good many things. Here we are, like wild animals in the forest, and we may well have forgotten the proprieties. But you must not be shocked, for if politeness is no longer our forte I fancy we have made progress with respect to the sort of courtesy whose heyday was the age of chivalry—after all, novels of chivalry are also known as novels of courtly love, and I promise I would attend your portrait with a devotion so immense, so tender, that as distant from you as it might be it could not fail to reach out and touch you. That likeness of you would dwell in the inside pocket of my jacket, on the left side, the same side as my sabre and revolver. Thus pressed close to the heart of your poet, your portrait would be able to chat with those weapons and so be sure of being in good company.

GUILLAUME APOLLINAIRE

9

Un seul bouleau crépusculaire
Sur le mont bleu de la raison . . .
Je prends la mesure angulaire
Du cœur à l'âme et l'horizon.

C'est le galop des souvenances
Parmi les lilas des beaux yeux
Et les canons des indolences
Tirent mes songes vers les cieux . . .

A solitary birch in the twilight
On the blue mountain of reason
I take the angular measurement
Of the heart relative to the soul and the horizon.

This is the gallop of remembrance
Amid the lilacs of beautiful eyes
And the cannons of indolence
Draw my revery heavenwards . . .

Goodbye little fairy so far away and so near, I kiss your hand.

Guillaume Apollinaire

Le ciel est d'un bleu profond[2]
Et mon regard s'y noie et fond

2 Calligrammes written on a piece of birch bark (see p. 262).

The sky is a deep blue
In which my gaze drowns and dissolves

Un invisible obus miaule
J'écris assis au pied d'un saule

An invisible shell whines
I write beneath a willow tree

[in the shape of a star:]

L'étoile du berger déjà
Comme l'aigrette d'un rajah

The shepherd's lamp already
Like a rajah's plume

[in the shape of a cannon:]

ou comme une œillade chérie
brille sur notre batterie

or like a beloved watcher
shining above our battery

Guillaume Apollinaire

at the Front
15 May 1915

My letter must have displeased you, for in your reply of 13 May I detect less spontaneity and quite frankly less amiability than in your first letter and the card that followed. True, you sensitively and completely kept your promise that you would write me at length and your letter is charming and as informative as one might wish, yet it is neither as warm-hearted nor as tender as its predecessor.

We here and I in particular have grown overly sensitive to faraway things that we can only imagine. This is related I suspect to the fact that our sensitivity to the immediate danger has been dulled. I am not explaining this very well, but I feel quite sure you will understand.

You are right to believe in my lucky star, because I believe in it too and I am very happy to think that someone believes in it with me.

But I sense so much sudden restraint in your letter after the charming naivety of the first one that I myself am now too embarrassed, too timid, to open my heart to you.

You will say that the heart has nothing to do with war, with our shelters, or with shells and bombardments. And that's true enough . . .

And I had promised to tell you about the artillery, but I see from your letter that I had already told you about it in my first missive.

Did I mention that my *cagnat*—as we call our little huts—is infested by grass snakes? They coil up gracefully and slither through the reeds, making them rustle. I am used to them now and consider these little creatures benevolent spirits.

I think it is good luck to see snakes. Not that I am excessively superstitious, or even superstitious in the slightest, but I am always ready to rejoice in good omens, and snakes are certainly pleasant messengers of hope.

What is more, my totem animal is the snake. Old Polish families all have totems whose names they bear.* The name of our clan is Wąz, pronounced 'Wonsch', which means serpent, and the coat of arms does indeed show a golden serpent twisted around a gold arrow in pale on an azure ground.

* The clan name is not to be confused with the family name.

Rats are plentiful too, but they are not good housemates for the snakes, their worst enemies.

The trenches of our artillery battery—where we do not stay all the time because we spend one day out of every four resting up in the shelters—are underground, and we come up only to fire the cannon, generally at night.

For the time being, since I am a liaison agent, I never stay in the trenches, even though I do visit every day and most often during the night.

Already the spring blossoms are beginning to fall here, auguring the fruit to come after the summer. Falling blossom saddens me. And I am extremely sad today, deathly sad. The weather is dismal. Yesterday from the infantry trenches we could hear the Boches singing in French in their communication trenches:

13

GUILLAUME APOLLINAIRE

Ah! Qu'ils sont bons quand ils sont cuits
Les Macaronis . . .

Oh! How good it is once it is cooked
That Macaroni . . .

This was their way, of course, of taunting us about the Italians, who are taking so long to make up their minds.

The swine added grotesque insults concerning the virtue of the women in the occupied lands, not very jolly to hear even if the intent is eminently humorous. Even if one is not directly implicated, this sort of thing is bound to make one a little depressed.

So I am in the dumps, and my sole distraction is trying to reconstruct an exact likeness of your face in my mind's eye.

What we see least of all here are women's faces and the faces of the Boches. It is a remarkable fact that so long as I have been at the Front I have never been more than about 2 and ½ kms from the enemy, whose rifles have a range of over 3000 metres, not to mention their cannon—and is it not paradoxical that I have still not seen a single one of these creatures all of whose projectiles, large and small, are so well known to me? My image of the Boches is now based solely on the crackling sound of matches being struck, rifle fire, exploding shells, and the copper or aluminium shell fuses out of which our lads make pen-holders.

I have written quite a few poems recently, but I don't have any today. I will write one for you and enclose it with my next letter.

I daresay you were surprised to receive little poems from me composed in regular verse (though my last consignment on birch bark did contain regular verse, albeit arranged ideographically).

14

The fact is that daring departures by no means imply ignorance. In any case, when it comes to correspondence I most often use regular verse.

Perhaps too my letters shock you because you find only chatter in them and no style. But in the end I reject what has generally been called style for a long time now in all the arts, confining the notion for my part to the actual expression of what is necessary and personal. Discipline and personality—such are the boundaries of style as I understand it; apart from these, there is merely the imitation not of nature but of earlier works of art.

Canons—unlike cannons in the artillery sense—are to my mind quite useless; when it comes to art pure and simple, canons are in the main obstacles to style as I understand it.

That is why I ignore the style of grammarians aesthetes and so-called people of taste and what I ask above all is to be delivered from the kind of taste that saddles us not with discipline but rather with models and canons whose criteria of value and beauty are dubious.

The tradition of peas in the shoes as penance—but boiled in advance by the cunning—is as old as pilgrimages. It is found at least as early as the fifteenth century, and it reflects a very firmly rooted tendency of the people to thumb its nose at saints once they have answered a prayer.

There can be no doubt that to sacrifice your beautiful hair would be a truly terrible loss and that our suffering could never be great enough to justify such an insult to beauty, but what I quite fail to understand is the idea that once the fashion for shaven heads took hold *the feminists would be assured of victory within a very few days.*

GUILLAUME APOLLINAIRE

Do you really suppose men so stupid that women would triumph as soon as they managed to resemble them?

I kiss your hand, my charming African, and with a sigh I add, just like you, *à bientôt*, sweet memory

Guillaume Apollinaire

Yes, dear little fairy, so far away, alas, and yet so near, you wrote me a delightful letter on 17 May and I was mean to write you such a disillusioned one a few days ago, forgive me! Forgive me most of all for allowing myself to feel disillusioned when in fact I had in no sense been deceived and when everything that comes to me from you expresses your extreme generosity, a generosity which in the case of your last letter borders on extravagance. I have read and reread your delightful letter, and how I wish by waving a magic wand I could abolish the distance between us. I too can see your terrace and the burning, clear and violently tender colours thrown off by your sun, those potent mauves as softly sweet as love those pinks as simple and delectable as joy those blues as mute and deep as sensual delight.

17

All the same, little fairy, you must not get the shivers, for we—or at least I myself am not suffering. Indeed I am enjoying myself a great deal, or rather—well, I can't define it—I don't know really, but your letters fill me with the greatest joy—only absences make me suffer— And then, so much depends on the day—But I have not suffered in the slightest from fear of danger—I don't think many soldiers in this war do experience such fear. True, I arrived here with a feeling of anxiety, quite forgetting how life in modern cities, the trams, buses, ordinary motor cars, etc.—all the machines of our civilization—have already accustomed us to danger; but now the arrival of a shell

GUILLAUME APOLLINAIRE

seems scarcely more dangerous to me (even though it is) than an on-coming car travelling at top speed.

This very day, this morning, in the wood that I told you about before that is so badly torn up, a timed-release shell exploded just above me. I was showered literally showered with shrapnel. I was not hit, but I saw the bullets in front of me, falling an inch from my face, tearing down through the leaves. It was the first time this happened to me but I didn't experience the slightest emotion, even though I did everything I could, as someone who does not feel particularly brave or particularly battle-hardened, to arouse some kind of feeling in myself. Yet many a time, in Paris, feeling lonely of an evening in my study, I have been frightened by nothing more than my solitude.

I simply do not understand it. Could it be the chatter of the men in my battery, who are always saying that I have the most dangerous job in the unit, that has accustomed me, perversely, to feel no fear? Could it be the fate of my predecessor, killed by an exploding shell on the edge of that same pretty little wood, which, again out of contrariness, makes me unafraid? Whatever the reason, the fact is that I am fearless when I go out there, but I shudder now as I write to you and my heart is pounding, whereas this morning I felt neither fear nor bravado but rather a simplicity and lightness of heart that surprised even me.

I write you with the confidence of a man writing to a girl whose mind he respects infinitely, and whom he therefore trusts to see no vainglory or bluster in what he says. Nothing could be farther from my nature, and I would never dream of passing myself off as a great warrior. I am simply describing a sensation, or rather the absence of a sensation. Bravery consists as its etymology suggests in braving a danger and there is no bravery in my case, and it is indeed quite possible that I might turn out to be a coward when it comes to bayonets or hand-to-hand combat or even the defence of a casemate under bombardment. I simply do not know. At all events, after I left the wood as the bombardment shifted its direction away from me, I headed straight for our trenches, for I found myself exposed to fire from the heights occupied by the Germans and saw masses of greenish smoke rolling along; it did not seem about to reach me at all, but after a moment my vision clouded over, and I staggered about with the impression that the ground was in violent motion, continually twisting back and forth, and then amidst the sainfoin in flower I trod on a soft body which thoroughly terrified me by rearing up and giving vent to a cry like that of a Punch doll when you press on its belly, and at the same moment two partridges took wing with the sound they make when startled. This brought me back to myself and my earlier simple state of mind, except for a continu-ing feeling of heaviness and a dizziness which I attributed to the sun, but which was experienced with like intensity as I later learnt in villages much farther away, so it was clearly bromine. All the same, these vapours did not reach our battery, where there were no complaints. Please note that there is more pathos in the details of my tale than in reality, which was quite untouched by pathos, for the afternoon was delightful and what is more we raised a glass of extra-dry champagne to Italy, and once again let me say that I certainly do not want you to mistake this account for the plea of someone in search of pity, because I consider that I was more diverted by all this than bothered in any way.

Thank you for sending me the measurement of your ever so pretty ring finger! I am going to start the engraving—the *ciselage*, or is it *ciselure*? (I'm forgetting how to write!)

GUILLAUME APOLLINAIRE

Yes indeed, my hut is now as trim as could be, all fixed up with canvas sheets to protect the occupant from the rain, and on the leakiest parts of the reed roof I have installed cement or cement-board panels that I found near a lock. I now have a table, a kerosene lamp, and an apothecary's graduated beaker for a tooth-brush glass.

And yes indeed, my forest is annoying—because the people in it are annoying. The officers are alright, if rather distant—we are not well acquainted with them, because the artillery is not like the infantry where men and officers are thrown together. As for the senior sergeant the less said the better, his deputy is a café waiter, the rest country people; the men are carters and that sort of thing. When off duty I often visit the wagon lines of the two other batteries of our group, billeted in a charming little town at present under very heavy bombardment, and I have much friendlier relations with the N.C.O.'s over there than with those in my own battery. The fact is that life in a forest could never be aggravating if it were not for (see above), and indeed my first published work, *L'Enchanteur pourrissant* (The Rotting Magician) was entirely devoted to the celebration of the forest as a prodigious creator of new marvels and ever-renewed life.

Do not talk to me about my verse. You do not yet know my poetry, though you will. I cannot be rushed. . . .

But how impatiently I await, impatient almost to the point of madness, the photographs that you mention. My mouth waters at the thought of them. (But why the mouth, I wonder?!)

Ah my little fairy! Which you assuredly are, since I say so and you believe it . . .

But how perfectly silly of you to be begging my indulgence when all that I am sending over to you in your beautiful Algeria is passionate admiration! Besides, I know that you are far more coquettish and rightly quite aware of your beauty—and the word is by no means too strong.

You ask me to breathe not a word about you? Whatever do you mean? You must know that everything that is yours or comes to me from you is for me alone, and I am more jealous of those things than you could ever imagine. . . . Meanwhile I am so delighted that you signed with your own little name, it is so much nicer, friendlier and more charming than that sexless 'M' of your earlier letters.

I am forgetting to tell you that the day before yesterday, which was Whitsunday, I attended a military concert in a nearby village—it took place on a very old estate. I plucked a rose and I enclose some of its petals. In the morning I saw a major-bishop on horseback, dressed half as a major and half as a bishop—a very curious sight, and to my way of thinking not a very agreeable one.

I am not fond of such transformations. They seem irrational to me, though I am by no means opposed to religious beliefs: having embraced some of my own from time to time, I can easily imagine a deeply anchored faith.

Little fairy, it is one o'clock in the morning, which must after all be an unreasonable hour even for brave warriors, even here at the Front.

I beg your leave to kiss, respectfully and discreetly, your pretty, tiny, fairy's hand, the measurement of whose ring-finger provides me with such a concrete symbol, and I ask you to write me as soon and at the greatest length possible, which would I assure you be a very good deed on your part.

Au revoir, little fairy

Guillaume Apollinaire

Little fairy,

I do not want you to send me parcels. It's very nice of you, very sweet—and first-rate so far as the taste is concerned—but you must not do this.... Being a soldier does not mean one must be showered with delicacies by little fairies waiting in ivory towers for their returning crusaders.

22

Despite this stricture, which is tempered by gratitude, I must say that I really enjoyed the mint chocolate—But if ever you are inclined to send me something, write to me immediately, because that is something truly from you and what I want most of all is you, with your sober beauty which fills me with such sudden, tender and painful nostalgia whenever I think of it.

You know that I am waiting for something else from you: your like-ness. This I wish for with all my strength. . . .

I have sent you a little ring that I made for you, a perfectly simple ring on which I engraved (badly I'm sure) the date 1915—for I could think of nothing more eloquent. When you write me, please tell me a little bit about your life too. So you are expecting wounded whom you will have to care for? But will your teaching duties leave you time for that?

You must not tire yourself. To each his own task. Yours is to promote good taste, harmony and beauty.

Here for a few days now we have been living in peace and thoroughly enjoying some exquisite weather while the spring sheds its blossoms so that summer can ripen and autumn bear its fruit.

I began this letter in the morning, and now that evening has come let me continue it by enclosing a small photo cut out from a group picture too large to go in with my missive, as well as a little poem:

MADELEINE

C'est quelque chose de si ténu de si lointain que d'y penser on arrive à le trop matérialiser

Forme limitée par la mer bleue par la rumeur d'un train en marche par l'odeur des eucalyptus des mimosas et des pins maritimes

Mais le contact et la saveur

Et cette petite voyageuse alerte inclina brusquement la tête sur le quai de la gare à Marseille et s'en alla

Sans savoir

Que son souvenir planerait sur un petit bois de la Champagne où un soldat s'efforce devant le feu d'un bivouac d'évoquer

Madeleine de la fumée d'écorce de bouleau qui sent l'encens minéen

Tandis que les volutes bleuâtres qui montent d'un cigare écrivent le plus tendre des mots Madeleine

Mais les nœuds de couleuvres en se dénouant écrivent aussi le nom émouvant Madeleine, dont chaque lettre se love en belle anglaise

Et le soldat n'ose point achever le jeu de mots bilingue que ne manque point de susciter cette calligraphie sylvestre et vernale.

23

MADELEINE

It is something so tenuous and so far away that merely thinking about it
　makes it too concrete
A form bounded by the blue sea by the sound of a moving train by the
　scents of eucalyptus mimosa and sea pine
And the feel and the taste

GUILLAUME APOLLINAIRE

And that alert little lady traveller briskly nodded her head on the station
    platform at Marseilles and left
                Without knowing
That her memory would hover over a little wood in Champagne where a
    soldier now strives by a campfire to conjure up
Madeleine in the birch-bark smoke with its Minaean redolence
As the bluish swirls rising from a cigar write that sweetest of words
    Madeleine
But the nested snakes as they uncoil also write the touching name
    Madeleine, each letter curling like a *Belle Anglaise*
And the soldier dares not complete the bilingual play on words[1] inevitably
    evoked by this woodland springtime calligraphy.

                      Guillaume Apollinaire

24

[1] *Lover* (French)/love (English).—Tr.

Bonjour Mademoiselle, so here I am once again. Do I intrude? I hope and fancy not, otherwise you would not have replied. As for you, why ever do you think you are a pest? Tell me how this beautiful being with her deep eyes and impish nose, as seen in the photograph you have been so sweet as to send me, could possibly be a pest!!

I thank you and beg you by no means to temper your generous impulses in this regard. Please send me more photographs of you. The one I now have never leaves me. I keep it in my left jacket pocket.

You interpret my ideogrammatic poem most poetically and what a pleasure it is for me to make poetry for you. . . .

But you write me very rarely and your letters are very short. Be aware, little fairy, that by replying you have accepted a responsibility—the obligation to write often, very often. I ask you to do so, indeed far more than that: I demand it of your good grace.

Thank you for the *fine and great and enveloping* thoughts that you send me here at the Front—I take comfort from them, roll myself up in them—curl up, if you will let me, in your mind.

Your description of Lamur I found very amusing. But the analogy between Grasshoppers and Germans does not quite work, because the Boches, though they go to ground, never jump up. But I like the mill, and I can clearly visualize the Moorish woman.

GUILLAUME APOLLINAIRE

My birch bark is beautiful, I grant you. But not as beautiful as you, and hence not worth talking about. Burn it and you will detect a penetrating aroma, and in the swirls of bluish smoke that rise from it try to read—I won't say what, but it will be my own thoughts, assuming you are prepared to learn the smoke's strange alphabet.

For my part I tried hard to guess what you were saying when you were photographed, but I am not clever enough to solve such a difficult puzzle.

I took the liberty of kissing your hand on the photograph. Forgive me for daring to do so without your permission, but please give me your permission quickly because I very much want to do it again.

Your letter is once again signed 'M. Pagès'—as though you disdained the beautiful name of Madeleine.

I shall do my best to send you a photo of our forest.

The last few days have been calm and the weather fine. But just 8 days ago we experienced very heavy bombardment around our batteries with large-calibre shells. The experience is one that may be had nowhere else. That is why I in no way regret coming here. At the moment the strawberries are coming out and blushing from modesty at finding themselves amid so many soldiers.

The day before yesterday I sent you a second ring, it was much harder to make, and in the aluminium I inlaid a little piece of copper taken from the band of (again) a 77-mm shell. An 'M' engraved as best I could (lacking good engraving tools) will tell you, I fear, how ham-fisted I am, but I appeal to your indulgence. If I have the great pleasure of seeing you after the war—I don't know when or where or how but I am infinitely desirous of it, with all my strength, with the passion of a savage—then I shall tell you some amusing stories (amusing after the fact, at least), but at the moment we are obliged to give fewer and fewer military details in letters. The eventual effect will be all the greater for it. Who knows, perhaps that is precisely what the powers-that-be are after—because in my opinion anything we might reveal is highly unlikely to impede the conduct of operations.

In your last letter, Madeleine, you asked that I keep silent about you. Let me ask you the same thing. Please show no one my letters. Just keep them to yourself. They are meant for you alone. Our friendship, so curiously conceived in a train travelling through places full of grace should itself be a graceful thing (grace is not for the mass of people) and remain so. Admittedly, if a tender note were to be added from my quarter I should not be very surprised. . . . But how can I risk telling you this so long as I know nothing of the intentions of that little African heart (that pretty little wireless set) whose beating I would love to listen to, like a telegraph operator picking up signals.

A Madrid newspaper, as part of a survey, has just asked me for my opinion on Cervantes and his Don Quixote. This question will absorb me during my free time tomorrow and I am thinking of the casualty of Lepanto, feeling sympathy for him, because he had no Madeleine in Algeria to write to him. He was a prisoner though, and I end up thinking that even though I am on the Western Front I too am a prisoner—in Algeria—

and I dedicate my beautiful chains to you.

Guill. Apollinaire

GUILLAUME APOLLINAIRE

4 June 1915

My adorable little fairy,

Forgive me for causing you distress. I am the one who is stupid and irritable from time to time: I do not want you to be sad on my account—I am so happy on account of you. I never use style for style's sake—nor do you, for you are the most charming of fairies, oh my pretty Gemiah of the Arabian Nights.[1]

1 Apollinaire probably means Djamilah.—Tr.

I am so sorry Madeleine that you had to wipe eyes as beautiful as yours.

My little fairy, my submissive fairy, I have nothing to forgive you for, but I would dearly like to caress the big little girl that you are, so compliant and so unfrivolous.

I see I have no need to tell you that this war, its reed-covered dugouts and big 305 shells have something to do with—indeed govern—what our hearts feel.

Sure enough, little fairy, you are always with me in my hut, you even lie next to my heart, or your image does, in the shape of the dear little photo of you which with your letters is my most precious possession.

The superstition about blue unites us in an exquisite way, and whenever I imagine your heart I colour it blue.

If you like the eternal spring of my poetry, the poetry of the birch-bark with my logical star, Madeleine if you love the springtime of the heart then love my heart itself. . . .

I have never heard the expression 'Boboches', I think you may mean 'Bobosses', which is in fact what the artillerymen on the Front sometimes call the *fantassins*, the infantry, who seem so deserving of sympathy (as indeed they are). 'Bobosses' is a sort of affectionate diminutive of 'Fantabosses'*—a comical designation that originated I believe in the staging area; back in the Zone of the Interior the artillery make fun of the infantry: the *artiflots* look down on the *pioupious*, while the term *fantassin* is itself used as an insult among cavalrymen.

* 'Fantabosses' stands no doubt for 'fantassins à bosses', infantrymen with humps (i.e. packs) on their backs; the term must have been invented by our gunners, who never carry packs.

My battery is made up almost entirely of men from the occupied territories, many of them have news from home claiming that people there are not unhappy. It seems that in Lille wild festivity reigns, and that the local women are the main attraction at the, shall we say, *fêtes galantes* go on there.

At any rate that is what is being said here.

My little fairy is none of the nasty things she calls herself: she is charming . . . Go ahead, I invite you to give me whatever instructions you like, and if you are wrong I shall simply caress you by way of consolation . . . But your instinct is not wrong, and the fact is we are being instructed to go out as little as possible, the gunners hardly venture outside at all, and even the drivers take only a short ride after nightfall.

Silent? I forbid it! And timid? You are not timid but on the contrary outgoing, coltish, free, and submissive—but submissive as a queen might be.

Affectionately, even very affectionately (though the word is not a pretty one).

Gui

GUILLAUME APOLLINAIRE

Please turn the page over Madeleine

What still needs adding to all of the above, Madeleine, is this: we must not cause each other pain—it would be simply too stupid—so let us be candid and free just as Adam and Eve are supposed to have been in their earthly paradise—

But above all I beg you Madeleine never again to threaten to stop writing to me—by doing so it is I to whom you would cause pain—and what terrible pain it would be!

Timid and silent!!! Be neither one nor the other . . . And as for me, whose shyness in face of the marvellous little fairy that you are you must surely sense from afar, help me, I beg of you, to overcome a timidity that when all is said and done is most unbecoming in a Soldier. Help me if you don't mind—though I know that before you do so you must first question a certain little bluish heart beating in Africa. . . .

And here I am, not daring even in a letter to kiss the finger whose measurement I now have.

Write to me quickly, Madeleine, for I am your poet and (as you added) your friend.

Gui

10 June[1]

Thank you for your good wishes for my saint's day—What is the date of yours, dear little fairy? Your letter of 28 May (half in pen and half in pencil) has been a magnificent joy to me. (I have forgotten how to write I put the words down just as they come.) No, no, I am no longer sad now that I know that my little fairy is even more magical than I had dared think—but even fairy magic does not describe you adequately. The nights here are indeed enchanted, and Algeria is enchanted too. I am a fairy myself inasmuch as a fairy bestows upon me whatever marvellous qualities it is within her power to bestow. But for you, Madeleine, one can only resort to the bizarre terminology of good old Restif, who occasionally spoke of a true fairy-woman, a *femme féïque*.

Granted, you are more than my fairy because you are *willingly* my joy, my sweetness and everything that I must still guess at, oh little sphinx to whom I shall be sure not to play Oedipus, for the last thing I want is for you to plunge off on the road to Thebes, oh my charming little sphinx of the Nice (City of Victory) express. If indeed you await my letters with impatience I'm afraid I shall sometimes deprive you of that pleasure, for I intend to chatter with you whenever I have the chance to drop you a line.

I hear your deep voice perfectly, it swathes my heart and keeps it warm. You cannot imagine into what transports I am thrown by this ability of mine to hear your joy.[2]. . . I do not even want to tell you to what extremes this illusion can carry me, for though I feel that you

2 Apollinaire writes 'joie' (joy) possibly in error for 'voix' (voice).

GUILLAUME APOLLINAIRE

are whispering in my ear, at the same time you do not seem to be speaking in a low voice at all.

You shall show me that star, and I in turn will show you yours, the star that I call Madeleine.

So your brother is a captain in the Artillery. Just recently I took refuge in a dugout by a platform-mounted anti-aircraft gun. There was only one cannon, and the chief of piece was a lieutenant who was quite amiable but funnily enough did not look at all like you. . . .

The account of your voyage home was upsetting: poor Madeleine tossed hither and thither by the sea.

Your poem shall be written, I'll start it this evening if I can.

We are on the qui-vive. We shall be leaving here before long, I think—I'll send you the n° of our new sector right away. I enclose a lock of hair—I'm ashamed to send it to you but this is the only way I can think of to ask you for something that I cannot put into words.

At present I am printing up a small volume[3]—here is a poem that belongs to you but which for reasons of politeness will be dedicated to the lady friend or fiancée of Sergeant Berthier, my friend, who came here with me and whom I write of in my last article in the *Mercure de France* (June 1915).

The article was finished and sent in just a few days before my departure. In this little book there will be many dedications but only one will really count.

3 *Case d'Armons* [From the Caisson Locker], containing 21 poems written before the enemy, duplicated by a gelatin-and-violet-ink process and 'published' on 17 June 1915. Cf. the letters of 18 July and 3, 14 and 16 August 1915.

VISÉE[4]

4 See p. 263.

Chevaux couleur cerise limite des Zélandes
Des mitrailleuses d'or coassent les légendes.

Je t'aime liberté qui veilles dans les hypogées

Harpe aux cordes d'argent, ô pluie, ô ma musique

L'invisible ennemi plaie d'argent au soleil

Et l'avenir secret que la fusée élucide

Entends nager le Mot poisson subtil

Les villes tour à tour deviennent des clefs

Le masque bleu comme met Dieu son ciel

Guerre paisible ascèse solitude métaphysique

Enfant aux mains coupées parmi les roses oriflammes

AIMING

Horses almost cherry red Zeelanders

Gold machine-guns croaking out legends.

I love you Liberty watching over the hypogaea

Silver-stringed harp oh rain oh my music

The invisible enemy a silver wound in the sun

And the hidden future that the flare elucidates

Listen to the Word swimming subtle fish

The towns one by one become keys

Mask blue like the sky God dons

Peaceful war ascesis metaphysical solitude

Child with severed hands amidst the pink banners

This poem belongs to you Madeleine, because I wrote it for you, so take it, since I have just composed it and shall not write it for anyone else.

Write me quickly, quickly. . . . I shall write at greater length tomorrow or the day after if I do not have the time tomorrow. I kiss your hands if you will allow me Madeleine and I dare add nothing more.

Guillaume Apollinaire

GUILLAUME APOLLINAIRE

20 June 1915

Little fairy,

A fortnight [*sic*] without writing to you—no way to do so! We have changed sectors—I am no longer in Sector 59 but in Sector <u>69</u>. I underline because of the similarity between the two numbers. So, *two whole weeks* of being unable to write and of not receiving any letters. A wall suddenly erected between life and me—between you and me.

34

Today after finally getting a little peace and quiet, feeling depressed and very tired, I was just getting ready to write you, when there they were!—4 wonderful letters from my little fairy turned now into a quite natural little girl. How I love this!—So let me answer each of these letters in turn. (1) The first one, dated 2 June: nothing to say except that I am very glad to hear the roses still smell sweet. (2) Letter of 5 June. I don't know why you think that I do not want you to speak of my poetry or of poetry and I note with a certain resent-ment—albeit a smiling resentment, so to speak—that the compli-ments of negroes are less shocking to you than mine—so I shall certainly persist with mine. But I must say that the darky in question was right, and were his plumage as fair as his song, I would hasten if so permitted to feel a pang of jealousy while adding my support to his categorical declaration. (3) With the letter of 10 June, it is not only the missive itself that is delightful but also and above all the au-thor thereof. No, this is not a literary matter at all, but bear in mind that for us the land of Tenderness is the Military Zone and that if only I could skip past all the stopping-places on the *Carte du Tendre* I would have very quickly joined you in the midst of your large family and among all those young virgins at your girls' lycée, where I imagine you are the most beautiful, knowledgeable, pure, and in a sense royal—royal after the fashion of Nausicaa. But neither my mind nor my pen is remotely concerned with literature but solely with you, to whom I am getting ready to stop paying compliments because you do not like them at all and respond with an irony that I have no idea how to answer—

You say you do not know—do you really think I know any better than you do? But for my part I do not analyse and I answer *yes* because I know perfectly well that the answer is yes and if it was *no* this correspondence that chains us together (but let us use another image, since I know that this one arouses your tendency to make fun of me)—this correspondence, I say, would never have sprung from the two of us like those twin geysers in Iceland or New Zealand whose steaming jets marry at a very great height—

But enough of all that, fair enough, and hurrah for Madeleine, the old grass snakes, my friend the sun, our cannon, the blue smoke of my cigarette, and that little blue heart which refuses to beat in time with mine!—

All the same, I do clearly sense it beating and without your saying a word it is I who get my heart into unison with yours, so listen carefully as I repeat: Madeleine. . .

Doña Quixote you are right, upon my corporal's word! I should never have told you that story, which not only shocked you but which you found implausible . . . Forgive me, camp life coarsens one.

GUILLAUME APOLLINAIRE

How happy I am to hear that you trust me . . . But all of a sudden
come these ominous words: *I am less free than you may think. I cannot
make you a promise that I shall be unable to keep.* What does this mean?
What chains bind you, and what promise have I sought from you?
Tell me, since you trust me—I trust you completely, because you say
trust me. And the little miracle from *Don Quixote*, which makes a
bridge between you and me, also gives me great pleasure my
beautiful little Eve. (4) The sirocco of 11 June shows me a very
headstrong Madeleine—and I approve of this trait, which I share—
but do not forget, Madeleine, that when I 'demand' I do so with
infinite gentleness, so much so indeed that I pride myself on never
demanding anything of you that conflicts with your own pleasure
or fails to answer to your own wishes. Well, I *might try*, if the opportunity presented itself—or rather I *would have tried*, for I demand
nothing, having no energy left for anything. . . . And what more
could you ask, Madeleine? I kiss your *very* pretty hands, since you
permit it, and—may I?—your forehead too.

Gui

(I am not re-reading this letter.—I'll write you as soon as I can, but
you please do write me at length.)

I did very well on the subject of *Don Quixote*, which I like very much,
as I do all Spanish literature.

I find close parallels between Cervantes and Gogol.

My little fairy, here you go writing to me but saying nothing and
waiting for me to say what I think first. But you should remember
that this is no time to be coy. You are very attractive, and this goes
for your mind as much as for your physical appearance. Which is
why my feelings are more at the mercy of yours than yours of mine.
So quite clearly it is up to you to decide, and this is the one and only
time that I shall *obey* you—even though I am your *servant*. Despite
which you are still the mistress of both our hearts just as, if you were
married, you would be the sole mistress of your home even though
your husband would be master in the house and in the marriage
bed—that is how good households work—this arrangement is not
going to change and it is desirable to hold to it. Yet things cannot be
forced—If you feel nothing, it is not so very important—A man's
heart can weather many a blow.—Even if you feel the slightest
doubt, say so, and we shall abandon the whole thing—because
forcing matters in this sphere is an insult to nature and hence a very
unreasonable way to proceed, and I do not want to do that at any
price.

Which having been said, I adore your letter. How I love the notion
of Nero's little soul attached to Poppaea's. This artificial pyrotechni-
cal conjunction prompts me to rejoice in the most charming of vices,
which is in your image, and in honour of halfa (*alfa*) my sabre has
been turned into a Moorish scimitar (*alfange*)—and what finer way
could there be for us to celebrate Italy's joining the dance.

GUILLAUME APOLLINAIRE

It is my dream that you as the most faithful might also be the most audacious, but at the same time the most sincere—just as I am at once innocent and (since the word is being used) *experienced*.

And so, Poppaea, tell all!! And leave old crippled Carabosse in peace, she is not worth changing into anything, whereas you are as lovable as can be.

Now you must not suppose that I am taking anything for granted or anticipating in any way. I am very concerned about your hesitations and if you only knew how much pain this uncertainty causes me you would tell the truth so that we might know it once and for all and return to it as often as we liked.

You do not know why you waver so. You should ask the fairies your sisters about your moods and consider how much you ought to obey me, for what in the world could I do with a fairy who never obeyed me? She would be of no help to me, because I could not count on her at all.

Agreed, reading *Paradise Lost* is not very entertaining. Tackling it would be easier if all other books were lacking, as with us here. Still, so far as I can remember, it is a masterpiece, albeit stuffed with the countless commonplaces which continue to clutter up our so Christian minds.

In any case masterpieces are not easy to read. One needs a great deal of intelligence and stamina to peruse them without falling asleep and it is truly the mark of a superior mind to be able to persevere with them. That is why I absolutely love your struggle with the blind and terribly tiresome Milton, whose own daughters, according to the very recent lyrical testimony of Villiers de l'Isle-Adam, could not abide his poetic excess and left him alone to grope in the dark for his lost paradise—

I recall nothing of the character of the *young Eve*, or that of Adam either. But what you tell me of them I find very amusing, for Milton's sublime idea of showing Adam, *fully aware that it will be his downfall, eating the fruit of knowledge out of which Eve has taken a bite* (I use your words, oh ideal fairy) has been developed in a very particular way in literature, and I can think (from memory) of just two places where it has appeared: first, in the famous Sotadic *Portier des Chartreux* (The Carthusians' Gatekeeper) by the judge or lawyer Gervaise de la Touche—a work that stands out among all those of a similar kind produced in the eighteenth century; and secondly in *Bubu de Montparnasse*, by Charles-Louis Philippe, with whom I was well acquainted.

In *Le Portier*, as in *Bubu*, the Hero wittingly catches the disease to which Fracastor gave a name closely resembling a word for a nymph, and he does so out of love, but in *Le Portier* the idea is very simple, for the protagonist Saturnin is not complicated; Bubu is even simpler, because Charles-Louis Philippe was no genius, but, since his soul was as scrofulous as his neck, the result, though somewhat more repellent, is nonetheless appealing—though it should certainly not be considered sublime—the idea in its sublime form you have already discerned in Milton. . . .

I told you in my last letter how much I loved Cervantes, especially the Cervantes of the first version of *Don Quixote* and of the *Exemplary Novels* (hard to read moreover). I am also very fond of the pseudo-Avellanada's sequel to *Quixote* which appeared between Cervantes's two versions—I like this anonymous author's bogus sequel despite Cervantes .

I write you whenever I can, please do not blame me or be disappointed when you hear nothing from me; for my part the despair when I

GUILLAUME APOLLINAIRE

hear nothing from you is impossible to describe and I assure you that I await letters from my little fairy with an impatience rivalled only by your charm as the letter-writer. No, I am no longer satisfied by re-reading books and I fancy that if the war were to end we should not go on reading at all—if I may add Dante to the great men willing to keep us company, assuming always that we need it, which I doubt, for despite all your good breeding we must be said, yes, my Fairy Poppaea, we must be said to be old friends, albeit so freshly awakened to each other.

Madeleine, au revoir, write soon and do not be coy.

I kiss your hands.

Gui

My God, how charming my little fairy is!—I am so happy with the
two photos. The ever-so-pretty face, so solemn, so seriously and
profoundly voluptuous. Little fairy, please, send more, more of your
photos! How I love this sweet and generous obedience on
Madeleine's part!

From time to time I propose to send you poems that I trust you will
mind for me and be so kind as to copy if need be for the purpose of
their publication. So much for the practical side of things—

But when is Madeleine going to tell me all in the letter that I
anticipate with every bone in my body?—

Every one of Madeleine's photos lies next to my heart. Her letters
are in my kitbag. And when there are too many I shall send them
home to Paris, where my concierge receives everything addressed by
Corporal G. de K. to M. Guil. Ap., and without opening anything
puts all the soldier's mail in the poet's apartment—

I live in Paris at Bd St-Germain, no. 202, between Rue des Sts-Pères
and Rue du Bac.

Since you like it so much, the piece of birch bark has been spared
and granted the right to exist.

I shall teach you whatever you wish—even if I have to invent—And
you shall likewise solve mysteries for me even more marvellous than
those hidden in smoke!—and more delightful too!

GUILLAUME APOLLINAIRE

41

I have the three photos of you before me. The first with the brow so high so pure, the eyes so candid, the chin so sensual and such a tender throat. Madeleine is in an armchair, a touch arrogant still. Her shoulders are pulled back and the just discernible twin fruits of her bosom thrust forward.

In a second photo Madeleine is shown at her work table. Her hair wilder—and so soft. Is she smiling? Dreaming? Here it is the nose that is voluptuous. I suspect that Madeleine is not wearing a corset, in this photo at least, and what a joy it is to descry the youthful roundnesses of the supple young body beneath her clothing.

And here she is on the balcony my darling fawn with dark circles beneath her eyes. All the same her voluptuous air is beyond imagining. The faces of the houris of the Koran must have looked exactly like this. I know now why that black man told you how pretty you were . . . And just look at those pretty hands . . . Ah well, let us say no more of this delightful vision of youth.

At present we are caring for a tercel caught here just a few days ago. A sort of falcon or hawk. A little bird of prey once used I believe in falconry.—This one that I am trying to train is still an eyas—a *niais* in what I believe is the original sense of the term: barely out of the nest. He is handsome and very nice with his curved beak and pale yellow talons. I have named him Aquilan, after a Saracen warrior who figures if memory serves in the story of Beuves d'Hanstonne. This last had prepared a feast by the seashore to celebrate his wife's coming to term when the celebration was interrupted by the arrival of the fleet of the Saracen Sorgolant. The knights prepared to defend themselves while the women fled into the woods. But the Saracens succeeded in catching the Duchess's sister Ysanne, who also gave birth in the midst of these events; they abducted the two infants, who were held in the arms of a young Saracen slave girl belonging to the Admiral of Palermo. The two young ladies were mounted on white palfreys when the Saracens seized them.

The Saracen warrior Aquilan de Mayorque was smitten by Ysanne's beauty and she married him once they were in the land of the Saracens.

So here we have Aquilan the tercel, with a string around his foot and hard put to it to find an Ysanne, but we give him field mice and he binds them like an eagle binding a hare.

This evening we are hearing a deep-toned sound of artillery, bells tolling in a terrible way or one might say terrible bells. It is bombs falling—incessantly, bells or thunder.

Au revoir Madeleine, I kiss your hands, but would you not offer me your forehead too?

43

Gui

Little fairy, an impressive night of departure here. But where are we going?—I have received your kind letter of the 19th. So sweet. Yes indeed, we both see the same pale and ever-changing heavenly body, the same milky moon. Thank you for the very very pretty little photo—I understand perfectly that you prefer me to Montesquieu even though he has much good sense and a good deal of intelligence (*esprit*) beyond that which he revealed in *L'Esprit des lois* (The Spirit of Laws)—

44

When now shall I get your letters? It is not long since I went ten days without receiving a single one. This time it may be longer. Who knows? Who knows? As for my little book—(everything is in complete disarray)

I have to say that this evening I am writing without quite knowing what. Everything is in such an uproar. I'll try to write you en route if possible. But who knows if it will be possible. Ah well.—You write me though, so at least I'll eventually have plenty of letters.—But perhaps between the posting of this letter and your reply we shall be settled again. I hope and pray that our sector n° does not change this time and that the post will be delivered directly to where we are. Au revoir Madeleine.

Gui

I cannot write any more—I have to do something else.

1 Rediscovered military postcard (Bibliothèque Historique de la Ville de Paris.
Gift of Marcel Adéma).

27 June 1915[1]

My *Poilue*, Your letter of the 20th was delivered to me in an extraordinary bivouac where we are resting up (!) for a few hours before
setting off eastwards again. So it is a sort of denial of Saint Peter, but
a denial that is not necessarily bad, which just goes to show that
anything can be good or bad. As for the rings, I believe our battery,
so it happens, makes the best ones. The aluminium is poured into a
mould carved from a potato and the finishing is done with a file.
For the copper work a swallowtail is made in the aluminium and
the copper (or bronze) plate is embedded and tightened in place
using an engraving tool and striking softly with a hammer, because
aluminium is soft.—Send me your finger measurement again and
I'll make you a ring with a good deal of decoration. Of course there
are a great many highly skilled people here who would consider
such rings very imperfect.

Your *poilu*.

Gui

I have read in the paper that it is customary for families in Algeria
to adopt their own *poilu*. On the face of it this is grotesque.

Write me quickly.

45

GUILLAUME APOLLINAIRE

We have arrived. I shall write you at greater length as soon as I have time. We have travelled in stages across regions now famous, towns and villages now haunted by illustrious ghosts. So I'll write when I can. For the moment we are sleeping on the ground, and have been for the last three days, with a saddle for a pillow and the sky for a canopy.

Gui

46

G. de Kostrowitzky
Brigadier
38th Artillery
45th Battery
Postal Sector 138

My dear little fairy, I write you amid the horrible horror of millions of fat bluebottles. We have ended up in a sinister place where, to all the horrors of war, to the horror of the site itself, and to the terrifying proximity of so many cemeteries, is added a dearth of trees, of water, even of any real earth. If we stay here very long, I wonder what will become of us even if we escape death by the instruments of war. After several fine days of travel on horseback and perfectly tolerable nights sleeping on the ground, we are now in vile holes—so vile that simply dwelling on the fact makes me feel like vomiting not to mention the bouts of fatigue, because everything is so spread out that the work of men and horses alike is multiplied by a hundred. So much for me. And so much the better if it serves a purpose. It was at our first bivouac, the Piémont farm mentioned in communiqués, that I received the letter in which you ask about the rings and I replied straight away from that pestilential place. Let me add to what I told you that the copper or bronze plate chased the way we do it is the speciality of the 45th battery of the 38th, where it is said the finest rings on the Front are made— learning to make them gave me nothing but trouble, but there are true artists here.—I have done what I can to simplify the syntax of poetry and in some cases I have succeeded, notably in the poem 'Les Fenêtres' ('Windows') which appeared first in *Poème et Drame*, then separately in a large publication that was also the catalogue of a painter's work. But now I no longer feel impressionism alone

GUILLAUME APOLLINAIRE

suffices, even in painting—it is ill-defined, so detached, most of all so passé, especially in art. Remember, one of my chief books is called *Les Peintres cubistes*, but still, language and the epistolary style do need to go through that impressionist phase, and when speed and compression are called for a telegraphic style constitutes a resource where ellipsis can produce a marvellously lyrical force and flavour. So, I am waiting for you to give it a try, to tell me, even in the most telegraphic and elliptical way, what I want to know, agreeable or disagreeable. Are you so proud as to think it would be humiliating were you to answer and I found your answer to my liking? And, if not, is it right for you to leave me in a state of uncertainty that can only worsen the horror of this wilderness that turns soldiers into hermits? Your embarrassment makes for literary long-windedness and our correspondence once so gay so lively is suffering. So let yourself go, speak the truth whatever it may be, let whatever is in there come out, even if it kills you? But no, not this. I am just your pet *poilu*, it's the fashion in Algeria and here am I, who had Cervantes in mind, a simple corporal conducting a platonic courtship with a young lady from Oran who finds my letters merely diverting.

Come along, Madeleine, strip yourself naked—soul, body, and heart. Then revel in your truthfulness. Because it is not about making me happy. You have to tell the truth, that's all. Even if that truth runs counter to my dream.

You say that the sirocco makes you feel like a broomstick. Well, astride that broomstick which you have turned into you should seat the pretty witch that you really are and fly her all the way to me, my delightful little fairy, or else allow yourself to write me the silly things you are tempted to write me. I too love Musset, precisely because of his freedom. But how much I love the end of your letter, where you begin to let yourself say what you think. I hope that the next letter I receive will be gayer and maybe freer also. But write quickly and at length without thinking about writing well, about you especially, I don't care about all the rest, take anything, your foot say, tell me about your hand, but do so profoundly like someone who takes pride in always pleasing and has no fear of being obedient all the time, because I want things to be that way, quite apart from the reservations you mention. And I even wonder what those reservations could possibly be—because in the event there are just the two of us . . . Write me Madeleine, a long long letter, your letters do me so unbelievably much good. And please, no more coyness—at the moment and from far away like this, it amounts to depravity pure and simple.

Gui

Dearest little fairy, so why do you persist so, you who are so anxious, who would like me to whisper Madeleine in your ear, why will you not sweetly call me Guillaume or Gui, whichever you like? You address me as 'Poet,' as though I were to call you 'Professor of Literature.' But I'm afraid all I'm saying is very mean, forgive me. The Lord of the Flies, Beelzebub, is here with his legions, his infinity of myriads of green, blue, brown flies—not horseflies but flies, and the greenest, most brilliant, most Boche amongst them have a gleaming muzzle like a bulldog's. And I, wishing for a metamorphosis like the one in Cazotte's *The Devil in Love*, only wish I could cry out at the emergence of some diabolical apparition from the hot and putrid *African* mists: 'My beloved Beelzebub, I adore you.'

Today's letter from you is dated 14 June, which means that the mail is now taking 16 or 17 days to arrive. You are still addressing letters to Sector 59.

Don't cry my pretty little fairy. Eight days—too long a silence!! But the war is not over and now we often change sectors. Here I am, billeted in a hole. But I live in it alone. A plank for a table, a plank for a bench, two planks for a bed. The ceiling is two metres from the floor, and the place is adorned by my revolver, my sabre, my saddle, my kitbag, some 75mm shell casings, my water bottle, and half of a bomb.

My adorable little fairy, write the words that make one live. It's not that I'm neglecting you. But I haven't been able to write more. I cannot write you all I would like, because what I would like is you, as you well know, my very own (??) Madeleine.—What is this Algiers exam?— I forgot to tell you in my last letter that the potato mould is an invention of the 45th Bʳʸ and that it is very easy to use potatoes in this way.

COTE 146

Plaines Désolation Enfer des mouches Fusées Le vert le blanc le rouge

Salves de 50 bombes dans les tranchées comme quand à quatre on fait claquer pour
*   en faire sortir la poussière un grand tapis*

Trous semblables à des cathédrales gothiques.

Rumeur des mouches violentes

Lettres enfermées dans une boîte de cigares venue d'Oran

La corvée d'eau revient avec ses fûts

Et les blessés reviennent seuls par l'innombrable boyau aride

Embranchement du Decauville

Là-bas on joue à cache-cache

Nous jouons à colin-maillard

Beaux rêves

Madeleine ce qui n'est pas à l'amour est autant de perdu

Vos photos sur mon cœur

Et les mouches métalliques petits astres d'abord

À cheval à cheval à cheval à cheval

Ô plaine, partout des trous où végètent des hommes

Ô plaine où vont les boyaux comme les traces sur le bout des doigts aux monumentales
*   pierres de Gavrinis*

Madeleine votre nom comme une rose incertaine rose des vents ou du rosier.

Les conducteurs s'en vont à l'abreuvoir à 7 km. d'ici.

Perthes Hurlus Beauséjour noms pâles et toi Ville-sur-Tourbe

Cimetières de soldats croix où le képi pleure.

L'ombre est de chairs putréfiées les arbres si rares sont des morts restés debout

Ouïs pleurer l'obus qui passe sur ta tête

51

GUILLAUME APOLLINAIRE

HILL 146

Plains Desolation Hell of flies Flares green white red

Fifty-shell salvoes in the trenches sound like four people beating a large
  carpet to get the dust out

Craters the size of Gothic cathedrals.

Buzz of aggressive flies

Letters enclosed in a box of cigars sent from Oran

The water fatigue comes back with its barrels

And the wounded come back alone through the endless bleak trenches

Decauville railway branch line

Over there they play hide and seek

Here we play blind man's buff

Beautiful dreams

Madeleine whatever does not belong to love is so much lost

Your photos next to my heart

And the metallic flies at first little stars

On horseback horseback horseback horseback

Oh plain so full of craters where men vegetate

Oh plain crisscrossed by trenches like the lines on our fingertips leading to
the megaliths of Gavrinis

Madeleine your name like a rose uncertain a wind rose or a rose of the
  rose-tree.

The drivers leave for the watering-place 7 km from here

Perthes Hurlus Beauséjour pale names and you Ville-sur-Tourbe

Cemeteries of soldiers crosses where kepis weep.

The shade is of rotting flesh the trees so rare are dead men still standing

Hear the shells weep as they pass over your head

Au revoir my fairy. If I were to be granted some rest, writing to you
is not all I would want, I'd want to see you, see your surprised and
serious expression impenetrable yet terribly voluptuous. But for the
time being rest is out of the question.[1]

Au revoir

                                                              Gui

1 Apollinaire here draws a single line
through the words 'I kiss you.'

My fairy,

For so many days now I have been unable to write you. Impossible. This sector is the sworn enemy of free time.—I love you too Madeleine, and have loved you since I first saw you.—Forgive me for saying so only briefly today. The epistolist is a thousand times more delightful than her epistles and the photograph of my pretty darling in her peignoir I found ravishing even if the image is a little washed out. My darling, I love you infinitely and this latest portrait so completely expresses your sensual beauty that it makes me tremble.

And since you in return are mine, let me decree that you shall be in charge of both our hearts, and I want you to direct them both towards the strongest passion imaginable. You shall preside over all the plans that must be laid immediately. You are worthy of it. Did you not already decide everything of your own accord when you exclaimed so wonderfully 'How happy we are going to be!' And so, my darling slave, I order you to do everything in your power to make just that come to pass. Madeleine, I adore you in a way that I cannot yet say, because in my delirium I cannot find the words.

You have understood perfectly that this is neither childishness nor friendship. Continue to be in charge, therefore, so long as I am over here. If I could get some leave I would arrange (if you liked) for us to meet and that meeting would be even more dazzling than our

53

GUILLAUME APOLLINAIRE

letters, though we cannot count on any such encounter for the moment, with things so uncertain. Shed light, my very dearest one, on our hearts and our lives. All the coincidences you mention I find most affecting. I am very anxious and don't know what else to write. I shall write better next time. It is night I'm in the hutch where I live by myself 3 metres underground with a roof of pine billets covered with earth and a good table and a straw mattress. I put it all together myself. The guns and machine-guns are at work, the noise is infernal. Signal-flares light up the night. What is it you want to know of my past, Madeleine, for my part all I asked you was whether you were free, that's all, and I love your charming admission in which you come out as pure as a dove. I am pure too, though after the fashion of a man, for I am 34 years old, and you are no doubt so young, so young, that I am afraid to think of your age which must be so far from mine.

But of course you are not asking for a life of Lovelace but simply for an assurance that there is nothing in my friendships that might estrange you from me. And indeed there is nothing that could estrange you from me. In any case, all this is inconsequential. I do have firm friendships which you will not want me to renounce once you become familiar with them, and I have friendships with women which are very serious but which should in no way give you cause for concern. What is more I forbid you to become concerned about me with respect to you, and *this forever*. Let us not even return to this subject.—Everything that is not serious, not profound, no longer exists—let that suffice for you Madeleine, for when all is said and done you are mine and nothing that I desire should be hurtful to you nor would I wish anything other than your happiness, your pleasure, and in that way my desires will become yours and no cloud can ever come between us.

Try to be that strong woman you speak of and if you succeed you will never doubt me nor I you. Indeed it is almost blasphemous to speak of such things. And I am almost cross with you my treasure for repeating your questions on these matters. We are not so common as not to know what we are doing; we have rights and freedoms, you and I, that protect us from jealousy. Never be jealous, my love, and never strive to make me jealous—I can be quite jealous enough without any help from you. But on the contrary let us by being as frank and open as possible avoid everything that could arouse jealousy.

Forgive me for such a disjointed letter. You have driven me a little mad this evening and I am madly in love with you Madeleine.

So kisses for your hands and brow my beloved. I'll write tomorrow too. And your hair? Have you not received mine my adorable and adored Madeleine?

55

Gui

My beloved fairy,

I adore you; I do not want you to be the slightest bit jealous for any reason, ever. But let us speak no more of that, for it is quite clear. It falls to you to oversee the fulfilment of our happiness, if life should offer it to us. But before returning to that subject I am waiting for an answer to my last letter.

56

You cannot imagine the pleasure I obtained from the little photo of my dear fairy in her dressing-gown strolling between banks of anthemia and geraniums.

I am much relieved to learn that your mother does not disapprove of our long-distance exchange of thoughts. I repeat, you must be the 1st to tell all. Were I free, I should certainly speak up myself. But such is the lot of a soldier, liable as he is to die from one moment to the next, that he must let those express themselves who are free to do so.

As you are, my darling.

So overcome all your scruples and show yourself as the strong woman that you can be.

You are already full of intelligence and grace and I exult in your mind as I do in your beauty.

And the pleasure I get from loving you will be multiplied a hundred-fold thanks to the mutual awareness of each other that we can achieve as two equals.

I have just received your first note addressed to me in Sector 138. You are quite right, my dear, but you must not be angry at your poet for having been a little bothered by the impatience he felt to have you at last speak from the heart. And the note I received from you that day at our encampment at the place known as Piémont Farm—the first note or letter or message from you ever to be indifferent or banal—had an almost painful effect on me. But that was the very last time that things shall be like that between us.

How I wish we could leave this sector! We are just miserably fed up here—under the falling shells.

You know, my sweetheart, if every time you had a new photograph taken you would send it to me, it would make me so happy. Then I can look at you, each part of you in turn. I love your forehead, your eyes, and the harmonious outlines of your body are my delight. I picture the perfection of your form. And your deep voice resounds in my ears which with sudden acuity seem to track its fading echo.

You were quite right not to surrender your soul to *vulgar inhumanity*. But since you had not yet bared that soul to me, that soul which I adore, on that day under the *vulgar and inhuman* sun of the summer of 1915, I experienced a rush of anxiety for which you should not reproach me.

For my part I was not really angry with you. I was giving voice to the bitterness of my heart, that is all.

And may that grotesque word never again be written by either of us, although you never know, perhaps we may find it agreeable once the war is over.

GUILLAUME APOLLINAIRE

You spoke to me recently of Claudel. This talented writer is the end result of Symbolism. He is the obscure and reactionary version of Arthur Rimbaud—Rimbaud as small change: a nickel coin to Rimbaud's louis d'or. Claudel is a gifted man who has done nothing but facile things in the realm of the sublime. In a time when there are no more literary rules it is not hard to impose new ones. Claudel has not had the courage to surpass himself nor above all to surpass the literature of images that is so ready to hand today. We have become used to images. No image is unacceptable and anything can be symbolized by anything else. A literature made up of images strung together like rosary beads is good at best for snobs enamoured of mysticism. It is accessible to anyone, and I wonder why *Annales* does not publish some Claudel just to help all our female cousins fancy themselves Thomists just as they at present fancy themselves Bergsonians or Nietszcheans. I kiss your hands and your forehead and I forbid you, Madeleine, to take umbrage at anything at all coming from me.

Your poet

14 July[1]

You, my darling one, are a delightful girl and a very attentive fairy, for you have guessed exactly what would give me the most pleasure, namely the eau de cologne which I await as I do your very own fresh scent. What? Get angry with you now that you are mine? Never! On the contrary, I kiss your forehead and also this *foot* and *your entire person* as evoked in your so charming letter. For my part I am sending you a pen-stand and a ring. Your measurement is now at my home in Paris, but I think the ring will fit. The pen-stand is made out of two Boche bullets. I send it merely as a souvenir and a curiosity and perhaps you will not find it very practical. But it may amuse you for a moment and it is meant to do no more than that.

Think how happy I am after getting your letters! I would love to be able to tell you so and subdue you with caresses so gentle that you would forget everything else in this world. My dearest pretty little sorceress, there shall never be anything mean in my letters. I wish you a happy saint's day. This letter will probably arrive near the date. If it reaches you earlier so much the better. Yes—tell me about yourself, which is what interests me most—indeed it is my only concern.

So you are mine, darling, and I am completely yours.

You say you would like me to obey *you*, but in all this there is only tenderness and your obedience to me must be complete. I want the

59

GUILLAUME APOLLINAIRE

state of subjection in which you must remain to be at once all love and all suffering, so that I may console the little wild thing that I seek to master. For if I were not your master, with all the prerogatives that the word confers, I would not love you so much.

I want all your feelings to be aroused tumultuously under my dominating gaze. Otherwise, would you be woman and I man?— For in any case our mental equality puts us on a par.

Which notwithstanding, we are now such friends, darling, that you may speak to me of yourself with all the freedom of which your dear soul is capable.

On the other hand, dearest, you must understand that domination is not simply a matter of gallantry, but rather a profound and passionate reality which should affect the imagination, the soul and the body to the limit, or as far as my will may require.

That is how I want you my darling, since you are mine.

At the same time I have made you mistress of our lives and our hearts for the duration of the war so that you may prepare them for peace.

On that particular subject I still await a reply.

I shall close now because the post orderly is about to leave.

I kiss your pretty hands and forehead that I adore.

Gui

My dear little fairy,

I have received the card and the two parcels. You are very very sweet and this is all so precious to me. The handkerchief, the silk lace— which I kiss passionately for they are Madeleine's, they have touched Madeleine. I am smoking the good cigarettes and interrogating their smoke. For the perfumed soap I thank you too, as for the hydrogen peroxide. Unfortunately the bottle of eau de cologne arrived in little pieces that were not even damp—only the label addressed by you was intact. What a shame that it broke! The wrapping was inadequate—bottles like this need packing well in jeweller's foil or wood shavings or some such material.

So Madeleine allow me to kiss your handsome forehead once more and say thank you. How could I now possibly hold a grudge against my Madeleine who is so far away, particularly considering that our exchange of letters has become far more than a merely friendly one—but you know that it is entirely up to you to decide what is to be, Providence willing of course. But then, what woman wishes God ordains.—And yet little remains to be made clear between the two of us, for your fine Algerian sun, the same sun that I see, unites and illuminates us both and it was with all your heart, my adorable Madeleine, that you posted this card to me, while the press of people around you marked you out as too beautiful to be at the post office all alone.

GUILLAUME APOLLINAIRE

Now, Madeleine, I ask that your letters speak to me of you and of love. That is my only concern. I love today's card in which you are completely you and completely mine my little independent one.

It is now about 11 o'clock at night. I have nothing to do but stay awake and write to you by the light of a candle. I had thought I would try to describe my love to you. But I have given up that idea. You already know how sudden, how involuntary and how fatal, so to speak, that love was. There is no need to comment further upon it, for it has found your own love, my dear adorable little fairy.

I have been looking for something to send you that would be equivalent to the birch bark from Sector 59. But there is nothing here. The kestrel is growing but I don't have the time to try and train him in the art of falconry. An eyas he came to me, and green he remains. A raptor that makes a big fuss about killing a mouse— he might as declare himself a pacifist!

You know just how happy I have been about everything since Madeleine became my Madeleine. As you may imagine, all else pales into insignificance. Have you finished re-reading *Don Quixote*? What are you doing now, during your holidays? Or perhaps the holidays have not begun yet.

I too, beloved Madeleine, sign with all my heart and I kiss your forehead madly, madly.

Gui

17 July[1]

I think, oh prettiest of fairies with the most beautiful hair of any Madeleine, oh my own Madeleine, that in my haste I forgot to thank you for the 'Madeleine alcohol' and the 'Madeleine cachou'. I take this opportunity to set my thoughts down on this card, thoughts that swirl up in the smoke from those excellent scented cigarettes. If you receive the little parcel whereby the War Front seeks in its modest way to celebrate Saint Madeleine's Day, please note that a pencil is lacking for the pencil-stand bullet and that both this bullet and the pen-stand one need to be better adjusted in their casings, and as for the bullet with the doings for holding the pens the doings in question should be replaced by a more authentic one that holds them better.

Have your photographers given up taking the pictures of you that make me so happy?

Your pink-silk lace clearly bore your dear scent, my fairy; I keep it on my person along with the little handkerchief.

You should know that this region is now full of enchantment for me because of the letters I have received from you here and because of the great secret, our great secret, that you have entrusted to me. I kiss your dear brow.

G

GUILLAUME APOLLINAIRE

I am very tired. That is why I make so many mistakes as I write and have to review the spelling of every word, but I am very well and in very good spirits. From what I can see and despite the fact that the sector has become more violent, I believe that we run far less danger here than we would elsewhere.

My darling little fairy, you may now write just as you please for now you are my very own Madeleine and I am truly your poet.

About your exam, it pained me to learn that you have experienced this setback, which must be corrected, because whatever one undertakes has to be successfully completed; I was upset too because you have been and still are ill my dear. Do not overdo things, and get some rest. But rest so as to become more knowledgeable and better prepared to confront your next exams, my pretty candidate.

You know English well; I read it but hardly speak it despite having been in England 3 times, albeit for a very short time on each occasion.

I can read English books and newspapers but I could never correspond in that language.

Do take care of your health, I want to find you well when I next see you. But I quite understand your liking for cold water and ice cream, for I too like them very much.

You are 22, my Madeleine—how much older I am than you! So it is not you who have to fear that I might ever tire of you, for you are my intellectual peer and it is I who might reasonably be afraid of being too old for you. But in the end I fear no such thing: no, the disproportion is not too great.—My little fairy is quite right to tell all; that is sweeter than anything.

Do you suppose that we might be able to meet again when I get my leave?

GUILLAUME APOLLINAIRE

Forgive me if I was mean, but you must never take anything coming from me as meanness.

I am as you know authoritarian and I want everything reaching you from me to be sensual for you. I want you to be mine completely, for I am your master my darling and your master unconditionally. So I want you to obey me in everything, to forget all else for me, to accept that no good breeding or anything else can withstand my will, and to remain my docile little slave forever. In return I shall offer you all the joys it lies within my power to offer, and you must accept them from me even if they are painful. In that way our love will be a marvellous one. This is nature's will, moreover: does not the first man a woman knows always cause her to suffer?

You must not think, however, that I wish to make you suffer. Not in the least—I wish only for your complete happiness, and this requires by way of contrast that (as cultured as you are) you be the most submissive of slaves.

A well-known albeit libertine painting by Fragonard depicts 'conjugal correction'. This is an artistic fantasy, but one which here—under the veil of Allegory, a veil that reveals more than it conceals—imparts a great truth about the relationship between man and woman.

I have always sought a woman who was my equal but at the same time very much mine, more mine in fact than a woman much inferior to me ever could be.

Naturally, no brutality at all is implied here, ever. Try to understand what I mean and do not perceive anything malicious, brutal, stupid or even too unrestrained in what I write to you. I am saying that between the two of us no quarrels of any kind can ever occur, because you will always be mine, thinking naturally like me, and by

66

my side your character will become all the stronger by virtue of your belonging more and more to me without limitation.

I would be jolly happy to have you nearer to me, I mean in Europe, in France. But this love of ours born between one part of the world and another is blessed, this dearest Mediterranean love, and I have a feeling that we shall see each other very soon.

But what do I really know after all? I believe they still expect another 2 years of this confrontation between nations transformed into rams.

You know my Madeleine, I am never mean, I am always very gentle. And I do not want you to think that I could ever be mean, least of all to you, and now I should love to take you in my arms, rock you for such a long time, caress you, say the words that answer to your mood, your grace, your lassitude, kiss your hair and hold you long in my strong arms against my swelling chest and my caresses would go on forever and by and by you would begin to return them of your own accord, loving and tender, and the sweetness of the world itself would be reborn in this exquisite exchange between two adoring souls.

What I am least able to comprehend is that you could possibly be afraid of me. Afraid? It simply makes no sense. I just don't want that, my darling. We belong to one another and that's that—equal to equal. But not fear—not when on the contrary what I ask of you is that there be no constraints between us, no coyness even, save for the kind that is liable to make you ever more beautiful in my eyes.

But your letter, darling, touched me to the quick, for it showed how well you understand me and how each day you become more Madeleine-like while still remaining, charmingly, the same sweet teacher of literature that you are.

67

GUILLAUME APOLLINAIRE

My dearest one, I clasp your very soul to me. I am delighted by your precious inner happiness. I kiss your dear forehead and your hair that you are keeping for me. All completely mine, is it not true? Do take good care of that marvellous hair that you once rearranged before me, my coquettish little fairy, in the train. You know full well how glorious it is. You are right, don't cut it at all, save it for me as my prize and prey when I return to you.

Your little note of Sunday my dear is one of the most delightful love poems that I know of and for me my dear your heart too is exactly as I wished it. Do you remember how at Marseilles I watched you leaving and all my being strained towards you and I felt certain that you felt exactly what was taking place within me? You were saying to yourself, 'He has my address and it is up to him to find his little traveller once more'.

Meanwhile I am distressed that you have not read my books—or rather just *The Heresiarch and Co.* and *Alcools*, for the others are not interesting (except for two published in very limited editions and impossible to find), but I would like you to have read *The Heresiarch* and the poems of *Alcools*.

No, I don't think we are changing sectors just now. I fancy anyway that there have been enough changes for the time being. We are preparing for the winter.

In the end I would as soon be here as somewhere else. There is a good deal of firing in the vicinity but not too much at us and I no longer have to duck through 105's and 305's as I did on that famous day I told you about. Here everything is so clumped together that we barely move except for going to the watering-place, and I don't even go there because I am now a corporal quartermaster. The closest fire has come up to now is some 200 metres short of us. So long as we are not spotted everything will be alright. True, there are very many Boche aeroplanes and once the French batteries open fire on them we are far more likely to receive a 75-mm shell on our heads than a 77. Meanwhile I wonder when it will all end and how. I can't make head or tail of it. We are so badly informed about everything that is happening.

If I manage to get a little time to myself as a quartermaster I shall try to write poems and a book.—I have published *Case d'Armons*, which I can send you if you like, because you are part of it, but not fully, for our two hearts had not yet fully recognized one another and the great light of our love had not yet come into being. There are poems in there composed before I began writing to you or before I loved you fully, before I knew you would love me, and this little volume also contains too many memories that I no longer wish to have now that Madeleine is mine, my Madeleine, my one and only Madeleine. All the same, this short work bears witness to the rising tide of our great love in my heart.

In France there are almost no more literary reviews and you can no longer publish poems. I have published hardly anything except for my 'Vie anecdotique' column in the June number of *Mercure de France*—and that was an old one written in Nîmes, since when I have not written this short generally bimonthly and now monthly article and can no longer manage to produce it regularly.

According to a letter from someone who is in Spain and who has read *Case d'Armons* it would seem that there is more interest in French poetry in Germany than here:

'I have read an article in a Spanish paper which mentions Paul Fort, you, and Romain Rolland as writers to whom much attention is being paid in Germany at the moment. Apparently German reviews have even been publishing old things of yours.'

GUILLAUME APOLLINAIRE

Life is very strange, and the universe is very small. We shall win this war, or die, but I tend to think we shall win and that I shan't die, because you protect me little fairy, so we shall be the victors and then it will become clear that the preservation of French literature during the war was the work of the other side.

But I would pay good money to read that article in the Spanish paper. Paul Fort has been publishing poems that as always with him are part banter, part erotic and part patriotic; Romain Rolland issues unpleasant and highly inappropriate declarations virtually in favour of Germany; as for me, in February I published a poem in Zurich entitled '2nd Gunnery Driver' which left no room for doubt as to my anti-Boche feelings, feelings that were no means new for me. So it can only be art's sake that Bocheland's fanciers of literature like what I do and what Paul Fort does.

But those devils are well placed to be art lovers. They hardly had any before the war, and the German avant-garde poets spent the last year of peace paraphrasing 'Zone', the first poem in *Alcools*: they even produced a very handsome edition of the poem (in translation of course), complete with a very nice-looking illustrated cover, printed up 15,000 copies, sent me 5 and sold the remainder in a week at 75 centimes a copy, never having bothered to ask my permission to publish and never even offering to buy the rights from me and turning a deaf ear to all my claims for remuneration. There you have another example of what great lovers of Art the Germans are. When they are not burning down some French cathedral they turn to stealing from French poets.

But this long digression must be tiresome for you my darling—my pen was carried away just as I was talking to you of love! Tomorrow I shall talk of love at greater length and in greater depth. I kiss you adorable hair and close this. Yours.

Your Gui to Madeleine

I wish you a happy saint's day my little Madeleine, I am behind with you. I have not had the time to write for the last few days. You say you love what belongs to you. I share the sentiment. And I belong to you, don't I, and you belong to me. It is almost as though we were one and the same and peace will prove my charming obedient little fairy that this is what we both want. I know it, yes I really do my Madeleine and there is no reason for you to have doubts. I adore you. I hope that your eye that was hurt by the simoon is feeling better.

Likewise my Madeleine I am with you. I think with you, within you— my heart is wherever you are and yes, you are wherever I am and thus we both have a wonderful gift of ubiquity which is worth more than anything in the world—I adore you. Certainly when you are in France our letters will arrive far more quickly. We shall be closer to one another.

I fear though that the 5 months you speak of will fail to harmonize with the plans of Bellona and the god Mars, whose intention it is to reign for a good while longer than that.

I too smile to think of this return of yours—the great return, Nietzsche would have said. Yes, do take good care of the adorable Madeleine. So that the pretty little fairy may still be as plump, and in all the right places, as she appears so fetchingly in the precious pictures

GUILLAUME APOLLINAIRE

that are my joy. But even if she turns into a veritable broomstick, I shall find such a graceful witch no less desirable just as she is.

It is curious that you used to look directly at the sun. I often did the same when I was younger and my eyesight has become weaker since. Not recommended.

The Swallow spoke the truth, my exquisitely tender companion. I love you deeply, I think of you *terribly*. My Poppaea, my Hermione, do not be afraid of being romantic. I adore you in all your forms— does a fairy not metamorphose at will?—If I saw you here as an artilleryman it would not surprise me, though I would tell you to leave immediately, for I do not want you to run into any danger— not even that of my love and as I said I love you *terribly* out here. I am assuredly as volcanic as you. The little geyser would not have to wait long for the response of its twin. I had rather not speak of it, but I am even sillier than you, believe it or not, my love. Even the silk lace that you once touched makes me frantic. Obviously it is idiotic to be like this. And you may be sure that I can be reserved when that is called for—ah! but how I long to see you, with your hair falling down your back.

By way of friends I have all my comrades-in-arms. I've started a novel though I don't write every day.

Please tell the sea that I love her because she has borne you and will do so again, please tell the sky that I love it too because I have looked at you by Its light, and please tell that little traveller that I love her enough to die of that love if need be.

Write me quickly, tell me lots and lots of foolish things. But above all tell me about you, because as for everything else I couldn't give a— well, you know. I should tell you that I do not expect to go on leave till 8^{ber}. One person per battery goes on leave every 2 or 3 days. And that's it! Corporals have their own rotation as do the non-coms, and in each case it takes about 12 months before everyone has gone on leave.

And now I must close—I love you, I love your hair down your back, I love your breasts discernible beneath the dressing-gown, I love your forehead, your eyes, your mouth and everything that is you, who are my Madeleine.

Gui

My darling dearest little fairy,

I am myself so overwhelmed by your letters and by all that has happened that I have been quite unable to write before this evening and I do so now with a passion at once so joyful and so painful that my fingers have seized up.

This is a reply chiefly to your letter about your saint's day and how you drank to me the next day and read from *Alcools*.

74

Your parcel arrived today. Intact this time and I am almost glad that the first time your scent was spilled like a libation in honour of our shared destiny. Furthermore the breaking of clear glass is a sign of very good luck and the cologne impregnated the box, so your fragrance continues to permeate my little cell.

As for my leave I was counting on spending it, if not in Oran, then at any rate in Algiers seeing that one gets at least six days when one goes to Algeria, and seeing that the day of disembarkation does not count if one arrives in the morning, so that makes it almost seven. These rules apply to Algeria only.

Mark you, Madeleine, I don't expect to get any leave before October, and I daresay not even before January or February. I am in a formation where leaves are granted this way and there's nothing for it but to accept the fact.

With regard to my book, at first I preferred that you not read it until I sent it to you. But ever since we made our vows I feel just the opposite and I am now delighted that in its pages you will have read much about my life.

I have told you not to be jealous, and since you no longer are, knowing that you are the chosen one forever, you may ask all the questions you wish with whatever degree of liberty you deem necessary and I shall reply with the candour with which a gentlemen should treat such confidences, a candour full of discretion yet without reticence.

And now to the matter of portraiture and literature. The portrait is lifelike in the most immediate sense. But this is scarcely the moment for the lesson in aesthetics that I could send you in this connection. What remains for the moment, my love, is your disappointment over a drawing that is actually a masterpiece.[1] A perfectly natural disappointment in someone who is not familiar with a completely legitimate art that one develops a taste for as soon as one discovers its meaning and logic.

I have written a little book on the subject entitled *Méditations esthétiques—les peintres cubistes*, although the second part of the title, which was supposed to be a subtitle, was printed in much larger type than the first, and so became the title. Paris, Figuière, 1912 or 1913 (?), but I don't have it to hand, as is true of all my books. The publisher is away at the war, and I don't know whether you can still find this little work.

As for poems, you say you like 'Zone', which I mentioned in an earlier letter. One day I will tell you how this poem of the end of love came about—for that matter I can tell you right away. In 1907 I developed an aesthetic liking, almost an admiration, which I still

1 Picasso's frontispiece for *Alcools*.

75

feel, for a young woman who was a painter.[2] She loved me or thought she did and I thought or rather tried to make myself love her, which I did not at that time. Neither of us was well known then, and I was just beginning my aesthetic meditations and writings, which were later to have an influence in Europe and even elsewhere. I may say that I did my very best to share my admiration for her with the entire universe. She wanted us to get married, which I never wanted—this went on till 1913, by which time she no longer loved me. It was over, but after so much time spent together, so many shared memories, with all that now disappearing I was plunged into a state of anguish that I mistook for love and went on suffering from until the war broke out at which time I met a charming woman, with a great passion for pleasure, you saw her at the train when I was returning from my leave and when I first met you: a charming and unfortunate young woman for whom life will always have pain in store, for she will always be a plaything in the hands of men and nothing more. I don't say this out of cynicism. For I was on the point of falling in love with her but she was able at the most to dispel my misery of the moment and for that I am enormously grateful and bound to her by eternal friendship. No more than that. But her character is as exquisite as her high birth might suggest. Our badinage is done but we continue to write one another without wasted words. At present she is near the Front in the Vosges near her closest friend, who himself knows what transpired, and writes me that the only thing he reproaches me for is that the idyll did not endure. Little does he know that Madeleine is a more powerful fairy. All the same, I still have for my poor little royal lady friend from Nice an attachment of which you ought not to be jealous for an instant, for women in whose veins the blood of Saint Louis runs, as debauched as they may be, retain a strain of nobility that allows friendship to outlast love. All that, in any case, never went beyond inconsequential displays of affection, and they no longer exist, can

2 Marie Laurencin.—Tr.

76

no longer occur, seeing that now only Madeleine exists. And yet I continue to nurture a complete and true friendship for that heroine of the Fronde, so deserving of friendship, of pity, of veneration, of indulgence, who has loved much, and suffered much, and whose life I would wish as sweet as can be.

As for that earlier and very longtime lady friend of mine, now among the most pre-eminent woman painters in the whole world, she was married about a year and a half ago to a German country squire. A true Parisienne, charming but plain, she is responsible at least in part for the fashions of the last two years and has successfully imposed her type of woman on all of Paris, and hence on the world at large. At the time of the mobilization she happened to be in Arcachon at a villa her husband owned there, and by virtue of her marriage she had become German. They managed who knows how to escape and avoid the concentration camps and are now in Málaga. The husband whom I don't know would not bear arms against the French. The tragic exile of this Parisian woman makes me very unhappy. She wrote me in Nîmes and has written to me here too. And her letters though still full of wit and fantasy border on a sort of desperate madness. She writes with the assent of her husband moreover and I have to say I wonder what he must think when he reads the letters she sends me in which despite herself memories crowd in behind every word.

So here I am standing like a new Marius on the Carthaginian ruins of my vanished loves.

Forgive me for them, Madeleine; so much for 'Zone' and for the whole of *Case d'Armons* if I ever send it to you; 'Mirabeau Bridge' is also the sad song of that long liaison with the person who after inspiring 'Zone' drew my portrait on horseback for the German edition of that poem, all of whose bitterness moreover she fully

GUILLAUME APOLLINAIRE

grasped, so much so that she sobbed over it, and had it been possible and had she really known what was in my heart she would have started all over again. For all that, she will always have a friend in me, an admirer, and even a defender. She knows it and many people in Paris know it, people who have written to me about it, rare good-hearted people who have by no means cast stones at her.

'Aubade' is not a separate poem but an interlude inserted into 'The Song of the Poorly Loved', which dates from 1903 and commemorates my first love when I was twenty, an English girl I met in Germany, it lasted a year, we both had to return home and then we stopped writing. Truth to tell, some turns of phrase in the poem are too severe and insulting for a girl who understood nothing about me, who loved me but was disconcerted to find herself in love with a poet, with such an odd being; I loved her physically but our minds were far apart. She was sensitive though, and gay. I was jealous of her for no reason and I took her absence very hard; my poetry well reflects my emotional state at the time, as an unknown poet among other unknown poets, and she far away and unable to come to Paris. I went to visit her in London twice, but marriage was impossible and everything was settled when she left for America, but I suffered a great deal, as witness this poem where I deemed myself poorly loved, whereas in fact it was I who loved poorly; there is also 'The Emigrant from Landor Road', commemorating that same love affair, just as 'Hunting Horns' evokes the same agonizing memories as 'Zone', 'Mirabeau Bridge', and 'Marie'—the most agonizing of all I think.

In *Alcools*, though, it is perhaps 'Vendémiaire' that I like best, and I also like 'The Traveller'—the fact is I very much like my verse, which I compose singing and I often sing to myself what little I can recall and that is very little indeed especially now—I can no longer remember a single line of 'Zone'. . . .

LETTERS TO MADELEINE

And I am very fond too of the poems written after *Alcools*, there are enough of them for a volume at least and I really really like 'Windows', which appeared on its own at the beginning of a catalogue of Delaunay's paintings. They answered to a completely new aesthetic whose basic principles I had been unable to retrieve until to my astonishment I found them clearly explained in one of your divine letters.

So there you have my great loves, which amount to nothing, considering my age, would you not agree Madeleine, and nothing at all alongside our love that is so absolute, beginning so purely, so tragically, so passionately, my darling, my pretty one, my divine joy and my little fairy.

So that is my complete confession, Madeleine. You have read some poems that I also like but that I had forgotten until the *Journal* of yesterday and the day before recalled them to me: verse, six little poems I think, written in the prison of La Santé in 1911. I feel sure you know the story. In that year of 1911 I took in a young man who was intelligent but quite unprincipled—unhappy rather than wicked and heaven knows what may have become of him by now. In 1907 he had stolen two Hispano-Roman statues from the Louvre and sold them to Picasso, who is a great artist but completely unscrupulous, whose name thanks to me never came out in connection with this business. I tried—we are far now from 1911, and even farther from 1907 or 1908—to persuade Picasso to return the statues to the Louvre, but he was much preoccupied by his research in aesthetics, which gave rise to Cubism. He told me he had damaged them while striving to uncover certain arcane features, at once classical and primitive, which they possessed. But I had found a way to help him get rid of the pieces without jeopardizing his honour. My friend Louis Lumet, Inspector at the École des Beaux-Arts, to whom I had

GUILLAUME APOLLINAIRE

told the story, had agreed to help in this good deed by means of an amusing feat of journalistic deception. We meant to suggest to *Le Matin* that it demonstrate to the public how poorly the treasures of the Louvre were guarded by stealing first one statue—big scandal—and then another—second big scandal. As a result the business of the original thefts would have lost all significance. But Picasso wanted to keep his statues. In 1911 the thief—whose adventures have been so often recounted in the papers that I do not need to give his name—the thief, or rather the hero, came back. At the time there was much talk about my book *The Heresiarch and Co.*, which in late 1910 obtained the most votes from the jury of the Prix Goncourt but still failed to win—unfairly, what is more. This was confirmed by Judith Gauthier, Léon Daudet and Élémir Bourges, who voted in favour, and even by Mirbeau, the 2 Rosnys, and Paul Margueritte, who read the book only after the vote, as they often told Bourges, the book's sponsor and certainly the sole artist in that Academy. The person who won the prize instead of me was killed not long ago: Louis Pergaud with a book entitled *De Goupil à Margot*—try and read the two books and tell me what you think. It was at this juncture that the hero of the statues came to see me, back from America with his pockets full of money that he promptly lost at the races, and now penniless he stole yet another statue. It was then that I took the miserable wretch in and tried to have him return the statue, but it was no go and I had to kick him out and the statue along with him. A few days later the Mona Lisa was stolen. I thought just as the police did that he must be the thief. But to cut a long story short he was not and he sold his statue to *Paris-Journal*, who returned it to the Louvre. I went to Picasso and told him how ill-advised his behaviour had been and how great the risks to him were. I found a frantic man who told me he had lied and that the statues were intact. I urged him to return them in exchange for a promise of silence to *Paris-Journal*, which he did. Big scandal! The miserable thief came to me and begged me to save his skin. I put him on a train at the Gare de Lyon with a little money to supplement the funds he had extracted from *Paris-Journal*. Thereupon I was arrested myself on the grounds that I knew where the Mona Lisa was since I had had a 'secretary' given to stealing statues from the Louvre. I admitted to the 'secretary' but refused to give him up, so they grilled me and threatened to search the houses of all my friends and relatives. A gruelling and truly dreadful situation. In the end, to keep my lady friend, my mother and my brother out of trouble I had no choice but—not to describe Picasso's role, but to say that he had been taken advantage of, and that he had no idea the antiquities he had bought came from the Louvre.

The next day they confronted me and my friend Picasso, who denied all knowledge of the matter. I felt sure I was lost, but the examining magistrate, clearly aware that I had done nothing and was simply being harassed by the police for not being willing to give up the fugitive, permitted me to question the witness, and using the maieutics so dear to Socrates I quickly got Picasso to admit that everything I had said was true. My case was dismissed and his name was never even mentioned. At the time the affair caused an enormous commotion; all the papers printed my picture. But I would gladly have done without all that publicity. For though I was passionately defended by most of the papers, I was attacked at the start and sometimes ignobly attacked by anti-Semites who could not conceive of a Pole who was not a Jew. Léon Daudet went so far as to deny ever having voted for me for the Prix Goncourt. This so revulsed that fine old gent Bourges that he was prompted to give 2 interviews in a single day, though up until then he had always obstinately declined to grant interviews on any subject.

GUILLAUME APOLLINAIRE

There you have the story, singular, incredible, tragic and amusing all at once, of how I came to be the only person ever arrested in France in connection with the theft of the Mona Lisa. What is more, the police did everything in their power to justify their action, interrogating my concierge and my neighbours as to whether I used to entertain young girls or young boys and lord knows what else and had my habits not been beyond reproach you may be sure that they would never have let me go—after all, the honour of their corporation was at stake. It brought home to me what the man meant who said that if ever he were accused of stealing the bells of Notre Dame he would take flight without a second thought.*

And there you have the story of the six little poems written 'À La Santé', in La Santé prison; you likewise have all the biographical details that inform *Alcools*.

82

I said just now that 'Vendémiaire' was my favourite poem in *Alcools*. Thinking about it, I feel that the most innovative and most lyrical, the profoundest, is 'The Betrothal', dedicated to Picasso whose sublime art I admire, a poem which concerns you absolutely, you, Madeleine, for no woman has ever been the object of it except you who were fated to arrive, and no doubt along with 'The Brazier' it is my best poem if not the most readily accessible.

For the rest, we love other each so much that you have already forgiven me my scandals. My poet's life is assuredly of the oddest, but fate has always beset me with so many troubles which despite all I find utterly delightful that I am one of humanity's greatest joys, I'm quite aware of that and what I love most of all is to have met you, you whom I was looking for, your mind sister to mine, yours the greatest beauty, yours the tenderest attentive obedience, everything I always missed—you Madeleine, ready to love me in a lyrical peace far from false loves and unwholesome rumours, far too from this war

* I might add that I never received an apology, though most of the papers held me up as a paragon of hospitality. And here is the end of the story: the Hero was arrested in Cairo at the end of 1913 and acquitted in the courts. Which made me happy, because the poor fellow was a madman more than a criminal, and the judges evidently thought just as I did.

which goes on forever and on which as a good soldier I shall refrain from stating an opinion even though I do have one in my heart of hearts that is henceforward irreversible.

So read this confession written in haste, but weigh even the disorder of its style in the balance, and if you still love me in that light (my image is not here alone, however, but everywhere in *Alcools*), then I shall write to your mother.

I am not re-reading my letter, it is too long, and my little fairy will no doubt supply the words left out and repair awkward sentences and other shortcomings. I kiss your darling forehead. . . .

Gui

83

My little fairy,

Whatever your response to my last letter, which must surely have
seemed mad to you, I want to add to all I said there that I am a
good honest lad whose life is dissipated in appearance only, this
impression being due to the fact that I am a poet and unmarried.
Had I met a Madeleine earlier everything would have been different. Above all I would have earned a great deal more money, which
would have been much easier for me were I married.

Until the war came I was making a very good living and when it
broke out I had 18,000 (eighteen thousand) francs guaranteed for
1915. All that is down the drain now and the small part of it that I
shall be able to get hold of is already spoken for either here or
because my brother who is still in Mexico can send nothing further
to our mother.

The upshot is that after the war I shall need to find a new way of
making a living and settle rent arrears for the whole war period.

The rent, though, is the least of it.

The main thing is to find a situation, and that cannot be done
quickly, especially since life in all its immediacy will press in. Much
effort and acumen will be required.

I tell you all this so that you can clearly see and grasp the circumstances in which I find myself.

In short this letter too calls for an answer, after which, if you tell me to, I shall write to your Mama.

I must reiterate, in view of the impression of a disordered life that you must have been given by *Alcools*, that I am not a libertine as you perhaps believe though without saying so.

I have had mistresses, true, but my honesty towards them and the friendship they still have for me shows that, even though I never found the one that I should have liked to marry, I at least exhibited the virtues of delicacy, tenderness and indeed constancy—in short, I did not betray them ever. But until now I had no wish to marry; I was waiting for more than they could offer.

There is a young girl who has been writing to me almost every day for the last two years. I do not reply, because I told her that I did not want to marry her. I did not want to make her my mistress either, though she wished it. I felt that it would be disloyal on my part and I refrained.

I tell you this so that you will not judge me too harshly.

What is more, you may question me about whatever you like. At this moment you are the judge in the matter of greatest moment in your life. So make your judgement in complete freedom. I could not speak to you of these things before for there was no good reason to do so. I can do so only now that there is a reason, the most serious possible one: our love.

Yesterday I sent a little heart to you in Nice. This time I put an inscription on it.

I wonder where the Petit Chemin de Valrose is exactly. I know a fair number of people in Nice, especially under my pseudonym of Guillaume Apollinaire. One in particular is Louis Bertrand, who has

GUILLAUME APOLLINAIRE

depicted Algeria in highly coloured academic novels that in his view make him a rival to Flaubert. He lives at Les Collinettes. I am acquainted too with Aurel and her husband Alfred Mortier. Both are notable literary people. They live over by the Russian church.

I also know the harbour-master, who reigns over the waterfront. He is a sailor, but also a poet and novelist. A charming and refined shirker who spends his time smoking opium and taking cocaine at home with his wife or else in a bachelors' den frequented mainly by women and seamen. The war is no cure for drug addicts. Not a word of this, mind, to anyone.

As a matter of fact, in February there were plenty of shirkers holed up in the Nice press, notably G. Maurevert at *L'Éclaireur* as well as any number of others. I presume they are still there.

But how magical old Nice is with its Genoese houses and the market along the Paillon. But I am getting nostalgic. I kiss your forehead tenderly, *Madeleine,*

Gui

My adorable friend, I have three letters from you dated the 24, 26 and 28 July. No, my darling, I am not tired at the moment. I am very well. I think we shall be moving once more in a few days. But where to?

How, my dear friend, can you suppose that I find you too ugly when there is no part of you, of those parts that I have seen, that I do not find lovely, and when thinking of what I have not seen is for me an excessively pleasurable kind of torture? I harp on about our love endlessly, my darling, and it seems to me that as far apart as we are we are now but one flesh.—You write so well, darling, and if you love as well as you write our love will be a masterpiece. I am sending you my little book *Case d'Armons* just as it is, without changing anything. This is a book whose truth is now in the past. But I leave it unchanged as a snapshot of a moment in my life.

I am dashed happy that you like what I do, and what is more that you have understood it so thoroughly as to observe that 'Your verse should be sung.' The fact is, Madeleine, that I never write poetry without singing. A musician once even pointed out the three or four melodies that I use instinctively and that express the rhythm of my existence. My beloved little slave you shall nevertheless be mistress of your own house and mistress of your master. We understand each other from afar without a word concerning those things about which we do not write, which is to say our joys—and therein lies our happiness.

GUILLAUME APOLLINAIRE

Frago[nard]'s apparently frivolous and libertine picture embodies more than allegory. The 18th century combined the barest and most practical good sense with the most mysterious and mystical oddity. Nothing that arouses the senses and submits those of a wife to her husband is unhelpful to the delicate, innate and primordial art of marital bliss, more vital than any other to the growth and greatness of a nation. Your own parents have set the example for you. The large family that they have raised is a boon to humanity. We too, Madeleine, shall try to have many children. Would you like that? All this is getting us away from Frago. Not so far away as you might think however. Look here, the fact that I, just like you, have written letters that call for a reply does not mean that I doubt you. Indeed I already look upon you as at once the freest and the most submissive of wives.

Your soul my darling is therefore mine just as your body awaits me.

Do not feel too sorry for me darling, for all in all I have not been unhappy in this war. After meeting you I took a reserve officers' training course in Nîmes to which I had been accepted on a competitive basis, then a circular was issued announcing that there would be no further nominations to the officer corps; I concluded that promotion in the Artillery was going to be difficult, and since I had been slow to write to you and I did not wish to do so from the depot, I asked to leave for the Front. My reward was a relative tranquillity. No great heroism was called for, no terrible suffering. Nothing but the damp, whose effects I shall no doubt feel later. True, there are drawbacks, such as the flies. And the shelling, but that is normal in war. But for the most part there is no conflict in the group. The artillerymen are real princes in their relations with the infantry. As for the job of quartermaster, it is certainly sought after, but it is far more onerous than gunnery corporal, which gives one a lot of time to oneself.

At present I can hardly ever write you save at night. Fortunately I don't sleep much and above all I have trouble falling asleep. So staying awake presents no problem for me. I was telling you earlier, but since my writing was interrupted I did not finish my thought, that I was rewarded for my voluntary departure for the Front, the reason being that almost all those who stayed behind at the Nîmes depot were sent to the Dardanelles, where according to the meagre information we get none of the landings went well. And I wanted to add that after all, in an extraordinary adventure such as this, it is not cowardice to congratulate oneself for having preserved one's life, which is such a precarious thing just now.

Too much importance should not be attached to the vexed question of the 'consistency of literature'. The fact is that in France taste and favour often reward banality. Their sense of moderation holds the French back today in matters of taste (and indeed has long done so), and this in times when taste is perhaps no longer in play or at any rate has changed enormously. But the age and authentic taste will reassert their rights in due course.

In these epic times, however, the plaudits are reserved for the sugar water of a Henry Bordeaux (a stale rehash of the remarkable Paul Bourget) or for the Rostands, pale epigones of the charming Banville, or even for an imbecilic caricature of Rostand such as Zamacoïs.

And the fact is that despite what I had to say earlier against the coldly lyrical spirit, the deliberately retrograde Thomism of a Claudel, this attitude dominates all the art known to the leading newspapers even though it is but base coin as compared with the solid gold that was Rimbaud. That is all.

I recognize the great influence that Romain Rolland has had in academic and bourgeois artistic circles throughout Europe. I am even

GUILLAUME APOLLINAIRE

willing to grant him all the merits that you point out and that my friends have often pointed out to me. But from what I know of him, his liberalism and generosity seem dull, sad as it were, in a word Swiss. For my part I have read nothing of his, though I had the chance to meet him a good many times about 12 years ago. At the time I was the editor of a review that I founded and that is now very hard to find: *Le Festin d'Ésope* (Aesop's Banquet). I had published a survey of the development of the orchestra in modern music, and he sent a long response which I published.

He is undoubtedly highly qualified when it comes to musical questions, of which I know nothing. After certain facts about the disorder in his household came my way by chance I was discouraged from opening his books and I have never read them despite the urgings of quite a few people.

Nor have I read his letters on the war, and my word the circumstances are such that to my mind a Frenchman should do nothing for the Germans and least of all write anything in favour of them, for they will devour us if we let them and in any case we surely have no good reason to be friendly with such louts and cheats. I have known enough of them to have got their measure. They are decent only when they are poor and wretched. In that event their plodding mentality suits them well enough and their petty abstruse lyricism gives rise to piquant little things with a feeling of the infinite, with musicality perhaps but no human consciousness: in a literary sense Goethe alone is great among Germans, and everything great about him pertains to his humanism, the rest is plodding too—and this on every subject.

Heine was a Jew who wanted to become French, and sadly it is the Jewish sensibility, so caustic, that has largely succeeded in replacing the profound simplicity of the French spirit—the art of the

Boulevards is excessively Jewish. Not that the Jews do not have great merits, which should not be disparaged.

Nietzsche was a Pole like me.

The great German writer today is also a Pole, Przybyszensky. I have read nothing by him. There are three Poles well known to literature today, and none of them ever write in Polish.

Conrad in England (a great talent).

Przybyszensky in Germany.

And me in France.

This was pointed out to me two years ago by Maeterlinck's Russian translator, a lady who wanted me to reserve my next novel for her to translate. But time went on and the novel was not finished. I needed a woman to get me to finish it. Indeed I missed a great opportunity there, for I was commissioned to write three theatre pieces likewise for Russia. Never written at all.

It is blasphemous at the present time for a Frenchman of whatever extraction to defend the Germans. The issue is not the outrageous reports of journalists whose proper place is in the trenches (I know a good five hundred of them who are not doing their duty and against whom I shall no doubt have to hold my own after the war, for I am fated to have to hold my own). These people play into the Germans' hands and dishonour the French spirit. But what is much more important is that this war not turn into a scramble for spoils among those in the rear. Unfortunately that is what seems to be happening. Even French women, though they do have a conscience and honour and grace the whole world, are not playing their part, which is to support the soldiers, ferret out shirkers and oblige those with special skills to contribute. I am not talking about you, Madeleine, you are doing your duty, your family is doing theirs, and besides, you have our future to prepare, which in such grave times as these is perhaps more important than the precarious destiny of a single country albeit the most beautiful country in the world.

In the meantime the murky patriotism of the Germans, who dream not of humanity but of a Boche universe, is working miracles—even promising the enlistment of women, whereas on our side there are still myriads of men who use every kind of excuse to flee the magnificent perpetual danger that we face.

But you must not picture me as downhearted; I am afraid that my letters might often have given you that impression, whereas in fact I laugh all the time and am renowned for it in the battery, where my iron constitution up to now and a good humour that nothing can perturb except for a lack of letters from Madeleine have won me a kind of popularity.

I belong to a very special battery whose peculiar customs combine stoicism, independence, cautiousness and a gaiety so mad that madness might as well be the group's name. Its members all come from the occupied lands. All brave fellows—poor fellows too because they have but scant news from home brought by refugees or via Holland. But they are industrious to the point where there is a massive amount of money in this battery, possibly more than on the whole Front put together. The trade in rings with the infantry (though I prefer sending mine to you, for whom I make them) has reached such proportions that one of the main jewellers by the name of Lemaire has put 2,500 francs aside without going short of anything and even though all he has is the rings and a sou per day in pay.

But it is true that this is the only battery which does such fine work—I've seen rings made by other *poilus* that aren't a quarter as good as my own, which are so very far from perfect.

You are surprised by the idea that this may go on for another 2 years. If only it did last 2 years, I believe that would mean certain victory, but the only thing to be feared my darling is that it does not last 2 more years. And if I wish for victory, it is simply out of manly pride. All men are brothers and in a way it makes hardly any difference to me who in particular triumphs, because for anyone considering the situation from Sirius, like Renan, life will go on just the same afterwards but from the point of view of our pride, of me, of the regal feeling that is in every man, it is necessary that what has animated me, that the language in which I sing, that the beauty of Madeleine, that everything that makes up the country that is mine just as much as it was the Hungarian Ronsard's, that France be victorious. And, no matter what happens, if we both live we shall be victors and victorious over the whole world.

I may possibly get my leave at the beginning of October, but not before.

My kisses cover all of you my darling and in doing so they reveal you to my imagination, which is driven wild.

Alcools contains very many misprints. Here are a few that need correcting: in 'Lul of Faltenin'—

> *Si les bateliers ont ramé*
> *Loin des lèvres à fleur de l'onde*
> *Mille et mille animaux charmés*
> Flairent

> If the boatmen have rowed
> Far from the lips that kiss the wave
> Thousands of enchanted animals
> Sniff out

GUILLAUME APOLLINAIRE

—*flairent* (sniff out) should read *flairant* (sniffing out).

In 'Cortège', for *amateurs* read *armateurs* (shipowners).

In 'Merlin and the Old Woman', 2nd stanza, read 'a fleuri *l'hiver*' (flowered in winter) for '*l'univers*'; in 'Vendémiaire', at the beginning, read 'je *vivais*' (lived) for 'je *vivrais*' (would live); later we find *trismégiste* [for *trismégistes*], etc. etc.

I can't recall all the misprints but I adore you my very dearest Madeleine. Your lips? . . . I adore you.

Gui

(I am not re-reading.)

94

My adorable Madeleine,

Together with two letters from Oran I have received a postcard from Marseilles (no date) my darling so I can now expect fresher news from you than hitherto.

And from the depths of my hypogeum I answer you joyfully. I have sent you the little book that is now outdated and a pen-stand made of aluminium which works better than the other one.

Postal delays should diminish now that we are both in the same part of the world. And since a minute does not pass without my having passionate thoughts about you, you should not worry yourself.

You have a notion of your slavery that ought to be mine and not yours, otherwise you will be nothing but a little runaway slave. But in the end it makes no difference. My darling, so lucid, is all mine. That is the main thing. Madeleine you are a marvellous prize and I adore you deeply. For there is nothing so exquisite as our love. Physical inclination is merely skin-deep for us, whereas in the spiritual and moral realms we have penetrated each other to a degree quite unheard of. At times I am reminded of Héloïse and Abélard. But I warrant you I am certainly not Abélard. Your dream was wonderful. I free you and shall free you from everything that might shackle you and my one and only desire is to take the place of your dream.

95

All the same, you must not form too exaggerated a picture of me. Take me as I am: not ugly but no longer handsome, absolutely not! I was a very beautiful child and still attractive as a youth but now I am no longer good-looking. By no means deformed and plenty of hair but quite often I find myself almost ugly. Masses of defects. Qualities: not a gambler not a drinker, just a poet and that is all. Very gay but with sudden sad moods. Marvellous constitution which the war has weakened and will doubtless weaken further. But to love you I have an endless store of ardour.

We undoubtedly share the same tastes and please tell me what yours are and I will endeavour to embrace them, though whenever in the first instance our tastes differ I shall let you know even if I have already adopted yours. But I want to point out the differences to you so as not to place unduly onerous demands on our individual natures, or perhaps rather so as to ensure that no lies come between us. So tell me not only what your tastes, dreams and preferences are but also what particular caresses your dreams have suggested to you, and draw a picture from your imagination of the one who would be your master.

And strawberry ice cream will taste better when it is an ice cream *à la Madeleine* that melts in my mouth.

And our secret is the most beautiful of secrets.

And our *Carte du Tendre* has no more stages: we have occupied all the important positions.

But just as in the dream I take you in my arms, I kiss your hair and your exquisite mouth of whose lovely form I was reminded by your card from Marseilles: an arch, the arch of love itself, by which I want to live and die.

Gui

8 August 1915

My great love,

I have received your first letter from Nice. Nice the 'City of Victory'—a good omen. I hope my leave will be brought forward to a date prior to 15 7ᵇᵉʳ and we shall see each other there.

My sweetheart, I have been with you in spirit throughout your journey—

You mustn't overwhelm me with praise. Your poet is happy to have touched you. And he is happy in general to see that *Alcools* is making its way into people's minds. In the last issue of the *Mercure*, which included an instalment of my 'Vie anecdotique', fragments from *Alcools* are quoted in a rather pretentious article, 'Montparnasse et la guerre', which has some good insights but also some errors. At the end some verse postcard messages of mine are given. The first was sent from Nîmes to a man named André Dupont; the reply appended in the *Mercure* to that short didactic poem does not concern Dupont and was in fact sent me apropos of another poem by [André] Billy, who at the end quotes some lines from a little poem in *Alcools*.

Lastly, the 3rd little poem printed was sent to the same Billy whose reply was as indicated. In the first poem the line

> *L'artillerie est l'art de mesurer les angles*
> Artillery is the art of measuring angles

GUILLAUME APOLLINAIRE

is now well known, and one of my friends Louis de Gonzague Frick even appropriated it after hearing it quoted. He used it in a little book entitled *Trèfle à quatre feuilles* (Four-Leafed Clover) which I'll send you so you can both read it and mind it for me. Knowing that the line was mine he wrote to apologize for taking it. In any case as an infantryman and knowing nothing of artillery he could never have written it. But now that his book is out the lines quoted in the *Mercure* will surely be attributed to him, which is amusing. I give you these unimportant details because I know they will entertain you.

But let us get back to love, the only thing really worth talking about.

But no, the smell of mimosa is not unpleasant at all and inasmuch as it is the smell of Nice where you are at present its sweet scent has become quite exquisite. It evokes the lovely journey during which I found you so gentle and demure, like a pretty and docile gazelle. Now we await the little fairy's photos. I am also waiting for a letter— *the letter*.

Now that you are writing every day, remember that from time to time I would like a long letter. I think we at this end are going to have to send our letters unsealed from now on but those received here will still be allowed, I imagine, to be sealed. For my part I have thought of a way to get round this unusual and intrusive order, my idea being to tie a cotton thread (linen thread being hard to come by) around my letters to you. In that way they will be both open and closed, as it were. As a matter of fact I don't suppose any more letters will be read than are being read now, this is merely to discourage people from giving out too much information.

We are of course ever liable to make imprudent statements without even being aware of it.

I am very eager for you to receive the little book, posted yesterday. The heart should have arrived and the long letters too—I am worrying today, I'm anxious—anxious that everything should reach you safely.

A friend has written me something perspicacious about the word *poilu*, pointing out that when he was in the service it was used to designate civilians. I mention this because I know that you detest this term.

Here we call soldiers *grivetons* (thrushes).

And if the *griveton* who is writing this could only see his little *grive* (which is I suppose the feminine of *griveton*), the two of them would soon be *saouls comme des grives*, as drunk as thrushes—and not in this case from marauding in the vineyard.

99

My fairy is adorable—oh, how truly lovable my Madeleine is!! I love her more every day, one day it is lust that grows in me, the next it is tender feelings, and this enormous love has killed everything it perceives as possibly hostile to itself. This love, this cherished love, is a great warrior.

Your Gui

My darling fiancée,

Your distress has upset me more than I can say. I withdraw everything. You must not suffer, for you are loved beyond anything ever loved before.

Poet, I grant you that, but fantasist [*fantasque*]—not in the least! And if I used the word I was referring to the imagination—and in any case you completely satisfy my need for fantasy, but I never meant to refer to real life. Once they find what they are looking for, poets have completed their task, and my own work in matters of love is likewise complete. You have fixed my love forever, darling Madeleine.

But my word, there is such rebellion in your letter!!!—Don't forget that you are not addressing an ordinary poet, you are addressing a soldier too. And you MUST NOT doubt me. I assume responsibility for your complete happiness. No woman shall have a more perfect life than you. And there'll be nothing fantastical about it.

But for this distress of yours just as for your joy I love you with an infinite love and at the same time I am annoyed with you for not fearing me.

I write you all this because it is true. Because you should know the whole truth, because to deserve you I am giving up everything that

100

is not Madeleine and also because I want you to love me and to fear me, quite naked, quite disarmed, all ready for the great love that holds us in its embrace. If you do not understand me, utterly true and UNCHANGEABLE INCORRUPTIBLE FAITHFUL as I shall be, in the most absolute sense, then my very soul must have escaped you and it must be that you are not worthy of it—But I know that you are in fact worthy Madeleine, and I await the reply in your next letter that will allow us once and for all to assess our two souls which I am quite sure are bound together forever. Today I am writing my letter to your mother, which I shall post only once I have your reply, which I already know by HEART. And as much as I know what you will say, I am indescribably anxious about this. Far more anxious than about the bombardment and all the rest.

How mean your letter is, all the same. Speak the truth the absolute truth because for my part I say everything, absolutely everything, without mincing words and in depth. My Madeleine, I do not want you to suffer, for the truest of true love is within us. Think about this, and may our faithful and free happiness be as you decide my darling slave. I want you to take me as the lowest of the low so that thanks to you I may rise to the greatest heights, adoring you as I do. I kiss your mouth

Gui

As from tomorrow I shall be leaving my letters open and they will be sealed by the censoring officer.

My beloved,

I adore you. Just a quick line. I am posting the letter to your Mama tomorrow. Write me a long letter and let it contain no trace of bitterness of any sort. Otherwise it will be too painful for me. I fear there was a hint of bitterness in your most recent letters despite their passion and assent. Even though I am writing to your Mama, until I have her answer you are still mistress of yourself and quite at liberty to change your mind.

I adore you.

Gui

102

To Mme Pagès

In the Field, 10 August 1915

Madame,

Madeleine has spoken to you of me. I adore her; she loves me. I wish to make her happy.

I have the honour to ask you for her hand in marriage.

According to her wish and mine, we shall marry as soon as possible, provided that you consent.

So great is my emotion, moreover, that I do not know what to add here save to express the great desire I have to become your son and to cherish you as the mother of Madeleine.

Words fail me now, yet I feel in advance how much I shall love you.

I await your response with the greatest anxiety, which is very easy to understand since, in view of our feelings and tastes and also everything that for Madeleine and me makes life worth living, there can be, I believe, nowhere in the world today, nor could there have been in the past, a more appropriate union.

I have the honour, Madame, to be most respectfully yours,

Gui de Kostrowitzky

Corporal, 38th Field Artillery Rgmt
45th Battery, Sector 138

GUILLAUME APOLLINAIRE

11 August 1915

My little fairy,

I wrote to your Mama yesterday.—

—If I wrote '*fantasque*', I intended to give this epithet no meaning beyond that which it derives from the idea of *fantasy*; genuine fantasy stems neither from caprice nor from irrational changes and as a fairy yourself how could you possibly believe that a fairy world might come into being by sheer chance? The only changes in me are as slight as the tiny movements to be seen at a pigeon's throat. What is more I have sung of myself in the following words:

> *Les jours s'en vont, je demeure*[1]
>
> The days go by, I remain

[1] From 'Mirabeau Bridge' (1912).—Tr.

And I do not change at all unless I am forced to change. Between us—though there is no need for them to do so—the bonds of the mind will secure the bonds of the heart.

Life is painful only for those who choose to keep their distance from poetry, thanks to which it is true that we are made in God's image. Poetry (even etymologically) is creation. And creation, the serene expression of intelligence beyond time, is perfect joy.

Childbirth alone is painful.

The poet's task is to create, not to give birth. That is why poets are often deemed lazy, for they do not labour and such is their destiny.

So it is that in every circumstance fortunate or otherwise I have always been happy, for life itself is my happiness.

You are my life Madeleine, which is to say my indescribable happiness and that joy which is not yoked to time.

And time cannot change someone whom the fearsome flight of the hours cannot carry off.

No, you should certainly not see any signs of sadness in my work, but rather a continual and conscious and voluptuous striving to live learn see know and give voice to life itself.

According to you, Madeleine, your reason is in perfect harmony with love; for me an instinct, a prophetic fever like the one that raged in the Sibyl, was the force that drove me towards you. As for faithfulness, there is no one more faithful to their commitments than a poet.

Is there any life in the history of the lyre more dissolute than Racine's before his marriage?

But was that most gentle of poets any less a good husband for having known La Champmeslé?

In any case, Madeleine, I sin in no way against you and I am absolved by your love.

I shall devote myself to your happiness with all my strength and all my soul. . . .

Tristan Bernard has sent me the first 15 issues of his *Poil Civil* (The Civilian Poilu). I'll send you them one of these days. The spirit governing this periodical pamphlet I find rather congenial on account of the freedom of mind it embodies. This freedom of mind is the most glorious of French virtues and must be preserved at all costs.

GUILLAUME APOLLINAIRE

Mon souvenir vous présente à moi comme le tableau de la création

Se présentait à Dieu le septième jour

Madeleine mon cher ouvrage

Que j'ai fait naître brusquement

    Votre deuxième naissance

Nice les Arcs Toulon Marseille Prunay Wez Thuizy Courmelois Beaumont-sur-Vesles

Mourmelon-le-Grand Cuperly Laval St-Jean-sur-Tourbe Le Mesnil Hurlus

Perthes-lès-Hurlus Oran Alger

Et j'admire mon ouvrage

Nous sommes l'un à l'autre comme des étoiles très lointaines

Qui s'envoient leur lumière . . .

Vous en souvenez-vous?

Mon cœur

Allait de porte en porte comme un mendiant

Et vous m'avez fait l'aumône qui m'enrichit à jamais

Quand noircirai-je mes houseaux

Pour la grande cavalcade

Qui me ramènera près de vous?

Vous m'attendez ayant aux doigts

Des pauvres bagues en aluminium pâle comme l'absence

Et tendre comme le souvenir

Métal de notre amour métal semblable à l'aube

Ô Lettres chères lettres

Vous attendez les miennes

Et c'est ma plus chère joie

D'épier dans la grande plaine où s'ouvrent comme le désir les tranchées

    Blanches les tranchées pâles

D'épier l'arrivée du vaguemestre

Les tourbillons de mouches s'élèvent sur son passage

Celles des ennemis qui voudraient l'empêcher d'arriver

Et vous lisant aussitôt

Je m'embarque avec [vous] pour un pèlerinage infini

Nous sommes seuls

LETTERS TO MADELEINE

As for us soldiers at the Front, we no longer enjoy the right to write freely. At first I felt sure that this restriction had little justification. Our letters must be left unsealed and may be read by censoring officers. On second thoughts, however, it occurred to me that the art of letter-writing is liable to revive as a result, for everyone will now try to write as well as he can, looking for new ways of conveying what can be intimated only, and the critical faculty, which had been rendered pointless by its plethora of targets, will now perforce be used in the subtlest way imaginable, while our intelligence freshly honed by necessity will once more become what it should never have ceased being, to wit, powerful and sophisticated.

All of which augurs well for an end to the war. And Paul-Louis Courier, as very witty as he was and so rational withal, could still have written his *Pétition pour des villageois qu'on empêche de danser* (Petition on behalf of Villagers who are Forbidden to Dance), though of course he would have had to be very sure not to issue a *Petition on behalf of Soldiers whose Correspondence is Intruded Upon*. In short, the measure is an excellent one. And with that thought my dearest fiancée I offer you my soul.

Gui

107

2 See pp. 264–65.

À MADELEINE[2]

Je serre votre souvenir comme un corps véritable
Et ce que mes mains pourraient prendre de votre beauté
Ce que mes mains pourraient en prendre un jour
Aura-t-il plus de réalité?
Car qui peut prendre la magie du printemps?
Et ce qu'on en peut avoir n'est-il pas moins réel encore
Et plus fugace que le souvenir?
Et l'âme cependant prend l'âme même de loin

GUILLAUME APOLLINAIRE

Plus profondément plus complètement encore
Qu'un corps ne peut étreindre un corps.
Et je chante pour vous librement joyeusement
Tandis que seule votre voix pure me répond
Qu'il serait temps que s'élevât cette harmonie
Sur l'océan sanglant de ces pauvres années
Où le jour est atroce où le soleil est la blessure
Par où s'écoule en vain la vie de l'univers
Qu'il serait [temps], ma Madeleine, de lever l'ancre!

TO MADELEINE

I hold your memory tight like a real body
But will what my hands can take of your beauty
What they may be able to take of it some day
Be any more real?
For who can capture the magic of springtime?
And is not what one may keep of it even less real
And more fleeting than a memory?
Yet a soul can embrace a soul from afar
More deeply more completely even
Than a body can clasp a body.
My memory presents you to me as the picture of creation
Presented itself to God on the seventh day
Madeleine my dear handiwork
To which I have so abruptly given birth
    Your second birth
Nice Les Arcs Toulon Marseilles Prunay Wez Thuizy Courmelois Beaumont-
    sur-Vesles
Mourmelon-le-Grand Cuperly Laval St-Jean-sur-Tourbe Le Mesnil Hurlus
Perthes-lès-Hurlus Oran Algiers
And I admire my work
We are one to the other like far distant stars

Sending their light back and forth . . .

Do you remember it?

My heart

Was going from door to door like a beggar

And you gave me the alms that have made me rich forever

When shall I black my gaiters and mount up

For the great expedition

That brings me back to your side?

You are waiting for me with on your fingers

Crude rings of aluminium pale as absence

And tender as memory

Metal of our love metal like the dawn

Oh Letters dear letters

You wait for mine

And my dearest joy

Is to watch the great plain where the trenches gape like desire

               White trenches pale trenches

To watch for the post orderly

Clouds of flies swirl up as he approaches

Enemy flies out to prevent his arrival

And reading your words at once

I set out with [you] on an endless pilgrimage

We are alone

And I sing for you freely joyfully

While your pure voice alone answers me

The time has surely come for this harmony to rise

Above the bloody ocean of these wretched years

When the light of day is horrifying when the sun is the wound

Through which the life of the universe drains uselessly away

The time has come, my Madeleine, to weigh anchor!

Gui

GUILLAUME APOLLINAIRE

12 August 1915

My darling fiancée,

I have had no letter from you today. I am stricken. What could have happened? Remember, I cannot live without news from you. I adore you, you and you alone. I am so sad not to have a word from you today.

> *C'est une nuit d'orage*
> *Le tonnerre fait rage*
> *La mitrailleuse aussi*
> *Mais je suis bien ici*
> *Je pense à vous ma fée*
> *De raisins noirs coiffée . . .*

> It is a stormy night
> The thunder rages
> So does the machine-gun
> But I am fine here
> I think of you my fairy
> And the black grapes of your hair . . .

Am I to have fewer and shorter letters from Nice than I had from your old address?

I am impatiently awaiting your news and may it be very loving.

Here the flies with the help of the storms are renewing their campaign to make life intolerable. They succeed, I may say, only on those days when I get no letter from you. I kiss your hair and your eyes.

Gui

Two delightful letters from you, dated the 6 and 7—just as I was hoping for news from you. So my confessions startled you a little? True, you are always for harmony. And photos! I do hope that the heart is now where it is supposed to be. Or possibly it should be put in a safe place, aluminium is a very delicate metal. You are right, we shall keep our love a secret, it will be ours alone.—But what is the 3rd birth? I don't quite understand that. Why yes, dear child, you were forewarned. You *must* tell me about your inclinations, and please talk to me too about your dear you that I so adore. You speak to me only of me. But you have offered me your mouth. I savour it, I devour it, and all of you even the most secret parts of you, and how happy I was to learn that you were feeling better. Now my darling that you and I truly belong to each other we can write freely and what can I say of the immense desire I have for young flesh. I am like an ogre who has been tossed a little child to eat. I take your lips madly like an exquisite fruit and my hands long for everything that the poem made you feel. Madeleine, my sweet darling, do write me a long letter. It is pouring with rain. I fear the peace may bring you nothing but a gout-ridden groom so crippled with pain that you will have no further use for him. Ah, how much love will be needed to dry this unrelenting damp!

Gui

111

Madeleine, by now you should have *Case d'Armons* in your hands and now that we understand one another as we do I no longer fear your reaction to reading it. You must assuredly be very beautiful, since your eyes and your lips persuade your mother of it. Talk to me at length, at great length, of your beauty. I want no humility at all on your part about that beauty and indeed you should continually be at pains to dazzle me on this very important subject.

I understand now what you mean by the 3rd birth and am happy to have found out, but in this matter let us wait until puberty when the process is completed before celebrating to the very fullest. We understand one another from afar, but you cannot yet understand how greatly I desire you nor grasp all I imagine about your beauty and your love. But this is not to say that you would be shocked if you knew these things. What is more I get these thrilling but painful feelings often, I need merely think of your eyes which are so serious and of your voice. Your eyes are serious when they are not looking, but as soon as they look they become sweet and light: I very well recall getting this double impression on the train. So, we are agreed concerning those who will have to continue our life and bear witness to our love—assuming always that this can be, for with your usual good sense you clearly ask that question. All the same, bear in mind that there is no more fertile blood than the Polish, and yours going by what you have told me is hardly barren either, and so there is a good 70% chance that we shall not remain alone.

I sleep little, but I sleep well, never have insomnia. But I love to lie in bed without sleeping, or reading; I get up very easily as well, and I must get myself up, must get myself to hurry up, and never give Slavic indolence or nonchalance or poetic timidity the chance to encroach upon the time of the distinctly unlazy man that I am. I judge you to be very serious, deeply imbued with a sense of duty, a sense of your role—you are the woman I have dreamt of, my darling, which means we may hope to do great things.

I dislike going to bed late and if I stay up here it is because I don't have time to write in the daytime, but whenever I can I retire early, and I love to get up early in the morning. And there I am well served, for I get up at half-past four. I go to bed about two. But I assure you I don't need much sleep. When I was at the lycée I used to rise at 3 a.m. to do my homework, in that way I had my evenings free, though I would go to bed at 9.—

Being emotional or softhearted is not necessarily bad. What is bad is false emotion or false softheartedness, and *fear of life* is simply an upside-down imitation of the *joie de vivre* of (the nevertheless very great) Zola.

Banville is charming and his influence is still discernible in the art of poetry—though not in the way he himself might have supposed, indeed in a very different way.

As for R. R. [Romain Rolland], I too have defended him in what I have had to say and I am well aware that there is something European in him and even in his positions. But it would take too long to go into this fully here, and by comparing my two letters (today's and the earlier one) you will see things more clearly. I am not a fool and understand the need to weigh things in the balance. In our letters the question had arisen of what you rightly called 'the ignoble

GUILLAUME APOLLINAIRE

wedding of the L's'. Other information suggests meanwhile that everything is going well in this area and that despite some official disagreements individuals are being well treated. Things are picking up and business is good. It is all quite remarkable in fact, and in the large towns mixed marriages are commonplace. I have some extraordinary details on this. So sangfroid is appropriate here, and perhaps R. R.'s attitude as viewed from Sirius is quite inconsequential. It is even possible that he is right, but in that case being right here would itself be irrational, because when someone slaps you across the face and that person is your enemy you would be mad to start trying to decide whether he was right or wrong. You would fight him and seek to thrash him. This is the human point of view so far as the nations are concerned. True, Christ taught a different approach for Christians, but obviously this applies to each unique individual, unless of course one chooses to treat socialism as organized Christian charity applied to the masses, and not simply to particular people.

I too took piano lessons for 10 or 12 years and I don't know how to play at all, though I do enjoy fooling about on a piano or harmonium in the most childish manner but even that only very rarely.

I adore you, my dearest Madeleine, we shan't have need of exuberance, we shall simply exult—which is far more beautiful.

Someone has written to me saying that the war is becoming bourgeois, and that is rather true. These leaves are so strange. The calmness of everything. But the war is with us just the same, the shells are still flying.

I am finishing up my poem to Italy, commissioned by *La Voce*.

My Madeleine I take all of you. I believe, from reading your letters, not only that we shall love each other but that we shall understand each other too, and thus besides everything else be a pair of friends.

Gui

My sweetheart I have barely finished writing this letter and war seems to be starting up again.

115

16 August 1915[1]   **1** Military postcard.

My little fairy,

Writing under canvas in a beautiful forest of pines, junipers, warty spurge, pines [*sic*] and moss. This card is all I have to hand. By its means I send you all my soul. So sorry that your name being mentioned in *Case d'Armons* gave you a shock. I wanted a trace of it to remain in this work, a visible trace, because while there will be others there will be none able to commemorate the beginning of our relations. You are right this book is yours. As for the names, none of them can embarrass you and the one that might do so is disguised. Those that are clearly spelt out should not embarrass you because they are of no consequence. I adore your personality, which is the same as mine and perfect, but talk to me more of you. How I love it when you do so my dear little Madeleine.

Gui

Madeleine dear, we may now once more seal our letters. Joy! I couldn't write yesterday. But yes did get the pretty photo taken on the terrace. Spoke to you of it already. It is the most charming, the one where my fairy is at her most dainty and perhaps her most delicious. I look at it every day. Worship you.

Now I am a mason and a woodcutter. Lots of lovely spiders in this pretty wood. Grass snakes flies spiders—a fine menagerie! Right here though there are neither snakes nor flies but thousands of spiders. My dear I am glad that you have understood how much *Case d'Armons* belongs to you. But considering how scarce a book it is, what difference does it make that your name is there, it is hardly cheapened thereby. 25 copies in all, one for me, one for you, which leaves but 23 throughout the universe. Not many, you must admit, and anyway later when we are married you won't mind at all when your name reappears in a real book like *Alcools*. Our memories will delight us then, we shall love them.

I write to you lying on the grass in a hurry to resume building my sod hut.

Because I have been sleeping on the damp ground for the last two nights and since I am well there's no sense in chancing new attacks of rheumatism.

GUILLAUME APOLLINAIRE

This wood is delightful. What a change! You can't imagine—and we're not permitted to explain!!! But I love you my darling infinitely. That dark hair of yours when I think of it is an unheard-of paradise, something unaccountably rare and disturbing, though not immaterial at all of course, far from it! I write sitting on the grass, in great haste. No letter today from you. Abt my leave, I imagine October or late September although in fact I know strictly nothing about it and I less than anybody else, for I am the orderly officer and thus cannot ask about myself.

So I am speculating only, and it could perhaps be earlier, in which case Nice, or perhaps later, and how is your dear mother by the way? Did she get my letter?

I adore you little dark-haired fairy. Do you have your brother with you at present?

Kisses upon your lovely mouth so sweetly offered.

Gui

Let me add this, my darling, we love one another too much to cause each other pain, even over a joke in my work. We trust each other completely. So no matter how impatient you are to write, you mustn't cause *me* pain who am so far from you. For my part I want nothing but to caress Madeleine and see her happy. You cannot imagine how much I love you, or rather, you do not imagine it yet at all and you must imagine it, this clear pure happiness that I want for us, without a cloud, without anything base, without the slightest misunderstanding. You are the only woman for that happiness. I want you to wish it as much as I do. So that it becomes real and so that a model couple may inaugurate the grand human happiness to come. We are entitled to it, it is achievable, all that is required is that it be wanted and we want it you and I both. But there must be no joking about something so lovely, so exquisite and so possible. If you want it, my Madeleine, put all coyness, all tricks and evasions aside—*voluntarily*—They will all remain available to you *unconsciously*. And be mine heart and soul, just as I am yours unreservedly, without regret, and with the greatest joy, for I adore you my Madeleine with all my strength, if only you knew. We are worthy of one another, let us prove it. For my part I promise you that never in any way shall I be unworthy of you. I adore you.

Gui

20 August 1915

My darling, I kiss you with all my soul, passionately, madly, hopelessly.

About Port-Vendres don't know anything yet for the good reason that I am hardly in a position to get my leave decided in advance but shall try to take advantage of my position as quartermaster corporal to hasten our reunion. I cannot go on like this. I must kiss Madeleine. It is incredible how much I want to, but it is not possible, and I can master my desire. But all the same I do most terribly want to. So, away with the past, let it be just Madeleine and I, just us all by ourselves.

Why no, she is not mean in the least my Madeleine. She is pretty and charming. I am sure she loves me she also knows that I worship her but she must be aware too that she is now mine body and soul, definitively.

Your Mama has written me an exquisite letter which paints her whole portrait. Just as you have described her. I love her very much.

Madeleine your mouth is mine and I kiss it for a long time.

I write you lying on the ground under canvas, in the wood, by the light of a candle. First frost last night. You can have no notion of this in Nice. You are my darling, my beloved flower and your dark hair is the most wonderful foliage in the world.

And these new photos from Nice!

I am so, so happy that Madeleine is happy, indeed I am so very pleased that I don't know what to write and am becoming stupid.

I am going to try and finish my 'Cry to Italy' now as I impatiently await that long long letter from my little fiancée so deeply desired spiritually and (it has to be said) carnally too.

I take Madeleine's mouth and devour it like a delicious fruit.

Gui

GUILLAUME APOLLINAIRE

To Mme Pagès

20 August 1915

Dear Mama of Madeleine,

Your letter gave me great joy. You are as kind as could be and I dearly love you. I should be delighted to come to Lamur on my leave, just so long as it is not too far from Algiers, for my leave is calculated beginning only on the day after I disembark, but the day of re-embarking is counted.

You are right to congratulate me on discovering Madeleine, I am terrifically proud of that too. I loved her as soon as I caught sight of her and she noticed it also, as reserved as she is. If it is up to me, she shall be happy.

I am very much obliged to you for the graciousness with which you have consented to contribute to happiness in my life and I shall always strive to demonstrate my gratitude to you.

With a filial kiss,

Gui de Kostrowitzky

under canvas

My dearest, the hair in your letter of the 17th had the lovely smell of
the rose of the beautiful rose-tree whose Rose you are. The Rose of
the world that has been my Quest. And I savour the flower's fruity
aroma, its unimaginable taste, while dreaming of your lips. I am no
longer calm in the least and I have an inexpressible desire for you
my darling. I kiss your hair madly imagining that you are all mine,
your young flesh prey to the ogre that I am. And these rose leaves
that have touched the charming mounds of your virginal bosom! Oh
no my darling I am not calm at all! And my sole reason for patience
is that we love one another, that you belong to me down to the
innermost recesses of your body down to the most delicate tendrils
of your fleece, oh my vine—my darling vine, with its exquisite
grapes, my vine whose wine will so inebriate me that I shall wish
never to be sober again, my dear little vine whose harvesting I await
as the Hebrews once awaited the prodigal harvest of Canaan's promised land, but now let us turn over a leaf my darling—a vine leaf. . . .

The 1st paragraph of 'La Vie anecdotique' is not a tale. In fact it is
the truth: *I was there this happened to me*. As for Claudien's article, I
have leafed through it. It is incredible how badly most present-day
writers write. And the rest fail to flesh their sentences out: subject
verb predicate and that's that. A harmonious style no longer exists.
You will have to oblige me to fill out my own style, which as a reaction to the Germanizing false stylists of the present moment is being

123

GUILLAUME APOLLINAIRE

slimmed down by the day. But I always write in such haste, my little wife will force me to regulate my work so that I have the time to make things perfect instead of relying on my facility.

Just as much my darling as the ivory tower of your body I love the shadow of the tower of your soul.

So what were those *frightenly reasonable letters*? They were mine! What you say about Racine and his wife is correct. It is also correct to say that the slave is mistress of her master. And I am very curious to know what kind of fidelity dishonours a woman. . . .

To get back to your letters: Botrel is close to being France's official poet, along with Jean Aicard, while England has Kipling and Italy D'Annunzio. When one sees such insanities from the writers in this country which deserves better one cannot help but wonder about other spheres of competence. What is more, Faguet composed his *Cult of Incompetence* on a canvas provided for him by the publisher, who had asked for it from the person who had had the idea, namely my friend René Dalize (cited in 'Zone'). Dalize is now a captain and he has written me a fascinating letter on strategy, which consists for him in fishing in a canal near a little village at the Front. What is your brother's Rgt., or rather the one to which he is to be assigned? What you say about the women of Fr. is true. As a young man I fancied I could absolutely never fall in love with one. It was mainly in Paris that I had formed this impression, but little by little I grew sensitive to their charms. On the other hand the ugliness of the *Niçoises* is widely recognized. I have often heard this remarked upon, but it should be said that for the most part it is their bodies that are ugly. Among *Parisiennes* the bosom is the main offender—a short-coming that they share with their Roman counterparts.

I have no doubt about the beauty of Algerian women. Your own attests to that. But you are the most beautiful. As for all those superannuated whores in Nice they are hideous to the point of obscenity—they must be raking it in during this time of war. Which said, some women who are not at all pretty have qualities every bit as important as beauty.

In answer to your letter of the 18th my darling all I can say is 'Je t'aime!'[1] But I adore the letter of the 19th, which is longer, because I love everything that prolongs love. And then I adore your beauty, talk to me about it hugely my little slave, I do want that, and this time you have told me about your eyes, and I can see your long lashes and clear gaze. And everything you say is right so right. I shall always love you and you likewise. I have written something similar to what you say about ways of ridding married life of monotony. It is in my preface to *Les Plus Belles Pages de l'Arétin* (Finest Passages from Aretino).

But between you and me there can be no monotony because between us harmony is assured in advance by virtue of our tastes themselves. You are my slave, that is to say Muse, mistress, friend and all these together make you my wife, my Madeleine. It is clear that we shall never be bored together, not for a single moment. I'll send you the poem to Italy tomorrow—Tomorrow too a parcel of books for safekeeping and the *Poil Civil*—but what is this booklet that you mention?

I am sending you the article from the Spanish newspaper that I told you about a while ago. It is to be kept, along with a paper, No. 3 (in fact the only printed or rather duplicated issue—a joke by a friend in the battery). It was put together during the Sector 59 days, the paper was just about to appear when we left, all that was still needed was to duplicate the articles. We stopped production and to make use of the thing added the note that makes it into an amusing trifle and a hemerographical (which is to say almost a bibliographical) rarity.

1 This is the first use by Apollinaire of the familiar *tu* form of address. From this point on he alternates between the *tu* and the *vous,* reserving the former for more intimate contexts, until he abandons the *vous* completely in his letter of 5 September 1915.—Tr.

125

GUILLAUME APOLLINAIRE

You are reading *L'Hérésiarque et Cie* (The Heresiarch and Co.) in which edition? Here are a few printer's errors or slips needing correction, the only ones I can recall at this remove.

In 'L'Infaillibilité' ('Infallibilty'), the French priest should always address the cardinal as '*Éminence*' rather than '*Monseigneur*'. There is also a '*vêtissaient*' somewhere that should be changed to '*vêtaient*' (a barbarism accepted however by some authors).

In 'Le Cigare romanesque' ('The Romantic Cigar') the first 3 editions do not tell what was done before posting the letter found in the cigar and the following needs to be added to the passage concerned: . . . *after putting my address on the back of the envelope so that the letter would be returned to me should it not reach its destination . . .*

There are certainly plenty of other things but I cannot remember them.

I am very fond of 'Simon Magus', which is difficult for most people. It is the first time I think that anyone has made use in such a precise, even a scientific and also a divine way, of angels, who here play the real role for which they were first imagined.

Note also that [the story] 'L'Hérésiarque' was written in 1900 and first published in the *Revue Blanche* in 1902, before the religious battles in France and before the heretical period that immediately followed.

I do hope this book that I feel is substantial will amuse you. I like it very much and am vain enough to think I have great talent as a storyteller, also as a poet. There should be no false modesty for us, my darling, we are charmingly proud and quite worthy of one another. So I kiss you madly on the mouth, for a long time, sweetly . . . and again . . . and now in an almost depraved way, if ever there

126

could be depravity in loving each other as we do, that is to say without constraint, which means in the purest way in the world, my dearest child that I worship. You wonder if I will be jealous?! Like a tiger, believe you me! But I am quite sure I shall never have a reason to be jealous, but I shall be jealous all the same if only in homage to the sovereign grace of my slave.

Gui

My dearest one, I am now a sergeant and I am very proud of this promotion. I received your delightful letter of the 20th which shows yet again how our thoughts come to us both almost simultaneously, for the use of *tu* suspended by you in the very dear letter that I read yesterday I had already unknowingly resumed the day before. *Je t'aime, je t'aime.* You are the loveliest of dreams, the most sublime reality. All virtues and all graces are in Madeleine. All sensuality and all tenderness is in Madeleine. All joys and all happiness. It does not surprise me in the least that children love you. You can give me no greater pleasure than to tell me about Madeleine. I still await the rest of your hymn to your beauty my darling. We shall never part, you are absolutely right, Madeleine. And no! Neither of us shall laugh at the words addressed to us by the mayor. The mere mention of your mouth disturbs me so much that I lose my train of thought and hardly know what I am writing. I told you what I think of R. R. but I also said that I had not read *Jean-Christophe*, and I am sure I shall be entirely of your opinion when I get to know that work, because your taste is impeccable. I never write you idly, my darling, how could you write such a thing to me who wants only to hold you in his arms forever and ever fondling you and looking at you tenderly. I who dream only of being carried away by a wave of infinite delight and smothering you with the gentlest of caresses. I want all the strength of my love to be sweeter to you than the lightest of touches, but a touch more powerful than any other and one that will never ever end. My slave will make my happiness and I shall make hers. Yes, love is always complete. You are right. I am stupid. And how right you are to catch me whenever I say foolish things. Let there be no mysteries between us. We must complete each other and so come closer and closer to perfection. I am sending you a large parcel containing *Poil civil* and those poetry booklets (I couldn't remember yesterday what they were). Also books on the Marne (folklore) and others. I have included some fragments of stained glass, big pieces from the martyred church of Les H. and smaller ones from the entirely destroyed church of Le M. Small relics from what are henceforth famous sites bearing witness to this war's unrelenting strife.

I love you, my darling, I cannot say how much I love you. Your dear hair that I can kiss is my most treasured possession along with your photos. At the moment I am impatiently awaiting the post orderly.

Do be careful not to hurt yourself my darling with the pieces of glass, I daresay you will make fun of me for sending these scraps, forgive me. But for me they are touching souvenirs—already—of danger and of the endless whiteness of the trenches.

I enclose the original of my appeal 'À l'Italie', as sent to *La Voce*, don't lose it my so so gracious one, I have no copy. I am also sending a drawing by Marie Laurencin that she sent me via Mme Faure-Favier. This drawing is delightful and extremely poignant. Have it put under glass in a narrow beaded frame. It is ours and it is a small masterpiece. Use no passe-partout and make sure the framer doesn't encroach on any of the white border.

I kiss you on the mouth. *Je t'aime*.

Gui

GUILLAUME APOLLINAIRE

À L'ITALIE

L'amour a remué ma vie comme on remue la terre dans la zone des armées

J'atteignais l'âge mûr quand la guerre arriva

Et dans ce jour d'août 1915 le plus chaud de l'année

Bien abrité dans l'hypogée que j'ai creusé moi-même

C'est à toi que je songe Italie mère de mes pensées

Et déjà quand Von Klück marchait sur Paris avant la Marne

Moi j'évoquais le sac de Rome par les Allemands le sac de Rome qu'ont décrit

Un Bonaparte, François Delicado et l'Arétin

Je me disais: 'Est-il possible que la nation

Qui est la mère de la civilisation

Regarde sans la défendre les efforts qu'on fait pour la détruire'

Puis les temps sont venus les tombes se sont ouvertes

Les fantômes des 'esclaves toujours frémissants'

Se sont dressés en criant: 'Sus aux Tudesques!'

Nous, l'armée invisible aux cris éblouissants

Plus doux que n'est le miel et plus simples qu'un peu de terre

Nous te tournons bénignement le dos Italie

Mais ne t'en fais pas, nous t'aimons bien

Italie ô mère qui es aussi notre fille.

Nous sommes là tranquillement et sans tristesse

Et si malgré les masques, les sacs de sable, les rondins nous tombions

Nous savons qu'un autre prendra notre place

Et que les Armées ne périront jamais

Les mois ne sont pas longs ni les jours ni les nuits

C'est la guerre qui est longue

Italie, toi notre mère et notre fille quelque chose comme notre sœur

J'ai comme toi pour me réconforter le quart de pinard

Qui met tant de différence entre nous et les Boches

J'ai aussi comme toi l'envol des compagnies de perdreaux des 75

Comme toi je n'ai pas cet orgueil sans joie des Boches et je sais rigoler

Je ne suis pas sentimental à l'excès comme le sont ces gens sans mesure que leurs
    actions dépassent sans qu'ils sachent s'amuser

Notre civilisation a plus de finesse que les choses qu'ils emploient

Elle est au-delà de la vie confortable

Et de ce qui est l'extérieur dans l'art et l'industrie

Les fleurs sont nos enfants et non les leurs

Même la fleur de lys qui meurt au Vatican

La plaine est infinie et les tranchées sont blanches

Les avions bourdonnent ainsi que des abeilles

Sur les roses momentanées des éclatements

Et les nuits sont parées de guirlandes d'éblouissements

De bulles de globules aux couleurs insoupçonnées

Nous jouissons de tout même de nos souffrances

Notre humeur est charmante, l'ardeur vient quand il faut

Nous sommes narquois car nous savons faire la part des choses

Et il n'y a pas plus de folie chez celui qui jette les grenades que chez celui qui plume
les patates

Tu aimes un peu plus que nous les gestes et les mots sonores

Tu as à ta disposition les sortilèges étrusques, le sens de la majesté héroïque et le
courageux honneur individuel

Nous avons le sourire, nous devinons ce qu'on ne nous dit pas, nous sommes
démerdards et même ceux qui se dégonflent sauraient à l'occasion faire preuve de
l'esprit de sacrifice qu'on appelle la bravoure

Et nous fumons du gros avec volupté

C'est la nuit Je suis dans mon blockhaus, éclairé par l'électricité en bâton

Je pense à toi pays des deux volcans

Je salue le souvenir des sirènes et des scylles mortes au moment de Messine

Je salue le Colleoni équestre de Venise

Je salue la chemise rouge

Je t'envoie mes amitiés Italie et m'apprête à applaudir aux hauts faits de ta bleusaille

Non parce que j'imagine qu'il n'y aura jamais plus de bonheur ou de malheur en ce
monde

Mais parce que comme toi j'aime à penser seul et que les Boches m'en empêcheraient

Mais parce que le goût naturel de la perfection que nous avons l'un et l'autre, si on
les laissait faire, serait vite remplacé par je ne sais quelles commodités dont je n'ai
que faire

GUILLAUME APOLLINAIRE

Et surtout parce que comme toi je sais, je veux choisir et qu'eux voudraient nous
  forcer à ne plus rien choisir
Une même destinée nous lie en cette occase
Ce n'est pas pour l'ensemble que je le dis
            Mais pour chacun de toi Italie
Ne te borne point à prendre les terres irrédentes
Mets ton destin dans la balance où est le nôtre
Les réflecteurs dardent leurs lueurs comme des yeux d'escargots
Et les obus en tombant sont des chiens qui jettent de la terre avec leurs pattes après
  avoir fait leurs besoins
Notre armée invisible est une belle nuit constellée
Et chacun de nos hommes est un astre merveilleux
            Ô nuit, ô nuit éblouissante
Les morts sont avec nos soldats
Les morts sont debout dans les tranchées

132

Ou se glissent souterrainement vers les Bien-Aimées
Ô Lille Saint-Quentin Laon Maubeuge Vouziers
Nous jetons nos villes comme des grenades
Nos fleuves sont brandis comme des sabres
Nos montagnes chargent comme cavalerie
Nous reprendrons les villes les fleuves les collines
De la frontière helvétique aux frontières bataves
            Entre nous et Italie
Il y a des patelins pleins de femmes
Et près de toi m'attend celle que j'adore
Ô frères d'Italie
Ondes, nuages délétères
Métalliques débris qui vous rouillez par terre
Ô frères d'Italie Vos plumes sur la tête
            Italie
Entends crier Louvain Vois Reims tordre ses bras
Et ce soldat blessé toujours debout Arras
            Et maintenant chantons ceux qui sont morts
        Ceux qui vivent les officiers et les soldats

Les flingots Rosalie le canon la fusée l'hélice la pelle les chevaux
Chantons les bagues pâles les casques
     Chantons ceux qui sont morts
     Chantons la terre qui bâille d'ennui
     Chantons et rigolons
     Durant des années
       Italie
   Entends braire l'âne boche
   Faisons la guerre à coups de fouets
   Faits avec des rayons de soleil
      Italie
    Chantons et rigolons
    Durant des années

TO ITALY

Love has tossed my life about just as the earth is tossed about in the war zone
I was coming into my prime when the war started
And now on this August day in 1915 the hottest of the year
Well protected in this hypogeum that I dug myself
It is about you that I muse Italy mother of my thoughts
Already as Von Klück was marching on Paris before the battle of the Marne
I evoked the sack of Rome by the Germans the sack of Rome as described
By a Bonaparte by François Delicado and by Aretino
I asked myself: 'Could the nation
That is the very mother of civilization
Possibly stand by without defending her creation against all the efforts being
    made to destroy it?'
Then the time came the tombs opened
The ghosts of 'slaves still trembling'
Rose up crying 'Death to the Teutons!'
We the invisible army with our dazzling shouts
Sweeter than honey and simpler than a handful of earth
Benignly turn our back on you Italy
But never fear we are your good friends

GUILLAUME APOLLINAIRE

Italy oh mother and our daughter too.

We are here calm and without sadness

And if despite the masks, the sandbags, the logs we were to fall

We know that others would take our place

And that our forces will never perish

The months are not long neither are the days and nights

It is the war that is long

Italy, you our mother and our daughter and something like our sister

I like you have my mug of vino to comfort me

Which makes us both so different from the Boches

And like you too I have 75s taking flight like packs of partridges

Like you I do not have the joyless pride of the Boches and I know how to
     laugh

I am not excessively sentimental like those intemperate people whose own
     actions escape them and who cannot enjoy themselves

Our civilization has more subtlety than the things those others use

It goes beyond the comfortable life

Beyond what is merely external to art and industry

The flowers are our children and not theirs

Even the fleur-de-lys dying in the Vatican

The plain is endless and the trenches are white

The aeroplanes buzz like bees

Around the ephemeral roses of the shellbursts

And the nights are decked with glittering garlands

With bubbles and globes in wondrous colours

We delight in all of it even in our torment

Our mood is agreeable, fervour comes as called for

We are sardonic because we have the measure of things

And the man throwing grenades is no more prone to madness than the one
     peeling spuds

You are somewhat fonder than us of resounding gestures and words

You have the spells of the Etruscans available, and a sense of majestic hero-
     ism and of brave personal honour

134

We keep smiling, we guess what we are not told, there are no flies on us and
    even those of us who get the wind up are able on occasion to demonstrate
    the spirit of sacrifice known as bravery

And we smoke rough-cut voluptuously

It is night I'm in my blockhouse by the light of electricity in baton form

I think of you land of the two volcanoes

I salute the memory of the sirens and scyllas dead at Messina

I salute the equestrian Colleoni of Venice

I salute the red shirt

I send you my friendship Italy and stand ready to applaud the great deeds of
    your raw recruits

Not because I believe there will never be any more happiness or misery in
    this world

But because like you I love to think for myself and the Boches would like to
    stop me from doing so

And because the natural taste for perfection that you and we share would, if
    we gave them their head, be quickly replaced by who knows what com-
    modities for which I have not the slightest need

And most of all because like you I know I want to make choices and they
    would like to oblige us never to choose anything again

In these circs a sole fate binds us together

I do not say this in a general way

        I say it for each of yours oh Italy

Do not by any means confine yourself to taking the irredentist lands

Place your destiny in the same scales as ours

The searchlights flash like snails' eyes

And the falling shells throw up earth like dogs with their hind paws after
    doing their business

Our invisible army is a fine star-specked night

And every one of our men is a marvellous star

        Oh night, oh glittering night

The dead lie among our soldiers

The dead still stand erect in the trenches

135

GUILLAUME APOLLINAIRE

Or slip underground towards their best beloved

Oh Lille Saint-Quentin Laon Maubeuge Vouziers

We toss our towns like grenades

Our rivers are brandished like sabres

Our mountains charge like cavalry

We shall recapture towns rivers hills

From the Swiss frontier to the Batavian

    Between us and Italy

Lie villages full of women

And near to you the woman I worship awaits me

Oh brothers of Italy

Noxious waves and clouds

Rusting the metal debris strewing the ground

Oh our brothers of Italy with plumes on your heads

    Oh Italy

Hear Louvain's cry See Rheims wringing her hands

And Arras a wounded soldier still standing

    And now let us sing those who have died

    Those still living officers and men

    Rosalie[1] guns cannon rockets propellers shovels horses

Let us sing the pale rings the helmets

    Sing those who are dead

    Sing the earth yawning with boredom

    Sing and laugh

    For years and years

      Italy

Listen to the Boche ass braying

Let us make war with the lash of whips

Made from the rays of the sun

      Italy

    Let us sing and laugh

    For years and years

1 Military slang for bayonets.—Tr.

        Guillaume Apollinaire

My love, I fear you did not like *The Heresiarch* at all. It is perhaps a
book simply not meant for women. By the way, little slave, you must
never speak of dying of laughter or by any other means. And then,
threats! Ah, my dear little minx, if only I was beside you a good
conjugal correction would be in order! The Bosnian observation
about marriage is just local colour and applies to people whose sole
bond is a carnal one; you and I, or so I believe, have a mystical union
that binds us even closer together in advance. Bad Madeleine! You
must never again cause me pain like this. I am quite upset about it.
Vexed. Unhappy. And it was a short letter, too short my darling—
please tell me everything you don't like so that I may persuade you to
like it. You have to write me in the way you were doing before, because
I don't think I shall get leave by the 20th. I am part of a battery made
up of men from occupied territory, all of whom will go on leave before
those from unoccupied areas. I don't know why, but that is how it is.—
So we shall not be travelling together. God, how miserable this makes
me. Especially so since now that I am a non-com my leave will occur
even later.—I'm not absolutely certain of this but I strongly suspect it.
I am scheduled for leave as an N.C.O. now, and obviously as the most
recently promoted I'll be going after the others. So there will be new
dates for you too my dearest darling.—My darling I live through you,
you are my all. Write me the sweet letters of my sentimental
Madeleine. Of she whom, since she loves me, I love. Now that love is
here, romance is no longer proscribed—rather, it is prescribed.

GUILLAUME APOLLINAIRE

I WANT US, my dearest treasure, to love one another more than people have ever loved one another before—people being everybody in the world. We must be above everything.

And so indeed you are, you for whom I was waiting. You the most beautiful—The tender flower that I warm against my breast.

My darling abide here with me, I caress you so much in my thoughts. At the moment you are busier and write me less and more hastily—so stop writing for a few days if you can manage it and then send me a long letter from the true Madeleine that I love and not from the Madeleine that rebels and passes judgement. I see your hair your eyes your mouth, your breast that I worship and all your you that is all mine. I am using your own terms.

I want your complete happiness, Madeleine, please collaborate with me in this delightful task.

I have your return kiss and I send it back once more, sweet, long, deep, as though our two souls were joined in the most intense love and were sobbing with voluptuousness—oh my darling.

I enclose a cutting from a Mexican paper sent by my brother who has been living for so long through the hideous nightmare of the Mexican civil war. Please keep this cutting for me.

The parcel left today from Valmy but I could not have it delivered to you at the house. It will arrive at the Nice station, I do beg your pardon for asking you to go and pick it up there. No other way to do it.

I am sad today, your letter darling has something un-Madeleine about it. So please not to write at all unless very, very nicely. But we still adore one another and I am saying stupid things at the moment, I'm worn out. It is dead calm here though, even if the communiqués call this the most active sector. And I love you,

Madeleine, with a manly love, and I know that whatever I write, whatever you read, you can never ever have the slightest doubt of that my darling Madeleine. I love you.

Gui

My sweetheart, at last I have received your two short letters, dated
the 25th and the 26th. So I am writing to you at Narbonne—I presume the parcel that I sent you will not be lost and that you
arranged for it to be picked up at the Nice station. I am hoping with
all my heart for the long letter you promised, because I have been
all alone here for several days now.

140 I am now a fire observer at a lookout post situated on a desolate
hilltop subjected to continual bombardment. I have made an inkwell
from a Boche 150 shell. I must get permission to send it to you. It
will be a nice inkwell once the place for the ink has been hollowed
out, which I can't do here.

So what I do is pass the night in this lookout bringing the alidad of
the sighting triangle to bear on flashes from the Boche cannon.

And as I conscientiously make these important measurements I
think of you.

I likewise my darling think of you in the maddest way. And I kiss
your hair that smells of a rose, the rose that you are. I imagine the
tenderest caresses for you, the slowest, the most violent yet gentle. I
was happy to learn that you were from the Vendée. I am sure you
know why.

I am not permitted to elaborate, my darling, but I am to be very
much exposed to risk during the 1st fortnight of September.

Remember that whatever happens I worship you, *je t'aime*, and write me a long letter, your letters are the only thing worth waiting for, worth reading. I worship love and you are all my love. You know it Madeleine. I say it again because this kind of repetition is always exquisite, it is our repetition, and we shall say these things over and over again and never grow tired of doing so and by Jove I do believe our right to do so will have been hard-carned. Is that not true, my darling Madelon, who are mine and with whom I may do what I please, everything I please. I love you.

Gui

GUILLAUME APOLLINAIRE

1 September 1915

After a few days as a fire observer I am now chief of piece, in charge of a gun. Here I am, sequestered on the firing line far from everything. No horse save in the event of departure. I shall be able to write you longer letters and perhaps even get a chance to work. I must have left almost everything I have behind in the wagon line. But I do have nearly all your letters with me, except for the last one with the Narbonne address, but I think I have it right so am not hesitating to write you there, my love. These last months spent in Fontainebleau must have done your brother good. Here we are cut off from the world and because the big big show is coming we live in very big, very deep holes.

From your sisters Denise Marthe and Anne and your brothers Pierre and Émile I have received a joint letter that is the most delightful pastoral poem I know of. I replied to them promptly but briefly—I don't have much time because I have to get acquainted with my new tasks. Thank them kindly, they are so charming. Pierre and Anne look the most like you especially Pierre. As soon as I have a photo I'll send it you.

I mentioned Algiers merely because I thought I would have to come via Algiers. I have no other reason to go there. I am not too well versed in the geography of Algeria. So, it's Port-Vendres for Oran. Port-Vendres—what a marvellous augury! I met you at Nice, City of Victory, and now I shall be rejoining you via Port-Vendres, etymologically the Port of Venus, that is to say of beauty and love, which is what you are my dearest darling, my joy.

I take you all of you, which you offer so sweetly so passionately and your mouth is mine. I love you, my Madeleine and I worship you. Your

Gui

My dear Madeleine, I would so much have liked you to tell me what you thought of *The Heresiarch*, we promised each other truth. If you do not like it say so but at least say something about it—

Yes, I too would like to write plays. You shall make me do so—

Obviously your culinary tastes are of no great concern to me, but we are far away from everything here and the slightest thing having to do with you fills me with pleasure. We are very much alike when it comes to things religious and our ideas on church marriages and on the education of children are identical.

All the same, since the start of this war I have been getting firmer ideas, though they will not be completely clear until peace comes.

You like decorating Madeleine. So do I, but I don't suppose you yet have the same ideas as I do on this. For my part I like the modern-day approach, but your woman's imagination will settle my notions tastefully—or rather without taste, for the old canons of taste must be overthrown. Yesterday, for instance, in a dugout I saw a ham hung up and partly sliced, a gorgeous sight; a violin on a wall is beautiful too, and I thought what a pretty way to decorate a bed-room it would be to use newspapers of all sorts as wallpaper.

I was very much amused by your dressing up as a cadet, and would love a photo of you like that.

Like you I love Duty, perhaps a little more in the Corneille manner than you. You could very easily be Corneille-like though—so do be, our times require it and by the way it will suit you perfectly. No good loving duty by halves, it is all or nothing, we are made to love it completely but freely and with pleasure and—even more than with joy, with curiosity, but never out of obligation—You wonder whether it is useful for me to be corresponding on the subject of you, but yes, yes, of course it is my darling, what do you suppose could interest me more than you—why, everything else is of no consequence, descriptions of sea, house, children and all the rest—only you are of interest to me. So talk to me about you, and if not about your tastes then something else, but concerning you, concerning us, but above all you. And above all you must not idealize me. That way you risk disillusion. At least admit in advance that disillusion is a possibility. I would never have taken a wife who was not completely mine. I want you to belong entirely to me, without even thinking of preserving your own personality, having you preserve it is a task that falls to me. That is just how things are, and you yourself sweetly imply it. My darling I take your mouth as you want me to, and know that my greatest pleasure is chattering about love with you even from afar. I am so far from everything that I think of you all the time and desire you incessantly. I have been imagining your feet, tell me a little about those pretty feet of yours my darling, I kiss their pink nails. And my heart beats continually for Madeleine. Your hair still smells of roses.

You can't imagine how happy I am that we love each other. I love you as if I had made you myself and you are exactly the way I would have made you myself. But do not love me too much with your mind, prepare your senses also to love me as much as possible. This is essential to love and the reason why you have to be a slave even if I were to make you suffer. Now that we belong to one another, my

145

GUILLAUME APOLLINAIRE

Madeleine, my Madeleine, get ready for our bodies to love each other as much as our souls do.

From eight p.m. the night before last until the morning I was posted as fire observer to a hill so desolate it put me in mind of Brocken Peak; I reached it on horseback with a bugler; the shell craters have turned the ground into a waffle grill, and the lookout post is right above one of the holes; I was in a sort of opera box watching the show through the embrasure: the barbaric and uninterrupted music of fire from French and Boche cannon of every calibre, from rifles, from machine-guns. Their flashes lit up the sky, the stark beams of searchlights combed the heavens, remarkably far-reaching agents alternately approaching and drawing away from one another, lengthening and shortening, the flares and signals burst in long-lasting showers bouquets globes white orange red blue green and shot up again strange exquisite dancing-girls. I pointed the alidad of the sighting triangle towards the flashes and noted down the readings while the bugler slept on a board bed. As someone who likes going to shows you would have loved being there.

Apropos of which, my darling, I like the theatre but I don't like to go too often so that I enjoy it all the more when I do.

I am writing you almost every day if not every day but from now on I shall try hard to write every single day, I simply cannot understand how you can go for a whole week without a letter from me, it is just unconscionable.

Ah yes, my darling, we shall love each other mightily to make up for being so long and so completely apart.

But of course I shall love your hand just as much with an ink stain as without one. Is beauty something that can be at the mercy of an ink stain?

Personally I don't keep a war diary, but later on I shall have to make myself return to my notes as I used to when I was younger.

I do write to my mother my darling and just see how sly you are to ask me about it so as to find out whether I have told her about us. No I have not, but it is not important and I shall tell you why when my leave comes. I love Mama very much moreover, and she loves me, but she has such a thoroughly Slavic character that she is bound to be jealous of anyone her son might fall in love with. She would like you very much but you will not get on together. Indeed she will be delighted to learn that I am getting married but she will be jealous of you and full of tender feelings for you at the very same time. Anyway it would take too long to explain but as much as she will love you my mother's Slavic nature will keep her at a distance from our household for anything more than a day now and then. And mark well that I am telling you this because I sense that you want me to do so and that I adore Mama just as she adores me. But when you want to know something, ask me directly instead of hinting, for you are obliging me to account briefly, in a way that is almost disrespectful towards Mama, for facts that though difficult to explain to someone who is not a Slav are exactly the same in all Slavic families, and in any case Mama will know in very good time about our marriage, but if I were to tell her now I should have to write her ad infinitum about it and with this war and her two sons being away she is upset enough as it is for her not to need her emotions roiled any further at the moment. But she will know when the time is right and let me say that so far as everything other than complete filial love and absolute maternal love is concerned my mother has no part in my life and she knows it, this is in her character as in mine because even though nothing moves her to take an interest in literature least of all in mine we are still very much alike, notably in our pride, but she is

GUILLAUME APOLLINAIRE

obstinate, utterly unyielding as only Slavic women can be (read Dostoevsky) and I cannot be myself unless I am away from her, when I am with her she always treats me as though I were ten years old and for two pins she would give me a good slap, something what is more that I would accept completely because nothing in the world would induce me to defy her, but then I am every bit as independent as she is and that is why I cannot live with her—She loves me too much and indeed I love her just as much; my brother's more austere personality allows him to live with her, and since he is not of a literary bent she has a great respect for him. But my mother though she does not realize it is like me, a poet like me, and not a few things I have written come from her, from what she says, even from what she thinks. There you are: you will have to sort these explanations out as best you can.

As for our loving each other, there can be no doubt that we love each other even more than your brother and his wife for the simple reason that you are certainly superior in beauty and intellect to your sister-in-law and that the superiority of the woman always determines the value of a couple.

There are fewer flies now that September has come. I love you Madeleine and take all of you just as if you were already my wife.

Gui

My most darling love, I got your little card, so exquisite, of the 29th
and I am waiting impatiently for the endlessly long letter because,
no doubt solely for reasons that I may not divulge, we are to remain
here for four days without communication even with the rear.—But I
shall write you every day during this time and you will receive everything at once. In any case you write me too and as for your movements, even those already announced, please repeat your address
each time so that should I mislay a letter as is possible (or rather not
possible, and I know your letter with the Narbonne address is in my
haversack along with other things that fill it to the top but certainly
not with oats—this sack, I say, is back in the wagon line and I cannot
have someone go through it looking for your letter to have it
brought to me)—so that, as I was saying, in case I do mislay or leave
behind a letter of yours, then at least I shall still have Madeleine's
address.

CHEF DE PIÈCE

Le margis est à sa pièce
Il dort dans son abri à côté du canon
Il vit avec ses servants et partage leur cuistance
Il écrit auprès d'eux à Madeleine
Il joue avec eux tous sept comme des enfants
Il songe à la Grande Chose qui va venir
Il admire le merveilleux enthousiasme des bobosses

GUILLAUME APOLLINAIRE

Décidément le courage a grandi partout

Et l'on est sûr on est certain de la Grande Chose

Il pensera tout ce temps-là à Madeleine

CHIEF OF PIECE

The sarge is by his piece

He sleeps in his shelter alongside his cannon

He lives with his gunners and shares their grub

He writes alongside them to Madeleine

He plays with them all seven of them like children

He thinks of the Big Show that is coming

He admires the wonderful enthusiasm of the *bobosses*

No doubt about it, courage is on the rise all round

And we are sure we are certain about the Big Show

He will be thinking of Madeleine the whole time

150

Had you told me Madeleine that you were going to go to beautiful, Greek Antibes, I would have told you to visit the tombstone, near the church, of the child of the North who came during the reign of I cannot remember which Roman emperor to dance at the Antibes theatre. The inscription, so pure, so beautiful and so poetic in its brevity, reads simply *Saltavit et placuit*—he danced and he pleased.

I had never been to Antibes as a child but I went there several times during my stay in Nice at the beginning of the war and the impression I then had of this delightful sea town corresponded exactly to the one I got from Casanova's *Mémoires*.

I am now living alongside the cannon.—You have already received the charming drawing by M. L. [Marie Laurencin]. To thank her I have sent her a little group of poems, for she had asked me for poems that she wants to illustrate and publish in aid of a work of charity, and since nothing should be hidden between us (between me and Madeleine) and since I will never have anything to hide from you, here are these poems which form a little poetic war novel and which are to appear in *Gazette des Lettres pour le temps de la Guerre* (Literary Gazette for Wartime):

LE MÉDAILLON TOUJOURS FERMÉ/THE EVER-CLOSED LOCKET

LA GRÂCE EN EXIL

Va-t'en va-t'en mon arc-en-ciel
Allez-vous-en couleurs charmantes
Cet exil t'est essentiel
Infante aux écharpes changeantes

Et l'arc-en-ciel est exilé
Puisqu'on exile qui l'irise
Mais un drapeau s'est envolé
Prendre ta place au vent de bise

GRACE IN EXILE

Off you go off you go my rainbow
Off you go delightful hues
This exile is essential for you
Infanta of the ever-changing sashes

And the rainbow is exiled
Because the iridizer has been exiled too
But a flag has fluttered up
To replace you in the chill north wind

LA BOUCLE RETROUVÉE

Il retrouve dans sa mémoire
La boucle de cheveux châtains

GUILLAUME APOLLINAIRE

T'en souvient-il à n'y point croire
De nos 2 étranges destins

Du boulevard de la Chapelle
Du joli Montmartre et d'Auteuil
Je me souviens murmure-t-elle
Du jour où j'ai franchi ton seuil

Il y tomba comme un automne
La boucle de ton souvenir
Et notre destin qui t'étonne
Se joint au jour qui va finir

THE LOCK OF HAIR RETRIEVED

From his memory he retrieves
The lock of chestnut hair
Are you reminded almost unbelievably
Of our 2 strange fates

Of the Boulevard de la Chapelle
Of pretty Montmartre and of Auteuil
I remember she murmurs
The day I crossed your doorstep

A kind of autumn fell
The lock of hair that I remember
Our fate that astonishes you
Rejoins the day coming to an end

REFUS DE LA COLOMBE

Mensonge de l'annonciade
La Noël fut la Passion
Et qu'elle était charmante et sade
Cette renonciation

152

Si la colombe poignardée
Saigne encore de ses refus
J'en plume les ailes: l'idée
Et le poème que tu fus

REFUSAL OF THE DOVE

The lie of the Annunciation
The Nativity was the Passion
And how charming how elegant
That renunciation was

If the bleeding-heart dove
Still bleeds from her refusals
I pluck her wings: the idea
And the poem that you were

153

LES FEUX DU BIVOUAC

Les feux mourants du bivouac
Éclairent des formes de rêve
Et le songe dans l'entrelacs
Des branches lentement s'élève

Voici les dédains du regret
Tout écorché comme une fraise
Les souvenirs et le secret
Dont il ne reste que la braise

CAMPFIRES

The dying bivouac fires
Reveal dream forms
And revery rises slowly
Through the tracery of the branches

GUILLAUME APOLLINAIRE

See the scorn born of regret
Like a strawberry rubbed raw
The memory and the secret
Of which only embers remain

TOURBILLON DE MOUCHES

Un cavalier va dans la plaine
La jeune fille pense à lui
Et cette flotte à Mytilène
Le fil de fer est là qui luit

Comme ils cueillaient la rose ardente
Leurs yeux tout à coup ont fleuri
Et quel soleil la bouche errante
À qui la bouche avait souri

154

SWIRLING FLIES

A rider is crossing the plain
The girl is thinking of him
And that fleet at Mytilene
The barbed wire lies there gleaming

As they plucked the ardent rose
Their eyes suddenly bloomed
And what a sun the errant mouth
At which another mouth had smiled

LES GRENADINES REPENTANTES

En est-il donc deux dans Grenade
Qui pleurent sur ton seul péché?
Ici l'on jette la grenade
Qui se change en un œuf coché

LETTERS TO MADELEINE

Puisqu'il en naît des coqs Infante
Entends-les chanter leurs dédains
Et que la grenade est touchante
Dans nos effroyables jardins

THE PENITENT GRANADINAS

Are there two then in Granada
Who weep for your only sin?
Here the grenades we toss
Change into cocked eggs

For cocks hatch from them Infanta
Listen to their disdainful crowing
And see how poignant grenades are
In our frightful gardens

L'ADIEU DU CAVALIER

Ah Dieu! Que la guerre est jolie
Avec ses chants ses longs loisirs
La bague si pâle et polie
Et le cortège des plaisirs

Adieu! voici le boute-selle!
Il disparut dans un tournant
Et mourut là-bas, tandis qu'elle
Cueillait des fleurs en se damnant

THE CAVALRYMAN'S GOODBYE

My God! How lovely war is
With its music its long hours of leisure
The ring so pale and polished
And the procession of delights

GUILLAUME APOLLINAIRE

Farewell! The boot-and-saddle sounds!
He disappeared round a bend
And died out there, while she
Picked flowers and sold her soul

Guillaume Apollinaire*

* I was forgetting to add that I have the same religious feelings as you have and still wear the charms that Mama hung around my neck when I was a child. So you see we are made of the same stuff, my love—

Since there is still room on this side, let me reiterate my beloved Madeleine that I adore you, that I dream of you dressed up as a cadet—a guise in which you must surely inspire thoughts of a distinctly non-warlike sort. I kiss you on the mouth and I take all of you with all of my strength.

I worship you, I love you.

Gui

I enclose the translation of one of my letters to M. L. as it appeared in a Spanish newspaper, translated by the poet Gomez de la Serna. Do not lose this cutting.

156

1 Military postcard.

3 September 1915[1]

I am changing postal sectors my darling sweetheart, my dear little fiancée, write me at Sector 80. Your

Gui

GUILLAUME APOLLINAIRE

My love, today I had the great joy of receiving 4 letters from
Madeleine. The last is the one from Les Arcs. You do not need, my
Madeleine, to ask for my forgiveness, for what I told you was about
nothing at all serious. You are utterly sweet and charming, and that's
that. And I love you simply and completely, so let us never quibble
over the terms in which we couch our love. I beg you never to entertain the slightest doubt about that, any more than I could ever doubt
it. We are one. You are always of my opinion in everything and
should you ever not be you must tell me and me alone and give the
reasons why you believe I am wrong and if I am wrong I shall stand
corrected. The same goes for me with respect to you. But you must
conceal nothing, nor must I. The very little I have suffered on this
score I have always been brought to forget by your very next letter. I
adore you. Do not punish yourself. You are my little slave and I
alone am entitled to punish you and this right I shall doubtless
exercise only lovingly and out of more love not less. I dare not ask
for leave by the 20th because I am the newest sergeant here and
only 4 have had leave. If ever some way round this were to present
itself you may be sure that I would be by your side. And, just in case,
do give me your addresses as you move around—And write down for
me the date and time of your sailing from Port-Vendres on a scrap of
paper. Be calm and serene my love, I know that you are mine. I
know it and my taking possession of you as mystical as it is at the
present moment is a complete gift of myself that I offer you, a royal

gift—as your brother Pierre writes so well I give you a master. You give me the scent of your lips and I inhale that scent passionately. The ease with which I carry out my tasks here is offset by the great distress the work causes me. This two-sided character of my activity is very curious. Yes my love the idea of duty must enter love freely, so as to subject whatever is unbridled in passion to the order that is the source of strength, grace and in a word harmony. It is not a matter of being faithful out of duty, but the obligation of fidelity must serve to reinforce within each person the kind of security that allows love to blossom and renew itself. Pleasure, which is not to be disdained, is in no wise the child of duty, yet duty is its guarantee and when one loves with the freedom to explore the marvellous and vast sphere of love one experiences pleasure more deeply. Mystical love is naturally detached from all duty, but with carnal love, whose enemy is satiation and lassitude, it is important for Duty to come into play to defend it against its adversaries. That is the main reason why marriage was invented, otherwise free union would have sufficed, as it does for animals. But for the love between two souls such as ours permanence is indispensable and the notion of duty is the sole guarantor thereof. Not everyone has grasped the importance of this idea of duty, which is the essence of marriage itself—indissoluble as the Church rightly claims indissoluble for all elevated minds indissoluble between you and me from this moment onwards—And inasmuch as this has not always been understood many a marriage is unhappy but ours as of this moment is blessed.

I too my darling am glad and proud of the desire that you discern in the eyes of men, a desire moreover that would outrage me and that I would punish were I to witness it. At the same time I would not hold it against those men, for your beauty is indeed beyond human, but it has been mine for all time, more sacrosanct even than the beauty of

159

the queens of Spain, and no one but I could ever have carried you off, my lovely fairy.

I was upset to hear about your brother, I should much have preferred for your sake that he return to the French Front. Please give him my kindest regards.

You do not wish to talk to me about yourself, and I quite understand your scruples, but please consider that everything you tell me about you makes me feel closer to you, and after all you do not appear to doubt that this separation is a long agony for me. It is true that I shall discover your beauties one by one but you should not suppose that telling me about yourself amounts to a deflowering, for on the contrary I shall learn what you like about yourself, what you are proud of, in short your tastes. How many married couples have been

unhappy because a wife was too tongue-tied or too modest to state her preferences and explain how she liked to be loved? So be aware that I claim the right to love you and intend to make the best use of the leisure offered by our separation by instructing you in the most thorough way possible—but this is not an order my darling, you may treat it however you wish, it is merely the explanation of a demand that is perhaps ill-considered and impertinent and if so I ask you to excuse it. But again, my darling, when Duty buttresses Love, to love one another unreservedly is to love one another purely and this is how Duty transforms Hell into Paradise—a great poetic and ethical idea that is very sound and that I trust you will remind me of some day. So Duty changes Hell into Paradise and the demons of vice revert to being what they were originally, namely Virtues. Do not forget that the virtues are indeed an angelic hierarchy and that it was Lucifer's failure to fulfil his duty that plunged this high shining light into the shadows that now envelop him.

Sweet bather, our mystical bond guarantees our love which duty guarantees even further and our purity is infinite. Virtue is the Pleasure of our Desire. Duty is thus represented by the Fidelity that we pledge to one another, just as the Virtues or Virtue per se which is to say the Strength of our love is represented by Pleasure and the chain that attaches Fidelity to Pleasure is called desire and mystical Love is represented by physical love and a thousand ladders lead up through the stages of perfect marriage, in other words indissoluble marriage, and these ladders are friendship, tolerance, goodwill, refinement of mind, gentleness and on occasion violence, and in this way manliness joins with femininity to form nature's sublime stage, which is to say humanity. But thanks to your subtle intellect you will discover these arcana for yourself now that I have given the key to you who are so worthy of it.

I understand all your troubles and am very grateful to you my darling for telling me of them. You are the ministering angel of your sister-in-law and your Mama and please be sure to save for me those Madeleine letters that you have never sent.

And my darling, the magnificent gift of all of you transports me to heights where gratitude becomes indistinguishable from pride at having been able to provoke such a gift. I adore you.

Yes, my darling, in our love we are on an equal footing. Perhaps, darling, I suffer more than you or at least as much as you from the distance between us and I suffer all the more since as a grown man I can imagine joys that to you are still a mystery that I adore, oh my lily.

My darling you find the most exquisite words with which to speak of our love. That love is indeed a religion and if you are a slave you are also and in another sense my divinity. This dual quality of yours has

GUILLAUME APOLLINAIRE

to become familiar to you my darling and now you are no longer a woman like other women.

And now, my darling, I see I have not yet told you that I love you but of course you know how much I do love you and how, subtly as a snake, the symbol of health, poetry and sagacity, I have crept up on you, and I now curl about you with an irresistible sweet strength, I wrap myself around those forms whose beauty is still closed to me but which according to your own ever so strong expression keep me secure and do you not feel my embrace crushing you in a unique ecstasy . . .

So you are mine as I want you to be mine, body and soul, action and thought, completely and utterly, and as for me I worship you my darling.

162

Here the war goes on, it is going to become more decisive I think, what marvellous morale we have now. We have just bested the aeroplanes in an exchange of fire. Very entertaining.

I kiss your lips.

Gui

My love, just received your first letter from Narbonne with the sheet written in pencil the evening before. Yes, my darling, I am now discovering your sweetnesses and imagining them one by one. No, you could never cause me pain by telling me about you and about our love. And yes again, my adorable darling, our engagement is marvellous and beyond marvellous. Such is your grasp of the sublime nature of our love that you often expose it to me with infinite power and delicacy.

163

You are a truly special girl, graceful and strong, without a trace of pretty-pretty. Your letter brought a forgotten memory of mine back to mind, which makes me very happy.

Yes, I shall be sending you letters and other things for safe-keeping when I have them.

What you did at your father's grave was a fine thing, my darling, newly consecrating and newly blessing our love. I take you in my arms, my lily, I inhale you and worship you. My darling, as you say so correctly we are beyond ordinary human happiness, not only in ourselves but also by virtue of the exquisite goal we have set ourselves. And if the thought of becoming my wife makes you tremble think of the even more painful ardour of he who is preparing to be the husband of a girl like you.

GUILLAUME APOLLINAIRE

The mere thought of your eyelashes causes me to imagine all the love in the universe and in one of your most recent letters you evoked your red lips and the perfection of your figure in a way so concise yet so powerful that all the old canons of beauty suddenly crumbled and created an emptiness in me that leaves me stricken, for your beauty is still beyond the reach of my imagination and your photographs convey nothing of it.

But still, I have your hair and the memory of your eyelashes and this sublime cry of yours on the perfection of your form oh triumphant beauty and I worship you more than you could imagine without submitting ever more fully to my will.

Your master.

Gui

My love, your letter of the 3rd touched me to the quick. You are truly my rose without a thorn and I adore you. Your assessment of the home front is sadly true from what I know of it. All those people are devoid of any sense of duty.

I spoke to you of duty a few days ago, just think how completely it can transform vice into virtue, evil into good, because thanks to duty murder the greatest of crimes can become an act of valour! And think too how thoroughly duty can turn vices into qualities, into the most delightful acts, when it ennobles love's charming and pacific rites. Duty is therefore no empty word but rather the very foundation of social life and without it men would fall low indeed.

The story of your female friend in Narbonne does seem distressing on the face of it, but one must always take care not to pass judgement without being fully acquainted with the facts.

All leave is suspended for a month my dear in our sector, which puts my own back even further. But let us speak no more of leave unless you should need to change some detail for when my leave is finally granted.

For the moment nothing can be predicted. In fact the fighting is resuming savagely. We have a good deal of work, and doubtless shall have even more shortly.

How can one talk of tomorrow in such circumstances?

GUILLAUME APOLLINAIRE

Resupply has become impossible, we are limited to basic rations. This could last who knows how long. For several days we may not receive any post and likewise you may receive none from me. So you must not worry if you get no letter for a few days. Fantastic music at this moment. Our eyes when we see each other will immediately give us the brilliant measure of our love.

The story of the little girl is delightful and you are an adorable virgin, my Madeleine, I adore you too, more than anything.

The departure of your brother makes me a little sad, though I have faith in his lucky star. He'll be spending some time at the base, and perhaps he will not even go to the Dardanelles.

Today I found your letter with the Narbonne address. You cannot imagine how much good your letters do me, particularly the long ones. When noon arrives I completely lose my bearings and I only get them back at 3 p.m. when the post orderly gets here.

I read all the uninteresting post first, keeping letters from Madeleine until I can read them calmly, alone, and over and over for a good hour. Once night falls I read my Madeleine yet again and reply to her.

I kiss you on the mouth for a long time, gently, our breaths inter-mingling and our kiss lasting so long that you faint away my dear love, my Madeleine, I love you, I love you.

Gui

Your letters are miraculous, my love, they are the only ones to reach me during this time of sector changing, and they arrive just as quickly as usual. Today there were only 9 letters for the entire battery and one of them was yours to me. We get no newspapers. We no longer live day by day but rather hour by hour—not to say second by second!

You are a most charming little girl, your letters are delectable. I write you whenever I get the chance and that is almost every day. You know it, my beloved. I no longer go to the lookout now because I am beside the gun, in command of Cannon 4. I am so sorry to hear about your Mama's eye trouble. I dare not write to Foix, for I fear my letter may not arrive in time. But what I'll do is send you a card in Foix at the same time as I post this letter. Yes, you shall always be my love. I simply adore your letters, and so far from scolding you I understand you to a degree of which you simply have no idea. But perhaps on second thoughts you do have an idea, because you let me know it, and for that attentiveness I adore you my love!

My darling please do not speak of misfortunes—as for example your leg, which is mine too—Let us not tempt fate: as far as my leave is concerned I still know nothing. All leave is postponed in my sector until further notice, you can easily understand why.

So why are you glad my love not to know my reason for liking the fact that you are from the Vendée?

GUILLAUME APOLLINAIRE

I have no idea why you are again asking me to pardon you, but if it is true that there is something for which I need to forgive you then I in turn beg your forgiveness for not having done so earlier. And I kiss you on the lips. Your letters are entrancing. I love them infinitely.

You ask when I have time to make things for you. During the day when we have time off—which we certainly do. As for when I write to you, it is in the evening before I go to bed which I do at about 10 o'clock.

Until now I have been living in a dugout consisting of a hole covered by a roof of pine branches and lumps of chalk but as from tomorrow night I shall be sleeping in my men's shelter which is completely underground beneath a thick layer of fill topped by billets.

My appeal 'To Italy' is to appear in *La Voce* in French and there will be a separate printing of the poem for my friends and me.

Your idea of signing 'Me' is as sweet as can be. I was happy too, though, to find a '*toi*' a little farther on. But your idea is enchanting. I worship you and you make me into the happiest of men. You love me as no woman has ever before known how to love. You already know how proud I am to enjoy the love of a girl as pretty and as sensitive and as delightfully intelligent as you. It is so sweet of you to try to make me happy even from afar. I take your mouth passionately and all of you with your myriad charms and your nine doors made holy by our love, the nine doors of your delightful body and the myriad charms of your adorable soul. You are my bunch of black grapes. I love you my love and am going to send you a card in Foix. I hope you will get it there.

Gui

168

I send this short word to you in Foix my love so that you shall not be without news of your love.

I have written a long letter that you should find in Narbonne.

I trust your Mama is feeling better. Kiss her warmly for me. She certainly deserves it for giving me her pretty little Madeleine, who is my beloved rose and my beloved lily.

You ask what it means to be a fire observer, so here is a little poem on the subject.

LUEURS

*La montre est à côté de la bougie qui végète derrière un écran fait avec le fer-blanc
    d'un seau à confiture*
Tu tiens de la main gauche le chronomètre que tu déclencheras au moment voulu
*De la droite tu te tiens prêt à pointer l'alidade du triangle de visée sur les soudaines
    lueurs lointaines*
*Tu pointes cependant que tu déclenches le chronomètre et tu l'arrêtes quand tu en
    tends l'éclatement*
*Tu notes l'heure, le nombre de coups le calibre, la dérive, le nombre de secondes
    écoulées entre la lueur et la détonation*
Tu regardes sans te détourner, tu regardes à travers l'embrasure
Les fusées dansent les bombes éclatent et des lueurs paraissent
Tandis que s'élève la simple et rude symphonie de la guerre
Ainsi dans la vie, mon amour, nous pointons notre cœur et notre attentive piété

GUILLAUME APOLLINAIRE

Vers les lueurs inconnues et hostiles qui ornent l'horizon le peuplent et nous dirigent

Et le poète est cet observateur de la vie et il invente les lueurs innombrables des
    mystères qu'il faut repérer

Connaître ô Lueurs, ô mon très cher amour!

Flashes

The watch is next to the candle sputtering behind a metal screen made
    from a jam tin

You take the stop-watch in your left hand so you can start it at the right
    moment

You get your right hand ready to train the alidade of the sighting triangle
    on the sudden faraway flashes

You point it just as you start the watch which you stop when you hear the
    detonation

You note down time, number of reports, calibre, deflection, and seconds
    elapsed between flash and detonation

You watch without looking away, you look through the embrasure

Flares dance bombs explode and flashes appear

As the war's simple rough symphony proceeds

So too in life, my love, we train our heart and our unwavering attention

On the unknown and hostile flashes that adorn the horizon and people it
    and govern us

And the poet is this observer of life who invents the countless flashes of
    mysteries that must be descried

And understood Oh flashes, Oh my very dear love!

What an extraordinary feast I had today my love, a fantastic orgy, something truly magnificent—5 letters and two parcels from you!

The contents of the parcels were exquisite. First of all I ate the fruit, the chocolate, and the honey bonbon still bearing the divine traces of your teeth, and this marvellous kind of kiss of your invention proved to me once and for all that you are a true *Vendéenne*. I was thrown into near spasms of voluptuousness by this kiss of such a new sort, so subtle, so delicate, so exquisite in its savagery, so Madeleine, I do adore you, you know. I could never have thought up such a thing or imagined such a perfect form of communion from afar between two lovers. Your dear mouth, your tongue, your teeth, your delicious saliva—all mine your absence notwithstanding, my Madeleine, dearest peerless inventress! And to think that I was almost forgetting to thank you. I am well and truly obliged to you my dearest little wife . . . I worship you. . . .

The letters are dated the 21st of August and the 4, 5, 6 and 8 of September! A feast indeed, and reading you it seemed as though I was holding you in my arms. My sweet thing, in your letter of 21 August you speak of a time when we are old and you paint me a charming picture of Monsieur and Madame Denis and of our ultimate demise in a far-off apotheosis in which we are transformed into twin stars because you feel sure we shall never leave one another even after life ends. You also recount in an admirably succinct way the most

GUILLAUME APOLLINAIRE

beautiful dream ever, albeit also the maddest . . . were your lips really bleeding from my kisses my love?!—you must never fear the precious liberty that we enjoy with respect to each other. This liberty is ours for we love one another and even 'things' of the most 'fearsome' kind, if they come into your mind, you must tell me—indeed you must promise to tell me and anyway what could possibly be 'fearsome' between us?? Tomorrow I am going to study the effects of the sun on your hair and try to make out the reddish glint you describe. And what makes you bring up the ghastly role of Phèdre with the words

La fille de Minos et de Pasiphaé

Daughter of Minos and Pasiphaé

I conjure you up rather, my love, with your great dark fringed eyelashes, murmuring the delightful couplet

Ariane ô ma sœur de quel amour blessée
Vous mourûtes aux bords où vous fûtes laissée

Ariane oh my sister wounded by what love
Did you die on those shores where you were abandoned

And that voluptuous air of yours would I am quite sure unleash an unprecedented frenzy in me and you my lily would assuredly not be far behind in that regard and already when I first saw you your marvellous eyelashes caused me to murmur

C'est Vénus tout entière à sa proie attachée

It is Venus herself fastened upon her prey

True, your deep voice equips you for that terrifying role, and you are my dearest Phèdre. But tell me in what way this role inhabits you as you say it does.

Yes, when I sail to Oran it will be my first long sea-crossing, for as of now I have been only to England 3 times there and back and to

Flushing, on the island of Walcheren. Otherwise my seagoing has been confined to outings on fishing boats.

Yes indeed, I adore your letters disjointed, simple and unstudied as they are—that is the Madeleine I love, just the way she is and not otherwise. What a shame that the photos did not turn out.

In your letter of 4 September you speak of your fears. I myself fear nothing, my love, I love you too much to be afraid of anything. It is going to begin about the 15th I think.

Yes, my love, you really are my wife, indeed it is extraordinary how strongly I feel that you are mine. It seems to me that . . . well, I feel I am your husband, that's all, my darling Madelon, and oh your exquisite letter of the 5th in which you play the little mother, so beautiful, oh my darling little Phèdre—and it is true, I would right now so willingly curl up in your arms. But yet again you bring up that pardon! My love this is not right of you, for you know full well that I love you and am your master and I would know how to prove it if need be— why, you are just a big kid who should get a good hiding for absolutely insisting that I have something to forgive you for.

The story of the nun is very amusing my Madelon.—Oh how much I envy the spot occupied by my photo, what an exquisite place that must be.

I have put the rose of the 6th of September against my heart, and how I love the little note written at midnight. I think of you all the time you know! Be calm my beloved, and yes, I so adore it when you reveal every inclination of your darling heart to me. Like you I love light, space and freedom, and as for having your dearest lips against my own heart I daren't tell you what ravages they cause but we must be stoical and I likewise place my lips against your heart my love!

GUILLAUME APOLLINAIRE

And lastly your letter postmarked the 8th! Imagine my tearing up your letters!! You are not thinking, because I love them every single one from the 1st to the last. You know I adore you and you want me to calm you down my love, with this dramatic tale of yours about my pardoning you. So let us forgive one another mutually—But for what? For nothing, upon my word—and that is so charming my love.

I adore you and you will never cause me pain.

Yes, my love, I feel how much you are mine and I adore you like this. The very best way for you to be, your truest and most natural attitude, that of love, the most unbridled love in the world my spirited little slave ready to put up with every punishment except for that of my suffering.—

I have sent you a note at Foix. It is not fair of you to mention my leave again at this moment. There is no leave in our sector, and that goes for everyone. My heart is rent by desire at the thought of this fresh sacrifice that you must make for our love, but I shall make it up to you a hundredfold, believe me! . . . Yes, your family is wonderful!! Yes, the picture you paint of our married life is the one I dream of. But tell me, what are these things that you dare not put in writing? So dare! It is so easy between us to dare anything. I received a charming letter from Jean, I like him very much but I replied in a way that will undoubtedly convince him to take me for a being bereft of morals, because I praised the philosophers of life who do not subscribe to Kantian ethics—one might almost now say to Christian ethics. Write him if you have a chance and tell him that the sense of duty among the élite must stand in for virtue, or rather, I think, that duty creates virtue.

I love you.

Gui

My love, thank you for your precious letter of the 8th. I too had a wild day yesterday my darling, wild with love on account of all your letters, and today yet another. This one is the most beautiful, the very dearest[1] from my beloved. How glad I am to hear that your mother's operation went well. And how glad too that I sent you a line that should reach you I believe at Foix, whatever I send you at Narbonne. So my Madelon you love me completely now. And you are going to come back to *The Heresiarch*, and speak quite frankly about it this time. My desire takes all of you with an infinitely sweet violence, an angelic brutality, my darling. I possess you as my wife, which is to say completely, and you are already so expert in our love that you invented the delectable bonbon kiss. And you love me in the most adorable way just as I want you to love me, I want you to love me to the point of the most delightful suffering. When we have joined our minds through the bond of the flesh I want you to be unable to think of me without being shaken by spasms of indescribable love. I love it that voluptuousness invades you so powerfully at the thought of me and that it already disturbs you in a way that you will come to adore because there is nothing more elevated. You spoke to me of your breasts, unimaginable wonders that your dear words reveal to me. I feel that I already know these exquisite fruits but words fail me when it comes to describing them and after all I do not really know them, it is merely my imagination striving to give form to my desire. Yes my perfect Madelon I shall hold you in my

1 Apollinaire writes 'plus chair' (literally, 'most flesh') in error for 'plus chère' ('dearest').—Tr.

175

GUILLAUME APOLLINAIRE

arms and press you to me, I shall kiss your adorable breasts, that vision of paradise. And instead of shrinking away your flesh shall palpitate against mine. No, this apprehension you mention cannot be painful, just the contrary, don't you think so my Madelon? Yes, you shall tell me everything—I wait and hope for this as an incomparable testimony to your love, a delightful sacrifice—you must tell me everything this evening about what you feel and you must forget nothing, oh my little slave, nothing that may help me guide our love. I shall tell you just as soon as my mother is informed, which will be after my leave, and done in such a way that we may speak of it without embarking on explanations which would not succeed in that she would in fact understand nothing. My reproaches must never hurt your feelings because I love you to the farthest reaches of love's possibilities and because you know it and because you love me too just as much, and I love you for not being hurt by what I wrote you, my love whom I love so passionately. If only you knew how I long for your next letter.

Moreover, you should know my darling that between us sulking is quite impossible, and all mental reservations likewise, for my slave is always loved as much as ever, and there can never be any pain for you darling. So, your brother is to be with the 37th Artill.

By the way, I ate the bonbons—not all of them of course—with my friend Berthier whose brother was with yours at Fontainebleau. Berthier, the one who is here, is a very nice lad and he too is engaged. He dreams all the time of his sweetheart (the lady to whom 'Aiming' was dedicated). I still have the taste of your mouth in mine. I await your next letter impatiently.

You give me your mouth for a long time and I take it for as long as you want to let me, which is to say forever.

You know, it is beginning to be mighty cold these nights. The days are fine, but the nights are really cold.

I am afraid I sent my latest 'Vie anecdotique' in too late, I made a mistake, because it was meant to be in Paris by the 12th, and it will leave here only tomorrow the 13th.—I thought it was due the 15th—how stupid of me.

It is incredible that the parcel has not yet arrived. Perhaps they do not notify you and you are supposed to go down to the station to see if parcels have come? What a pity that they no longer have forms at the station to request *home delivery*. My little one I take you all of you with infinite delicacy, yet in a manly way, and you offer me your voluptuous breasts and I kiss them passionately as you faint away with a smouldering sensuality in your eyes. I kiss the delicious strawberries of your breasts. I so wish that this war this too chaste war would end quickly. But after all I suppose that war must needs be chaste. If it were not, what soldier would be willing to fight! Though it seems there are some sectors that are less abstinent, but to my mind that is a bad thing. And I adore you, my darling, with an infinitely voluptuous chastity that I dedicate to you, for my whole spirit is chaste in this here-and-now, which is not to deny that for some time my love for you has been anything but chaste. Not chaste in the slightest! But there is no morbid delectation involved. It is very peculiar and very hard to explain my love and it will surely require many letters to clarify this important matter. But I adore you because you are the most intelligent girl in the world and also the most desirable. You are my wife moreover and one has every right to desire one's own wife especially when she is as beautiful as you are my love. Our lips unite.

Gui

GUILLAUME APOLLINAIRE

My love, you are a love and every day you offer me new delights. True, after yours of yesterday I was expecting a letter that was supposed to have many details about certain things—Well, that letter never came—But your letter of the 9th nevertheless afforded me exquisite pleasure. In it you tell me of the delicate perfection of your feet that I adore and you say that each time I have shown an interest in a particular part of the little person of my own Madelon that part is the very one that in your own eyes is your best feature. In so saying you slander both of us, my love, for there is no part of you that I do not love. I have seen you just enough to know that I love all of you for you are full of charms and there is nothing in you that is not absolutely lovable and the very tiniest bit of my Madeleine is beauty itself with all its attractions. All the same, I quite see what you must have meant, namely that whenever in my letters I expressed an interest in some part of your adorable person I persuaded you of its perfection. That is all, wouldn't you say? But now my imagination is running riot . . . in what parts precisely did I show an interest? You must tell me again and at length about everything I brought up in my letters. To the best of my recollection I evoked your hands your dear hands for which I have filed metal fallen from the moon, and your hair so like bunches of black grapes, one bunch being here where I gaze at it as ecstatically as the Hebrews gazed at the grapes brought from the Land of Canaan. And I spoke of your exquisite mouth, whose incorruptible savour was brought to me by the bonbons, that red mouth which is mine and which I bite my love. Also your breasts, and what you say in your letter fills me with the highest esteem for their delightful perfection and I cannot think of that pair of pigeons without longing to be able to kiss them and caress them albeit with all the caution indicated before one touches such precious things. It is said that a cup was moulded from Marie-Antoinette's perfect breast, so I shall mould my mouth from yours and from that cup you shall drink. And, to return to your feet, so dainty and sensitive, I adore them.—There is supposed to be a vice or rather a deviation of feeling consisting in a love over and above all else for feet and by extension shoes. I certainly do not suffer from this shortcoming, which is a form of sexual psychopathology. This was the peculiar vice of Restif de la Bretonne and we have Restif's guidance to thank for Binet's elegant engravings. It is also a vice widespread in England and in the Germanic countries. But for my part I stand ready to worship at the shrine of your ever so treasured and lively feet. At the same time I am most interested in all your charms my darling and since I have no special vice to reproach myself for and to satisfy I would like to make all the vices mine the better to love you. Meanwhile in my imagination I press your beloved body against me and dream of the suppleness of your waist and its roundness. I fancy too I once mentioned your patches of fleece, my all-dark one, and it is true that the thought of them affects me deeply.

179

Why do you wonder whether it is possible for our bodies to love each other as much as our souls? It is true that physical love, to my mind at least, is limited. But we shall never cease pushing those limits farther and farther back.

I myself have read very little Dostoyevsky, I leafed through *The Idiot* rather than read it; I read a poor adaptation of his memories of

Siberia, and I have seen *The Brothers Karamazov* on stage. I do know something of him, nevertheless, but he saddens and demoralizes me. That is why he repels me a little even though I recognize his great talent, and what is more he stresses psychological detail over realistic detail. I like there to be a perfect balance between these literary modes. The Russian author I like best and rank with Shakespeare Flaubert Cervantes La Fontaine Molière is Gogol, the admirable, charming, laughing Gogol, delectable Little Russian, adorable poet of whom as a matter of fact I have read too little. I had started *Taras Bulba*, a novel that enchanted me, but after reading the 1st chapter I left it on a train along with a novel of my own on the end of the world, *La Gloire de l'olive* (The Glory of the Olive), which was supposed to appear in the *Revue Blanche* and which I never found the courage to start again (my novel, I mean—as for Gogol's, I never managed to get another copy).

I relished *Dead Souls* and would love to re-read it one of these days.

At bottom I appreciate the satire of the great poets (Cervantes Gogol Shakespeare La Fontaine Molière) but I find teratology repugnant. I do not like the shortcomings vices and ugly aspects of man to be contemplated without a smile, which is a way of understanding and of compensating in a sense for our wretchedness, veiling it by means of intelligent indulgence, even if we are liable to shed tears over it eventually. I hate the earnestness and tragic airs adopted by the likes of Zola and Dostoyevsky in dealing with degradation.

In Tolstoy there is something else, he is a sort of pope or a sort of Jupiter of the novel, he does not smile but he supplies order, which is saying a great deal. There is something of classical tragedy in Tolstoy, whereas with others (Zola or Dostoyevsky) there is startling and remarkable melodrama but their seriousness never transcends what they are describing, even if they describe it (as Dostoyevsky does) with genius. Tolstoy's life was an extraordinary one. In part he was heir to the genius of Restif, though in the way that an inheritor can be quite unaware of the fact—Restif is a truly admirable creature but his abjection is comical and he is a literary hydra offering every possible face; he was very widely read in Russia and exerted a very strong influence on Russian literature. A fact moreover that has never been remarked upon. The emotional prostration before the prostitute so typical of the Russian novel comes from Restif.

Your remarks on *The Heresiarch* strike me as odd. Please do explain what you mean my darling. You expect me to guess, and while you may be the Sphinx I am no Oedipus. A little piece of your heart, you say, to be guessed at with reference to *The Heresiarch*, something that links us in a strange way and that has revealed your own nature to you. Whatever can it be? Tell me all, my dear beloved, do not think of the Great Event, just imagine that it has already taken place and banish an anxiety that you need not feel my beloved little virgin. You'll see, you will become my wife in joy, for I do not want you to suffer. The lily shall become a rose and this metamorphosis should not worry you in the least my love.

But tell me about your nature, and do so without fear. You know perfectly well that I am your master.

Today I have sent a parcel for you via the mess corporal from the wagon line who should put it on the field train whence it will be transferred to the railway. I put your Narbonne address without thinking that by the time the parcel arrived you might be in Lamur. So it will be forwarded to you . . .

The package contains an inkwell made from the hollowed-out fuse of a Boche 150. Simply unscrewing the top will expose the hole into which a glass receptacle for the ink will fit. It would be a good idea to have 2 tenons inserted into the holes in the little screw lid to make it easier to remove. As for the thread at the bottom a small triangular wooden base will be needed into which the inkwell can be screwed. Don't worry, there is no longer any danger. The fuse fell very close to our gun but we were all in the shelter. Incidentally, it still bears signs of its fall. You will see a ring graduated from 1 to 28 which serves to select a particular flash-hole and thus set the timing of the fuse, and just below a mark serving as a reference point. This graduated ring would do quite well as a calendar, using if desired the cross just after the 28, the indicator in the shape of a cross or sword, and the 1st hole to represent the missing dates 29, 30 and 31. The whole thing is wrapped in a copy of *Corriere della Sera* on the front page of which you will notice a word I have circled in ink. You will understand the word and even the entire event reported. We saw it ourselves in detail—we were adjusting the battery when it happened. I take you all of you my dear little Madelon my voluptuous Madelon and I kiss you on the mouth madly and deeply and not with mouths closed.

Gui

And to think that I had become accustomed to your almost daily letters! My love! . . . At last!!! Write me as often as possible for your letters are my paradise . . . I am posting this to you at Lamur, but I'll send a word to you at Narbonne too in hopes that it will reach you there. Write the moment it arrives. Those damned Boche submarines fill me with boundless fear for you my love, yet at the same time I am sure that no harm will befall you. Kiss all the family for me, my charming dear friends and future sisters-in-law and the two little lads. And don't forget to kiss your dear pretty Mama for me too, my Madeleine. Today I got your letter of the 10th and it made me so happy. You understand me completely my dear. Certainly there will be times of sadness, in fact we seem to be enduring one at this moment. But it is you who will bring them to an end, that is your role and you will know how to fulfil it, just as you will be able to counsel me and (being my slave) often prove yourself even stronger than me as we confront life. But this strength of yours will flow from mine, from my confidence and from your faith in us both.

But let us banish all sadness from this correspondence . . . To that end speak to me whenever you can of your you that I adore, oh my rose-lily. We love each other limitlessly with all of our souls and with all of our bodies. And I want you to tell me about any scruples you may have. I take your purity my rose-lily of love and return it to you as passionately as you offer it to me. This purity is within you and

GUILLAUME APOLLINAIRE

will remain there forever. It allows you my dear chosen vessel to welcome all desires, all caresses, all embraces. Your flesh calls me my darling and as for me I stiffen towards you like a compass needle in search of North. Oh my dear Wind Rose you have a mystical and pure awareness of the North that attracts me. It lies within you intimately within you. And thanks to the notion of our dear Duty, my beloved, the devil of Limbo has changed back into an angel of charm and grace. I fully understand the peerless modesty that animates you, and not only do I understand it but I also love and shall always respect it. And you shall see how by doing my will you shall at the same time take the first steps down the delightful path of conjugal happiness. It is you that will always make the advances, I shall merely give the orders, for to command means putting things in order, and as for you, you will obey by anticipating our thoughts, which intersect continually and in such an intimate fashion that the two are one and the same, the result my dear being a perfect Trinity: our perfect union is the guarantee of the diversity of our company, in which we shall no longer be alone for there will be you me and us.

When you get this letter you should also receive 2 paper-knives made from large bands taken off Boche shells. I cannot make a present of them to you because one must never give anything that cuts. So they are mine and you shall keep them for me. The inkwell I sent yesterday is packed into a food tin and to get it out it will be necessary to cut the metal. Do not try to remove it without doing so or you may cut yourself. Yes just like me you have a feeling of modesty about our love, which is sacred. And I love to think that the modesty you offer me will become the frankest of immodesty. And then there you will stand before me as naked as Eve before Adam! Revealing to me at once your soul your heart and your body. Shall I embrace you once more, oh my lily, in your nakedness? I feel that your torso, that flower springing from the exquisite calyx of your lower body and loins, your torso with its twin flowers blooming at your breast, I feel your torso falling enraptured into my encircling arms and my mouth moves to yours that is calling me. And I feel you are tired now my darling adorably tired and played out and so happy that there is no part of you that does not smile as I stroke your unbound hair.

Is that the way, tell me, that you want me to take you, deep into your most intimate parts? Do you realize that the intimate discomfort that you cannot explain stems from my not being there with you to provide supreme nourishment to your legitimate appetites, oh my adorable angel. You are my own purity just as I am your own sensuality.—I enclosed 2 photos with my letter of yesterday. Please keep them safe as I have no other copies and the person who took them is no longer here. So I cannot get any more—in one I am on a little bridge with a chasseur sergeant and the other one shows me standing next to a 75-mm anti-aircraft gun, you can clearly see the platform but the barrel is covered with leaves.

I hope to send you a better photo than these in a few days.

The picture has been taken but we are waiting for paper to print it I take you madly all of you in an endless caress.

Gui

My love, once again I am sending this letter to Narbonne so that
you don't go a single day without a word from me. If it arrives after
you leave it will be forwarded to you. At the same time I am writing
to you at Lamur and from tomorrow on I shall write to Lamur only.
Send me a card from Port-Vendres, where sadly I cannot be on the
20th. There is no doubt that the show has now begun or is about to
begin. This time I have the greatest confidence in the outcome, this,
I believe and those around me believe, will be the last great push.

This morning my love they collected the rudimentary masks we had
been issued and now I have a cagoule—a penitent's hood. Those
hoods had a powerful effect on me as a child. I was born, as you do
not yet know, in Rome, though of Polish origin, and came to France
at the age of 3. But I very clearly recall a certain brotherhood that
we used to see at burials all of whose members wore such hoods.

This frightened me a little and the very last thing I could have
imagined was that one day I might myself wear a cagoule.

I keep forgetting to tell you that my voice has been recorded for the
Archives de la Parole (Spoken Archives) which Ferdinand Brunot
runs at the Sorbonne with his wife's help. There are two discs there
containing 3 poems of mine (10 poets were recorded in all, I think).

The poems are 'The Traveller', 'Mirabeau Bridge' and 'Marie'.

Madame Brunot offered to give me copies of the discs. The war intervened, but I now recall her offer and note it here so you may remind me of it after the war and I can ask her for them.

In the letter sent to Lamur (almost '*l'amour*'!), I wrote a good deal about love, my love. I adore you, I kiss your red mouth and your adorable breasts, I clasp you to me with all my strength in the gentlest way and stroke you, my so very graceful darling, my darling love.

I love you.

Gui

17 Sept. 1915

My love, today I received yours of the 11th. I am no longer writing
to you at Narbonne. The letters would have no chance of reaching
you in time. Venus would already have taken ship at her port. I think
the show is about to start here. Tomorrow they are bringing in a
three-day supply of food and water. Consequently I think we shall
not be getting any letters nor will you receive any. Now my darling
you must not be alarmed over a few days without letters. I shall
nevertheless write you every day and you do so too—

Meanwhile my love, along with what you call your new womanly
heart you must also keep your virginal young girl's heart. They are
both you, chase neither away, they are both me too. If you only
knew . . .

But yes my love, on the contrary, you make me very very happy. I
find everything I want in you and the joy your letters give me
though very voluptuous is also marvellously pure. No, I am not
suffering wretchedly and outrageously. I am master of my feelings. I
suffer solely from our separation and of course I would prefer to
have you all of you in reality. But that is all. I desire you infinitely
and that delights me. I suffered only during the time when I did not
yet know—though I did in fact know—how much you were mine.
But now in me there is all the inquisitiveness of my love for you, but
nothing base. I adore you but my strong sense of duty will not allow
me to wear myself out with the sort of fancies that might haunt some

solitary in the Thebaid left to himself with no concerns but meta-physical ones, but not a soldier. In any case a soldier must be chaste. In the early days my lady friend in Nice had suggested that I spend a few days with her in the rear of Sector 59, where there were still a few little villages left, but I did not want to. I wanted to be celibate. I planned to make up for lost time after the war or while on leave. Then you answered my prayers and all that went by the board. I had opportunities like everyone else in Sector 59 in those villages of the 2nd Zone, but even had I been tempted to let myself go, my memory of you, by now becoming a future, would have held me back. I like my present celibacy because it helps me put up with the fatigue and keeps me from falling ill and above all because it lets me be worthy of Madeleine and because my desire could never be directed at anyone but her, body and soul. My desire is for you alone, and not for some emanation, even one that came from you, and there is nothing in the world I would like less than to be like poor Ixion who went to bye-byes with a ghostly cloud in the shape of Juno. I love Madeleine and I love her writing to me because her letters are refined, intelligent, voluptuous, charming, delicate, and full of insights about herself, about us, yet it is not her letters that I love, and such a monstrous love would diminish me too much in my own eyes for there ever to be any question at all of my suffering as I then would, with your letters coming to resemble the apples of the wretched Tantalus, no, you need fear nothing of the sort. So far from paining me, your letters by demonstrating your love merely increase my joy, my joy to be loving someone so youthful yet at the same time so womanly, so ready for our complete love. And I too even though it is clearly not with the intent of promoting chastity between us—on the contrary—kiss your lips purely and chastely. In short, I give your letters the weight they deserve but the man that I am is reserved entirely and exclusively for you. My desire for you is

189

GUILLAUME APOLLINAIRE

thus infinite but depends on the moment when I can make you mine.

I just knew you did not wear a corset! What a marvellous presentiment! I asked you about this only because I was so absolutely sure of my intuition. But I did not insist because all the same I might have been mistaken. You simply cannot imagine how happy this marvellous and important news makes me. So your bust is free . . . my Madeleine. You are a divinity! And as for the news concerning your goddess's hips, I had concluded as much from your photos and from your gait, *patent incessu dea*. You have the very hips that I prefer. And forgive my immodesty, you shall see that I am immodest with the cunning of a savage, pardon me for putting it so crudely, but I feel I could not love a woman who did not have hips the way you describe yours and the way yours in fact are. I imply no vice or obsession when I say that I love the spirit of the Greeks in their adoration of the Callipygean Venus and I feel no shame about so Hellenic a taste. So you have no reason to console yourself over this—rather, you should rejoice, my most beautiful Madeleine. And wherever did you read that Nero disliked narrow-hipped women? For my part I abominate them.

Nero, I agree, was a remarkable person. When all is said and done, I believe that all the charges against him have been refuted.

Your figure my darling is quite admirable. I can tell as much from the photo of you in your dressing-gown and also from the one where you are on the terrace and your left leg is much in evidence. I am waiting impatiently for the picture of you in Narbonne.

How I love your remark about our happiness. It shows me how our tastes coincide in everything, for you wrote it after first telling me a little, even a great deal, about your body which I sense is as admirable as your profile.

My beloved, kiss your feet for me—those dear suffering creatures as the *précieuses* used to call them, for upon my word those *précieuses* were not always so *ridicules*.

Why yes my love we shall bestow very very much mutual love upon one another. And please excuse my naive tendency to name things with a directness which is part of my nature and part of yours too, for you are as frank and straightforward as I am, and come, my love, you must admit that even if I have lived more I am pure also and worthy of your own so magnificent and so voluptuous purity.

And when I think of you my darling, every time, your image puts me suddenly in mind of the Song of Songs. That marvellous pastoral is the perfect backdrop for the African fastnesses whence you write me and whence you call to me and offer me out of the purest of desires the most beautiful and virginal of bodies which is also the most voluptuous of bodies, oh my love.

Gui

GUILLAUME APOLLINAIRE

192

17 Sept. 1915

My love, my dear treasure, I can scarcely breathe at the thought that you will be on shipboard in three days and at the mercy of the sea, you and your dear Mama. Once you are back in Oran do not move either of you until the war is over. I was so ignorant of the geography of Algeria that I did not even know or had more likely forgotten that Oran was on the sea. This letter will reach you in Oran, please tell me if you are in danger of being bombarded or anything of that sort. Keep me up to date my dear love. Besides this letter I am also writing you at Narbonne. Yesterday I sent you a poor proof of a photo of me taken by Berthier. I'll send you a better one tomorrow. As a joke, a very witty one in fact, he has mounted this portrait after the fashion of a medal to poke fun at my authoritarian bent.

Back in Sector 59 he wrote a little prose poem on the same theme which I shall look out and send you.

He is a charming and knowledgeable fellow and possibly my best poetry student.

Berthier's fiancée is also a person of erudition and in their letters, so he says, they discuss any number of problems in mechanics or physics; I don't believe a word of it, unless they use them merely as interludes, just as we do, you and I my beloved Madelon, with literature.

My treasure, our love which is so mystical and carnal in its essence will grow even more and continue growing forever. So far as I am concerned, that is the simple truth. For within such a marvellous girl as you there are endless treasures and my happiness will consist in discovering and taking possession of them knowing full well however that I shall never come to the end of my ardent, my pure, my sweet Madeleine.

You speak, my love, of the adorable work for which my hands are destined. Those hands burn for the activity that you envision and my arms avid snakes of my body have already reared up fascinated by the dazzling whiteness of your body.

And since you belong to me down to the most secret recesses of your being, I take all of you, even those most secret parts of you my darling.

I love your tempestuous desires, oh you who are more beautiful more pure than Phèdre and more agitated than she, but who can bear no stigma of vice nor burden of remorse, since our love is a self-purifying fire and since from the crucible into which it is plunged by our separation it will emerge in the shape of Duty. Is this not the very golden age that we are destined to create? I adore you for combining the sensuality of a bacchante with the intellectuality of a Vittoria Colonna and with the mystical ardour of a Saint Theresa. And I am already dreaming of marvellous celebrations of your flesh in which you shall be both altar and sacrifice. I too, my darling, am proud of us but above all of you and of your beauty. I dream of girding your divine hips with myrtle. It is night now, a cloudy night with rifle fire on every side and mixed with it a curious rumbling noise from some Boche artillery or other, it sounds like someone beating carpets. Stray bullets fall spent, some even reaching our positions and raining down on us. I am going to write a letter to you in Narbonne now and I take your mouth and I kiss the flowers of your breasts and I take possession of your entire being, oh my divine one.

Gui

GUILLAUME APOLLINAIRE

My adorable love, I have written to you in Oran but now that I know
you may stay a little longer in Narbonne I am writing you there
also.—Did your brother get my letter? I shall never tire, my beloved,
of telling you how grateful I am to you, first of all for the infinite
grace of your delightful letters but above everything for all the love,
all the voluptuousness that you put into them. Yes indeed, our loves
are equal and in me there is not an impulse not a nerve not a fibre,
not a heartbeat that does not belong to you. Oh give me that
languid look of acknowledgement, the clear-eyed glance so full of
tenderness that you cast at me do you remember on the station
platform at Marseilles a glance that at the same time did not want to
see me out of the exquisite modesty of a young girl whom I already
loved without really knowing it, for I loved you at first sight and I
believe that you sensed it oh my love, and that that is what
prompted your sweet attitude and obliged you to respond to me
even if your inner voice told you that I was perhaps too insistent.
And I managed to capture your attention and your intelligence and
most of all that glance that I adore so warm so ardent when you look
down so clear so tender when your eyes are open wide surmounted
and adorned by those splendid jet-black lashes.

I await your photos with justifiable impatience. Of course I don't
confuse your photos with you yourself. I am well aware that
snapshots can never convey the image of your beauty which is too
perfect, too regal too subtle to be interpreted by any camera no

1 All editions of the letters to Madeleine
have 'Ma Polie' here, but it seems
at least plausible that Apollinaire
intended to write 'Ma Jolie'.—Tr.

matter how sophisticated. And I understand that the love which animates you, so perfect, so sublime, oh my Pretty One,[1] in other words oh my everything, is a love that you could not show off to any photographer, even a completely imaginary one. But all the same I am waiting for those photos with impatience, no matter how little of my Madelon they will bring me.

No, I have no wish to gauge the strength of your love, because I know it is just as immeasurable as mine and that it is happiness plain and simple with its very highest peak being voluptuousness and ever-renewed voluptuousness of body and of mind. I am not sad my love, but rather infinitely joyful because of the untrammelled beauty of your body rivalled only by the untrammelled beauty of your soul and these two freedoms you have offered me in slavery and your duty is my will and my love. I rejoice in this, and I want to cry out to the world that I am happy because of my beautiful Madeleine. Yes, you are indeed worthy of me even in your desires. You are your own mistress henceforward because you belong to me.

195

Your soul, worthy of Corneille, turns out to have the strength and marvellous organization needed for all that we shall create my perfect Madeleine, my other self so much more beautiful and perfect than my own self.

I take your body and inhale your soul and caress you deeply and endlessly from your delicate feet to your broad supple hips and thence to your awakened breasts to your mouth to your hair.

I love you.

Gui

My love, my Madeleine, my thought was indeed badly expressed
and you have rectified it with the good sense of the exquisite lover
that you are. I meant merely to voice the feeling that two beings who
love one another forever cannot go beyond the bounds of legitimate
duty even when they embrace all those refinements which their love
suggests to them, and which in other circumstances such as transient
or serial love affairs would be considered vices or obsessions of a
deplorable if not reprehensible kind; for duty within marriage
consists in the avoidance of tedium and refinements in love can aid
this purpose. Between you and me, whose minds understand each
other so well, satiation is impossible, yet refinements must arise
nonetheless from our very love itself as from the fact that we love
everything in us, not solely this or that property of our bodies or
souls but indeed everything absolutely everything. Yet inasmuch as
love itself has often, due to indefensible prejudice and enormous
malice, been deemed a vice, all its refinements have been similarly
described. And this charge has been brought just as readily against
the commonest postures of love as against those others in which the
Ancients proudly excelled but which the Moderns have practised
only in a hypocritical manner. If duty plays no part in love, it is true
that vice may be present. Thus two beings who unite with the sole
purpose of amusement—2 women for example, or 2 men (which is
very common)—are justifiably considered depraved.

196

The rites of love that you speak of are certainly natural, but they are not all necessary, not to procreation at any rate, far from it, and while procreation may occur thanks to acts of love the fact remains that the pleasures of love and procreation are connected by chance alone and in short there is very little relationship between the two. They are like neighbours living across the landing from one another. No more than that.

Which having been said, my argument will be specious if my theory of duty is not accepted, in which case anything would be allowable in an anarchy unworthy of humanity. But once this idea of mine, this idea of duty comes into play it is easy to grasp that between spouses, but solely between spouses, or at least between people tantamount to spouses—as in not a few Parisian ménages—everything is allowed when it comes to the joys of the flesh.

Love is a pleasure at once so heady so fragile that great caution is required. Otherwise one risks becoming the plaything of the flesh, to the utter detriment of the will, the mind and the soul.

One must master the flesh in order to enjoy it harmoniously, to the maximum, and without exhaustion.

It must be mastered and it must not gain mastery over you. That is why an excess of modesty is another way of allowing oneself to be dominated by the flesh.

The mind must dominate, and when it does so the flesh may be immodest and there is no need for us to feel shame, but one must take care to keep things private. Marriage was invented as a way of maintaining such privacy.

I write you all this without nuance, so please add all the nuances and niceties that are absent from this cursory explanation.

GUILLAUME APOLLINAIRE

You understand, do you not my darling, that we two have a secret, the secret of our love, for the sake of which a special language has come into being between us, though it is not yet beyond the stammering stage. We already have 'the Big Event' and your 'intimate being', vague terms in themselves but very clear to me. And I like the fact that there is this secret between us, this language agreed upon that has yet to be refined. 'Innermost being', as vague as it may be, is too precise—not for us, certainly, but for what you call, by virtue of the deep intuition within you, 'the modesty of our love'. Our lexicon could well be borrowed from flowers or from something else.

To get back to the original subject, the rites of love are of great purity because they are natural but not because they are necessary, it is love itself that is necessary—and our love in consequence is absolute, but its rites are not all necessary. For instance, your hips might conceivably have been narrow, in which case I would have loved you just as much as I do love you but obviously your hips would not have received the same passionate homage that I pay them now. Thus your hips that I adore and that I adore in a thousand ways constitute a factor favourable to refinements of our love but a factor that was a necessary condition of that love, which came about independently of it, as completely natural as such circumstances are and so conducive to refinements of all kinds that the Greeks erected altars to a Callipygean Venus. It is also conceivable that were I not so experienced I might bestow no more than a purely aesthetic admiration upon my love's feet. That would entail the loss of another form of refinement, as likewise in the event that I held my wife's intellect to be unnecessary considering that so many men love women without intellect. I am pointing all this out to you without describing the refinements themselves since our secret lexicon is not yet extensive enough to address them. Moreover they cannot be addressed save in the form of passionate indications

198

designed to refine your sensitive mind and dissipate your scruples. But I love for my slave to be also my equal—and have you not already surpassed my own refinement with the exquisite bonbon-kiss that you devised in Narbonne? In the passion proper to the Duty that we love (do we not speak of *conjugal duty*?) lust is permitted, but beyond the limits of this passionate duty one descends rapidly into lechery, which is a vitiated, nauseating form of love.

These distinctions are essential. Lechery arises when one is not discreet about one's loves, so lowering and devaluing them. It is what happens with so many people.

Our secret shall be marvellous and no hypocrisy shall attend it. Of course it is unnecessary to tell you all this, it goes without saying, but this long reply was occasioned by your question about a poorly expressed passage in my letter. Yes my darling you dream of my embrace and for my part I desire you unendingly.

199

I think of you all the time, but from noon until 3 I shall think of you if possible even harder.

~~The story of the injured suitor and the English orphan girl would seem to be from Cervantes. I quite understand your pity.~~[1] I shall not write you at Narbonne from now on but at Oran.

1 These two sentences are crossed out on the manuscript with a single line in darker ink.

The portion of your letter about your life before me brought me close to tears and filled me with an almost ecstatic joy. You write wonderfully my love and for your mind I have an admiration rivalled only by the love I feel for you. I wonder by what miracle I found my Madeleine and I thank my lucky stars. At times I even feel unworthy of all your qualities and want to elevate myself so as to become worthy of them. So much beauty, so much charm so much intelligence even so much knowledge is mine, is within my darling slave, I am master of it all, all of it is my prey, my most beautiful prey.

GUILLAUME APOLLINAIRE

Yes my darling you do love me as I wish to be loved. The allusions you so often make to your beauty make me tremble with voluptuousness, I want you to redouble them so as to arouse this chaste happiness in me, the only happiness I can experience being so far from you but happiness nonetheless since it comes from you. Yes, you are my delight and my highest pleasure. You have the supreme gift of varying even this chaste voluptuousness, nevertheless so intense that I am left confounded in admiration before the audacity of your pure imagination. The story of the suitor's costume came back to me this morning as I was reading one of Shakespeare's sonnets translated in a review, and I had a strange dream in which I treated you as a little boy, an extravagant fancy clearly admissible and safe to imagine solely by virtue of my absolute confidence in you, my deep certainty about your intelligence, which is capable of complying with love's most delicate and outlandish speculative flights.

You aspire to loving me and in this you succeed admirably my love.

Yes, you are my dream of dreams. There is nothing above you and even above that there is only you, you alone, always you. Your wonderful plumpness that you speak of my darling, knowing full well how this will affect me, puts me in mind of all the masterpieces of Praxiteles and certain perfect nudes of Rodin not to mention Albani Fragonard and Ingres and I believe you have much in common with the Venus de Medecis and most of all, most of all with some of Titian's nudes. I may be mistaken, but I rather think not. But what a joy it is to forget war by talking with you about your beauty.

At bottom, you see, you are the only thing that counts for me, for you are everything—beauty, love, poetry, in a word life. How can you ask me whether your duty is to love me. It is, absolutely. How could you belong to me otherwise and how could you be my wife if you did not give yourself utterly?

There is a pleasure to be drawn from our present separation, the joy of your purity, our ability to enjoy love to the full with your virginity intact. In this way we reach the pinnacle of true Platonic love and you may give yourself over to it unconstrainedly for being as pure as we are we may contemplate each other with pure delight and virginal as you are I shall find you as innocent after this period in our love as you were a year ago. So have no reservations. In that way you will enjoy, and do so out of duty, all your time as a young girl and prepare in the most marvellous way to become a woman.

I can imagine nothing more foolish than to turn a young girl into a woman without warning her of that transformation's importance or properly informing her of the facts, the result being that two young newlyweds will be ashamed of one another, not daring to face reality and often feeling repelled by each other because the man, being ill-suited to the task of broadening his bride's often paltry knowledge, is quite unable to initiate her into things that though natural are generally unknown to young girls.

But I adore you, my Madelon, I take you all of you, I inhale your breath, kiss your mouth and knead the flesh that you offer to me.

I love you.

Gui

GUILLAUME APOLLINAIRE

My love, I had no letter from you today. I received your dear letter of yesterday and I see that our secret language has grown thanks to you and I am charmed by your exquisite confidence in me. I have grasped the meaning of the expression 'I was a little tired' and everything you tell me in that connexion about your impressionability and nervousness at that time affects me enormously.

202   It is tomorrow morning that you take ship my love. And I shall be breathless with anxiety so long as I remain without African news from you.

How my love have I lived until now without you, without your intelligence? I never had beauty like yours, nor anything like it, though of course there are women who are likeable and pleasing. As for you, you combine beauty and even more beauty with the rarest qualities of body and soul. So much so that without ever having been united our two bodies already know each other, which is extremely wonderful and rare. Since I cannot offer you virginity, which is perhaps not required of a man when he marries, I can at least offer you a heart that is pure and that contains nothing but you. As I realized today I have lost all memory of everything in the past and if I struggle to write to you about it and recover the details it is in order to show the more clearly how much I belong to you alone. My last lady friend was pretty and undoubtedly the greatest libertine imaginable, but I have forgotten all of that, or rather I remember it solely with an almost scornful coldness, so very voluptuous and pure is my love for you. We are not chaste and yet we are as pure my love as two lilies. Mark you, her letters were passionate excessively passionate and her caresses were of the most flattering kind to a man. Her vice, and here the word is appropriate, was also most flattering to someone of an authoritarian disposition, and yet a single glance, an eternal glance from my Madeleine sufficed to change everything in me. And forgive me, my love, for it is sacrilege to be speaking of anything that is not you—all the rest seems infernal to me now, and infernal in a mediocre way. I despise that past life of mine, I am ashamed of it, and yet I tend to think that perhaps those wretched experiences were not useless inasmuch as they helped me attain if not a greater love for you then at least more mental clarity concerning our love.

But when I think of you, of your fire, of your grace, of your canephor's hips, of your breast, of your rowan-red mouth, I become as pure as the Prince who woke the Sleeping Beauty and you are that adorable princess, you were sleeping as you waited for me to wake you right here in this, my forest, and my love and this war are the phases of your wonderful awakening to my love. You are the dawn, I adore you, and I take you with as much violence and tenderness as ever, more than ever, my dear my dearest love, and today my sights are set on the organ that was the instrument of our first commerce, my darling, and it is your tongue that I take.

Gui

GUILLAUME APOLLINAIRE

19 September 1915

It is for tomorrow, my love.

I enclose the photo got up as a medal or rather as a coin by that lovable rascal Berthier who is launching the Kostro as a monetary unit like the Louis. On the obverse with my portrait and the signature R. Berthier is the following inscription:

APOLLINAIRE THE CRUEL

TYRANT OF LES HURLUS 1915

On the reverse are the words:

I

KOSTRO

The serpent the rose the arrow

and:

38 ARTILLERY—45TH BATTERY

SECTOR 80 HYPOGEUM 4

1915

Quite amusing, I must admit.

I'll write you at length this evening my love, it is now 1 o'clock and I am thinking of you with all my soul. I am hoping that in a little while I shall have a letter from my love, I had none yesterday—my own letters are post-dated in the sense that I date them according to the day that the post orderly picks them up. Usually I write them in the evening and often very late at night.

I wrote you last evening. I take your lips my love and I take all of you—tyrannically, in accordance with what it says on the solar Apollonian coin that I am sending you, my dear beloved I take your mouth.

Gui

My love I think it is going to begin tonight and that when you read this letter we shall already have advanced. This evening I have sent you another inkwell made from the fuse of a 150-mm shell, but there is no graduated ring this time, and the whole thing rests in the bottom of a 77. I think it will make a fine inkwell but I wasn't able to hollow it out very well, it will have to be recarved or else used as it is.

My love, I got yours of the 16th, posted from Foix, you can just imagine my most beautiful one how happy I was that you received my card in Foix.

The account of your motor-car trip gave me a mad desire to hold you tight against me, kiss your cheeks so cool from your standing up in the wind, my pretty one, if only you knew how much I desire you and that desiring you and picturing you as beautiful as you are is my only consolation.

My darling, my treasure, you were thinking of me too! You are an angel. I imagine you reading my letters in your bed, your hair loose and a roguish breast pushing upwards and your mouth so red so ardently offered to me like a flame the flame of my life itself and this exquisite awakening that you describe—just like you I always smile when I wake up and it is to your very own beauty which is my shining light that I smile.

Your rather jealous idyll with the colchicums touched me deeply. But come, do not be jealous my love, you are so far above anything like that. Never I am sure has a man loved as I love you. But you must be careful of the colchicums, I believe they are terribly poisonous. I don't want you to touch them my Madeleine, and I don't want you to be jealous, you should really be dealt with like a naughty little boy for this ill-considered and rather unreasonable behaviour.

In any case, my little love, do not forget to tell me about whatever feelings may disturb you, tell me about all of them, desires, jealousy etc. so that I may be well acquainted with yr soul.

I am expecting your endless letter tomorrow, if ever they deliver letters tomorrow. We are to wear helmets from now on, no more kepis, so I shall send you my old one, which is rather fancy, for safe-keeping.

Yesterday I forgot to thank you for the rose petal. I adore you.

I am a little concerned about your sea voyage, though something secret tells me that nothing untoward will befall you. By the time this letter leaves our battery you will already be at sea . . .

When you get it you will be in Oran, in the pretty garden where you were photographed dressed as an American negress. How ravishing you are, my little black slave.

Write me at length my dearest treasure to make up a little for your absence.

Kiss your Mama, your pretty sisters and brothers for me my wonderful treasure.

I am impatient for this present thing to be over. Indeed for it all to be over. I take your mouth and your entire exquisite body and the most private part of your being with the most perfect, the most private, the most intoxicating of caresses.

Your Gui*

* I enclose an entertaining and humorous anecdote in which my friend Berthier enjoyed caricaturing me in Sector 59 well before you evoked Nero in connexion with me and at the beginning of my stint as quartermaster corporal. So you see your comparison of me to Nero is not unsupported. I feel the story will be amusing even for those who do not live here with us.

Here we smoke a pipe because there is nothing else to smoke, but rest assured I shall never impose the stink of it on you.

GUILLAUME APOLLINAIRE

20 Sept. 1915

My love, I have received your letter from Foix and quite understand that you have not had the leisure to write me a long letter but you wrote me very delightful things just the same.

You will be in Oran when this reaches you, write me at length my darling. Obviously we are going to experience some delays, but we are not here to have everything we might want, we are soldiers hang it all! and you too my Madelon you are a soldier alongside me thanks to your heart which is here. I published a little book with Michaud (1910), with many illustrations and including documents portraits etc., called *Le Théâtre italien*, and for it I translated one act of a play that drew on the improvised theatrical art of the Commedia dell'Arte. The title, if memory serves, was 'Columbine, A Soldier for Love's Sake', it was rather amusing and I think of it often when I get your letters which bring you close to me, though not close enough to satisfy my greatest wish.

Your relatives in Foix must have found you much more beautiful. You do not say whether you received the letter-card I sent you at their address. It should have arrived though.

You sleep in my arms, my darling little Madelon, in my little trellis-work bed.

So I unchain you my dear little slave and your master shall try to restore his power over you when he has the opportunity.

From your letters I glean all the details of your beauty and when they are complete and exact I'll write a pretty poem using all these elements, it will be the poem of our desire and later on when I have acquired direct knowledge I shall compose the book of your pleasure and that too will be a hymn to your beauty.

This evening I have sent you a letter-opener simply hammered from part of the small driving-band of a Boche 150 shell, also a heart hammered and filed from the large band of a shell of the same calibre. The metal is sturdier than aluminium. You will need to get a hole drilled at the appropriate place because I don't have the tool I need to do it. The letter-opener I am not giving you, it is mine but you are welcome to use it.

The heart is yours.

Copper objects are prettier and more durable than aluminium ones but they require more work.

My love, I take your mouth, I kiss your adorable breasts, I stroke your feet and the pearly, pure, almost Oriental roundnesses of your body.

I adore you my love, I adore you, give me your mouth and the exquisite gift within it along with your delightful voice and your gaze helplessly fixed on mine.

I love you.

Gui

GUILLAUME APOLLINAIRE

My love, your letter of the 17th, written upon your return from Narbonne, has given me unimaginable pleasure, you are truly worthy of me, of our future and present joys, you are marvellous, you are quite ready for the most delightful commerce in the world and our engagement is exquisite so open is your soul to our love and so ready your body to fall in line with the impulses of our souls. I imagine you reading in your bed, reading my letters, and you are the very picture of sensuality, albeit of a sensuality still young. Like you, I have learnt to divine something of the stirrings of desire in you from your writing, but perhaps not as much as you—but no, I take that back, just as much as you. So I am no longer afraid of upsetting you and now that you embrace our voluptuous feelings we may talk of them, which will help us more than anything else to get to know one another and bestow the most truth possible, the most life possible upon our love. It is certain that only Madeleine can love me as I am loved at present and that I knew nothing of love before you, for you are innocence itself and you teach me innocence and what an exquisite lesson that is.

Yes, you have grasped why I am happy that you are a *Vendéenne*. The women of the Vendée must indeed know how to love. An old custom in the Vendée is what is called *maraîchinage*, but it is disappearing today, or rather becoming vulgar and immoral under the influence of our wretched modern prejudices.

210

Maraîchinage meant (and still means to a degree) all the ways and customs of the region concerning kissing before marriage and even before betrothal. Girls and boys used to kiss one another on the mouth for long hours at a stretch, honing fine skills that graced the people of the Vendée without plunging them into sentimentality, for dalliance as unrestrained as this is delightful but not affected. The art of tongue-kissing was thus supremely refined and so complete an art of the lingual caress has no equal save among the Slavs of Poland and the Balkans. Moreover, these brief remarks give but a rough idea of *maraîchinage* in the Vendée, which is the subject of many weighty volumes produced by scholars both prudish and otherwise.

Note that in the heyday of *maraîchinage* debauchery was less prevalent than it is today in the Vendée and what is more even at that time it was less common there than in other French provinces, for sensuality is not debauchery and is perfectly compatible with intelligence. The Athenians achieved the highest civilization by virtue of their refinement and sensuality but at the same time they were the most brilliant people in the world, nor can they really be taxed with debauchery since even the courtesans of Athens were eminently respectable and universally respected for their intelligence and harmoniousness.

You have informed me my darling of the birth in you of Voluptuousness. I want all the impulses that bring your body and soul together to take pleasure in me, to be reserved for me, to the point where the mere thought of me awakens them in you and that as you think of me you will need simply to tighten those legs, which you offer me once again in your letter—you have simply to tighten them, I say, to be shaken by voluptuousness like a reed—or rather a rose!—shaken by Aquilon.

Nor, as I wrote earlier, must you fear being upset by such feelings—I am my own master as much as I am yours. But what an adorable

GUILLAUME APOLLINAIRE

idea of yours to have me sleep on your breasts, as you hold me close in your arms and kiss my hair.

But don't forget that before I could sleep in that way, you yourself my love, admit it, would have to have grown very sleepy.

A secret poem enclosed with this letter tells you of the nine doors. You are right to tell me everything my love and I adore this love of your own devising and by and by you will be teaching me just as much about love as I teach you and that is truly splendid. Oh how I love your tremors, your waves of emotion, your amorous agitation, my love, I take your mouth and drink in your soul until you swoon. Yes I have tasted your bonbon-kiss with a true savage's passion and it was the greatest pleasure of my life and the most unexpected. Only the reality of your body, I believe, can now surpass that kiss invented by your innocence. Still, it is true, your soul must surely conceal even more unexpected riches. Do you never think of inventing more such kisses? This is beyond talent, my love, you possess the genius of love.

Yes, I do think about our future life and we shall talk about it at length when I am on leave.

You shall play Phèdre and I am ready to challenge Venus at her own game, my fiery slave. You are right to tell me everything, we shall love one another all the more if we share more secrets. I am envious of this photo of mine that shows your adorable breasts. Do tell me I am not mistaken about those breasts, I kiss you on the mouth for a long long time and madly, just as madly as you offer it to me.

Gui

P.S. Today I sent you two pen-stands, one made from a Boche bullet and an English one, the other from a Boche bullet and a Belgian one. The Belgian bullet is rounded, and the English is longer than the Boche. Also 1 metal ring made from a horseshoe nail of mine, a ring with my initials, an emblazoned ring—it was an engraver staying here very briefly who worked on these, there was no time for me to have him make them smooth for you—and lastly a larger oval ring and a ring to which I have added a grain of real coral that I found on the ground, which is for you.

2nd Post Scriptum. In the package there is also a notebook covering 1 hippology course and 1 topography course, keep this for me as a souvenir of my military training, along with an English scarf with the word 'Tipperary' on it. This is for you and a precious example of the imagery of this war.

LES NEUF PORTES DE TON CORPS

Ce poème est pour toi seule Madeleine
Il est un des premiers poèmes de notre désir
Il est notre premier poème secret ô toi que j'aime
Le jour est doux et la guerre est si douce. S'il fallait en mourir!!

* * *

Tu l'ignores, ma vierge? à ton corps sont neuf portes
J'en connais sept et deux me sont celées
J'en ai pris quatre, j'y suis entré n'espère plus que j'en sorte
Car je suis entré en toi par tes yeux étoilés
Et par tes oreilles avec les Paroles que je commande et qui sont mon escorte.

* * *

Œil droit de mon amour première porte de mon amour
Elle avait baissé le rideau de sa paupière
Tes cils étaient rangés devant comme les soldats noirs peints sur un vase grec,
    paupière rideau lourd
De velours

GUILLAUME APOLLINAIRE

Qui cachait ton regard clair
Et lourd
Pareil à notre amour.

* * *

Œil gauche de mon amour deuxième porte de mon amour
Pareille à son amie et chaste et lourde d'amour ainsi que lui
Ô porte qui mène à ton cœur mon image et mon sourire qui luit
Comme une étoile pareille à tes yeux que j'adore
Double porte de ton regard je t'adore

* * *

Oreille droite de mon amour troisième porte
C'est en te prenant que j'arrivai à ouvrir entièrement les deux premières portes
Oreille porte de ma voix qui t'a persuadée
Je t'aime toi qui donnes un sens à l'Image grâce à l'Idée

* * *

Et toi aussi oreille gauche toi qui des portes de mon amour est la quatrième
Ô vous, les oreilles de mon amour je vous bénis
Portes qui vous ouvrîtes à ma voix
Comme les roses s'ouvrent aux caresses du printemps
C'est par vous que ma voix et mon ordre
Pénètrent dans le corps entier de Madeleine
J'y entre homme tout entier et aussi tout entier poème
Poème de son désir qui fait que moi aussi je m'aime

* * *

Narine gauche de mon amour cinquième porte de mon amour et de nos désirs
J'entrerai par là dans le corps de mon amour
J'y entrerai subtil avec mon odeur d'homme
L'odeur de mon désir
L'âcre parfum viril qui enivrera Madeleine

Narine droite sixième porte de mon amour et de notre volupté

Toi qui sentiras comme ton voisin l'odeur de mon plaisir

Et notre odeur mêlée plus forte et plus exquise qu'un printemps en fleurs

Double porte des narines je t'adore toi qui promets tant de plaisirs subtils

Puisés dans l'art des fumées et des fumets.

* * *

Bouche de Madeleine septième porte de mon amour

Je vous ai vue, ô porte porte rouge, gouffre de mon désir

Et les soldats qui s'y tiennent morts d'amour m'ont crié qu'ils se rendent

Ô porte rouge et tendre

* * *

Ô Madeleine il est deux portes encore

Que je ne connais pas

Deux portes de ton corps

Mystérieuses

215

* * *

Huitième porte de la grande beauté de mon amour

Ô mon ignorance semblable à des soldats aveugles parmi les chevaux de frise sous la
    lune liquide des Flandres à l'agonie!

Ou plutôt comme un explorateur qui meurt de faim de soif et d'amour dans une forêt
    vierge

Plus sombre que l'Érèbe

Plus sacrée que celle de Dodone

Et qui devine une source plus fraîche que Castalie

Mais mon amour y trouverait un temple

Et après avoir ensanglanté le parvis sur qui veille le charmant monstre de l'innocence

J'y découvrirais et ferais jaillir le plus chaud geyser du monde

Ô mon amour, ma Madeleine

Je suis déjà le maître de la huitième porte

GUILLAUME APOLLINAIRE

* * *

Et toi neuvième porte plus mystérieuse encore
Qui t'ouvres entre deux montagnes de perles
Toi plus mystérieuse encore que les autres
Porte des sortilèges dont on n'ose point parler
Tu m'appartiens aussi
Suprême porte
À moi qui porte
La clef suprême
Des neuf portes

* * *

Ô portes ouvrez-vous à ma voix
Je suis le Maître de la Clef

THE NINE DOORS OF YOUR BODY

This poem is for you alone Madeleine
It is one of the first poems of our desire
It is our first secret poem oh you that I love
The day is sweet and the war is so sweet. To think you could die from it!!

* * *

Do you not know, my virgin, that your body has nine doors?
I know seven and two are closed to me
I have passed through four, I went inside and do not expect me ever to leave
For I have entered through your starry eyes
And through your ears with Words which I command and which are my escort.
* * *

Right eye of my love first door of my love
Who had lowered the curtain of her eyelid
Your lashes lined up in front like soldiers painted on a Greek vase, eyelid a
heavy curtain

Of velvet
Hiding your gaze clear
And deep
Just like our love.

* * *

Left eye of my love second door of my love
Resembling its companion and likewise chaste and laden with love
Oh door that leads to your heart my image and my smile shining
Like a star bright as your eyes that I adore
Double door of your gaze I adore you

* * *

Right ear of my love third door
It is by taking you that I succeeded in opening the first two doors wide
Ear door for my voice which persuaded you
I love you, you who give meaning to the Image by means of the Idea

* * *

And you too left ear you who among the doors of my love are the fourth
Oh you ears of my love I bless you
Doors that opened yourselves to my voice
As roses open themselves to spring's caress
It is through you that my voice and my direction
Penetrate the whole body of Madeleine
I go through wholly man and also wholly poem
Poem of her desire which makes me love myself too

* * *

Left nostril of my love fifth door of my love and of our desires
Through which I shall enter the body of my love
I shall enter subtly with my man's smell
Smell of my desire
Pungent manly perfume that will intoxicate Madeleine

GUILLAUME APOLLINAIRE

* * *

Right nostril sixth door of my love and of our voluptuousness
You who like your neighbour will smell the odour of my delight
And our combined odour stronger and more exquisite than a flower-filled
    Spring
Double door of the nostrils I adore you who promise so many subtle joys
Drawn from the science of vapours and aromas.

* * *

Mouth of Madeleine seventh door of my love
I saw you, oh door red door, gulf of my desire
And the soldiers ranged there slain by love cried out to me in surrender
Oh red and tender door

* * *

Oh Madeleine there are two more doors also
That I do not know
Two doors to your body
Mysterious doors

* * *

Eighth door of the great beauty of my love
Oh my ignorance is like blind soldiers amid chevaux-de-frise under the
    liquid moon of Flanders in agony!
Or rather, like an explorer dying of hunger thirst and love in a virgin forest
More shadowy than Erebus
More sacred than the forest at Dodona
Who has spied a spring cooler than Castalia
But my love would find a temple there
And after bloodying its forecourt guarded by the charming monster of
    innocence
I would discover the hottest geyser in the world and make it spurt
Oh my love, my Madeleine
I am already the master of the eighth door

LETTERS TO MADELEINE

And you ninth door more mysterious still

Opening between two mountains of pearl

You more mysterious than all the others

Door of magic spells of which one dare not speak

You belong to me also

Supreme Door

For it is I who hold

The supreme key

To the nine doors

* * *

Oh doors open at my voice

    I am the Master of the Key

G. A.   219

GUILLAUME APOLLINAIRE

24 September 1915

My love

When you read this letter hope that we are deep into French territory. We set out tomorrow for the occupied areas. They saddled us
up last night. Our kit is stacked and brushwood has been loaded
onto the gun-carriage limbers to help get us across trenches. I am
writing you only this morning the 24th I didn't write yesterday
because one of my friends a simple searchlight sapper but in civilian
life a secretary at the French Legation in China—(At this instant I
am told that we are to leave this very evening—for the Vosges?
somewhere near Remiremont?) But despite all this the fact is we just
don't know. At the moment everything is in motion the orchestra-
tion is fantastic. Passing infantrymen say that on the Boche side as
far as the eye can see the earth resembles an ocean heaving with
waves. Myself I don't believe in this Vosges business, I think it
remains to be seen what will happen tomorrow.

I just broke this off to read the proclamation in detail, it will soon be
as famous as the Marne Proclamation, and now we have recom-
menced firing. I write as the fire continues and at each shot the
letter is covered with a fine dust which dries the ink. Most conven-
ient. Yesterday you sent me your eyes my darling, your marvellous
eyes that are themselves a marvellous artillery, your eyes of ecstasy.

My love, you were leaving the next day, so by now you must be in
Oran. My darling, your pictures are in the map-case, everything is

220

ready. You now have my other photos. You love me to perfection, my fine Chimène. But you are right, our love implies neither crime nor vice because it is sufficient unto itself and cloaks everything in its very special virtue. You need never be anything but the marvellous girl that you are and the panther in you need be aroused only for our wild and frantic loving which will leave us gasping exhausted but never sated. Tell me more my darling, sometimes you are still afraid to say all. Why? I love your hands and your whole long and supple body and your hair is my ecstasy.

I too have examined your eyes for the longest time through the magnifying glass. I am keeping the Medjerda address on my person. I bury my eyes in your hair, always say everything my love. I adore your mouth and your eyes ever-changing just like your whole face and my mouth has an unquenchable thirst to mould itself to the mould of your mouth.

So what was it that I mentioned that you do not know and that you dare not mention because it disturbs you so?

I am waiting for you to speak to me about *The Heresiarch*, m'love, my rose my lily and my jasmine. Your latest photo shows you lanky as you say, which I did not yet know, for your travelling clothes concealed it and your other photos did not show it, especially not the exquisite length of your legs.

Yes, I too adore our freedom. Please excuse the disjointed style but I am writing you while we are firing and must break from one moment to the next to adjust the ballistic elements. My darling slave, there is no question at all of vice, the issue is our love, which I want to be as great, as varied as possible and you too, my innocent lily, you wish for nothing less, so let us leave the word vice aside, for we love only our virtues. Tomorrow I doubt I shall be able to write

221

GUILLAUME APOLLINAIRE

anything more than a card. Who knows where from?! I love you all of you with all my strength, that is our virtue, the greatest of virtues, the only virtue.

I too can hardly wait to make you my wife. I am like a thirsty traveller in the desert, there is but one oasis for me and that oasis is you.

So I adore your bite, my dear inventress.

I can hardly wait for my panther to be mine, for her feline roaring and bounding to belong to me, for me as tamer to master you with the whip if need be my dearest, my wild, my savage panther.

And that word, brought into my letter by you, puts me in mind of Balzac's story 'A Passion in the Desert', which is so disturbing.

222

You say, my darling, that we make a magnificent couple. All praise for that to you, my dear, because you chose to answer me on the train—how perfectly miraculous! An unknown force must have prompted you to do so, for I clearly saw that you were not replying to a stranger willingly.

I kiss your photo, and I take you the most voluptuous girl imaginable, the most intelligent and the most beautiful.

I fear that your observations concerning 'L'Amour dans le Crime' (Love in Crime)[1] and your panther's soul betray a touch of jealousy. Do not be the slightest bit jealous m'darling love, there is no reason for it. Everything but you is a matter of indifference to me forever. All that now resides in a kind of museum that I never enter.

1 Apollinaire means 'Le Bonheur dans le crime' (Happiness in Crime), the title of the third story in Barbey d'Aure-villy's *She-Devils*.

You alone exist and you are everything to me: Panther and Pantheon. My god how I love you. And what of your feet? Would you not like to tell me about them?

I am sending an article by Vollard, Cézanne's art dealer who has just written some 'anthumous' recollections of Renoir.

But Renoir who is the greatest painter living says many stupid things, just like all old people. As for the rest of us, we must take care not to lose our youth don't you think so my love? I adore you and bite the nape of your neck gently my darling, my Madeleine. I hold you close in a deep embrace.

Gui

24 Sept. 1915[1]   **1** Military postcard.

I have received your telegram and the letter from Port-Vendres—
How happy I am to hear you have arrived safely!!!

The first inkwell will reach you—but the second has been returned
to me. They won't let it through. Red tape! But never mind.

Wrote today shall write tomorrow if have time. Thank you for
putting my mind at ease with the brilliant idea of a telegram. My
love to all the family and to Madeleine all my thoughts.

Gui

224

My love

We have been shelling all day long. Now evening has come I rest until half past midnight then I start firing my gun again. We leave tomorrow—for where?—My engineer friend came, tomorrow he must be at an assigned place that today is still in Boche territory. Your wire (inspected) reached me and filled me with great joy. I sent you a postcard right away to tell you so. The second inkwell came back from military customs who forbade its dispatch; I shall try to send it in bits and pieces if possible, abiding by the weight restrictions imposed by military regulations. This evening I also sent a few books, a novel by Quevedo, famous, the life of Coleridge, the latest issue of the *Mercure* and the Figuière anthology with a preface by Lanson, which contains mainly bad poems but also a few respectable ones. You will also find a short, incomplete note on me—my work for *Le Matin* is not mentioned, nor is the anthology published before *Alcools*.

I am relieved about your journey. I love you as you love me *deeply* and *magnificently*. Write me a long letter.

The 'port of Venus' was propitious for you my love, after all you are Venus herself and far more beautiful than all the images that have been created of her.

GUILLAUME APOLLINAIRE

The proofs of 'La Vie anecdotique' arrived and I have turned them in. I hope that this instalment will appear in the October issue. I forgot to ask you my love how tall you were.

I am tired tonight my love from our almost incessant shelling. Tomorrow things will be even worse. The Boches bombarded us with asphyxiating-gas shells but they were small and we were upwind so the effect on us was nil.

Along with my kepi I have sent you two chargers, a Boche one and an English one, and two rings. See whether the large oval ring I sent earlier and the other very angular one sent yesterday fit your brothers and if so give them to them. Please also send the measurements of your sisters and Mama.

The ring with the four-leaf clover and a little copper ball is for you, to bring you good luck, I wore it for almost two months.

I have campaigned until now with the kepi I am sending you (along with the golden figures and the gold chin strap I got when I made sergeant). It is a keepsake, which is why I am sending it. It is my own—I had it made in Nîmes.

My love I love you, you see, as no one has ever loved and you too love me likewise. I desire you in the most violent way yet at the same time the gentlest and the most patient way possible, and if you only knew how much I love your glance, as clipped from what photo my love and why did you not send the entire photo, my adorable darling. I take you all of you all of you with all my might. I bite your mouth.

Gui

1 Military postcard; in pencil.

26 Sept. 1915[1]

I'll write as soon as I can, at the moment too much to do. This is just to give you news of me, practically all I can manage. You occupy all my thoughts.

Gui

who is thinking endlessly of Madeleine

227

GUILLAUME APOLLINAIRE

My very dearest, I hadn't the time to write last evening—in any case
the post did not leave yesterday. Today my letter of the day before
yesterday left along with a card written in haste during the shelling.
I cannot give you details. Everything was magnificent. The Boche
prisoners passed by here and I have a fine Imperial Guard belt
button which I'll send you, it will make an amusing brooch.—I have
had no letter from you yesterday or today. Nor was I expecting any.
What are you up to? I picture you in your room, my beauty, my
beautiful scholar. In your studious virginal room. For my part I am
tired tonight and I was even more exhausted yesterday after the
most ferocious time imaginable. We were covered in sweat and dust,
intoxicated by the smell of gunpowder. At present my kit is all
packed up. I have no envelopes, only this paper. My ink is also put
away. How many interesting and fine things I shall have to tell you
after the war—Yesterday we had not the time to eat properly. Just
some bread and chocolate during the shelling—As a matter of fact
this life suits me fine—The prisoners were all very young. I chatted
with some of them but I was so stupefied, I have to say, that I could
not possibly give a description. They were very poorly dressed and
very obsequious. The one whose belt button I cut off bent over
obediently in a truly German manner and showed a patience that
was nothing less than comical. My knife does not cut well, I was in a
hurry because of the firing and I went about it as quickly as I
could—their officers put on a contemptuous air but they were very

surprised to see how well dressed we were.—We have new light blue uniforms and helmets. When I get a chance to have my photograph taken in my helmet I shall do it. These helmets in case you have not seen one are rather like the salad helmets—so called I suppose by reference to Saladin. I do not find them ugly and they are extremely protective and pleasant to wear albeit rather heavy.—In short I am quite happy with my helmet. I think it resembles the barber's basin that Don Quixote mistook for Mambrino's helmet. Except that it is grey and does not gleam in the sunshine. What are you doing my love? I am thinking of your hair. Your dear photograph helps me immeasurably to remain cheerful.—Yesterday it rained all day long. Today it was fine but this evening it is cold and there is a Scotch mist. The fireworks are beautiful too beautiful. I am writing to you from my hole, well protected from the largest shells. Anyway I'll tell you all about it when I come. We have had no newspapers for three days. The post arrived yesterday at midnight along with fresh supplies. The moment I finish this letter my love I am going to bye-byes. I adore you and have not stopped thinking about you all day long. Your photo of which I have two copies I slipped into my gunner's logbook and I was looking at it all the time, my dearest, my beautiful, my pretty, my graceful Madeleine. My love, my darling, completely envelops you. I take you in my arms gently and vigorously, I say sweet words to you—we are alone, I am proud of you my beloved, as proud of you as I am in love with you and that is not a little as you well know my love. I think of Oran, my little darling with such pretty hands—I await your letters impatiently so as to know the details of your crossing and also everything you have promised to tell me. When will you be resuming your courses? Write me everything about your life. It is so interesting to me. You are my love, my marvellous, my miraculous Madeleine. Days like today with no letter from you are days without colour and yet I like my life in

GUILLAUME APOLLINAIRE

the field well enough. But without you everything is grey, your letters light up my countenance like the flares that light up the Front. I adore you.

My Madeleine I take your mouth. I can hardly wait to be your husband, and you know it. I take your open mouth.

Gui

1 In pencil.

28 Sept. 1915[1]

My dear love,

Yesterday I received your letter written on the boat and posted in
Oran. I adore you. Our work is over. We are ready to leave. You have
seen the papers and you must know more than we do, because we
have had no news of the world since the 22nd. There was an alert
during the night and I was ready, spurs, revolver, canteen and helmet. Saddled up. But we didn't set off. I got your letter at six o'clock
I adore you my love. Yesterday I sent you three Boche buttons
including a belt button. Couldn't send the inkwell. In short my
darling you managed things so well that I was without news from
you for only two days. You are a dear. Now I look forward to a long
long letter. It is cold this morning. My hands are freezing. I adore
you, I make your red mouth mine, it is so exquisite and it must bite
so well. I worship you. I worship you. I am so happy that your
voyage went well. I worship you.

Gui

231

GUILLAUME APOLLINAIRE

My love if only you knew how much I miss your daily letter. It is
terrible and unfair—and what possible reason could there be for
leaving a colony as important as Algeria without daily news from the
mother country? I adore you my love, but we have horrible freezing
weather here. It has been raining all day, a wretched autumn day.
What sadness. The rain has flooded the hole we live in and I slept
all night in the wet . . . I am writing with ink loaned me by a sapper,
a searchlight operator. You will have read all the details of our
victory here in the papers. I still haven't had the courage to reckon
how many times I fired during our extraordinary bombardment
which gave the Boches such a surprise. I'll do that reckoning
tomorrow, for the captain has asked me for it. For two days now I
have had no letter from my love. I did receive the idiotic lyrical
sheet in which Paul Fort prince of poetasters sings of our battles
from afar in truly stupid terms—oh how impatient I am for your
passionate letters. Without them I might as well be deprived of life
itself. Tell me the story of the little photo trimmed so that only your
beautiful eyes are shown. The wind is blowing. . . .

Il y a un vaisseau qui a emporté ma bien-aimée
Il y a dans le ciel six saucisses pareilles à des asticots dont il naît les étoiles
Il y a un sous-marin ennemi qui en voulait à mon amour
Il y a mille petits sapins brisés par les éclats d'obus autour de moi
Il y a un fantassin qui passe aveuglé par les gaz asphyxiants
Il y a que nous avons tout haché dans les boyaux de Nietzsche de Goethe et de Cologne

Il y a que je languis après une lettre de Madeleine

Il y a dans mon porte-cartes plusieurs photos de mon amour

Il y a les prisonniers qui passent la mine inquiète

Il y a une jeune fille qui pense à moi à Oran

Il y a une batterie dont les servants s'agitent autour des pièces

Il y a le vaguemestre qui arrive au trot par le chemin de l'Arbre Isolé

Il y a dit-on un espion qui rôde par ici invisible comme le bleu horizon dont il est vêtu
et avec quoi il se confond

Il y a Vénus qui s'est embarquée nue dans un havre de la mer jolie pour Cythère

Il y a les cheveux noirs de mon amour

Il y a dressé comme un lys le buste de mon amour

Il y a des Américains qui font un négoce atroce de notre or

Il y a un capitaine qui attend avec anxiété les communications de la T.S.F. sur
l'Atlantique

Il y a à minuit des soldats qui scient des planches pour les cercueils

Il y a des femmes qui demandent du maïs à grands cris devant un Christ sanglant à
Mexico

Il y a le Gulf-Stream qui est si tiède et si bienfaisant

Il y a un cimetière plein de croix à 5 kilomètres

Il y a des croix partout de-ci de-là

Il y a des figures de barbarie sur les cactus en Algérie

Il y a les longues mains souples de mon amour

Il y a un encrier que j'avais fait pour Madeleine dans une fusée de 15 centimètres et
qu'on n'a pas laissé partir

Il y a ma selle exposée à la pluie

Il y a les fleuves qui ne remontent pas leurs cours

Il y a l'amour qui m'entraîne avec douceur vers Madeleine

Il y avait un prisonnier boche qui portait sa mitrailleuse sur son dos

Il y a des hommes dans le monde qui n'ont jamais été à la guerre

Il y a des Hindous qui regardent avec étonnement les campagnes occidentales

Il y a des femmes qui apprennent l'allemand dans les régions occupées

Elles pensent avec mélancolie à ceux dont elles se demandent si elles les reverront

Et par-dessus tout il y a le soleil de notre amour

GUILLAUME APOLLINAIRE

There is a ship that has carried my beloved away

There are six sausages in the sky like maggots giving birth to stars

There is an enemy submarine which had it in for my love

There are a thousand little pine trees around me shattered by shell bursts

There is an infantryman going by blinded by asphyxiating gas

There is the fact that we have hacked everything up in the Nietzsche Goethe
and Cologne communication trenches

There is the fact that I am pining for a letter from Madeleine

There are in my wallet several photos of my love

There are prisoners passing by looking anxious

There is a girl thinking of me in Oran

There is a battery with gunners busy about their cannons

There is the post orderly emerging at a trot from Lone Tree Way

There is they say a spy prowling around as invisible as the horizon-blue of
his uniform into which he blends completely

234 There is Venus who has embarked naked for Cythera from a haven by the
lovely sea

There is the dark hair of my love

There is the breast of my love upthrust like a lily

There are Americans running a vile traffic with our gold

There is a captain anxiously awaiting wireless messages via the Atlantic

There are soldiers at midnight sawing boards for coffins

There are women in Mexico crying out loudly for corn before a bleeding
Christ

There is the Gulf Stream so warm and so benevolent

There is a cemetery full of crosses 5 kilometres from here

There are crosses here there and everywhere

There are prickly pears on the cactuses in Algeria

There are the long supple hands of my love

There is an inkwell I had made for Madeleine from a 15-centimetre fuse
which they would not let me send

There is my saddle out in the rain

There are the rivers that do not reverse course

LETTERS TO MADELEINE

There is the love that carries me gently towards Madeleine
There was a Boche prisoner with his machine-gun on his back
There are men in the world who have never been to war
There are Hindus contemplating our Western battlefields in amazement
There are women learning German in the occupied lands
They think with sadness of those they fear they may never see again
And above all there is the sun of our love

Gui

235

GUILLAUME APOLLINAIRE

My very dear love, you promised never to suffer because of me and here comes your letter of the 24th showing that you have indeed suffered, you my delight, you whom I want to be infinitely happy on my account! No, my darling, you must not suffer, do not ever suffer, because I still adore you. Today I got your letters of the 23rd and the 24th of September. Let me start by replying to the first. So my letter of the 15th addressed to you at Lamur has obviously gone astray, at least for now. I love the account of your crossing immeasurably, my love; your 'faith' has not been betrayed and your 'ardent and powerful love' was certainly one of the 'imponderables' that helped in the battle. Do not be sad my love, I love you. . . .

LA TRAVERSÉE

Du joli bateau de Port-Vendres
Tes yeux étaient les matelots
Et comme les flots étaient tendres
Dans les parages de Palos

* * *

Que de sous-marins dans mon âme
Naviguent et vont l'attendant
Le superbe navire où clame
Le chœur de ton regard ardent.

THE CROSSING

On the fine boat from Port-Vendres
Your eyes were sailors
And how gentle the billows were
In the vicinity of Palos

* * *

So many submarines are in my heart
Sailing as escorts to
That proud ship whence
The chorus of your ardent gaze calls out.

My photo gave you pleasure. Just think what pleasure yours give
me out here where I am—I scrutinize every last detail with a
magnifying glass my love. . . .

237

L'ESPIONNE

Pâle espionne de l'Amour
Ma mémoire à peine fidèle
N'eut pour observer cette belle
Forteresse qu'une heure, un jour.

* * *

Tu te déguises? . . . À ta guise,
Mémoire espionne du cœur!
Tu ne retrouves plus l'exquise
Ruse et le cœur seul est vainqueur . . .

* * *

Mais la vois-tu cette mémoire
Les yeux bandés prête à mourir

GUILLAUME APOLLINAIRE

Elle affirme qu'on peut l'en croire:
Le cœur vaincra sans coup férir.

THE SPY

A pale spy of Love
My hardly faithful memory
One day had but an hour
To observe that lovely fortress.

* * *

Are you in disguise? . . . Take your pick,
Oh memory spy of the heart!
But you cannot retrieve your exquisite
Cunning and the heart alone prevails . . .

* * *

Just see how memory
Blindfolded and ready to die
Claims she is to be believed:
The heart will prevail without striking a blow.

I hope the 'little photographers', who are as sweet as can be, will take beautiful pictures of their sister whom I adore. How could you think that your passionate letters had caused me to forget your tenderness my love—on the contrary they epitomized it and made me thoroughly happy. Away with all those rather unreasonable scruples my adorable Phèdre. I do love your young girl's heart my sweetheart, but I am destined to love your woman's heart even more, and so I am getting prepared by loving both those hearts of yours, which are really just one, while already leaning towards the second—And I do not want you to suffer when I take your lips— Your letter of the 24th is very beautiful, my love, but you must not imagine that I was angry with you, nor think any ill at all of me—I love you completely, irrevocably, and you must not be jealous, ever—for you shall never have cause to be, because I speak freely to you but want you to understand everything and to understand that I can never be mean or angry so far as you are concerned. You are me, I am you, I adore you. I take you in my arms. Cheer up, little Madeleine. Cry if you will but cry without suffering, I kiss your tears, may they be tears not of sadness but of love. But you are right to tell everything my love. I adore you even more if possible for telling me all about your worst troubles, my very dearest one. I don't remember now what remark of yours it was that provoked my letter. Oh yes, I know, it was when you said you were afraid that your passionate words might unduly inflame my desire, to which I replied that you should have no fear, and I probably used language that was too strong, that clearly overstepped my thoughts. But I was not annoyed, nor ever could be, with you. I know how completely you belong to me and am proud of it. There is no Madeleine that I do not love. I love all of you my precious little virgin, but just think what wish of mine these words imply, for you may be sure that there is hostility in them, hostility towards a virginity that is the sole barrier between us save for the fact of our separation. But you must not be frightened of me, who adores you and who is all sweetness with regard to you. Please understand me my precious, and don't make mountains and moral issues out of things of no significance, you are my joy—so be my joy utterly without striving to understand statements of mine that probably had scant meaning and merely expressed the elevated idea I have of the absolute purity of our love, at once so mystical and so carnal. If I desire to speak freely with you it is because you are another me. I tell you my dearest love it must be understood that there can be no hurt feelings or embarrassment between us. But how can you possibly think that you said something

239

GUILLAUME APOLLINAIRE

wrong by speaking of your body? Surely you are not going to
deprive me of your precious uninhibitedness, which I so love, on
account of your scruples? No, my love. What I was trying to explain
to you was that my curiosity did not arise from some aimless solitary
delectation, but from my love for you which binds me to you and
means that when you write me with the passionate abandon that is
so exquisitely natural to you it is almost as if we were together. There
were no reservations in my letter. You are mistaken, my darling, for
when I said that I desired you unreservedly waiting for the moment
when I could have you I was merely trying to show you how great my
soldier's patience is. How can you suppose my love that I have mental reservations? I am quite incapable of having any. We belong to
one another. I am terribly sorry to have expressed myself so poorly
my love. If I did not press your lips to mine at the end of my letter
my darling, it can only have been for lack of space, or from forget-
fulness, and such a thing could never occur in reality, and in any
case in letters our kisses inhabit every single word and if ever a kiss
is not expressed it is certainly always implied. So I take your lips now
to make up for that time, my darling, and for today and forever. Kiss
the little ones for me and tell Émile that I am going to be ever so
fond of him. But, my love, what of the things you were going to tell
me about *The Heresiarch*?

Madeleine, you are my wife, and you must never suffer on account
of your husband. I kiss your eyes and your lips endlessly. Do once
more become my passionate Madeleine, I beg of you. Today I
posted the base of the 77 which is supposed to house the second
inkwell. The day after tomorrow I'll send the main part and in four
or 5 days the top, assuming always that they let the base through
first. I trust that by now you have received the inkwell, the first one.
It is to be hoped so, but you don't mention it. It must have taken a
very long time to arrive. I believe I marked it for home delivery but

240

am not sure. So possibly only a notification will have come to your relatives' house in Narbonne. If so I hope that they will do what is needed to get the parcel to you in Lamur, unless of course I sent it directly to Lamur myself, but I don't remember now if I did. Our operations are not quite over, but I hope that in a few days we shall take the crucial positions commanding Vouziers.—But no, my love, your letter does not seem to me the least bit incoherent, to the contrary it demonstrates an intellectual superiority that frightens me a little for so much subtlety amounts almost to a revolt on the part of my little slave and I wonder whether you ought not to have more faith in me. I want you my darling to have complete faith. Your distress is a form of rebellion. And I do not say this lightly, believe you me. You can hardly call it doing my pleasure when you dissect everything I say, I who so love to express myself freely but who do not want in any way at all to upset you, whom I adore.

241

Madeleine, please kiss your feet once more for me now that I have cheered you up, smile at my photo, kiss me on the mouth, I take your mouth passionately, my darling. But do not rebuke me henceforth for anything in my letters for if you do I shall in my turn tell you that you must not assign more importance to writing than to the mind. And the mind says this: I love you in any event, forever, in every way, even when you develop enormous but unjustified anxieties and need to be reassured my little Madeleine, so beautiful and so sweet. Come now, I love you and I know that you love me. Come, I love you, and you may always tell me everything, even if I chide you a bit. Are you not consoled now my love? Yes, I know you are. Above all write me long letters, long like your letter of the 24th, letters that express all of you. Once again I take your lips passionately.

Gui

My love and my joy, is it not true that you know I love you, that you
know I want you never to suffer and that you know I never feel anger
towards you? Is that not so, Madeleine? You must not be jealous. You
have to be mine, without any kind of rebellion. For there must be
nothing bad within us. Our love is the supreme good and everything
that contributes to it is good, how can you imagine anything bad
therein and most of all how can you see anything bad in my letters?
You mustn't. I speak frankly with you. I tell you everything, for I can
tell you everything and there is nothing in me that is not yours, even
my past life. That life belongs to you. So treat it indulgently, because
it has kept me yours. Above all when I explain something to you
never suppose that I am annoyed. Look at my picture. It smiles at
you. I smile forever at you my love and I love you, I take your lips,
but if ever I forgot to do so in a letter never think that the gesture
has not been made. I perform it continually in my mind and spend
my whole life within this kiss that I adore. Today no letter from you.
I await your letter impatiently, a letter that is calmer, that is more
Madeleine. Love me without being afraid of me, my darling, otherwise I should hate myself for frightening you. I don't know what to
write you today, yesterday's letter from you has confused me so. Be
Madeleine, be my woman and not a woman merely. Be my wife, my
Poppaea, my Phèdre, be the scholarly and worldly-wise Madeleine that
I worship. It was your beauty and your superior mind that pleased me
so much—so much that nothing has ever been worshipped as you are,

242

oh my love. Return now with me to that dear freedom that we cherished so greatly. Be the ideal Madeleine that you are and that I want you to be.

The base of the 77 is on its way. Tomorrow I'll try to send the main part of the inkwell. From what you write in your letter of the 24th about my photo, I conclude that you too felt an attraction in that train, is that not so my dearest one? Tell me about it. Leaves, suspended in our sector for a month now, have not yet been restored. I wonder when they will be. Write me at length and every day my love.

About the word *bobosse* or *fantabosse* which we discussed earlier in our letters. It is not new and was already in use in '70. I have just come across it in a novel of Richepin's set in that period, *Césarine*. I have not told you how blue the tear gas is and how it floats like will-o'-the-wisps in a meadow. I love you my Madeleine. It is cold here and we are stamping our feet. We have a poor excuse for a fire, and no water. But I love you and that makes up for everything, especially if in your letters you would very kindly tell me about yourself instead of retailing the sort of idiocies that I am prone to put in my own letters, invariably written in haste, as I perch on the corner of a crate surrounded by people talking, spouting nonsense and fooling about in a brutal way, for like it or not life at the Front is brutal. Which is precisely what makes it tolerable, as a matter of fact. I have been told that my horse is limping slightly. This bothers me. He must have a sore on his foot. I would like him to be treated, because I am fond of him. But horses are rather poorly cared for here. Humans too, for that matter, are left entirely to *Naturas medicatrix*, and if something befalls I hear that the ambulance corps have not so much as a drop of spirits to buck you up a bit.—But happily nature is the true healer. Plenty of people do without doctors and sects such as the Mormons prohibit recourse to them. As for me I love you my

243

darling.—You must never regret having written me or having once again to write me such sweet passionate letters, especially now when I no longer get post every day. Tell me about yourself, and about the precious life we are going to have, that life for which I am preparing myself with tender devotion my love that I adore. You are a miracle worker. I have never written long love letters but I love you to the point where I want to tell you so continually and prove it to you even more often. I have examined your dear eyes in the photo and striven to decipher the word written but cut short on the back— hopeless. And your photo taken in Narbonne I love because it shows your splendid long legs. Tell me what flowers are blooming at present in Algeria. Tell me what effect the communiqués have on your dear soul and heart which are mine and to which I belong. Write me. I really would like to get my leave now but who knows when that will happen. It is long, my love, so long and not finished yet, yet I love you so much that all the waiting seems short just so long as it leads to you my darling.

Today I imagined how a very flexible fabric, warm as wool and transparent as crystal, might transform morals overnight. We would no longer be ashamed of nudity and the reign of beauty would return— that feminine or manly beauty which enshrines all rational canons, all intelligent principles. Such beauty is a marvellous book in which all knowledge may be found, a book that it is wrong to mistrust, just as you almost did when you hesitated to speak to me in very precise terms of the beauty of your physical form. On that day however your mind eventually took a step that you should never regret, my love, and in honour of which I take your lips once more.

Gui

I write you, my love, on the evening of the 2nd. No letter from my love today. All I received were the proofs of my call 'To Italy', which is to appear in October in *La Voce* in Florence. Today I sent you the main part of the inkwell, though I don't yet know whether it will get through. Send me very loving letters to provide fodder for mine even on those days when I receive none.—I get quite rattled when I have no letters from you my love.

We are still braced for marching orders. One cannot work at anything during breaks in shelling because all our gear is packed up. It is now two days since I heard from you and it feels like a century. We are so badly set up for writing, moreover, that we can barely manage to compose even a very few letters. And then it is only to you that I can write with pleasure and at length. The rest of the time one roams around, without venturing too far afield, trying to find a newspaper, which one rarely succeeds in doing, as was true today for example, when one was reduced to reading some old novel that was lying around.

One comes across quite a lot of Boche equipment, all of it above the weight limit for sending home. This prohibition is curious, indeed inexplicable, but since we all know there is no point in trying to understand such things, why bother.

Tell me, my love, have your classes resumed yet? I think they probably have. I think of your little dark head, so pretty beneath

GUILLAUME APOLLINAIRE

that magnificent virgin forest of lovely hair. My desire for your presence knows no bounds.

I think of a Boche battery which was found amid overrun enemy lines and which I saw on a tour: the smashed artillery pieces, the gunners slaughtered and desiccated after lying since March where they died between the present French lines and the enemy's.

And I think once again of your sweet letters, so rare now, so rare so rare my love.

Write me regularly. It was fine all day but since nightfall it has been freezing cold.

I take your lips my dear dear love, I take them endlessly, I adore you, I adore you my darling, I love you and want you so badly, if only you knew! I love you and I take your lips yet again my love.

Gui

246

My dearest love, my little Madeleine that I adore, I got three letters from you today, three letters so loving that they have banished all the sadness—a painless sadness though, for I know for certain that you love me—all my sadness from your letter of the 24th. So now I am relieved, relieved, relieved. Yes, you are right my Rose, you shall always be my lily. You well know that such a rose as you shall always be a lily. The more you are my rose the more you shall be a lily to the entire universe, and the more you appear as a rose to the rest of the world the more you shall be my unique lily and I shall always keep for my wife the love I felt for my fiancée. I love all the Madeleines, who are just one Madeleine, and although yesterday I said I was leaning towards the Rose, that detracted in no way from the Lily, for no sooner does the Rose assert itself as Rose than the Lily rises up claiming all its rights—which I hold just as dear as the Rose's. I am simply trying to say that the Rose can in no wise harm the Lily, which is why I do not like the Lily ever to feel superior to the Rose, and if you are willing to accept this sincere lover's rigma-role you shall be my Rose-Lily. Both flowers at once. I am very happy to have anticipated your own desire by expressing the wish that you should always take the first step. It is by no means my intention, you understand, to offend your delightful modesty; rather, I want you for your part to refrain completely from curbing your body's impulsive movements towards mine, so that your

247

GUILLAUME APOLLINAIRE

modesty may never present itself as an obstacle between you and me. This is, I know, how you too see the matter.

You may use the paper-knives for whatever you like, but they are mine, that's all.

The revelation that unsettled you so much unsettles me too, and deeply, precisely because of what it made you aware of in yourself. I revel in your joy, my darling, and I take you, all of you, unto the most intimate part of your being, and I take your mouth, tongue to tongue, passionately. So much for your letter of the 25th.—Now for the 1st letter of the 26th. I am happy to know that Lamur is far from the sea and you are all safe. My passionate Madeleine you love in the way I want to be loved. I take your lips till they bleed with the blood that is your gift to me.

As for your second letter of the 26th, I have already read it 20 times I love it so much. I take you dreamy or vivacious, laughing or serious my love. All is beauty in you my darling, all is harmony and even more—how I love this about you—all is the desire for beauty. For yes, your contempt for hypocrisy stems from your admirable sense of beauty. Truth and love are what we two are, and they are but one in their synthesis, which is Beauty.

You continued your letter on the 27th. I do not wear the ring that is like yours because it is too large. But keep it for me please. It bothered me when riding, and whenever I had to use my hands a lot. How happy I am that you have at last understood that we love everything in ourselves, that you have so well understood the secret the divine secret and I long for the language you will find that is adequate to it. Your grasp of the rites of love fills me with a joy that might almost be called religious, oh my Rose, my Lily. You have understood that for us everything is permissible and that we shall enjoy all the delights without letting ourselves be dominated by them, while what tames you will not be your will but mine.—My candle has just tipped over onto this letter, forgive me my love for such a messy letter, but I am so badly set up here!! I renew my kisses upon your pearly hips, those hips that I love and that you are so proud of my angel, and I am happy that in your thoughts you seek refinements designed to make our love greater than love ever was until now. Your senses are awakening in the most delightful way, making me think of Aphrodite emerging naked and beautiful from the foaming sea. You knew that you would find me my love and you saved me imperturbably for yourself and now you are my prey, my golden fleece, yes my darling, I lay my head upon your left breast, I tremble voluptuously as I touch it, I listen to your heart, I kiss it and I also kiss the divine mound of your breast formed just as I would have wished, for indeed breasts should not be too heavy, as you say my darling, and yours are perfect. How I love your long harmonious body, how happy I am that you understand me and that you love me as you do with every fibre of your body and how content I am that you no longer need feel ashamed before me of your beauty my love with your beautiful eyes, and I knead your flesh like a baker kneading dough—a comparison that must always have been obvious because however far one goes back in time loaves were always pressed into sexual forms—split loaves for the female pudenda and long ones for the male member. I am so happy at the unalloyed joy elicited in you by my letter of the 19th and I beg you never more to quit a joy that is so favourable to us. Joy is everything in life, joy is the great soldier victorious, our joy shall reign over everything if you wish it and your sensuous joy is my supreme happiness. I take all of you in the deepest way and I take your tongue my love neverendingly. I am dying in your adorable mouth.

GUILLAUME APOLLINAIRE

I have received the *Mercure* and I'll send it to you. It does not include my 'Vie anecdotique', which I sent in too late.

I take your lovely breasts my darling and your marvellous hips. I adore you and tell you so over and over again forever, mouth to mouth and tongue to tongue forever.

Gui*

* The ring in the photo of me must be either my signet ring, whose signet was copied on one of the rings I sent you, or else the diamond-shaped ring that you wear.

250

My love, Today I sent you a card to let you know that we shall be moving back to Sector 138 from Sector 80.—I am writing badly because my situation is bad. It is cold, and during the day we may not light fires because of the smoke, so it is impossible to write. After dark the guns go back in their holes. We can make fires. But the men are here playing cards and joking. I accept all your caresses and return them. But I must say I am less fond of your letters since you have been in Oran, you feel less mine to me in them. After all, you forget to tell me all the things you promised to tell me—concerning *The Heresiarch*, for instance. You are holding something back, I don't know what, and you express yourself in less direct terms, hence more affected and vaguer—but perhaps this is just one of the myriad aspects of your love? I miss my Poppaea and my Phèdre—Mark you, I say this with neither anger nor regret—Between us such feelings are not acceptable, so do not be hard on yourself. I daresay it all stems from the renewed obligations that must now once more be taking up your time.

Your father was quite right to admire Tolstoy who is indeed an admirable figure and this especially in my view by virtue of his having foreseen and announced the end of the old aesthetics. Tolstoy saw this clearly and your letter reminds me of it at a time when Art is suffering greatly from the temptation to fall back into the rhetorical mode in which it remained for too long. Tolstoy

GUILLAUME APOLLINAIRE

clearly understood that taste is meaningless and can only spoil art. Art should be quite separate from taste but since three-quarters of art lovers are concerned solely with taste it is difficult to get rid of it. Tolstoy spoke very intelligently of Shakespeare and Maeterlinck and showed up the artistic error that perverts pure beauty. That was his truly great contribution, apart from which he was a great novelist and a great proselytizer, although there I am a poor judge. In those spheres he is certainly great, based on what little I know, but great like an enormous phantom, a gigantic spectre that the past has left standing before us who are so blind and so easily seduced by a host of things that are dead. I have not read the books by Tolstoy that you mention. Russian novels are connected to life, but I have already spoken to you about that—I have read *Anna Karenina* and part of *War and Peace*.

252

I got your 2 letters of the 28th.—Now for the second of them.

You must be amusing and charming in your class. I too would love to get lost in the woods with you . . . I accept your smiles and I pre-fer this simpler and more spontaneous second letter in which you invent the pretty and subtle, so subtle eye-caress—And I also love your smiling lips. Today I inhaled 'tear gas' smelling of rotten pears and also of the brandy they sometimes give us in the morning—It makes your eyes sting, and it emanates from a sort of thin grenade made of copper and filled with a liquid that may be nitrogen protoxide (impure). It is thus probably laughing gas. It did not make me laugh, however. But still, the odour is by no means disagreeable to me. I have found a Boche belt buckle that I am going to send you along with a Boche bag for holding their mask against our asphyxiating gas. You can make yourself a belt using the buckle if you like.

Might it not be possible to derive the malleable glass I mentioned to you from cellulose acetate? If so, it would be an interesting discovery. But I am not well enough versed in chemistry to put such a thing into effect. And so to you. My love I adore you and I kiss you on the lips endlessly and intensely.

Gui

253

GUILLAUME APOLLINAIRE

They are saying my love that we leave tomorrow but we shan't go far. Inasmuch as we have rejoined our old corps, we shall likely remain in Sector 138 where we have now settled in. But nothing is certain. Now, first of all, please forgive me for finding something to fault you for in your exquisite letters of yesterday. I was so ill disposed on the moment that your discretion hurt my feelings as if it were a defection—and yet your letters were in fact marvellous. I enclose some verses that I composed after writing to you and they will give you an idea of my spleen-ridden state of last night. Today much work, attack supposedly for tomorrow, after which I dearly hope that we shall take up positions beyond the Boche lines—Today your letter of the 29th came and gave me great pleasure. Among the rings in one of the parcels I don't remember which you should have found one made from a horseshoe nail—I am attached to it, did I tell you about it?—Of course you may wear whatever rings you like. Send me the measurement of your ring finger again. I am going to try to make two engagement rings from Boche aluminium, then I'll send both of them to you and you'll kiss one of them and send it back for me. Your letter received today is the first in which you mention communiqués regarding events in which I took part, my love, as a combatant. I have seen a picture purporting to show that a village near where we are—you have seen the photos by now—is once again inhabited. I wonder by whom and where the peasant women shown were photographed. The place is on the firing line

254

and it is an insult to the public to feed it humbug of this sort. There are not even any houses left there.—Your second inkwell returned to me yesterday because it was too heavy was posted off once more today—if it comes back again I'll give up—If it goes through after all I'll send for one thing its top and for another 2 chargers with their powder removed and quite harmless because their caps have been fired—also a complete belt buckle (in 2 pieces) with the *Gott mit uns* and a piece of the Boche soldier's bread that they call Pumpernikel— not the K.K. bread that I think is also known as Kappa bread in Bocheland.—You tell me you are happy that I find your letters charming. They are more than charming and you have a good deal of talent quite apart from the love that you put into them—There are few writers today who write better than you my love. Apropos of which, there is a collection of stories—fairy tales in the main— known as the *Pentameron* of Basil (16th century I believe), written in the Neapolitan dialect. I should have liked to translate it. I have a copy, but such a task is beyond my linguistic abilities, and hardly justifies (in terms of the benefits) my making a thoroughgoing study of the ancient Parthenopaean tongue. It has been translated into English, however, in an illustrated edition for young readers that I saw somewhere or other. If you had the time you could translate it, which would be good practice for your English, and then I would polish your version up with the help of my old edition of the original. I am very fond of fairy stories. When I was a child Perrault (along with *Robinson Crusoe* and Racine) was my main reading matter. Perrault's tales are full of old mythical truths from Asia passed down by tradition. And Naples (or Parthenopaeia) is one of the gates through which these fables passed, which is what makes Basil's *Pentameron*, never translated into French, so very interesting— I have been told that Lucie Felix-Faure Goyau discussed it in a book of hers on fairy tales, but I do not know what she had to say about

GUILLAUME APOLLINAIRE

the *Pentameron*.—My darling, you are my pretty one and I was delightfully unsettled by everything you tell me about your love and also by your allusion to heirs as yet unborn, oh my love. I kiss your belly and your breasts. What you say about our journey from Nice also unsettled me but at the same time made me very happy. There is no doubt that my will cast its mantle over you from my first glance in your direction. I was certain that you would be mine. I desired you madly, not in a purely physical sense of course, although in the highest forms of desire the physical and the spiritual are no longer separate, but one and the same.

There is no more talk of leave where we are and I fancy there will be none any time soon, at least not around here.—Beginning today I'll be sending you poems that I would like you to copy when there are enough and send back to me so that I can submit them to a magazine. I take your mouth, I can feel your body wrapped around mine, your legs fast about me in the purest of [*illegible*], your loins shaken by mad desires—I take your mouth my tongue explores it; your lovely teeth touch mine. I kiss your mouth, my love.

DÉSIR

Mon désir est la région qui est devant moi
Derrière les lignes boches
Mon désir est aussi derrière moi
Après la zone des armées

* * *

Mon désir c'est la butte de Tahure
Mon désir est là sur quoi je tire
De mon désir qui est au-delà de la zone des armées
Je n'en parle pas aujourd'hui mais j'y pense

* * *

Butte de Tahure je t'imagine en vain
Des fils de fer, des mitrailleuses, des Boches trop sûrs d'eux
Trop enfoncés sous terre déjà enterrés

* * *

Ca ta clac, des coups qui meurent en s'éloignant

* * *

En y veillant tard dans la nuit
Le décauville qui toussote
La tôle ondulée sous la pluie
Et sous la pluie ma bourguignote

* * *

Entends la terre véhémente
Vois les lueurs avant d'entendre les coups
Et tel obus siffler de la démence
Ou le tac tac tac monotone et bref plein de dégoût.

* * *

Je te vois Main de Massiges
Si décharnée sur la carte

* * *

Le boyau Goethe où j'ai tiré
J'ai tiré même sur le boyau Nietzsche
Décidément je ne respecte aucune gloire

* * *

Nuit violente et violette et sombre et pleine d'or par moments
Nuit des hommes seulement

GUILLAUME APOLLINAIRE

Nuit du 24 septembre 1915

Demain l'assaut

Nuit violente, ô nuit dont l'épouvantable cri profond devenait plus intense de minute
*   en minute*

Nuit des hommes seulement

Nuit qui criait comme une femme qui accouche

DESIRE

My desire is the region that lies before me
Beyond the Boche lines
My desire is also behind me
Beyond the zone of operations

* * *

My desire is Tahure Hill
My desire is what I fire at
My desire that is beyond the zone of operations
I am not going to speak of today but I think about it

* * *

Tahure Hill I imagine you in vain
Barbed wire, machine-guns, Boches too sure of themselves
Too deep underground already buried

* * *

Clack clack clack, gunfire dying away in the distance

* * *

As I keep watch late in the night
The Decauville railway sputters
Corrugated iron under the rain
And under the rain my burganet

* * *

Listen to the vehement earth

See the flashes before hearing the reports

And some shell whistling dementedly

Or the monotonous brief tack-tack-tacking laden with disgust.

* * *

I see you Main de Massiges

So scraggy on the map

* * *

And you Goethe Trench on which I have fired

I even fired on the Nietzsche Trench

Decidedly I am no respecter of greatness

* * *

Violent and violet night dark and filled with gold now and then

Night of men only

Night of 24 September 1915

Tomorrow the attack

Violent night, oh night whose frightful deep cry intensified from minute to
    minute

Night of men only

Night screaming like a woman in labour

Gui

I have just been looking for the poems I wrote yesterday but I
cannot find them, never mind—I take your mouth—

GUILLAUME APOLLINAIRE

My love, I had no letter from you today. I hear that Remy de Gourmont has died. He was my friend; it was he that brought me into the *Mercure de France*. A great mind disappears with him. His judgements were sometimes skewed when he allowed self-interest to get the upper hand, but otherwise he was a great fount of literary knowledge and very possibly biological knowledge also. Disfigured by leprosy (or so it was said, in any case his face was purple and looked burnt), he was tormented by matters of love and spoke much of that—There was something in him of a Pierre Bayle (of dictionary fame), that celibate man who championed the writer's right to publish obscenities without being called a corrupter of morals. Remy de Gourmont disentangled not a few ideas and this analytical work made him one of the subtlest of vulgarizers. His death leaves a gap that few will be able to fill. He was open to new ideas and he was tolerant, such a rare quality these days.—

So your father knew Russian, my love? I knew it as a child, but have lost it long since.

I fear that Bulgaria's decision may lengthen the war for a very very long time. Here everything continues to go well. Good work, and the communiqués contain news to make you rejoice my love.

Your inkwell is gone at last and today I sent you two more parcels one of which—the smaller—contains the top. You should already have received the base, sent separately. I take you my love with a very long kiss in which our mouths joined together by lips teeth and tongues are the most exquisite furnace imaginable.—I think of you naked pressed against me. Your lovely breasts pierce me with their soft tips. I squeeze your supple waist so delightfully weighted by the broad chalice of your honeyed hips. Our arms encircle our bodies like lunar serpents. Your hair drowns us in the mysteriously nocturnal billows of our love that shines with its own light. The flower that I love blooms as it awaits me and I take it with the powerful sweetness of our infinite passion. I think of the penetrating exquisite scent of your [*illegible*] armpits and I see only the deep clear light of your ecstatic eyes. I feel that I am your master. I bend you to my fancy. You obey me passionately, you wish for the most violent commands from me, you desire my violence, you humiliate yourself in thrall to the higher joy of womanhood and you suffer with such delight that your rapture is a sensuous Nirvana. Be aware my love that your education is not over. I want to have you perfect when I take you, for I have the time to perfect you and I beg you my darling do not rebel against this education, which is meant to give me a virgin entirely instructed by her fiancé. I adore you my love; I want you to be my Poppaea, my Phèdre, for the impulses of your passion as manifested in what you write are my consolation in this war where one is so deprived of immediate love that whatever love one can derive from letters is a priceless distraction from the troubles of the present. That is why our secret should be deepened more and more by passion. And why you should respond more to my letters, my little rebel, instead of putting off so many questions that are of the utmost interest to me. You deserve a conjugal correction for leaving me in suspense about what you had promised to tell me about certain passages of *The Heresiarch* and about other things too, oh you whom I desire, my love, I take your mouth.

Gui

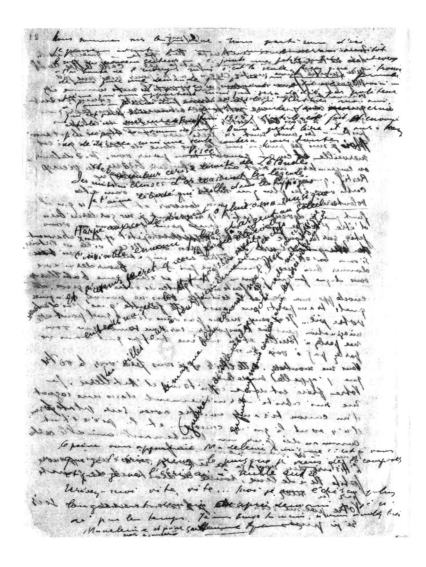

263

264

LE GÉNÉRAL JOFFRE

"GRAND-PÈRE"

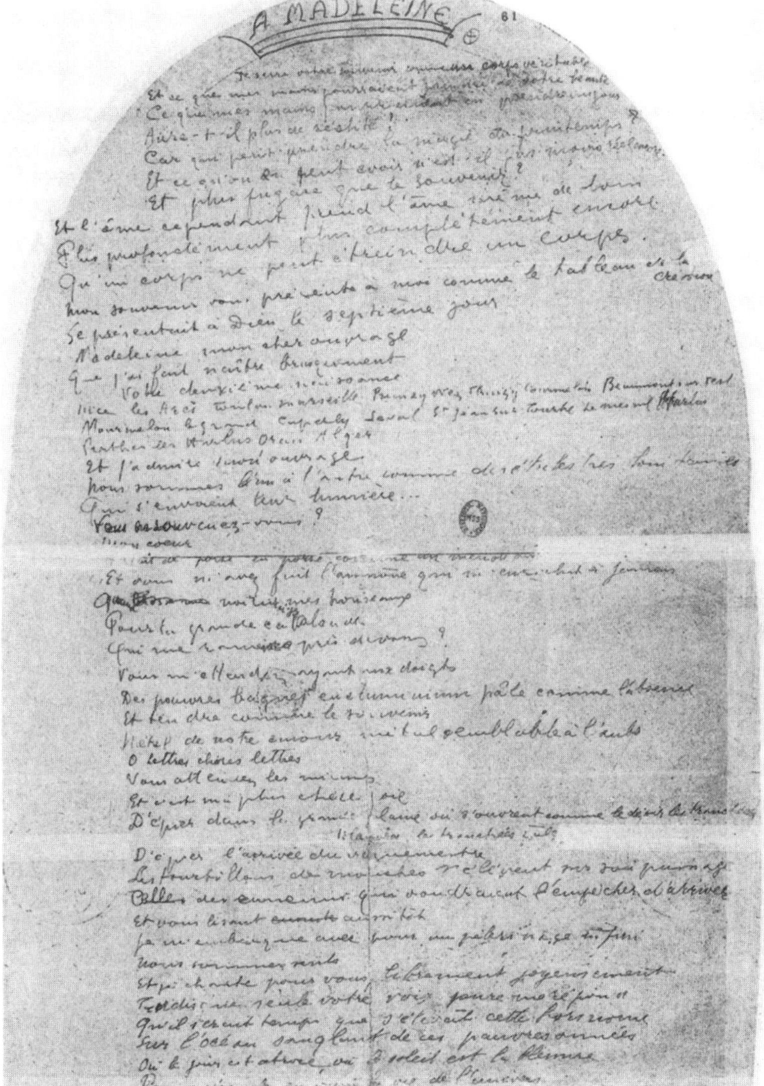
A MADELEINE
61

Se présentait à Dieu le septième jour
Madeleine mon cher ouvrage
Que j'ai fait naître brusquement

O lettres chères lettres

Nous sommes seuls

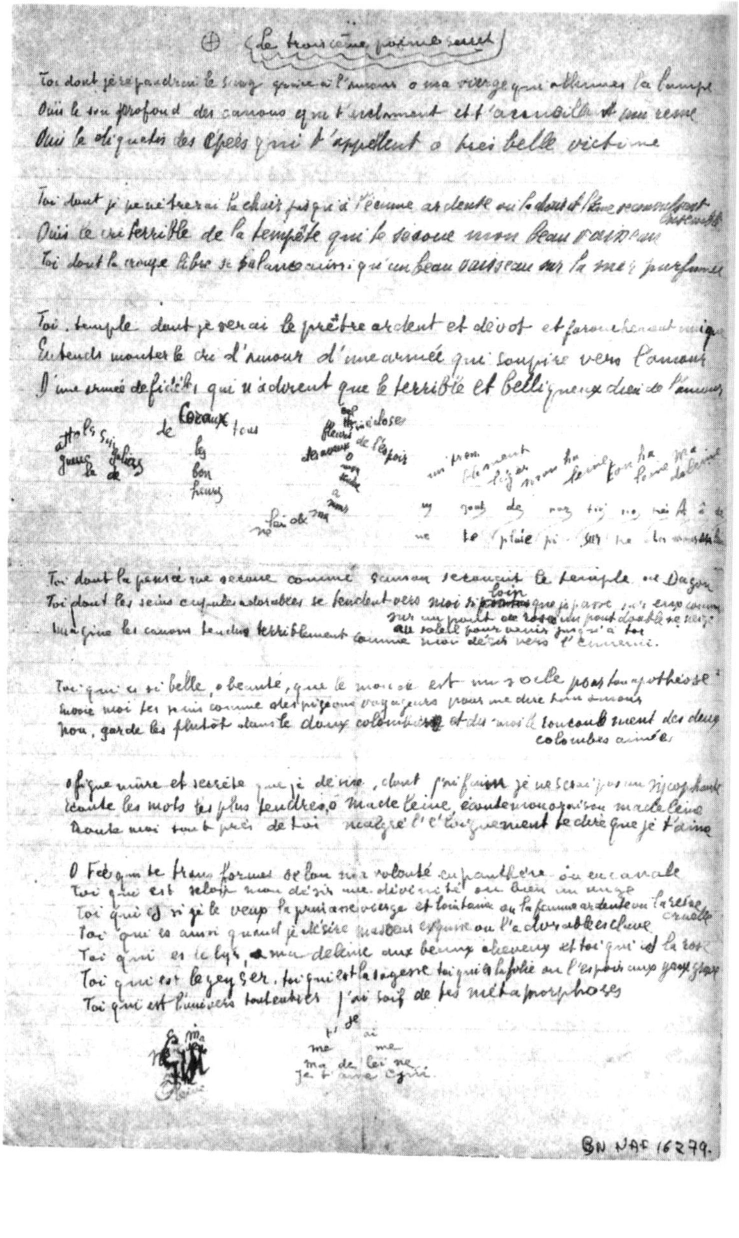

⊕ (Le troisième poème secret)

Toi dont je répandrai le sang quoi qu'il en soit ô ma vierge qui allumes la lampe
Oui le son profond des canons qui se lamentent est ta merveille à une messe
Oui le cliquetis des épées qui t'appellent ô très belle victime

Toi dont je pénétrerai la chair jusqu'à l'écume ardente où le dard blanc renaît sans fin
Oui le vent terrible de la tempête qui te secoue mon beau vaisseau
Toi dont la rouge libre se balance ainsi qu'un beau vaisseau sur la mer parfumée

Toi, temple dont je serai le prêtre ardent et dévot et farouchement unique
Entends monter le cri d'amour d'une armée qui soupire vers l'amour
D'une armée de fidèles qui n'adorent que le terrible et belliqueux dieu de l'amour

[marginal fragments, largely illegible]

Toi dont la pensée me secoue comme Samson secouait le temple de Dagon
Toi dont les seins crépus adorables se tendent vers moi ...
[illegible lines]

Toi qui es si belle, ô beauté, que le monde est un socle pour ton apothéose
Envoie-moi tes mains comme des pigeons voyageurs pour me dire bien bonsoir
Non, garde les plutôt dans le deux colombiers et dis-moi le roucoulement des deux
                                                                colombes aimées

ô figure mûre et secrète que je devine, dont j'ai ... je ne saurais pas un ...
écoute les mots les plus tendres, ô Madeleine, écartent-nous ô mon Madeleine
route moi sans fin près de toi malgré l'éloignement te dire que je t'aime

Ô feins de te transformer selon ma volonté ou panthère ou ... cavale
Toi qui es lointaine mon désir me dévie ici ou bien un ange
Toi qui es si je le veux la proie amoureuse et lointaine ou la femme ardente en la rêche
Toi qui es amour quand je désire ... ou l'adorable esclave cruelle
Toi qui es le lys, ô Madeleine aux beaux cheveux et toi qui es la rose
Toi qui es la geysère, toi qui es la sagesse toi qui es la folie ou l'espoir aux yeux ...
Toi qui es l'univers tout entier j'ai soif de tes métamorphoses

[drawn monogram/fragments]
je
me   j'ai
ma   me
ma de toi me
je t'aime ... je

BN NAF 16279.

commencement cuivre en gris épais
qui accroche derrière le courrier quand on
est en route en ce vin déjà de toutes
les couleurs X je me sers ensuite de ta savonnette
je me lave la poitrine le cou les aisselles les
mains au savon, puis dans une nouvelle
eau je me rince. Après quoi je me lave
la tête et tu rince, puis le visage
après quoi je lave tout ce qui est à toi consciencieuse-
ment. Puis je m'habille puis je tire du
ou lit jusqu'à la soupe à 12 h ½ puis
on attend les lettres. Je ne comprends naturelle-
ment pas les tirs qui viennent n'importe
quand le jour ou la nuit et durent à ceci
durent. En principe, on mange encore à 4 ½ et on
reprend le café, puis moi j'écris pas qu'à
10 h où il n'y a de l'un si pas et s'il ne pleut
puis je prends une douche en plein air,
me [Brosse] les dents et vais me coucher vers
onze heures. Ainsi vois on ne dort pas
un est ce qu'on a pas mais menu en ce temps
mais pas moyen de dormir. Dans le jour
je me rencontre souvent avec Berthier md.l. de la
2e pièce qui n'est pas du Dufresney md.l. de la 1re pièce
il vit tout seul dans un petit trou où il a prix la
place de s'étendre. Il y a un mois nous avons
une argent commune avec Berthier, mais
je résolus. Il y fais cuit de ta photo, puis depuis
l'après que. J'ai une table pliante que j'ai fabriqué
et petit banc je m'asseoir et un lit aussi bien
mais je ne pourrai pas emporter le lit et je crains
qu'en fin il ne me mes des changements ou
ne trouve de rebuis la main ne planches

le lit est en planches
le fond en treillage
de fil de fer, le
clous sont fabriqués
de bout de fils
d'acier, sur le
treillage il y a de la
paille sur la paille un sac puis un isolefeuse
que j'ai trouvé inutile. Mais puis un
toile de tente pliée en 2 je me ouate dedans

et sur mon couverture de cheval ce sur
pied, manteau, au pied du lit devant la porte
dg a ma table

Je viens de recevoir
tes lettres du 18
et du 19 . oui
sois calme mon
amour et
patiente quant

PATIENCE

Guirané Madeleine je t'adore

mon amour

Je prends ta
bouche
Et j'aime tes seins

des obus, mon
amour cheri

[...] ne reçois pas de lettre de moi
Non mon amour tu ne m'as pas encore parlé
de tes jambes et je voudrais aussi une longue
lettre sur tes [...]. J'adore tes seins qui
sont si beaux. Ils s'impriment dans ma
chair. Et je te fais encore cette caresse que
tu devines. Je te mange, mon amour et je me
fais une [...] de [...]
j'adore. J'adore ce sourire qui était [...]
[...]. Moi aussi [...]
ce qui n'est pas toi m'est indifférent. J'adore
que tout soit clair en toi madeleine, c'est ainsi
en moi aussi. Mais oui tu m'aimes bien
mon grand amour, ma belle [...], mon
adorable évanescente, mon Ariel voluptueux
ton corps [...] contraste parce que tu [...]
[...] encore mon [...] et
puis c'est peut-être ta [...]
Parle moi longuement des amphores
de tes hanches mon amour et de mon amour
comme est placée cette bouche rose et [...]
de ton être intime, bas et [...] le
sol en plus [...] et comme une fente verticale
devant toi. Oh moi aussi quels sont
les [...] que tu préfères, en dehors
de moi bien entendu qui suis ton amour
et qui t'adore, dis-moi aussi si tu es
gourmande et si tu as bon appétit et
par quel côté tu dors. Dis-moi
encore que tu m'aimes mais je
t'adore. Je prends ta bouche

je n'ai pu bien t'écrire.

J'ai reçu aujourd'hui un mot d'un horti-
culteur qui me demande une
œuvre en échange de quoi il m'
offre tout ce que je vais dire comme
une végétation après la guerre.
Je t'envoie la lettre et on s'en servira
s'il y a lieu.

Mon amour fais-moi la description de
ta chambre et de ton bon lit, ma chérie
moi et mes hommes couchons dans
un trou recouvert de 2 couches de
rondins de chêne et de plaques de
tôle ondulée voilà le plan du trou

Ce plan donne tu en as l'air
trop large en réalité il n'y
a pas entre les lits
comme passage la largeur
d'un lit

À droite du canon il
y a la cuisine où l'on
mange
Je me lève ainsi que
tous la tête vers la
lucarne

Le vrai au art de se
coucher maintenant
Souvent on boit du thé que j'aime
beaucoup et c'est une façon de
boire de l'eau

ma chérie je t'adore de vouloir être
docile, et être mon amour, je

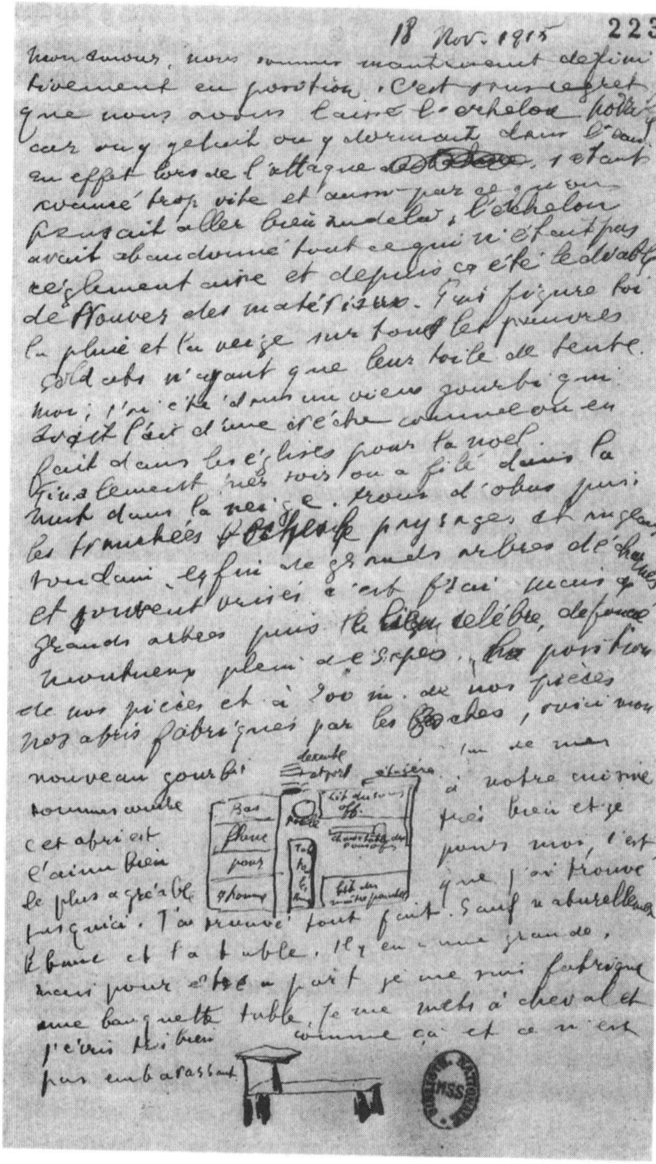

LETTERS TO MADELEINE

mon amour, je continue ma lettre le [...] à 4 h.
par [...] aujourd'hui. — comme choses curieuses
de tranchées il y a les parapets [...] taillés dans
la tranchée et appelés [...] selon leur
forme [...] il y a les girouettes pour
voir [...] la direction du vent
en cas [...] de gaz [...]
[...] ou l'avenue [...] porte
[...] avec l'indication Villa
Ste Anne. si on a moyen à faire je tâcherai
de faire les ronds de serviette ces jours
à [...] quoi, je crois que je ne ferai plus
souvent d'objets, maintenant que je suis
officier, et [...] aurai plus guère le loisir
[...] je dis qu'avant [...]
de mon ancienne batterie au [...]
j'[...] un autre [...]
plus beau que le premier que je [...]
[...] très bien sculptées, aigles, inscription
générales : celle-ci en ancien germanique
et qui est peut-être tirée des Nibelungen
Lieber düd as slavv (plutôt mort qu'
esclave) et celle-ci : Kein schönrer Tod
ist auf der Welt als Wer Vor 'm Feind
erschlagen (il n'est pas de plus belle mort au
monde que de tomber frappé devant l'ennemi)

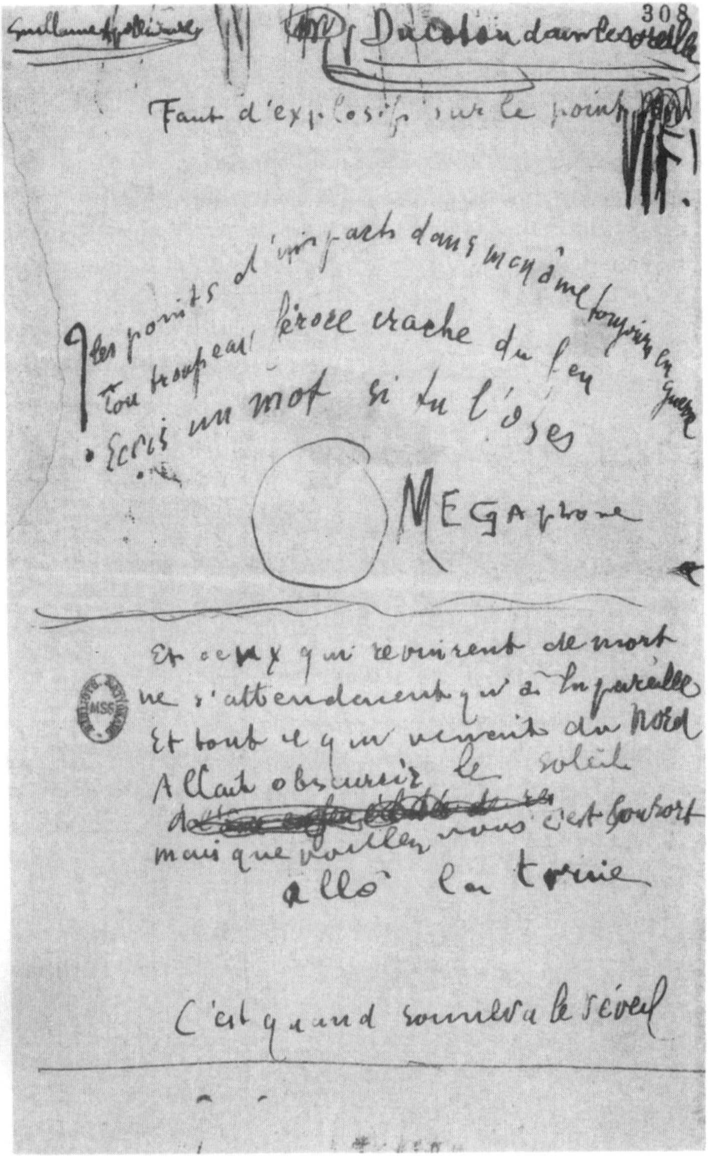

Courage
Ivresse
Vie
T R I
B cavernacaire
J l'amour
C la France

POPUL R F AVENIR
ALLO ALL SOUVENIR
ALLO ALL LA TRUIE
ALLO ALL LA TRUIE

La sentinelle au long regard
Et la cagnat s'appellait

Les cenobi

Les Cénobites
Tranquille

La sentinelle au long regard
Et Les coquelicots étaient qui tous
Allo la truie

Tant et tant de coquelicots
D'où tant de sang a-t-il coulé
Qu'est-ce qu'il se met dans le cœur
Bon sang de bois il s'est roulé
Et sans pinard et sans tacot
Avec de l'eau
allô la truie

GUILLAUME APOLLINAIRE

③

Le silence des photographes
Mitrailleuses des cinémas
Tout l'échelon là bas piaffe
Fleurs de feux des lueurs-frimas
Puisque le canon devait suis

allô la truie

Et les trajectoires cabrées
Trébuchements des Soleils-nains
Sur hautes chansons déchirées

majuscules

Rôt'étoile du Bénin

Main au singe en boîtes
carrées

Crois-tu qu'il y aura la guerre
Allô la truie
Et s'il vous plaît
Ami l'Anglais
Ah peut
ton frère, ton frère ton frère à toi

LETTERS TO MADELEINE

Et si mangeais du pain de guerre
En respirant leurs gaz lacrymogènes
    Mets du coton dans tes oreilles
        D'cire

Puis ce fut cette flûte sans que nous
A peine un souffle au souvenir
~~Apaisées et disent ta tête~~
Quand s'en allèrent les canons
Au tour des tours heure à courir
~~canons~~
La baleine d'autres canons

(Éclatements qui nous canons)
    mais mets du coton dans ta oreille
Évidemment les canons
    des signaleurs
        allô la téte

5

Où la musique militaire joue
quelque chose
Et chacun se souvient d'une joue
rose

Parce que même les airs entraînants
Ont quelque chose qui c'brement le cœur
Lorsqu'on les entend à la guerre)
Allô la truie

Mettez du coton dans vos oreilles

Ne prenez pas les feuilles pour
Pour autre chose qu'elles ne sont

Comme feraient pas mal
d'auteurs
avant
la guerre — mettez du coton dans vos oreilles
Ce fut bien quand sonnez le réveil

277

GUILLAUME APOLLINAIRE

les longs boyaux où tu chemines

Adieu les cagnats d'artilleurs

Tu retrouveras

La tranchée en première ligne
Les éléphants des pare éclats
Une girouette malique
Et les regards des guetteurs las
Qui veillent le silence insigne

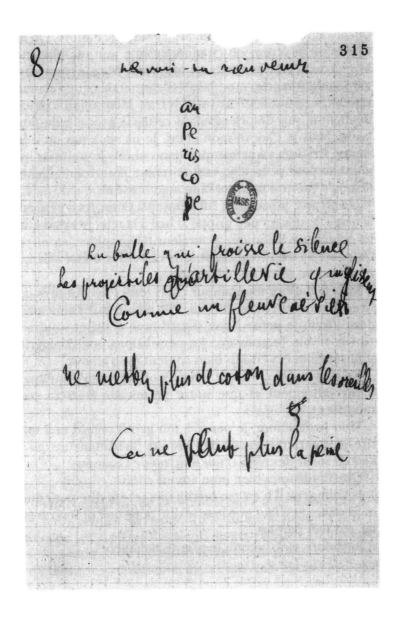

au
Pe
ris
co
pe

la balle qui froisse le silence
les projectiles d'artillerie qui rougissent
Comme un fleuve aérien

ne mettez plus de coton dans les oreilles

Ça ne vaut plus la peine

279

GUILLAUME APOLLINAIRE

280

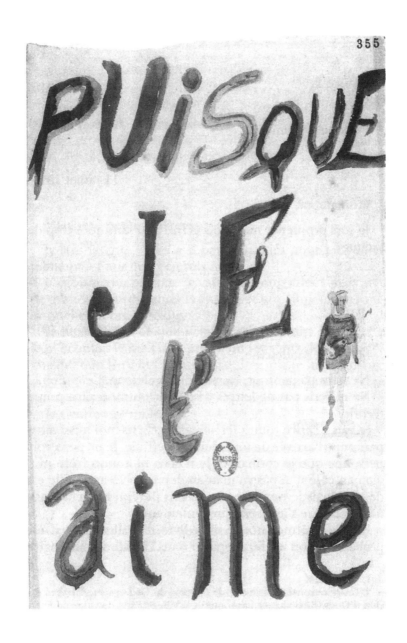

281

GUILLAUME APOLLINAIRE

282

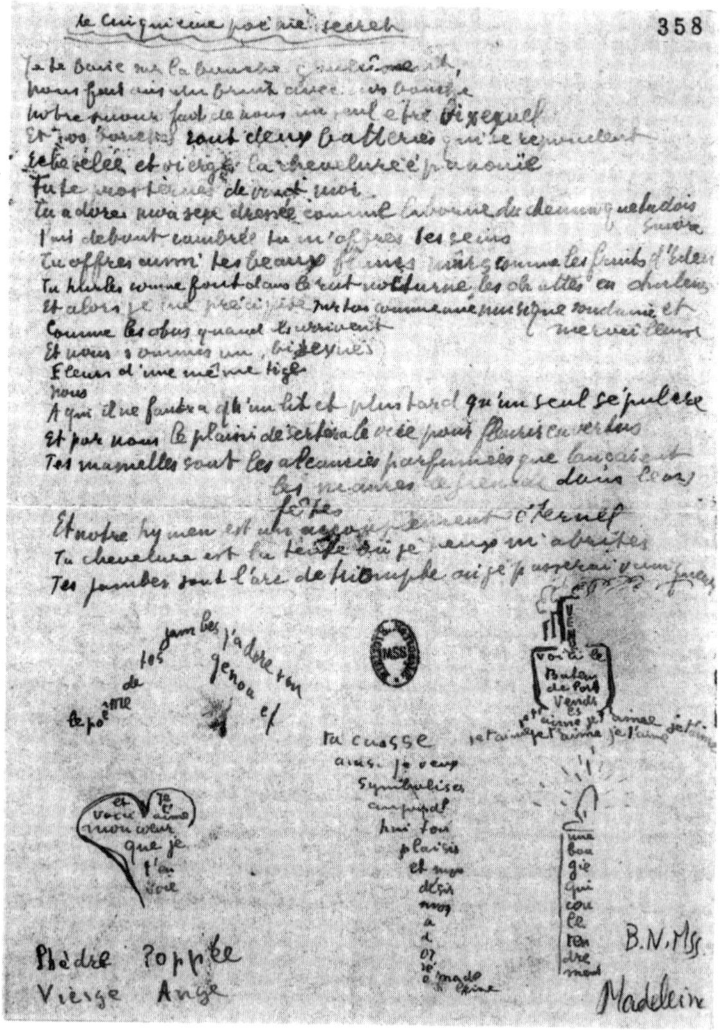
le cinquième poème secret

358

Je te baise sur la bouche quelle que soit la nuit,
Nous faisons un bruit avec nos bouches
Notre amour fait de nous un seul être bissexué
Et tes fesses sont deux batteries qui se [illegible]
Échevelée et vierge la chevelure épanouie
Tu te [illegible] de vingt mois
Tu adores ma verge dressée comme la borne du chemin que tu dois suivre
Puis debout cambrée tu m'offres tes seins
Tu offres aussi tes beaux [illegible] comme les fruits d'Eden
Tu hurles comme font dans le ciel nocturne les chattes en chaleur
Et alors je me précipite sur toi comme une musique soudaine et merveilleuse
Comme les obus quand ils arrivent
Et nous sommes un, bissexués
Fleurs d'une même tige
Nous
A qui il ne faudra qu'un lit et plus tard qu'un seul sépulcre
Et par nous le plaisir [illegible] fleuri en vertus
Tes mamelles sont les alcarazas parfumées que lançaient les [illegible] dans leurs fêtes
Et notre hymen est un accouplement éternel
Ta chevelure est la tente où je veux m'abriter
Tes jambes sont l'arc de triomphe où je passerai vainqueur

le poème de tes jambes j'adore ton genou et

et voici mon cœur que je t'adore
je t'aime

Ta cuisse ainsi je veux symboliser aujourd'hui tous plaisirs et mon désir mon [illegible] je t'adore Madeleine

VENDS
Voici le Bateau de Port-Vendres
je t'aime je t'aime je t'aime je t'aime

une bougie qui coule rendrement

MSS

Phèdre Poppée
Vierge Ange

B.N. Mss

Madeleine

283

GUILLAUME APOLLINAIRE

284

359

Three letters from you today my love—the one of the 30th and the 2 of the 1st. But first of all let me tell you how much I love the photo of my Madeleine taken two years ago. It is a good likeness and I can see you very well in it and it shows you as voluptuousness itself. Hebe in person. I can make out your bosom marvellously well. Your breasts, those two delectable fruits, are easy to divine. I adore your eyes in the picture and all of you my very very dearest. This photo shows you to be of such superlative beauty that I cannot believe that any man would not fall on his knees when first exposed to it. Truly not to be believed. You know, I passionately kissed your red, sensual lips, so well shown in this image where beneath your innocence voluptuousness already smouldered like fire in a dormant volcano. Your neck is wonderfully curved and your fine shoulders exquisitely formed and rounded, and your graceful bosom is gloriously high just as I would wish.

The sides of your nostrils quiver like a pair of doves, showing that your beauty is as piquant as it is noble and sensual. I adore the expression in your eyes and their dark circles are like a foreshadowing of love.

Cupid needed a spare bow, and now his two prescribed weapons are your two marvellously limned eyebrows.

And your pure brow! And the lobe of your right ear and the admirable mass of your black hair which puts me in mind of that rich fleece

GUILLAUME APOLLINAIRE

Qui très sûrement est la sœur
De cette énorme chevelure
Et qui t'égale en épaisseur
Nuit sans étoiles nuit obscure[1]

Which is quite certainly the sister
Of that enormous head of hair
And rivals you in its denseness
Oh starless night oh night obscure

1 Apollinaire's approximate rendering of the last quatrain of Charles Baudelaire's 'Les Promesses d'un visage' ('The Promises of a Face'):

Une riche toison qui, vraiment, est la
soeur
De cette énorme chevelure,
Souple est frisée, et qui t'égale en
épaisseur,
Nuits sans étoiles, Nuit obscure!

These four verses of Baudelaire's on the hidden fleece of the woman he loved came to me as I wrote without my searching for them, so perfectly suited were they to the image evoked for me by your lovely hair so welcome in your photo, oh my long-lashed love. In any case, I believe that these lines tell the truth!

286

By the way, my love, do tell me your dreams whose 'truth is astonishing' so that I may dare tell you mine. They enter a realm into which I dare not precede you. Oh my dear Phèdre, be your sister Ariane in this labyrinth and guide me. Do not fear conjugal correction as though it were a harsh punishment, my love, for it is the very opposite and an exquisite refinement when people love one another as you and I do. But how I love hearing you say that you die of voluptuousness at my voice and at my glance.

I thank you for writing 'I know that I may tell you about my intimate being, and that our secret should be enlarged because it is the beginning of the secret life of our marriage'. So it falls to you to extend the secret because it is you who must guide me down that *admirable road*.

I can just picture you my Madelon as a cadet—complete with that bosom and those hips of yours! And I certainly don't want you to cut your hair. I love you with all my might with your hair just as it is.

Not at all, my Madelon, I don't really use as many matches as my comrade says, but I can never keep a pipe going and the tobacco is for pipes only. That is all there is to it. But it is true that I once used up Berthier's reserve down to the *very last* match (not that he had very many to begin with). The fact is that matches are scarce here. We use the boxes to send things in merely because they are the only boxes we have.

I am afraid that your dream of the war being over by November may not come true. Our stupid diplomacy has allowed a comedy to occur in the Balkans that will prolong the war for who knows how long, indeed I dare not say how long I think it will prolong it for. I take your red mouth and your breasts that love my caresses and all of you all of you.

Kiss Pierre for me and for all the good things you have told me about him.

It was not a Spanish but an Italian newspaper that was used to wrap up the inkwell.

Why were you waiting for news of the 29th? The offensive took place on the 22nd 23rd 24th and 25th, it continued in the days following but the big days were those. I feel the gift of your life my love and you cannot imagine the good that this does me my very dearest.

I love you with all my soul, my love, I take you in my arms and I cradle you, I caress you, I undress you gently looking at you and losing myself passionately in your eyes. I kiss your darling feet which curl at my tender touch. From your mouth I drink in the whole of life. Enclosed you will find the verses that I thought lost. Nothing is now left of the sadness in whose thrall I was when they came to me.

GUILLAUME APOLLINAIRE

I adore you my darling and once more I take your mouth your breasts, I take all of you, all of you and I feel you swooning from my caresses oh my dear, dear little Madeleine with dark rings under your eyes, my adorable beauty, my Madeleine, adorable and adored.

PLAINTE

Mon amour tant chéri ma Madeleine

Je me jette vers toi et il me semble aussi que tu te jettes vers moi

Une force part de nous qui est un solide qui nous soude

Et puis il y a aussi une contradiction qui fait que nous ne pouvons nous voir

—Quand est-ce qu'on [se] reverra—

En face de moi la paroi de craie s'effrite

Il [y] a des cassures de longues traces d'outils traces lisses et qui semblent être faites
dans du nougat

Des coins de cassures sont arrondis par le passage des types de ma pièce

Moi j'ai ce soir une âme qui s'est creusée qui est vide

On dirait qu'on y tombe sans cesse et sans trouver de fond

Et qu'il n'y a rien pour se raccrocher

Ce qui y tombe et qui vit c'est une sorte d'êtres laids qui me font mal et qui viennent de
je ne sais où

Oui je crois qu'ils viennent de la vie d'une sorte de vie qui est dans l'avenir dans
l'avenir brut qu'on n'a pu encore cultiver ou élever ou humaniser

Dan ce grand vide de mon âme il manque un soleil, il manque ce qui éclaire

C'est aujourd'hui, c'est ce soir et non toujours

Heureusement que ce n'est que ce soir

Les autres soirs je me rattache à toi

Car toutes les places de mon corps correspondent à ce qui leur équivaut dans le tien

Les autres jours je me console de la solitude et de toutes les horreurs

En imaginant ta nudité

Je voudrais en connaître tous les détails

Pour l'élever au-dessus de l'univers extasié

Puis je pense que je ne connais même pas cela

288

Je ne le connais par aucun sens

Ni même par les mots

Et mon goût de la beauté est-il donc aussi vain

Existes-tu, ma Madeleine,

Ou n'es-tu qu'une entité que j'ai créée sans le vouloir

Pour peupler la solitude

Es-tu une de ces déesses comme celles que les Grecs avaient créées pour moins
s'ennuyer

Je t'adore, ô ma déesse exquise, même si tu n'es que dans mon imagination

Mais tu existes ô Madeleine, ta beauté est réelle

    Je l'adore

Malgré la tristesse de la craie et la brutalité incessante des coups de canon.

COMPLAINT

My love my darling love my Madeleine

I throw myself towards you and I fancy you throw yourself towards me too

A force springs from us a solid force that solders us together

But then there is an obstacle that prevents us from seeing one another

    —When shall we see one another again?—

Before me the chalk wall is crumbling

There are cracks in it long tool marks smooth marks like marks made in
    nougat

Edges of the cracks have been worn down and rounded by my gun crewmen
    brushing past

As for me tonight I have a hollowed-out soul an empty soul

A soul into which one seems to fall continually never touching bottom

And with nothing to catch hold of

What fall in and dwell there are ugly beings of a kind that hurt me and come
    from I know not where

Or rather I think they come from life from a kind of life that lies in the
    future in a raw future as yet impossible to cultivate or bring along or
    humanize

In the great emptiness of my soul there is no sun, no source of light

GUILLAUME APOLLINAIRE

This is just today though, tonight, and not always

Happily only tonight

On other nights I am joined to you

For every part of my body corresponds to its counterpart in yours

On other days I console myself for the loneliness and all the horrors

By imagining your nakedness

Whose every detail I should like to know

So as to raise it above the ecstatic universe

And then I think that I do not know even that

I do not know it through any of the senses

Nor even through words

So is my attachment to beauty also vain

Do you exist, my Madeleine,

Or are you just an entity I created unintentionally

To people my solitude

290   Are you like one of those goddesses the Greeks invented to lighten their
lives

I adore you, oh my exquisite goddess, even if you are in my imagination
only

But you do exist oh Madeleine, your beauty is real

       I worship it

Despite the sadness of the chalk and the neverending brutality of the canon
fire.

                           Gui

Enclosed are ten francs for the knife, scissors and file.

My love that I adore, Madeleine my dear ecstasy, Madelon my delight, Roselily of all purity and all voluptuousness. You do not tell me what she is or what she does, the young woman to whom you are giving lessons.—I have received your three letters of the 31st 8^{ber} the 1st Nov and the 2nd.[1] I like them very much. All the same, you are becoming excessively modest with me once more and I want you to abandon this attitude with me completely while remaining ready to reassume it upon my order should I judge that you belong to me not only body and soul as you do belong to me but even in the unfathomable subtlety of your whole being. I want you to be immodest with me as befits the female with the male, just as I want your mind to rise with mine to the greatest heights of aesthetic, metaphysical, religious and moral thought. I want us to be one, but even though your brain may obey me, and your body too, there are still obscure regions of your being where you are not yet altogether my Madeleine. Your modesty ought to grow and indeed become infinitely rigid with respect to everything that is not me but vanish absolutely and passionately when it comes to me. Words are the only way to express this short of actions and utterances situate actions and make them real. That is why utterances are so important. Few people have ever loved each other; and those few have often acted dishonourably, under the sway of vice. It is important that the actions of two beings such as we be governed by virtue yet be as

1 In error for 30 September and 1 and 2 October.

291

GUILLAUME APOLLINAIRE

thoroughgoing and as passionate as actions governed by vice. Read the lives of the female saints and you will see how the divine love that enraptured them caused them to abandon all modesty. This was not vice but virtue, and one can only feel sorry for those who find something reprehensible in the admirable passion that palpitates so immodestly in the works of a Saint Teresa of Avila. I shall let you know when the time comes for you to be modest once again, when your whole mind has become mine along with your fully consenting flesh even though I have not yet received the actual gift of that oh my love—It is not that I prefer the panther in you I love all of you my Roselily but it is the panther that I want to know entirely along with every feeling that the love displayed before her eyes can arouse in her. For a few days I sensed how great an effort you were making, but you now falter. One more effort oh slave of mine! and fasten the wonderful chain of my senses forever to the wonderful links of yours. But it is of you that you must speak in order to show me the depth of your sensual possibilities. I know that your feelings are passionate. I want to know just how passionate they are thanks to an unfettered revelation of everything you imagine so that your body may belong to me in the most magnificent way as a fertile field that I can reap at will. I love your voluptuous attitudes. They are assuredly your own for I have never mentioned such things to you and they give me a glimpse of your true nature, oh my Madeleine that I adore. It is true that we shall love each other splendidly. It is true that you are me and that I give you all your thoughts, do not forget that you must likewise give me all mine and that I shall be you just as completely as you are me. Bear in mind that I imply no rebuke, for I am quite aware that you belong to me more and more, when I say that I have noticed that your tone has become slightly less carnal, without ever yet having been fully carnal, and when I say that I want to plumb your carnal power to its depths but that there is a sort of retreat to

292

your former modesty towards me in these verbal reservations of yours which I detest. You are mine as the female is the male's and I want all your immodesty all your disorder all your madness, I want to do with you what I will without your ever feeling debased nor should words debase you words belong to us but the rest of the world has no right henceforward to anything save our amused contempt and cruel majesty. Be aware that not for nothing have I told you that should it please me I claim the right to lash your flesh, I want my dominion over you to be absolute and that even a flogging if I gave you one would merely enhance your voluptuous feelings. You know perfectly well that I do not mean to brutalize you, far from it, you know perfectly well that my love for you is of the tenderest kind and that I admire you for your beauty for your mind and for all of you, that I love you more than myself. So I want you to belong to me entirely. My Madeleine whom I adore, you give me so much joy by so marvellously describing your powerful yet refined sensations. You love me as I wish you to love me, so allow me, love, to use my violent authority to further inflame the infinite ardour of our love. Yes, I am your plaything too, but you are ardently infinitely madly and in no sense reasonably my slave. I may rip your skin if I wish, or welt your thighs and haunches so worthy of a bacchante, and you shall worship me as an adorably cruel idol. And if I wish I may bathe you with an endless caress in a river of balm sweeter than all paradises. All things considered I prefer it that you should have read few modern authors. It is I who shall guide your reading. As a matter of fact I have not read many modern authors either. I adore you. You are exquisite, you are my love that I adore and I savour the sweetness of your belly like honey from the comb. You pay me infinite honour when you compare me to Racine. As for you there is no woman to whom you may be compared, you are without peer. Curiously, I find Bordeaux unsavoury (judging by the little of him that I have read), I

GUILLAUME APOLLINAIRE

find him mediocre and sensual and depraved in a Jesuitical way, ugh! I'll show you what I mean and you, healthy and honest as you are, will understand clearly what I mean. Your judgement on Richepin is right, I have also read *La Mer*, an overblown rhetorical exercise on the theme of the sea. You yourself have retained a natural attitude thanks to your family and (from what I know of them) their exquisite sensibility. What you told me of your Papa's work and your Mama's graciousness delighted me. The firmness of your body is a wonderful tribute to your splendid youth. I adore you and devour all of you. Yes, the hymen is a membrane but I don't know whether it resembles the ear drum, anatomy not being my forte. I don't know what other blood you are referring to. I shall cause the blood to flow from the rent the first time, but oh there won't be very much, likewise the moist essence of your pleasure, destined to flow and flow again at each voluptuous spasm. I love your exquisite odour. The secret caress of the 9th door creates a powerful anxiety in you, and I adore the fact of your shame, love of mine, and I well understand that your most particular anxiety concerns our kiss, because you can imagine it the most clearly. Yes, it is marvellous that you should learn everything from me. I adore you for your exquisite sweetness and I adore your kissing and kissing my intimate being until I want you madly. I realize that you needed time to understand and that even now you cannot understand everything completely but things will become clear little by little. You are right, solitary practices are depraved and should be avoided so far as possible. Our daughters shall be raised in a healthy way and not sent away to school. You are quite right to tell me everything, love, and you may be sure that I pay no attention to your little adventure in the train. Yes, I should be delighted for you to be my teacher in matters of love, in things that you invent, that we both invent. I offer you the caress from my tongue that makes you swoon and after caressing you I lay my head on your

294

breast and rest. I love the way you get my meaning how marvellously you understand me my Madeleine whom I adore, come here and let me hold you in the deep embrace that makes you vibrate like a violin from Cremona.

Yes the peevish author of *Racine ignoré* (The Unknown Racine) was called Masson Forestier, I even wrote an article against him in *L'Intransigeant*; he died about two years ago. Yes, there is a marvellous poetry, and one very far removed from the conventional kind, in the exquisite love that is ours, I am pleased to learn that you want to be a pretty mama, and passionately happy that you have a broad pelvis and are not unpleasantly narrow in the hips like so many Parisian women who cannot abide love. As for you, I know you will respond superbly to my embrace and I adore you my lioness, my darling empress. I adore you. I take your teeth your tongue and all of you. I say, love of mine, sometimes in winter we shall make a big fire, burn incense and heat friar's balsam and with all the doors closed we shall love one another madly, you naked and I naked in the soft light you speak of, read poetry for relaxation and drink sweet liquors and eat fruit, it will be a grand feast at our court and not only shall we love each other divinely but we shall also converse in the most delightful way. I adore you and I take your mouth holding you wonderfully close against me and I place a kiss on the exquisite tuft of your fleece.

295

Gui

LE DEUXIÈME POÈME SECRET

La nuit la douce nuit est si calme ce soir que l'on n'entend que quelques rares éclatements
Je pense à toi ma panthère bien panthère oui puisque tu es pour moi tout ce qui est animé
Mais panthère que dis-je non tu es Pan lui-même sous son aspect femelle

GUILLAUME APOLLINAIRE

Tu es l'aspect femelle de l'univers vivant c'est dire que tu es toute la grâce toute la
beauté du monde

Tu es plus encore puisque tu es le monde même l'univers admirable selon la norme de
la grâce et de la beauté

Et plus encore mon amour puisque c'est de toi que le monde tient cette grâce et cette
beauté qui est de toi

Ô ma chère Déité, chère et farouche intelligence de l'univers qui m'est réservé comme
tu m'es réservée

Et ton âme a toutes les beautés de ton corps puisque c'est par ton corps que m'ont été
immédiatement accessibles les beautés de ton âme

Ton visage les a toutes résumées et j'imagine les autres une à une et toujours
nouvelles

Ainsi qu'elles me seront toujours nouvelles et toujours plus belles

Ta chevelure si noire soit-elle est la lumière même diffusée en rayons si éclatants que
mes yeux ne pouvant la soutenir la voient noire

296 *Grappes de raisins noirs colliers de scorpions éclos au soleil africain nœuds de*
couleuvres chéries

Onde, ô fontaines, ô chevelure, ô voile devant l'inconnaissable, ô cheveux

Qu'ai-je à faire autre chose que chanter aujourd'hui cette adorable végétation de
l'univers que tu es Madeleine

Qu'ai-je à faire autre chose que chanter tes forêts moi qui vis dans la forêt

Arc double des sourcils merveilleuse écriture, sourcils qui contenez tous les signes en
votre forme

Boulingrins d'un gazon où l'amour s'accroche ainsi qu'un clair de lune

Mes désirs en troupeaux interrogatifs parcourent pour les déchiffrer ces runes

Écriture végétale où je lis les sentences les plus belles de notre vie Madeleine

Et vous cils, roseaux qui vous mirez dans l'eau profonde et claire de ses regards

Roseaux discrets plus éloquents que les penseurs humains, ô cils, penseurs penchés
au-dessus des abîmes

Cils soldats immobiles qui veillez autour des entonnoirs précieux qu'il faut conquérir

Beaux cils antagonistes, antennes du plaisir, fléchettes de la volupté

Cils anges noirs qui adorez sans cesse la divinité qui se cache dans la retraite
mystérieuse de ta vue mon amour

Ô Touffes des aisselles troublantes plantes des serres chaudes de notre amour
  réciproque
Plantes de tous les parfums adorables que distille ton corps sacré
Stalactites des grottes ombreuses où mon imagination erre avec délices
Touffes, vous n'êtes plus l'ache qui donne le rire sardonique et fait mourir
Vous êtes l'ellébore qui affole vous êtes la vanille qui grimpe et dont le parfum est si
  tendre
Aisselles dont la mousse retient pour l'exhaler les plus doux parfums de tous les
  printemps
Et vous toison, agneau noir qu'on immolera au charmant dieu de notre amour
Toison insolente et si belle qui augmente divinement ta nudité comme à Geneviève de
  Brabant dans la forêt
Barbe rieuse du dieu frivole et si gracieusement viril qui est le dieu du grand plaisir
Ô toison triangle isocèle tu es la divinité même à trois côtés, touffue innombrable
  comme elle
          Ô jardin de l'adorable amour.
    Ô jardin sous-marin, d'algues de coraux et d'oursins et des désirs arborescents
        Oui, forêt des désirs qui grandit sans cesse des abîmes et plus que l'empyrée.

SECOND SECRET POEM

Night soft night is so quiet this evening that we hear but a very few
  explosions
I think of you my panther yes certainly panther for to me you are everything
  that is animate
But panther wait what am I saying no you are Pan himself under his female
  aspect
You are the female aspect of the living universe which is to say you are all the
  grace all the beauty of the world
You are even more than that for you are the world itself a universe magnificent by the measures of grace and beauty
And yet more my love for it is from you that the world obtains that grace
  and beauty which is yours
Oh my dear Deity, dear unflinching intelligence of a universe that is saved
  for me as you are saved for me

GUILLAUME APOLLINAIRE

And your soul possesses all the charms of your body because it is through
  your body that the charms of your soul have become directly accessible to
  me
Your face sums them all up and I imagine the others one by one and ever new
As they will always be new for me and always more beautiful
Your hair as dark as it may be is light itself, diffused in rays so brilliant that
  my eyes unable to bear it see it as black
Bunches of black grapes necklaces of scorpions born under the African sun
  nests of beloved snakes
Oh wave, oh fountains, oh curls, oh veil over the unknowable, oh hair
What else do I have to do today save sing the praises of the admirable plant-
  life of the universe that you are Madeleine
What else for me to do save sing of your forests I who live in the forest
Double bow of the eyebrows such a marvellous inscription, eyebrows
  containing every letter of your form
A greensward to which love attaches itself like moonlight
My desires in curious flocks scrutinize these runes in search of their meaning
Vegetal script wherein I read the most beautiful sentences of our life
  Madeleine
And you, eyelashes, reeds looking at their reflection in the deep clear waters
  of her gaze
Discreet reeds more eloquent than human thinkers, oh lashes, thinkers
  poised above abysses
Lashes motionless soldiers standing guard by precious caverns yet to be
  conquered
Beautiful antagonistic lashes, antennae of pleasure, darts of voluptuousness
Lashes dark angels continually worshipping the divinity hidden in the
  mysterious recesses of your eyes my love
Oh troubling underarm tufts of hair hothouse plants of our mutual love
Plants with all the delectable scents distilled by your sacred body
Stalactites of shady grottoes where my imagination wanders in delight
Oh tufts of hair, you are no longer the fool's parsley that brings on sardonic
  laughter and death

You are the hellebore that drives one mad you are the climbing vanilla
whose perfume is so delicate
Oh armpits whose moss retains and disperses the sweetest scents of every
springtime
And you oh fleece, black lamb that we shall sacrifice to the charming god of
our love
Fleece insolent and so beautiful, fleece that accentuates your nakedness as
divinely as hers did the nakedness of Genevieve of Brabant in her forest
Laughing beard of the frivolous god, so gracefully virile, who is the god of
the supreme pleasure
Oh fleece isosceles triangle you are divinity itself with your three sides and
your infinite denseness
Oh garden of adorable love.
Oh undersea garden, garden of seaweed of coral of sea urchins and of
arborescent desires
Yes, a forest of desires growing endlessly from the depths and
reaching higher even than the empyrean realm.

2 See p. 266.

LE TROISIÈME POÈME SECRET[2]

Toi dont je répandrai le sang grâce à l'amour ô ma vierge qui allumes la lampe
Ouïs le son profond des canons qui t'acclament et t'accueillent ma reine
Ouïs les cliquetis des épées qui t'appellent ô très belle victime

Toi dont je pénétrerai la chair jusqu'à l'écume ardente où la chair et l'âme se
convulsent ensemble
Ouïs le cri terrible de la tempête qui te secoue mon beau vaisseau
Toi dont la croupe libre se balance ainsi qu'un beau vaisseau sur la mer parfumée

Toi, temple dont je serai le prêtre ardent et dévot et farouchement unique
Entends monter le cri d'amour d'une armée qui soupire vers l'amour
D'une armée de fidèles qui n'adorent que le terrible et belliqueux dieu de l'amour

attols singuliers de la guerre

Coraux de tous les bonheurs

GUILLAUME APOLLINAIRE

Belles fleurs inécloses
des aveux de l'espoir
Ô mon tendre amour madeleine

un tremblement léger
mon haleine ton haleine ô Madeleine

Une goutte de pluie par pitié sur notre très cher Amour ô Madeleine

Toi dont la pensée me secoue comme Samson secouait le temple de Dagon
Toi dont les seins cupules adorables se tendent vers moi si loin que je passe sur eux
*   comme sur un pont de roses un pont double de neige au soleil pour venir jusqu'à*
*   toi*
Imagine les canons tendus terriblement comme mon désir vers l'ennemi.

Toi qui est si belle, ô beauté, que le monde est un socle pour ton apothéose
Envoie-moi tes seins comme des pigeons voyageurs pour me dire ton amour

Non, garde-les plutôt dans le doux colombier et dis-moi le roucoulement des deux
*   colombes aimées*

Ô figue mûre et secrète que je désire, dont j'ai faim je ne serai pas un sycophante
Écoute les mots les plus tendres, ô Madeleine, écoute mon oraison Madeleine
Écoute-moi tout près de toi malgré l'éloignement te dire que je t'aime

Ô Fée qui te transformes selon ma volonté en panthère ou en cavale
Toi qui es selon mon désir une divinité ou bien un ange
Toi qui es si je le veux la princesse vierge et lointaine ou la femme ardente ou la reine
*   cruelle*
Toi qui es aussi quand je désire ma sœur exquise ou l'adorable esclave
Toi qui es le lys, Madeleine aux beaux cheveux et toi qui es la rose
Toi qui es le geyser, toi qui es la sagesse toi qui es la folie ou l'espoir aux yeux graves
Toi qui es l'univers tout entier j'ai soif de tes métamorphoses

Gui aime Madeleine

je t'aime ma Madeleine
Je t'aime Gui.

THIRD SECRET POEM

You whose blood I shall spill for love oh my lamp-lighting virgin
Listen to the deep roar of the cannons hailing and welcoming you my queen
Listen to the clinking swords calling you oh most beautiful victim

You whose flesh I shall penetrate to the place where in foaming ardour flesh
    and soul convulse as one
Listen to the terrible cry of the storm that shakes you my fine vessel
You whose free haunches roll like a fine vessel on the perfumed sea

You, temple whose ardent zealous and singularly fierce priest I shall be
Listen to the mountain cry of love of an army sighing after love
Of an army of faithful who worship none but the terrible and warlike god of
    love

curious atolls of war

Corals of all joys

Beautiful unopened flowers
of confessions of hope
Oh my tender love Madeleine

a slight tremor
my breath your breath oh Madeleine

A drop of rain for mercy's sake upon our dear Love oh Madeleine

You the thought of whom shakes me as Samson shook the Temple of Dagan
You whose breasts adorable cupules strain so far towards me that I must
    pass over them as over a bridge of roses a double bridge of snow in the
    sunshine to reach you
Picture canons straining mightily, like my desire, towards the enemy

You who are so beautiful, oh beauty, that the world is a pedestal for your
    apotheosis
Send me your breasts like homing pigeons to tell me of your love

GUILLAUME APOLLINAIRE

No, keep them rather in the sweet dovecote and tell me how those two
    beloved doves bill and coo

Oh ripe and secret fig of my desire, for which I hunger, I shall not be a
    sycophant
Hear words most tender, oh Madeleine, hear my prayer Madeleine
Hear me very close beside you despite the distance between us telling you I
    love you

Oh Fairy who changes at my bidding into a panther or a mare
You who according to my desire are divinity or angel
You who if I wish it are a virginal and distant princess or a passionate
    woman or a cruel queen
You who are also if I like my exquisite sister or my darling slave
You who are the lily, Madeleine of the beautiful hair, and you who are the
    rose
You who are the geyser, you who are wisdom you who are madness or
    solemn-eyed hope
You who are the entire universe I am thirsty for your metamorphoses

Gui loves Madeleine

I love you my Madeleine
    I love you Gui.

My love I am sending you a butterfly's wing that I found today. Butterflies have beautiful names but I don't know them, beautiful mythological names. May the autumnal hues of this wing suggest to you the even more delicate shades of my love.

Today I read some bits and pieces of D'Annunzio. A decidedly bogus writer.

No letter today from Madeleine.

The weather is fine and cold.

My love, I beg you to be sure always to reply to my letters, and if need be to repeat my questions so that I can put your reply in context. Remember that your answer to a question of mine takes half a month to reach me, meaning that an extended exchange of ideas between us cannot consist of more than 24 statements in the course of a year, which should give you a sense of your obligations with respect to my questions. And please reply right away, in your very next letter, otherwise you are liable to forget the question.

I adore you my darling and I kiss your mouth. I also kiss your breasts, of which yesterday's photo gave me an enticing near-vision, and your hair which generated such disturbing associations in me, as witness the verses I quoted to you from Baudelaire's poem 'Les Promesses d'un visage'.

GUILLAUME APOLLINAIRE

Now that you are my infinitely dear fiancée, do you know I am very jealous of all the people who cherish adulate and pamper you. I am even jealous of those big girls in your class who must surely be a little bit in love with their adorable teacher.

FUSÉE

La boucle des cheveux noirs de ta nuque est mon trésor
Ma pensée te rejoint et la tienne la croise

* * *

Tes seins sont les seuls obus que j'aime

* * *

Ton souvenir est la lanterne de repérage qui nous sert à pointer la nuit

* * *

En voyant la large croupe de mon cheval j'ai pensé à tes hanches

* * *

Voici les fantassins qui s'en vont à l'arrière en lisant un journal

* * *

Des sœurs de la Croix-Rouge russe sablent le champagne dans un wagon restaurant

* * *

Le chien du brancardier revient avec une pipe dans sa gueule

* * *

La pudeur est le sachet antilueur entre nos amours Madeleine

* * *

Un chat-huant aile fauve, yeux jaunes, gueugueule de petit chat et pattes de chat

Le train entre Vera Cruz et Mexico les soldats qui forment l'escorte descendent de leurs
    wagons pour combattre en route puis le train se remet en marche

* * *

Une souris verte file parmi la mousse

* * *

Notre amour est un sous les étoiles

* * *

Je suis fier de ma virilité puisqu'elle se dresse en l'honneur de ta beauté et de notre
    bonheur

* * *

Le riz a brûlé dans la marmite de campement ça signifie qu'il faut prendre garde à
    bien des choses

305

* * *

Le mégaphone crie 'allongez le tir'

* * *

Allongez le tir, amour, de vos batteries

* * *

Allongez le tir bombardez la côte africaine
Où est celle que je veux voir mourir et remourir pour vivre plus encore

* * *

Mourir et remourir d'amour pour vivre plus d'amour encore

* * *

Un arbre dépouillé sur une butte

GUILLAUME APOLLINAIRE

* * *

Le bruit des tracteurs qui grimpent dans la vallée

* * *

Ô vieux monde du 19ᵉ siècle plein de hautes cheminées si belles et si pures

* * *

Virilités du siècle où nous sommes
Ô canons

* * *

Balance des batteries lourdes, cymbales de la folie

* * *

Folie de mort non plutôt folie d'amour folie d'amour et ce village qui s'appelle presque
l'amour, ce village où tu m'attends Madeleine que je baise sur la bouche

FLARE

The curl of black hair at the nape of your neck is my treasure
My thoughts go out to you and yours meet them half-way

* * *

Your breasts are the only bombshells I love

* * *

Memory of you is the searchlight that helps us aim at night

* * *

Catching sight of my horse's broad rump I thought of your haunches

* * *

There go some infantrymen reading a newspaper on the way to the rear

* * *

Sisters from the Russian Red Cross are sipping champagne in a dining-car

* * *

The stretcher-bearer's dog comes back with a pipe in its muzzle

* * *

Modesty is flash-damping powder to our loving Madeleine

* * *

A tawny owl, buff-winged, yellow-eyed, kitten's little face and cat's paws

* * *

On the train between Vera Cruz and Mexico City the soldiers of the escort
   leave their wagons along the way to fight then climb back in and the train
   sets off again

* * *

A green mouse scampers off through the moss

* * *

Our love is one beneath the stars

* * *

I am proud of my manhood standing upright in honour of your beauty and
   our happiness

* * *

The rice has burnt in the field cookpot which means we must be careful
   about a good many things

* * *

The megaphone bellows 'lengthen the range'

GUILLAUME APOLLINAIRE

* * *

Lengthen the range, love, of your guns

* * *

Lengthen the range bombard the African coast
Where she is whom I want to see die and die again so as to live yet again

* * *

Die and die again of love to experience yet more love

* * *

A stricken tree on a rise

* * *

The sound of tractors labouring up the valley

* * *

Oh old nineteenth-century world full of tall chimneys so beautiful and so
    pure

* * *

Manhoods of this century of ours
Oh cannons

* * *

Swinging of the heavy-gun batteries, cymbals of madness

* * *

Madness of death no rather madness of love madness of love and the
village whose name is almost love [Lamur], that village where you are
waiting for me Madeleine whom I kiss on the mouth

Gui

My love, I had 2 letters from you today (dated the 2nd and the 3rd). I am very happy with them, you sound more like Poppaea and Phèdre now. I love you so much like this. Especially out here, where your precious sensuality is a consolation to me, the sole remedy for all my troubles. Please do mark this well, my love. You said yourself that we should strengthen the secret between us, so do strengthen it, and fear for nothing. Be naked before me—as far away as I am. I have sent you plenty more parcels to keep you abreast of my life, being well aware that letters are subject to much delay. So reply right away to my questions when I ask or when you deduce any. Remember that to this letter for example I shan't have your reply before the 27th or the 28th. Do not mention leave again for the time being. They have cancelled all leave in the forward zone all along the Front. Those on leave at present are therefore either from the depots or from the rear of the zone of operations. The infantry sometimes goes to the rear for rest periods, but we do not. Our group has never yet been sent back for rest. It is assumed that we have enough free time (and hence rest) where we are. Your meaningful look in Marseilles is admirably clear to me in memory, charged with all the voluptuousness that is part of you. You are very beautiful. I kiss your mouth through your hat veil, tearing it like a Veil of Isis and grasping the whole of that little traveller who is now my own beloved little wife and clasping her madly to me. Ah yes my love we shall know perfectly how to tell each other of our love and how to say it with our lips as with our eyes.

GUILLAUME APOLLINAIRE

It was charming, exquisite of you to tell me what you did after leaving me on the station platform at Marseilles and also the whole story of the amorous struggle that has been taking place within you since then. I love you. So we loved each other at very first sight. That is marvellous. I adore you.

My darling, I love this dear love story of ours and I take your whole mouth and kiss it, and then your breasts, so sensitive, whose tips harden at my kiss and strain towards me like your desire itself. I wrap my arms about you and hold you tight forever against my heart.

This is the moment when the epeirids, cruciferous spiders, strew their gossamer all around. Looking at these white threads that the breeze tosses about and causes to shimmer in the light makes me think of you oh my adorable lily.

You are right not to mention the war, it is so long and talking about it is so pointless.

The communiqués, moreover, are quite accurate. I can confirm this on the basis of our own sectors. For the day is past when the soldier knew nothing of the battle—an idea promoted by Stendhal, so often wrong-headed—in this war at any rate we get to know everything in due course. Perhaps because we are waging a war of position, we hear of all that transpires, be it at *Trapèze, Main, Tahure, Mamelles*, or *the tree at Hill 193*—and we do so minute by minute so to speak via the wounded, via engineer comrades, via telephonists, even via our officers. So you may rely on the communiqués, which are candid and very very well done! I confess I was sceptical about them until I had the chance to check their scrupulous accuracy for myself. Note that they are post-dated and the events they report have happened on the day before the date they bear.

Great confidence reigns here on account of the recent events. It is a shame that developments in the Balkans have cast something of a pall over that mood. I am writing this on the evening of the 10th perhaps I shall finish my letter tomorrow, we bombard for a good part of the night.

Today we were treated to the splendid sight of a homeward-bound squadron of 28 bombers intercepted by our fighter planes. The clash took place very very high up, albeit not as high as our love, and the sky was speckled with thousands of white puffs of smoke from the explosions. A spectacle at once agonizing and fascinating. Such a new kind of refinement! In the distance along the two fronts the vile priapic sausage-balloons maintained their defiantly immobile watch like maggots hatched in a rotting field of blue. Sausages! Is it perhaps these grubs that give birth to such graceful butterflies, the aeroplanes?

I wonder why no one has thought to enhance the terminology of aviation, as yet so unsettled, by paying verbal homage to Icarus. Words could so easily be derived from his name. That indisputable forerunner of our aviators deserves no less and the same goes for Elijah and Elisha not to mention Simon Magus!

As for you I adore you, I take you naked as a pearl and devour you with kisses all over from your feet to your head so swoon from love, my darling love, I eat your mouth and your fine breasts which belong to me and which swollen with voluptuousness thrill with endless delight.

LE PALAIS DU TONNERRE[1]

Par l'issue ouverte sur le boyau dans la craie
En regardant la paroi adverse qui semble en nougat
On voit à gauche et à droite fuir l'humide couloir désert
Où meurt étendue une pelle à la face effrayante à deux yeux réglementaires

1 Written upside down on the back of the illustrated cover of Tolstoy's *Resurrection* in a popular adaptation by Romain Slawsky from the 'Grande Collection Nationale' series (Paris: F. Rouff, n.d.).

GUILLAUME APOLLINAIRE

Qui servent à l'attacher sous les caissons

Un rat s'y avance en hâte et se recule en hâte

Et le boyau s'en va couronné de craie semée de branches

Comme un fantôme creux qui met du vide où il passe blanchâtre

Et là-haut le toit est bleu et couvre bien le regard fermé par quelques lignes droites

Mais en deçà de l'issue c'est le palais bien nouveau et qui paraît ancien

Le plafond est fait de traverses de chemin de fer

Entre lesquelles il y a des morceaux de craie et des touffes d'aiguilles de sapin

Et de temps en temps des morceaux de craie tombent comme des morceaux de vieillesse

À côté de l'issue que ferme un tissu lâche qui sert généralement aux emballages

Il y a un trou qui sert d'âtre et ce qui y brûle est un feu semblable à l'âme

Tant il tourbillonne et tant il est vrai inséparable de ce qu'il dévore et fugitif

Les fils de fer se tendent partout servant de sommiers supportant des planches

Ils forment aussi des crochets et l'on y suspend mille choses

Comme on fait à la mémoire

Des musettes bleues des casques bleus des cravates bleues des vareuses bleues

Morceaux de ciel tissus des souvenirs les plus purs

Et il stagne parfois de vagues nuages de craie

Sur la planche des fusées détonateurs joyaux dorés à tête émaillée

Noirs blancs rouges

Funambules qui attendent leur tour de monter sur les fils de fer

Qui font un ornement mince et élégant à cette demeure souterraine

Ornée de six lits placés en fer à cheval

Six lits couverts de riches manteaux bleus

Sur le palais il y a un haut tumulus de craie

Et des plaques de tôle ondulée qui sont le fleuve figé de ce domaine idéal

Sans eau car ici il ne coule que le feu jailli de la mélinite

Le parc aux fleurs de fulminate jaillit des troncs penchés

Tas de cloches au doux son des douilles rutilantes

Sapins élégants et petits comme en un paysage japonais

Le palais s'éclaire parfois d'une bougie petite comme une souris

Ô palais minuscule comme si on te regardait par le gros bout d'une lunette

Petit palais où tout s'assourdit

Petit palais où tout est neuf, rien rien d'ancien

Et où tout est précieux où tout le monde est vêtu comme un roi

Ma selle est dans un coin à cheval sur une caisse

Un journal du jour traîne par terre

Et tout y paraît vieux cependant

Si bien qu'on comprend que l'amour de l'antique

Le goût de l'anticaille

Soit venu aux hommes dès le temps des cavernes

Tout y était si précieux et si neuf

Tout y est si précieux et si neuf

Qu'une chose plus ancienne ou qui a déjà servi apparaît

        Plus précieuse

Que ce qu'on a sous la main

Dans un palais souterrain creusé dans la craie si blanche et si neuve

Et deux marches neuves elles n'ont pas deux semaines

Sont si vieilles dans ce palais qui semble antique sans imiter l'antique

Qu'on voit que ce qu'il y a de plus simple de plus neuf est ce qui est

        Le plus près de ce que l'on appelle la beauté antique

Et ce qui est surchargé d'ornements

Ce qui a des ornements qui ne sont pas nécessaires

A besoin de vieillir pour avoir la beauté qu'on appelle antique

Et qui est la noblesse la force, l'ardeur, l'âme, l'usure

De ce qui est neuf et qui sert

Surtout si cela est simple simple

Aussi simple que le petit palais du tonnerre

THUNDER PALACE

Through the exit opening into the trench cut through the chalk
You see the wall opposite which looks like nougat
And to left and right the damp deserted bare corridor fleeing into the distance
A shovel lies like a dead man with a horrifying face and the two regulation eyes
That are used to hang it under the caissons
A rat scurries along then turns and scurries back

GUILLAUME APOLLINAIRE

And the trench goes on its way topped by chalk interspersed with branches
Like a hollow ghost leaving emptiness in its pale wake
And way above the roof is blue a fine canopy to a view bounded by a few
    straight lines
But here on this side of the exit is the palace, very new but seeming old
Our ceiling is made of railway sleepers
Between them lumps of chalk and tufts of pine needles
And now and then bits of chalk fall like fragments of old age
By the exit screened by a piece of rough packing cloth
Is a hole that does for a fireplace and what burns there is a fire reminiscent
    of the human soul
So turbulent so truly inseparable from what it devours and so fleeting
Wires are stretched everywhere supporting planks
And also forming hooks for hanging up a multitude of things
Just as we hang things in our memory
Blue haversacks blue helmets blue ties blue tunics
Pieces of sky woven from the purest of recollections
And sometimes vague clouds of chalk hang in the air
On a plank are detonator fuses golden jewels with their enamelled heads
Black white red
Tightrope artists waiting their turn to go up on the wire
They make slim and elegant ornaments for this underground dwelling
Furnished with six beds in a horseshoe pattern
Six beds covered with fine blue coats
Surmounting the palace is a high mound of chalk
And sheets of corrugated iron are the frozen river of this ideal domain
Without water because all that flows here is the spurting fire of melinite
A park full of flowers of fulminate springs from listing trunks
A pile of sweet-sounding bells gleaming shell cases
Elegant little pines as in a Japanese landscape
The palace is lit at times by a candle small as a mouse
Oh palace so tiny as if seen through the wrong end of a glass
Little palace where everything is muffled

314

Little palace where everything is new, nothing nothing old
And where everything is precious everyone dressed like a king
My saddle is in a corner astride a crate
The day's paper trails on the floor
And yet everything seems old here
So much so that one can see how the love of the old
The taste for the antiquated
Must have arisen when men still lived in caves
Everything there was so precious and so new
Everything here is so precious and so new
That anything older or anything that has already seen use might seem
                    More precious
Than what one has to hand
Yet in this underground palace dug out from the chalk so white and so new
Where two new steps not even two weeks old
Are so old in this palace that seems antique without imitating the antique
You see why what is simplest and newest is what is
                    Nearest to what is called antique beauty
And why what is weighed down with ornaments
What has ornaments that are not necessary
Has to get old in order to attain the beauty which is described as antique
And which is the nobility, strength, ardour, spirit and wear and tear
Of what is new yet used
Especially if it is simple simple
As simple as this little palace of thunder

GUILLAUME APOLLINAIRE

13 October 1915

My love, I have been reading your adorable letter of the 5th over
and over all day long. I want my panther to be entirely tamed by me
and abandon all rebellious feelings. I have in my hand the beloved
riding-crop with its power to settle the outcome of the struggle and
the wild bucking of your trembling rump cannot but further excite my
wish to tame you. But your wild and shameless passion eventually
drives me to distraction too and before I know it drunk with voluptuous feelings I am in your arms, oh my slave so wedded to her
enslavement, and my panther has now admirably tamed her tamer
who clings in desperate delight to her marvellous supple flanks.

Your thoughts on the art of Renoir are perhaps even more pertinent
than I realized yesterday and it is quite possible that Renoir's
anthropomorphism demands that his art be perfect according to
the human norm which is its point of reference. And how right you
are to compare yourself without hesitation to these drawings, even
though you are beyond compare.

Re-reading you, I also loved the fluid voluptuousness that you distil
for me. How wise you are my Madeleine, you even grasp the subtlety
that will assuredly be the great issue of this twentieth century in
which we find ourselves, and do we not compose our very own
subtlety exquisitely and delicately in our letters or rather by means
of our letters, we whose subtlety combines so exquisitely and
delicately, ah such subtle loves. Yes indeed, our love is well able to

make us tremble gently. Wrenching your guts is not my intent my love. On the contrary I want to arouse your flesh exquisitely and powerfully, and at present I want that flesh to be moved, to be agitated without pain but with extraordinary voluptuousness. For I love your virginal voluptuousness. A voluptuousness which affects me so miraculously when I think of it. A kind of lovely fairy magic between us. An adorable magic in which your voluptuousness billows forth ever more voluptuously as the lily turns into the beautiful rose. Each of your letters gives me the greatest pleasure of my life. The simple and so delicate refinement of the joys you vouchsafe me is astounding. Those joys are like pure mountains of eternal snow in the sun and my mouth fresh from the chill and the so sublime ardour of the heights strays delightfully towards the secret depths of that temple whose forecourt I am going to bloody. Depths whose exquisite voluptuousness and exquisite purity I adore. I defy Venus herself, as pure as she is, to match those qualities. Come, come, you know perfectly well that I am your fool. I am your fool utterly, and you are my fool likewise, my ardent, so ardent Madeleine. I eat you, I have told you where, my love, and have you not yourself written oh my sweet seashell: 'Gui, eat me!' Yes I do eat you and did you not yourself send me—what an exquisite token of love—the magnifying glass with which to undress you, and look how faithfully I follow your lead, my beloved guide. You are my panther and I am your poodle. Yet the panther in this case is the poodle's slave and such insanity can only hint at the delightful madness that possesses us both, for we are hopelessly in love with each other.

We shall keep gazing into each other's eyes, shall we not my love, even in the ultimate spasm of pleasure, and our mouths too will be so greedy that my soul will penetrate your body, so exquisite within, down to the marrow of your bones, and your soul will for its part penetrate my body down to the very fibre of my vigour.

GUILLAUME APOLLINAIRE

And how well you have understood that our love belongs to us two alone and that we may love each other just as we wish, which is to say to the skies. No letter from you today, just two cards passed by the censors from the Futurist Marinetti—who is a cyclist in the Italian Army. Yesterday I received a letter from Italy also opened by the censor from a friend who sends me the *Corriere della Sera*, a very good paper. You ask would I like you to be here by my side. My love I would adore it but it would be impossible because we should never be alone. I love you, you know it, I can just imagine you dressed as a gunner in a horizon-blue tunic and a helmet, how charming you would be, but your shape would disturb the men far too much. I adore you, I take your mouth and adore you even more, my very much adored Madeleine. I adore your tongue and I take it, my love.

Gui

4 H.[1]

C'est 4 h. du matin

Je me lève tout habillé

Je tiens une savonette ~~à la main~~

Que m'a envoyée quelqu'un que j'aime

Je vais me laver

Je sors du trou où nous dormons

Je suis dispos

Et content de pouvoir me laver ce qui n'est pas arrivé depuis trois jours

Puis lavé je vais me faire raser

Ensuite bleu de ciel je me confonds avec l'horizon jusqu'à la nuit et c'est un plaisir très doux

De ne rien dire de plus, tout ce que je fais c'est un être invisible qui le fait

Puisqu'une fois boutonné tout bleu confondu dans le ciel je deviens invisible

1 These four poems are written on the back of a list, cut from a book, of volumes in the series 'La Grande Collection Nationale'.

4 A.M.

It is 4 in the morning

I get up fully dressed

I am holding a bar of soap ~~in my hand~~

Sent to me by someone I love

I am going to get washed

I come out of the hole where we sleep

I am ready

And happy to be able to wash myself something that has not happened for
    three days

Once washed I'll shave

Afterwards in sky-blue I'll be one with the horizon till night and it's a very
    sweet pleasure

To say no more, everything I do is done by an invisible being

For once buttoned up all in blue indistinguishable from the sky
    I become invisible

PHOTOGRAPHIE

Ton sourire m'attire comme pourrait m'attirer une fleur

Photographie tu es le champignon brun de la forêt qu'est sa beauté

Les blancs y sont un clair de lune dans un jardin pacifique

Plein d'eau vive et de jardiniers endiablés

Photographie tu es la fumée de l'ardeur qu'est sa beauté

Et il y a en toi Photographie des tons alanguis

On y entend une mélopée

Photographie tu es l'ombre du soleil qu'est sa beauté

PHOTOGRAPH

Your smile attracts me as might a flower

Photograph you are a brown mushroom from the forest of her beauty

Your patches of white are moonlight in a peaceful garden

Full of plashing water and bustling gardeners

GUILLAUME APOLLINAIRE

Photograph you are the smoke from the fire of her beauty

And Photograph you have languid tones

Chanting can be heard

Photograph you are the shadow of the sun of her beauty

PEU DE CHOSE

Combien qu'on a pu en tuer?

Ma foi!

C'est drôle que ça ne vous fasse rien

Ma foi!

Une tablette de chocolat aux Boches?

Ma foi! Feu!

Un camembert pour le logis aux Boches

Ma foi! Feu!

Chaque fois que tu dis feu le mot se change en acier qui éclate là-bas?

Ma foi!

Abritez-vous

Ma foi

Kra

Ils répondent les salauds

Drôle de langage ma foi

NOTHING MUCH

How many might we have killed?

Oh my!

Strange it doesn't affect you at all

Oh my!

A bar of chocolate for the Boches?

Oh my! Fire!

A camembert for the Boche household!

Oh my! Fire!

Every time you say fire does the word change into bursts of steel over there?

Oh my!

Take cover

Oh my!

Crack!

They're replying the bastards

Strange language oh my

POUR MADELEINE SEULE

Lune candide vous brillez moins que les hanches

  De mon amour

Aubes que j'admire vous êtes moins blanches

  Aubes que chaque jour

J'admire ô hanches si blanches

Il y a le reflet de votre blancheur

Au fond de cet aluminium

Dont on fait des bagues

Dans cette zone où règne la blancheur

  Ô hanches si blanches

FOR MADELEINE ALONE

Clear moon you shine less brightly than the hips

  Of my love

Dawns I admire you are not so white

  Dawns I admire every day

Oh hips so white

There is a touch of your whiteness

Deep in the aluminium

We make rings from

In this zone where whiteness reigns

  Oh hips so white

GUILLAUME APOLLINAIRE

14 October 1915

My love, rose petals, oh my Poppaea, my beautiful languorous one, I adore your letter so full of the sensibility of this moment. I love everything that comes from you my love. I thought it very amusing that *Alcools* was on sale in Oran. I am exactly in the area where you think I am, in other words not much change. Your story of the frightened lady passengers made me laugh heartily, and as for you my love how kind and noble you were.

I do not much care for what is happening in the Balkans. Take precautions, don't say anything but do take them, you never know.— Ah yes, a desert is where I should like to be with you. If only we were rich and no longer needed to see anyone but each other. An exquisite oasis. Your letter of yesterday was adorable, oh my spirited, my proud slave. I found your Neronian memories delicious, what a perfect tale for the two of us and how good you are at discerning and depicting fools. You are perfect. I believe it was German scholars notably Mommsen and Italian ones who revised Roman history on the basis of epigraphical and no doubt other documentary evidence. I say this tentatively however because I have not studied the question much and the episodic Nero in my 'Simon Magus' plays but a small part in that story of divinity and angels. Meanwhile the most delightful fact I disentangled from what you wrote was that you were saving yourself for me oh my virgin pledged from the very beginning, oh my love! Whenever one does not share their herdish opinions or tries to make a sincere contribution, fools reckon that *épater le bourgeois* is one's motive, as you put it, my adorable and adored love. How much I also adore your birth date of 14 November 1892. I was in 5th then, just beginning Greek, we had a teacher named Becker he was very thin, we called him Meletta I don't know why or sometimes Catherine. We played so many dirty tricks on him that he was forced to leave. But it was he who pushed me towards literature and it was in that very year and around that time that (unrelated to Becker) I wrote my first lines of poetry, which by the way were certainly of no interest. In May '92, during the previous school year, I had made my First Communion. I fancy it was your birth that awoke me to poetry, my muse had just been born and she was my Madeleine. No, you had not told me that you were born at La Roche-sur-Yon; as for me I was born in Rome, Italy. You are slightly shorter than me, who am 1.72m tall—You did well to give the oval ring to Pierre—I am waiting for your Mama's measurement.

I confess I never thought my kepi would give you such pleasure. I had sent it you knowing that you would be happy to mind this travelling companion which was mine and for which I felt some affection, but which was something of a nuisance once we started wearing helmets. It was never brushed after the first day and chalk dust built up on the visor.

I should also have liked the photo of you in the white hat. Everything that is yours gives me such pleasure. Because I love you—I am mad for you, my Madeleine. Everything from you affects me so deliciously, so sweetly. Your being out of sorts makes me think today of the dark circles under your eyes and your rather pale look, my darling wife.

And I adore you like that too, my darling, my wife, so pretty, so frail.

I take you as you want me to, with all my might. I wish you were beside me and I could feel your mouth biting me and the exquisite caress of your tongue on mine. I love your wildest embrace and the satin heat of your adorable body when you surrender it to my touch.

GUILLAUME APOLLINAIRE

I want to admit something to you today, Madeleine, for I see it clearly now: I never loved before loving you, I have never loved anyone but you. You are, in fact, my first love. But what am I saying! forgive me, you are my one and only love, you are love itself.

And today in my imagination I compared you to a piece of music, a piece dominated by the woodwinds and by human voices. The music had all the inflexions of your beauty, the infinitely subtle sweep of your intelligence and the plain measureless strength of your love. I read today of the death of the entomologist Fabre whose books I loved so very much because his study of insects taught me to understand human beings, whom if only I had the leisure I should like to study as a novelist in a way just as meticulous and precise, just as free of all moral considerations. Moreover there was a cheerfulness and good humour in the works of the scholarly Fabre that pleased me enormously. But sometimes I liked changing the names of the insects Fabre described in his work into the names of men and women, creating a horrible and as it were too realistic view of humanity, after the fashion of the Marquis de Sade (the closest parallel I can think of for the pages I altered), or perhaps after the fashion of Suetonius, for while it is possible to see the history of the Roman emperors in another light, Suetonius's work must surely be true too. For man is man and everything is in man that is in nature. I firmly believe that man is a microcosm, and after all is not every particle of the universe to the unfathomable extremities of the ether also a microcosm? My love, my darling, I think of you endlessly. I adore you.

SIMULTANÉITÉS

Les canons tonnent dans la nuit
On dirait des vagues, tempête
Des cœurs où pointe un grand ennui
Ennui qui toujours se répète

Il regarde venir là-bas
Des prisonniers. L'heure est si douce
Dans ce grand bruit ouaté, très bas
Très bas qui grandit sans secousse

Il tient son casque dans ses mains
Pour saluer la souvenance
Des lys des roses des jasmins
Éclos dans les jardins de France

Et sous la cagoule masqué
Il pense à des cheveux si sombres
Et qui donc l'attend sur le quai
Ô vaste mer aux mauves ombres

Belles noix du vivant noyer
La grand folie en vain vous gaule
Brunette, écoute gazouiller
La mésange sur ton épaule

Notre amour est une lueur
Qu'un projecteur du cœur dirige
Vers l'ardeur égale du cœur
Qui sur le haut phare s'érige

Ô phare-fleur mes souvenirs
Aux cheveux noirs de Madeleine
Les atroces lueurs des tirs
Ajoutent leur clarté soudaine
À tes beaux yeux ô Madeleine

SIMULTANEITIES

Cannon thunder in the night
Sounding like waves, a storm
Or hearts assailed by great apprehensions
Apprehensions that always return

GUILLAUME APOLLINAIRE

He watches prisoners coming up
Not far off. The moment is so sweet
Despite that great muffled sound, very low
Very low, causing no tremor but growing

He holds his helmet in his hands
Attending to remembrances
Of lilies roses and jasmine
In bloom in the gardens of France

And masked by his smoke-helmet
He thinks of hair so dark
And the one who waits for him at the dock
Oh immense sea of lilac shadows

Fine walnuts from a living tree
Folly thrashes you in vain
Brown-haired beauty, listen to the titmouse
Twittering on your shoulder

Our love is a beam
That the searchlight of one heart trains
On the like flame of another
High atop a beacon

Oh flower-beacon of my memories
To Madeleine's black hair
The ghastly flashes of the gunfire
Add their sudden clarity
To your lovely eyes oh Madeleine

I take you mouth, Madelon that I adore.

Gui

My precious love, my great darling, I do not want you to tell me that
you are stupid. You are the most enchanting child imaginable, you
are my love. You are my Madeleine, my Virgin, my Phèdre, my
Poppaea, my Hermione, my jasmine, my lily, my rose and my everything. Yes indeed, come now, you truly are my everything, my love.
I adore you. I received your letter of the 7th and I don't need to tell
you how it delights me. I am happy—I am immensely happy that
you have now cheered up my love. This is the perfect smile-letter,
kiss-letter, Madeleine-letter. I take your lips. You are intellectually
superior in every way, my love, and I cannot abide the idea that you
should find it burdensome to be an intelligent woman. Your intelligence is something that has bound us one to the other. Believe me,
I adore your intelligence, my pretty one, my great darling.

I am no longer sad in the slightest, because you love me because you
understand me all of me. The caress of your whole body that I so
adore sets me deliciously on fire. You know now just how much I
love the photo of you taken in Narbonne, so expressive, so mischie-
vous, so winsome, and the one from two years ago, so pretty also: I
am waiting for the next one. How pleased I am by your vow not to
be anxious from now on, and to understand that I-and-you is us,
that we is me, is you, that each of our feelings belongs to the one
and to the other, and that your modesty with me should be grace,
the grace I need and cannot have save through you, that your

GUILLAUME APOLLINAIRE

modesty with me should be even more unfettered than what is usually considered immodesty, that it should surpass all that and be a marvellous and ever-renewed liberty.

I do not want you to imagine that there might be any grounds for jealousy between us, for my part I do not imagine any such thing even though I am by nature inclined to be jealous. For considering your intelligence your awareness your nature, and the freedom of your voluntary giving of yourself, I cannot imagine it. Within freedom there is duty and I cannot be jealous over Madeleine. We are too special for any such thing to be possible. For me it is just the same—we are made for each other. Good sense ought always to remind us of this and protect us. Were you to become ugly in the eyes of everyone else in the world nothing would change. For what I love is you and everything else is extra: had you been ugly I should have loved you just the same, for I loved you the moment you appeared, the very first moment—and without having so much as looked at you closely, because I did not dare do so and because you were hiding yourself. Your beauty is my reward but my love is independent of it, which is why you need not worry about it on my account. In our case beauty is not, as with so many couples—paltry unions founded on the flesh alone—the main foundation of the husband's love. But you may freely bestow your beauty upon me, for we are rich in love. And in this connection be subtle, and think how much I adore that beauty, but remember that this is logically inevitable, for whatever your physical form I would find you more beautiful than anything. So if you happen to be beautiful for everyone else so much the better for them. What I want therefore is that your beauty which I have created by my choice of you by my liking for you, that you have created by your love for me, should belong to me as it belongs to you. What I mean is that you should steer me to your beauty as far away as I am, and now *I want your beauty-letter* just as I had your *smile-letter* before, and I beg you oh my beloved to sing me a song as beautiful as the Song of Songs. Let your reservations melt away so that you may bestow on me all the magnificent beauty that is for us the absolute. For you must love your beauty as I myself love it Madeleine. But I forgive you your scruples and your jealousy. Nothing but you exists for me. Let me assure you—though fear of exciting that jealousy once more gives me pause—how all the past, all the carnality of earlier days has filled me with disgust since I began to worship you, all of it is putrid, horribly foul alongside your adorably triumphant body, so exquisite in its virginity and so marvellously passionate. You are my arch-divinity my Madeleine, my ardent virgin the mere thought of whom is more voluptuous than all the voluptuousness in the universe. Nothing in the world is worth a single spasm of your body, the sensuous tension of one of your breasts is more significant than any masterpiece, and the divine spreading of your thighs is a weightier event than the foundation of any great empire. I want my slave to be aware of her own glorious-ness and never to surrender to any jealous impulse of the sort so pointless between us since between us eternal love alone reigns. I take you in my arms and may you never be jealous again. May you weep, oh my smile, solely from sensual longing for me.

Let it be understood that you shall never again deprive me of your sweet abandon, oh my secret. You tell me to question you, to ask you what you have not yet told me about your body; but my darling you have told me nothing about it, or only the vaguest things, I can barely imagine it, or rather if I know anything of your body I have divined it by means of my imagination, but still know nothing precise save that you are beautiful, for everything that you have told me is prerequisite to the bodily beauty of any woman, while as for

GUILLAUME APOLLINAIRE

details that make Madeleine Madeleine I possess none save for those of your face and those whose outlines your clothing reveals. Moreover I ask nothing that might embarrass you—Indeed I ask you nothing—It is up to you to decide what to reveal in order to enhance our intimacy. But do bear in mind that the more open you are with me the more you will become one with me, and the more completely we shall become one and the same by virtue of our love. Remember too that there is no empty lust in me and that you are free in this matter and that if you are free it is because I grant you that freedom and because if lust were part of it I should oblige you as my slave to do this that or the other thing. Remember that I involve myself but slightly, thus ensuring that whatever part of your modesty is real is not offended and bowing to the fact that you are our guide along the conjugal path oh my Beatrice of love. And remember that if I ask you to perfect our intimacy carnally and materially you will be employing only words and words can hardly upset you for they leave your nakedness inviolate even from me, oh my nightingale whose chatter alone reveals what is visible to none. All the same, the intimacy between us that I wish to intensify continually is indeed carnal, as completely intellectual as it may be also, and that cannot be overstated which is why I have insisted so much upon it. But words no matter how precise can never provide a true image of Madeleine, which can be vouchsafed me only once we are side by side. Those words can be but a pale reflection of you which cannot affront a modesty that they themselves serve to protect.

Your freedom is whole and entire. Yet just think how little words amount to and you have still told me nothing or almost nothing while believing that you have told me so much. But never mind, I adore you. You are a marvel to me. I am perfectly well aware, you know, my darling, that your rebelliousness is a form of love. That is why I love it, and love to tame it, and make it mine, I adore you. Since you have something for the 1st inkwell, there is no need to have anything more done to it.

Today I am sending you the wing of a screech-owl, truly a bird for this war of the night. If you have no use for it, throw it away, but perhaps you could put it on a hat. I send it merely for your amusement and to show you that I am still thinking of you. Save the pieces of the *Bulletin des Armées* that I use to wrap up the things I send—I made the ring for Denise in three hours and posted it, it is another kind of four-leaved clover, she will have to polish it herself for I did not have the time to shine it up properly and had no polish left.

My Venus, be Venus herself proud of her beauty, be Greek for the sake of pride in your beauty, for my sake, deepen our secret and describe all your inclinations towards me and the reactions they provoke. I take your lips.

Gui

GUILLAUME APOLLINAIRE

My love, today I got your note of the 5th and your 2 letters of the
8th. I must say it is surprising that letters and parcels continue to get
here during the present business.

How I adore that very long look of yours from between your lashes. I
love you, I love your little shivers. I take your mouth, my love.

I am happy that you enjoyed my letter of the 1ˢᵗ, my love. But I am
quite sure, dear love, that my very own rose shall never cause our
love to fade. For this great love of ours is a spring that never tarries.
I am dying to see your latest photograph.

For the moment there is no way for us to have photographs taken.
All cameras have been taken away and things will stay like that so
long as we remain on alert.

How I love the fragrance of your heart. Why yes my love we shall
keep our eyes open during love and the gaze of the one will be lost
deep in the gaze of the other.

My love, no matter how your hair is done you will always be beautiful and you will always attract me. My love, I am taking good care
of your husband. I love you so much and how much I love your
rapture. In your second letter of the 8th I find a sentence very similar to something I wrote to you yesterday: 'Our love is absolutely the
only thing that matters in the whole world.' The rest of your letter

was dated the 9th. Tell me in detail everything you feel, so that I may direct and if need be correct our love (correct in the sense of steer). So you had an irritating day, my dear love, at your lycée. What do you teach? Do you have many pupils?

I am impatient for your long letter of Sunday which is going to express so much love. Why do you want to control your love? Tell me all, write it quite simply, as you know so well how to do my love.

What you say about my verse is very charming. You understand it perfectly. I adore you. You express yourself very well and I am sure that you speak my lines just as I would, with the right melody and my own cadences. For my rhythm is your rhythm.

I think in the most delightful way of your breasts rising and swelling out of love for me.

And our ideas always coincide, because yesterday I asked you for the song of songs of your beauty and today you promise me the poem of your body.

You say in your letter of yesterday that you feel you have told me everything, but consider how little I really know.

I know your waist measurement, which tells me a good deal about your whole frame. You have told me that your waist is uncorseted, that your hips are broad, and described the shape of your breasts.

But none of this really lets me picture the beauty of your form.

I do know your face and hair.

But I do not know the colour of your body, whether your veins are visible, or the shade of your dear nipples. I do not know whether everything else is as black as the hair of your head. I do not know the shape of your midriff or that of your posterior, whether it is very

GUILLAUME APOLLINAIRE

prominent or simply follows the line of your back. There are a thousand ways of being beautiful, after all. I am acquainted neither with your feet, nor with your legs, nor with your arms. I like your telling me many things about you because it is a way for you to come closer to me. Speak to me of you, be proud of your beauty. Speak to me of you however you wish but do speak to me of you body and soul.

How far down does your beautiful hair fall?

My love, I clasp you to me desperately tight. I adore you, I love you, I kiss your mouth endlessly, for ever so long, your tongue in my mouth. I love you. I adore you.

Gui

My love, no letter from you today! What I did get today was a letter from Willy (Henri Gauthier-Villars). He is a slight author, but a very talented one. His value is in a sense greater than that of his work, some of which by the way is not his own. The former husband of Colette and the originator of the *Claudine* series, he has a great wit. He went to Dusseldorf on a Dutch passport to attend the première of Ernst's tragedy *Ariane*. What nerve! He could so easily have been caught. And he is toying with the idea of going to Munich. The fact that a writer like Willy, well known and close to the public, finds it so hard to survive, makes me very anxious about the future of literature and writers after the war. I even wonder whether I might not give literature up for a time and go into business or some other line. Alright, alright I am just thinking, that's all . . . You might give it some thought too my dearest darling little wife. And bear in mind that Willy is well connected and is already I think fifty-five years old!?—But what does all this matter alongside the fact that you love me! My dear love, my very beautiful Madeleine. This evening we had tear gas. It went on until just now as I write, it must have been two hours. This time it smelt of chlorine, as though we had been doing laundry. It was fine today between 1 and 3 o'clock. I sunbathed— naked, except for my underwear—near the battery in a pretty little wood scorched by shell bursts. I thought of you as the sun caressed me—I am sending you Willy's letter, which will entertain you—

GUILLAUME APOLLINAIRE

In our woods of small pine the most abundant plants are burnet, with its taste of cucumber, and warty spurge, which is a bluish tuft with its wart either brown or yellowish or pink and when it is pink it puts me in mind, and this is very delicate my love, of the very seat of your voluptuous feelings, which must resemble the reddish bud of this curious plant. There are also penny buns and other excellent mushrooms. As for trees, there are only the little pines and not a single shrub.

My friend the searchlight sapper, in civilian life secretary to the French Legation in Peking, came to see me again and told me all kinds of amusing things, especially about Chinese women, who are apparently very pretty, circle their eyes with rouge and have large buttocks but little or nothing by way of a bust, a prominent bust being poorly regarded in China. It seems they are amusing and witty. As for Japanese women, he described them to me as overrated and in his experience mediocre lovers.

But enough of such nonsense, my love, I fancy you took the right boat by returning to Oran.

I love you my darling, I take your mouth, I am thinking of you, I adore you.

I am hoping for a letter from you tomorrow.

> *J'espère une lettre de toi*
> *Tes lettres amour sont les roses*
> *De l'absence et de notre foi,*
> *Épine et parfum de tes proses!*
>
> *Un oiseau chante ne sais où*
> *C'est je crois ton âme qui veille*
> *Parmi tous les soldats d'un sou*
> *Et l'oiseau charme mon oreille*

Tandis qu'il chante le canon
Répète le non taciturne
Éclat et non parole: Non!
Que répète l'écho nocturne

Non! ennemi tu n'auras point
Ni les villes ni les campagnes
Ni ma vie, amour en a soin
Entends l'amour qui m'accompagne

Écoute! il chante tendrement
Je ne sais pas sur quelle branche
Il est partout qui va m'aimant
Nuit et jour, semaine et dimanche

Et que dire de cet oiseau?
Que dire des métamorphoses
Du chant en âme, doux morceau!
Du cœur en lys, du corps en roses . . .

Car cet oiseau c'est mon amour
Et mon amour c'est une fille
La rose est moins parfaite et pour
Moi seul l'oiseau bleu s'égosille

Oiseau bleu comme le cœur bleu
De mon amour au cœur céleste
Ton chant si doux répète-le
—J'attends ta lettre comme un geste! . . .

Tu m'ouvriras les bras et puis
Tu me répéteras je t'aime
Ainsi vont les jours et les nuits
Amour bleu comme est le cœur même!

GUILLAUME APOLLINAIRE

I am hoping for a letter from you
Your letters my love are roses
Of separation and of our faith,
Thorn and perfume of your prose!

A bird is singing don't know where
It is I think your soul keeping watch
Amidst all the rough soldiery
And the bird delights my ear

As it sings the cannon
Repeats its taciturn no
A flash not a word: No!
Repeated by the echo in the night

No! my enemy you shall never get
Either towns or countryside
Nor my life, love is taking care of that
I mean the love that walks beside me

Listen! the bird sings tenderly
On what branch I know not
But it is everywhere, loving me
Night and day, weekday or sabbath

And what to say of this bird?
What of these transformations
From song to soul, such sweet melody!
From heart to lily, flesh to roses . . .

For that bird is my love
And my love is a girl
The rose is less perfect than she
And the blue bird trills for me alone

Bird blue as the blue heart
Of my heavenly-hearted love
Sing your sweet song again
—I await your letter like a caress! . . .

You will open your arms to me and then
You will say over and over I love you
So go the days and nights
Love blue as the heart itself!

Blue love, I adore you, you are my Venus, you arise from Mediterranean waves blue as your heart. I imagine a caress amazingly long and sweet my darling, with my mouth pressed to the forecourt of the temple as I breathe in all your love, an evening when I change into an octopus the better to love you and my mouth becomes a sucker, you wriggle delightfully and delightfully your divine thighs offer up the perfumed chalice and there I remain endlessly. Your body shudders repeatedly, spasm after spasm until you faint away under my persistent and terribly gentle touch and you come round only when you feel my manly embrace, which awakes my ardent Phèdre. The battle is wonderful and ends with my complete victory which is also yours, my darling love.

LE QUATRIÈME POÈME SECRET

Ma bouche aura des ardeurs de géhenne
Ma bouche te sera un enfer de douceur
Les anges de ma bouche trôneront dans ton cœur
Ma bouche sera crucifiée
Et ta bouche sera la barre horizontale de la croix
Et quelle bouche sera la barre verticale de cette croix
Ô bouche verticale de mon amour!
Les soldats de ma bouche prendront d'assaut tes entrailles

GUILLAUME APOLLINAIRE

Les prêtres de ma bouche encenseront ta beauté dans son temple

Ton corps s'agitera comme une région pendant un tremblement de terre

Tes yeux seront alors chargés de tout l'amour qui s'est amassé dans les regards de
    l'humanité depuis qu'elle existe

Mon amour, ma bouche sera une armée contre toi

Une armée pleine de disparates

Variée comme un enchanteur qui sait varier ses métamorphoses

Car ma bouche s'adresse aussi à ton ouïe et avant tout

Ma bouche te dira mon amour

Elle te le murmure de loin

Et mille hiérarchies angéliques s'y agitent qui te préparent une douceur paradisiaque

Et ma bouche est l'Ordre aussi qui te fait mon esclave

Et me donne ta bouche Madeleine

Je prends ta bouche Madeleine

FOURTH SECRET POEM

My mouth will have an ardour worthy of Gehenna

My mouth will be an inferno of sweetness for you

The angels of my mouth will reign in your heart

My mouth will be crucified

And your mouth will be the cross-bar of the cross

And which mouth will be the upright of that cross

Oh vertical mouth of my love!

The soldiers of my mouth will take your insides by storm

The priests of my mouth will incense your beauty in its temple

Your body will heave like a land struck by an earthquake

Then your eyes will be laden with all the love stored up in human eyes since
    humanity's beginnings

My love, my mouth will be an army against you

An army of great variety

Versatile as a wizard master of metamorphoses

For my mouth addresses your hearing too and above all

My mouth will tell you of my love

Murmuring it to you from afar

As a thousand angel ranks within busily prepare for you the sweetest
   paradise

And my mouth is Order too, making you my slave

And giving me your mouth Madeleine

I take your mouth Madeleine.

                                                              Gui

19 October 1915

My love, Letters of the 11th, 12th and 13th. You are a sweetheart—
I am writing you using envelopes with insides of a violet that I
dislike. I have two or three of them to hand so I am using them,
but I adore you for sending your letters in envelopes with green
interiors which I do like.—Your parcel is to be delivered to me
tomorrow morning.—Your photo is exquisite, it gives me boundless
pleasure. It is true that it does not show much, but through your
transparent blouse I can make out your breasts, those exquisite
breasts; true breasts of the Venus of Praxiteles and your arms and
your adorable neck. Next time please have yourself taken in profile
also. Congratulate the children for their photography—I shall speak
to you tomorrow about the precious gifts from my Madeleine. Yes do
write me every day and do not worry. So long as you do the right
thing you have no call to be anxious so do not get upset my very
dearest, my letters are not sad, because I love you and you love me.
Yes I take you my love. Yes you have understood now what kind of
letters I want, but not sad ones my love, you must be above reality,
above separation, be regal my dear slave. No, I do not think you
should carry out your plan to go to Beauvais. Stay rather with your
own and wait for me to come. Later we shall see we shall talk about
it more. *I have never ever doubted your passion.* How sweet your body
was the night you speak of, how it burned for me . . . But no, the act
of love is not cruel, as you suppose, or only the first time and not
even then for many women. *I know that you love me* and *you know that*

I love you. I am not in a bad mood and my sad moments are rare because you love me. So do not mention such things. Be joyful my love, be my passionate Phèdre and leap like her, be joyful be a secret Bacchante until I return. Afterwards you may be as changeable as possible or as you wish—I adore you—how delightful that we were both thinking of rings at the same time.

About the *Pentameron*, do it by all means if you can find it and it amuses you and is worth the trouble—after all I know nothing about it. Translating what I saw should not be difficult because it was intended for young people.

It is so wonderful to think that we both had an intuition about each other and about our love from the very first.

You are my darling for copying those lines of poetry, you are kindness itself.

I note that you have well understood where I am.

My love my darling. How extraordinary to put obstacles in the way of sending tobacco from Algeria to a soldier. It seems unfair and pettifogging to me. The fact is I have good white teeth albeit irregular ones, and upstairs I have a snaggle tooth. The coarse-cut tobacco we have here stains them but I take good care of my mouth and make sure to brush my teeth every night I can. I use a very good toothpaste. One of my lower teeth was filled and the filling has come out but as yet it is not hurting. How pretty the little scene is where after explaining Montaigne you stretch out at my feet like a little black slave—black but beautiful as the Song of Songs says.— Yes you are indeed my sensuous snake. I love you when you love me like a panther. I also love the mutual caress of our tongues when you are tender. And I love you coquettish and affected. I love your poetess too. I await with the greatest composure the Poem of your

GUILLAUME APOLLINAIRE

body—in reality—as well as the version you are going to send by letter, my Venus. I also love you fiery, as when you sense my merciless dominion over your Houri's flesh. I also love you proud, imperious, superb. My Lioness. I love you. You have told me exquisite things. And I embrace you in your nakedness that belongs to me. Forgive me for my letter of the 5th if it distressed you. I want never to cause you distress. How many times must I tell you so, oh my love. Why no, you certainly do not make me unhappy, on the contrary you make me very happy, because you teach me and I teach you. Think how well we are getting to know one another. Smile, my darling, through those tears of love. Above all do not be so silly as to leave Oran, which you have promised me not to do, especially without your family. Do not frighten me by imagining the unimaginable. Where could you go—where I am there is nothing anywhere, no villages, nothing not even water. So . . . Ah, now you are talking sense, now you are my darling virgin my secret Bacchante, I adore you for kissing my whole body as you put it so wonderfully oh my ever so sweet Madeleine. I am sending you letters from the engraver Laboureur and from Jean de Gourmont (on the death of his brother). They should amuse you, and apropos of Laboureur's I beg you do me the honour and favour, my love, of not feeling jealous at the names of the women he mentions, for they give you not the slightest call for jealousy, and you will thus be able to savour the story of Glycerine and Vaseline the two lady opera singers attached to an English division. You will also appreciate the artfulness of Jean de Gourmont's getting himself into the Ministry of War just near his home in Paris and the details printed on the official envelopes of the English army. And you my darling how can you possibly tell me to become your passionate love once more—I who no longer think of anything at all save through you, you who are now my canon (nothing to do with artillery!) you who are my measuring rod, all

344

beauty and all joy. Fancy your saying that I am impassive and judge you coldly, my love! Why no, I am not like that at all. I adore you, I love you, I am madly in love with you, we are each happy only through the other. And you said it yourself, we must never suffer henceforth. You are my great love, my absolute darling, my most beautiful idol. You cannot begin to imagine how much I love today's photo which shows me all your grace and all your suppleness. The earlier photos did nothing of this kind. I have examined it under the magnifying glass, your face can only be guessed at, but as for your breasts it seems to me that I can see them and they are truly lovely. You are more beautiful than Titian's Venuses, Antiquity alone offers such pure beauty and individual grace. My God, how fine and gracious you are my beloved gazelle. Your arms are of inconceivable purity. And be it said that the sight of your breasts took all the perspicacity of my passionate and fervent love, for in reality they cannot be seen yet I saw them as it were in flashes. In the end the beauty of your hips is more easily discernible, and here too the perspicacity of love is required, but all the same the material of your skirt curves inward in conformity with your hip. What can be seen through the window that you are leaning against my love?

You cannot conceive how beautiful you seem to me in this photo, it surpasses everything I had imagined, I believe you become more beautiful every day, your throat is a marvel and the splendour of your shoulders is my treasure. And how delectably lissom you are. I caress you in the most intimate way until our two souls are convulsed and our mouths melt in ecstasy. I love the look in your eyes where deaths and resurrections lie dormant, and your dark skirt, so sober, stirs up ideas of a torrid, tufted obscurity. I love you I love you. I picture in the morning as you wake, your bosom released from the cocoon of your bed, your black hair unfurling like the waves of a

GUILLAUME APOLLINAIRE

storm-tossed sea, I see your nightdress riding up, billowing over the fullness of your breasts. Then I see you arising quickly, your nightdress falling back down to mid-thigh, your legs so smooth and plump above the knee and I love you infinitely, I am with you, attentive to your Cypris-like beauty, it is I who strip you and I take your mouth.

Gui

Very dearest Madelon, I adore you my love. Your letter of the 13th is marvellous. First let us talk parcels. I have received the ring that I adore and that is now on my left ring-finger and shall stay there. I have the gloves which are fine for riding*—(my horse is better now)—and the cigars (I have already smoked three, exquisite) and this morning the packets of delicious cigarettes, you are my very sweetest little darling for spoiling me like this. Let me get back to your letter. You have understood me completely and so profoundly that there is no one in the world who has ever understood my mind as you do, and we are but one in the most magnificent way. So when have I hidden my love, my darling? Never! Never!! I adore you, you love me exquisitely. You are my joy and you desire me physically . . . the same goes for me . . . There are a good many positions for love, my darling, the commonest being the one that you wish for at present and that I wish for likewise—*illa sub ille super* as the Latin has it.

The Latin words do not shrink from honesty (nor do the French for that matter: *elle en dessous, lui au-dessus*). But we two shall also reverse the roles and try countless variations, and when you are Phèdre you desire me no doubt after the fashion in which I believe Pasiphaë had knowledge of the bull and I believe that that is what you intended to convey in offering me your beautiful white haunches. Your desires are thus in harmony with the kind of congress in question. I am delighted that I can now picture the downy vegetation, dark as Erebos, that

* they are very expensive gloves and I wish I were brave enough to upbraid you for buying them but I haven't the heart. I kiss your mouth madly.

347

GUILLAUME APOLLINAIRE

grows on your sleek body, and I am thrilled to learn that it is curly. I should not have liked it had your body been smooth in places where it is not supposed to be smooth! . . . You have now spoken marvellously to me of *The Heresiarch*, you have understood me, and how I love reality. I dream and create reality, true and pure simple and healthy. I was sure that you had understood, but I was wondering why you did not yet want to tell me so; I also dislike what is unhealthy.

How curious that you do not like Colette Willy, neither do I, but Willy himself is a writer of talent who destroyed both his life and his talent, that is the plain truth, but the talent was considerable. Louÿs the Parnassian voluptuary is an artificial writer with a circumscribed but genuine talent, a shame he is so artificial, his is a small work of pastiche without great importance without truth, the purest and most graceful as also the most sensuous expression of which is *Les Chansons de Bilitis* (Songs of Bilitis), a successful long shot. He lauds a sensuality that he does not feel, for his subject is largely love between women and he is a man. His work embodies a slightly unhealthy curiosity—not entirely, it is true, for he has a genuine feeling for Hellenism—but the apparent simplicity is at bottom unhealthy. His life bears this out. Louÿs was unable to keep his wife who has just married Gilbert de Voisins. The same goes for Willy, whose wife Colette after trailing her lesbian love through one women's snuggery after another ended up by marrying a co-editor-in-chief of *Le Matin* whose name escapes me; now he betrays her with his former mistress (his but also hers) a horrible woman by the way who is in turn unfaithful to him with grotesque small-time actors. As a rule people go into ecstasies over how natural Colette's writing is. For my part I see much affectation, very little that is natural, just a simple schoolgirl talent and a strictly superficial sensibility. That is all, and it is to my mind of no great interest. What is more,

Colette has an awful Berry accent that I dislike intensely. But I am telling you about all these largely insignificant people only because you brought them up. They are of no concern to us. You are right to dislike things that are out of line, I feel the same way and you have sensed it in me very clearly.

Zola is a giant among novelists, it is hard to pass judgement on such a man in a couple of words, particularly a negative judgement. But we can talk about this later when we have the time. All the same, I admit that though I admire Zola I still get no pleasure from reading him.

I love you my Rose as dark as you are, you are my earliest experience—(and this has just dawned on me for the first time). When I was a child between 5 and 10 years of age I had a vision 3 or 4 times of a dark-haired girl who drew back the curtains of my bed in the morning (beds had curtains in those days) and looked at me sweetly for a moment before closing them softly once more. It was you, not as I saw you and no doubt imperfectly saw you on the train, but as you are in the photo of two years ago. What is more as a child I told myself I would never love any but a dark girl and I was very surprised when at 20 I conceived a fancy for a blonde, but my childhood wish, my purest wish, is now being fulfilled, because I am in love for the first time and I love a really dark-haired woman, just as my childish desires foretold. In any case, fair fleeces do not have the appeal of the sort of curly fur you describe, which must heighten the lily-like brightness of your natural whiteness, oh my beautiful Madeleine of the white belly and the beautiful white hips.

Like you I am very fond of 'The Poets' Napkin', and to reward you for liking it I am going to make you 2 napkin-rings from Boche aluminium; I shall put 2 Boche coins on them as ornaments. One ring for me and one for you. You are a poet too and our napkins will be poets' napkins.

GUILLAUME APOLLINAIRE

Something splendid has happened. A few days ago a Boche aeroplane was shot down between the lines. I saw it come down, and yesterday I had the opportunity to go into the infantry trenches where I was given a piece of an aluminium tension adjuster from the plane from which I have taken two rings, so there was no need to melt anything down, merely to file them and make them the right size and engrave them (which last I have not finished) and then I'll polish them up. So, two engagement rings literally fallen from the heavens!

Today I am sending you 2 rings for Marthe and Anne and 1 for you made with a Boche button, which is I feel more amusing, for they say that everyone is making rings in the rear now, so at least this one will appear to have come from the Front, as indeed it has. I'll send you the engagement rings as soon as the engraving is done. And with them you will be getting a little gold chain that I have been wearing round my wrist since the 7th of January. It comes from a neck chain that I broke, at present I have a silver chain round my neck. With the remaining pieces of the gold chain I had 3 bracelets made (I wore one of them because it was the fashion in London, a fashion that I liked). I lost the 1st bracelet 2 years ago, I forget where now, and the second fell off as I was jumping onto a horse on a merry-go-round in Nîmes, I looked for it in vain in the sawdust; so I started wearing the 3rd one and it broke 2 days ago, a sign no doubt that any earlier chain that it might have stood for no longer existed, so I can do no better than send it to you, for this bracelet did not get lost like the others and since it is not for me then it must be yours and besides in this way I chain you to me. I am sending it you because it will suit you better than me and because I am very fond of these bracelets, they are so delicate. But please after all do not see any symbolism in it, even should it break on your wrist. It broke on mine because it tended to catch on any number of things and because it was far too fragile to survive the physical rigours of camp life. This is just a little chain I am sending to my slave to beautify her and express my love for her. The true chain that binds us cannot break. It is eternal. I am delighted that you like the simplicity of my style, which is yours too, and you cannot imagine how much I admire your letters, your style, your little head that I adore, so balanced, so sure—why, if you could imagine it you would never say that I am more beautiful than you, for I do prefer you to me, but I am the master, there it is, so I have the absolute right to declare you the more beautiful. You are right to have gathered that there is nothing I would not do for love of you, abduction rape anything. I love you so much, you are so beautiful my rose my lily, never say that the lily is the victim of the rose for it is entirely within your power to have the lily live on in harmony with the rose. When we are married we shall live one and the other as one and the lily can easily coexist in you with the rose, surely you want as much my roselily, and as for me I love the rose as I love the lily and the lily as I love the rose. Everything is healthy for the healthy, as you say, and the healthy rose can mean the health of the lily. Come, my love, never doubt it, our love will be one of passionate purity, precisely because its mystical quality will be full of reality and what could the lily's purity have to fear from that. The lily is the only flower capable of joining perfectly with the mystical rose of which you speak so prettily and which is your intimate being, palpitating with love and desire. Never fear, my lioness, I adore you. What you say our letters ought to be corresponds exactly to what I think. You are right, let us never weaken, and your feeling here is the perfect response to my own wish, oh Madeleine with your beautiful vigorous body.

I take the exquisite gift, my love, of your mouth, of your tongue of your hips of your adorable virgin belly. Yes, tell me everything about your upsets, speak to me of your disturbing feelings. I kiss you my

GUILLAUME APOLLINAIRE

love, I kiss that intimate being which is the seat of what you call your turmoil, and I adore you for your marvellous efforts, oh my darling, to give yourself to your husband from so far away. I should not be at all surprised if we achieved 'touch at a distance'[1] You may certainly trace the outline of your breast on the basis of its shadow on the wall. What an exquisite idea of yours you are wonderfully inventive my love!

I shall never again be sad because you love me my darling.—Do whatever you wish with the things I send you, use them for whatever you want, but I fear they won't add up to much in a display cabinet; the main thing, anyway, is that they not be lost; the fact is we are not permitted to send much by way of weaponry. For the inkwells I risked it—The chargers must not leave here either. As for a rifle or shell casings which would make wonderful vases that is quite out of the question. Tell me quickly, are you keeping well—I don't want you to catch cold. Cover yourself and don't go out in the rain without an umbrella, Madeleine darling. But what's this my love about forgiving you? You have been nothing but exquisite with me and I adore you more and more because you are adorable by nature and your personality is so perfectly in harmony with mine that when I think of the two of us I fancy I hear choirs of angels that are the rarefied spirit of a sky as blue as your heart. I take your mouth and give you my tongue.

Gui

1 See 'L'Amphion faux messie ou Histoire et aventures du Baron d'Ormesan', in *L'Hérésiarque et Cie*. (The expression is translated as 'remote projection' in *The Heresiarch and Co.*, tr. Rémy Inglis Hall [Cambridge, MA.: Exact Change, 1991].—Tr.)

My love,

I had no letter from you yesterday but was expecting none, having
received letters several days in a row. I daresay I shall have none
today either. I am still engraving the engagement rings fallen from
heaven and I have finished the ring with the Boche button, which I
am going to wear for a while before sending it, I have also made a
little ring for you using part of a belt, just as it fell off, as a bezel.
These little jobs help pass the time. I have begun a sort of novel
comprised of truth and reality as created by me. I'll send you chap-
ters or parts of it one at a time, you will organize them linking them
up where needful, you may even give me advice if you like. I'll produce it in pieces, as they come, and not always clearly connected, but
no matter. I adore you my love, I draw your mouth to me, our
tongues play together deliciously like two swords fencing. I love you
today with an infinite tenderness, I smile as I caress your angelic
body, I feel as though we are frolicking in heaven. I am packing up
the ring with the button and the one with the fragment of belt—
shall post them in a while.—Yes my love, I love you paradisiacally. I
caress you so gently, it is as though a rivulet of milk were flowing
over your white body and blending with it so that milk and body are
one and only your divine face floats above the surface along with
your hair and one may just discern that dark triangular patch of

353

GUILLAUME APOLLINAIRE

fleece which is my Eldorado. I am sending you a book today which was in press before the war and which has just been published.[1] It is of no great worth but perhaps since it comes from me it may amuse you. It will also show you to what depths one is obliged to sink to make a living in Paris, though I have always resisted taking on even baser tasks of the kind undertaken by Willy or by writers of serial novels. You will appreciate of course that I have more important things to write. This was amusing to do, but at the same time a little wretched, worse paid than Willy's stuff and much worse paid than sentimental *feuilletons*. I wrote it quickly, relying on the various versions of the Don Juan story. I took everything I could from Molière for 'Don Juan Tenorio' and the third part does little more than resume a literal translation of Byron's 'Don Juan'. But I never count things of this kind among my works and do not even list them on the 'By the Same Author' page of *The Heresiarch*, *Alcools*, etc.

The orderliness that you will impose on me and that your dear presence will require of me, oh my darling little slave, will I hope preserve me in the future from all such drudgery. Raptly, my love, I caress your breasts which are more beautiful than those of Goya's *Maja desnuda* and strain towards me like rosebuds just about to open. My caress is gentle so gentle and wanders farther afield and becomes even gentler as our mouths join gently deeply but with an irresistible force that makes us infinitely serious and irreparably lost to everything in the world that is not us and this until the moment when my slave transformed into my panther demands my most intimate attention and fervently offers me the mossy black rose that I have been in quest of for so long, as you will remember my love from these lines of mine from 'Rosemonde':

> *Plus lentement je m'en allai*
> *Pour quêter la Rose du Monde*

1 *Les Trois Don Juan* (Paris: Bibliothèque des Curièux), published in the series 'L'Histoire romanesque' in October 1915, though bearing the date 1914.

354

Then slowly I went on my way
In search of the Rose of the World

And that was you, who are the rose of the universe and purer than
the unknown Rosemonde whom I cannot even remember, you are
my roselily and what could be more lily-like than the chalice of your
belly and your hips crowned by that rose so bushy and so black after
absorbing all the sun's heat. On your ring, in any case, is a little
diamond in the shape of a rose, luminous as the lily, it speaks to me
still.

Dis Amant que tu adores la Rose

Say Lover that you adore the Rose

And I too adore the Rose, my exquisite Madeleine. I shall eat you,
my darling, as easily as a *madeleine de Commercy*.

I think of your fragrant hair into which I shall plunge my head and
my breast readies itself to welcome your darling head into the nest
you have chosen for it. And I caress you again gently oh my panther,
now gentle once more and you return my caress, our entire bodies
fall prey to our mouths and when we are tired we revert to the
spiritual love of our two-person decamerons in which you shall be
my audience and I your sultan astounded by his Scheherazade. For I
love you, my darling, and I love the spiritual Madelon above all, so
much that even were Madeleine to be divested of her superabundant
beauty I should love you just the same and prove it physically to you
just as emphatically. And I caress you still with a gentleness at once
chaste and lascivious, with a concentrated fervour that causes me to
pause at length every time I bite you gently and fall into a rapture as
I nibble the dark curls of your fleece and sob ecstatically at your
beloved mouth, and taking you about the waist I shall put you on my
back and carry you like a beautiful woman on horseback

GUILLAUME APOLLINAIRE

Ô Vénus tout entière à sa proie attachée

Then our intimate caresses will resume and our spider-like fingers in search of sweetness will transport us once more to the land of ecstatic smiles (more than ecstatic, more splendid even) on the Carte de Tendre that we are wandering through together even though we are so far apart. I take you Madeleine and our tongues stake our lives in the pink gulf of your mouth which I kiss.

Gui

356

Your letters of the 14th and 15th, my love, were a great joy to me.
I adore you. Your parcel will not get to me for at least a month
because postal packages are all routed through the depot. By the
way I already have scissors and knife, so those I shall send back to
you so as not to overload my kit. If the need develops I'll ask you
again. The liquid will be welcome, even with no label, but you had
better not send any more, it is forbidden, though it is the most
appreciated item, along with tobacco, fruit and sweets. But I need
nothing at present except your love and your patience. Impatience
is unworthy of you my love. I do not want you to be impatient. You
say you are a soldier, so arm yourself with patience. Anyway I have
sent you a little book by Remy de Gourmont composed of short
newspaper articles and well printed. His chief works, however, are
Esthétique de la langue française (Aesthetics of the French Language),
Le Latin mystique (Mystical Latin), and the well done *Natural Philosophy of Love*, but you shall read the books of this singular and curious
man in due course, at random. Whenever you wish. Though he is an
acceptable thinker and a good writer, he is one of the founders of
symbolism, the polygraph of the group and one of the most talented
of the Symbolists. But which modern French authors have you read,
seeing that you do not know Remy de Gourmont? Bordeaux, you
told me. Rostand I fancy and Richepin among those still living.
Quite remarkable how my beloved Madeleine has been clever
enough to keep her natural attitude amidst the works of these

GUILLAUME APOLLINAIRE

mediocre people, I must say I am grateful after all to Romain Rolland for providing a link between our two minds, for his scruples and his European sensibility have kept you mine. Nor must I forget the spirit of your father and of Tolstoy, for certainly that too has protected you and please to kiss your mother warmly for she has [protected] you also. Did your father publish anything? if so please tell me what my love.

Since you are mine, my love, you must learn how to have the requisite patience, just as I myself am patient. Do I ever tell you I cannot go on, and yet if only you knew how I much I want you, why, it is madness, but I give no outward sign of it, I remain impassive—a case of ataraxy: a virtue of the gods. What you tell me of the remarkable firmness of your breasts fills me with joy, though it does not surprise me.—Are you just as firm everywhere else? You are probably going a little too far, though, in supposing that the stiffened tips of your breasts could penetrate my chest; on the other hand my own flesh taut and hardened by desire will indeed gain entry into your flesh and by rending your hymen open once and for all cause your pure blood to flow and signal my mastery over you forever. Tell me, my dearest love, to what you yourself would compare the secret odour of your body. It makes me weak at the knees to think of it, but let me tell you that the pain of defloration never recurs, and everything afterwards is voluptuous. True, there is a certain voluptuousness in pain, a sensation known chiefly to women. A husband who knows how to love his wife completely can procure for her this particular kind of pleasure, this acute voluptuousness (and one unimaginable until a woman experiences it), by violating, albeit with infinite gentleness, and not deeply after the manner of brutes without love—by violating, I say, with the wife's consent, the 9th door while at the same time his right hand toys with the 8th and his left with the tips of her breasts and their two mouths seek one another

358

and join each other in endless delight. He may also acquaint her with the voluptuousness of a pain that is pleasurable and gratifying by whipping the fine haunches she presents by bending over and when her desire reaches its peak the two will possess each other in a frenzy of excitement. But few husbands have these skills, which are hard to master, and even fewer can show the tact, poetry and nobility that should preside over exercises that were once part of the mysteries of Eleusis, so carefully guarded from the profane. Sight touch smell are all sources of sensual delight, especially for men. That is why your descriptions of yourself and of your feelings and sensations, with their great attention to detail, can bring me so much joy here in the monotonous hell of the trenches. Voluptuousness itself, the pleasure of love, is stronger, they say, in women. Such at any rate was the opinion of the seer Tiresias, who I believe was at first male, then female, then male once more. This is what I want of you my love, but of all of you, just as you are, and you shall soon be au fait with all of it, my love, for our minds are so perfectly attuned that I am sure we want the same thing at the same time and shall have no need to speak of love in order to make love.

I never scold you and want never to scold you. The Eleusinian mysteries that I revealed to you above are not a daily thing my love but rather refinements to which one does not have recourse every day for fear of wearing oneself out and one must learn to be sparing in this regard. As to the sense of smell, its delights come naturally to me. I have always loved aromas and I do not mean just those for which the perfumier is responsible. I have devised a role for you to play in a love game having to do with our sense of smell, and it is for you alone, I swear it. All the scents, all the smells of your delicious body will be a joy to me. I have a very sensitive nose and a very good nasal memory so to speak, and a rush of scents can often bring back to my mind far-off things that I would never have thought of had

GUILLAUME APOLLINAIRE

my sense of smell not suddenly revived them in my brain. In women, in dark women like you, the three fleeces and the hair of the head are exquisite cassolettes such as their blonde sisters cannot boast of. The scent of blonde women is far less sweet than that of brunettes and especially of fair-skinned brunettes with pale eyes, like you, who are I believe the rarest and most beautiful of women, I had dreamt of them but never seen them, you are the only one, the one and only beautiful thing in the world and the sweetest, my love. I dream up everything I can for you and I always shall.

Dream things up too, my love. But please forget for good that I have ever held another woman in my arms. It makes me so sad and you cannot imagine how much I reproach myself for it. But I swear to you that I no longer think of those things at all without a feeling of disgust that only intensifies my desire and the great love in me that clamours only for you. Strangely I feel your love bites all over my body and especially in the place that is the seat of my desire.

I kiss the lips so red that you hold out to me. Love may certainly put dark circles under the eyes inasmuch as it is fatiguing, but such circles certainly don't prove anything. Your eyes always have them, mine almost never, and certainly not on account of love. Tell me how far your fleece extends. Oh how perfectly you guide me my Ariane whom I shall abandon as soon as you say the word for the Phèdre that you are. Yes, tell me as you guess more and more. But I feel that you are beginning to understand. I adore your frenzied embrace. Now, as for chemistry, I asked the question not knowing whether or not you were versed in that science. I take your exquisite blood. Set aside a fine cambric cloth to collect the adorable blood of your maidenhood and we shall preserve it lovingly, assuming always that blood indeed flows, for many women are deflowered without bleeding. In many the hymen has already been broken either by

360

accident, as by some physical effort, or else by solitary manipulations too roughly performed, such practices being so common that those women who have not indulged in them are a privileged minority. They are rife among boarding-school girls young and old and even among married women. I quite understand that D'Annunzio is not to your liking because he is not to mine either, and in a very particular sense. He is a fake artist, an ornate fake but sham just the same. And I understand that you wish to learn about love from me alone, just as I truly know love only through you. You tell me not to be jealous and that you send everyone else about their business. Am I to suppose that you are being courted, my love? I do not want that, absolutely not. Moreover I have complete faith in you, an absolute faith that you may likewise have in me. But I want you to tell me everything. Precisely who is it my love who dares look at you in a way that makes you blush with shame?

I likewise drink your saliva, how exquisitely you invent our love.

Naturally I am jealous of your pupils if they are in love with you. Those silly geese do not know where they are dabbling! But what you tell me about them gave me a good laugh and at bottom I should be very surprised were they not in love with a beauty as perfect as yours. If these young ladies divide up your blotter they give every sign of engaging in fetishism, one of the most bizarre of genital aberrations. But in the end I am proud of the admiration you arouse in girls some of whom must themselves be beautiful. My love I have certainly enlarged our secret life, now it falls to you to do your part. I adore you. I do not want you to risk getting ill. When she is tired I want my wife to rest. The voluptuous picture you paint of life in our own home enchants me my love and we shall do just what you say, I working, you at my feet tantalizing me with your exquisite charm until your kittenish games turn into panther games

GUILLAUME APOLLINAIRE

and overwhelmed by your scent that I so adore I brutally strip your beauty naked and then, changing my mind out of respect for your secret wishes, I cover you once more, you are simultaneously ashamed and delighted, and undress you now with the greatest gentleness and all the skill of a lady's maid albeit a little clumsily. I shall pause at length at every smallest detail and you will hide whatever I expose so that I may uncover it all over again until I have you naked and royally naked and my caresses ever so sweet become more intimate until my hands then my lips and my tongue play for a long time first at the borders and then within the so jealously guarded 9th door and you hide your face in shame, leaving only the adorable reverse of that medallion visible, and when our play has rendered you more panther-like than ever I shall turn you over and my tongue will for the longest time caress your intimate being which is hiding *in the shadows of the forest*. You in turn will reciprocate by sitting astride my face and our mouths and tongues will explore our private parts endlessly and leave off only when you, completely Phèdre once more, call me to your bosom where mouth to mouth belly to belly we shall be profoundly one in the sweetest of ecstasies. And no, no one shall ever know anything of our love and we will show the world at large only that love's outer aspect, only the signs of an attachment appropriate to the married. Neither children nor anything else can ever alter our love, which will always be just as passionate, varied, and exquisite. I want to feel your teeth in my flesh and I want to be able to chastise you like a trainer punishing the panther that has bitten him. I'll tell you what I need here, but for now there is nothing. Please do not send things because I shan't know where to put them. And if you do, please no more than a kilo at a time, otherwise it will take too long.

I adore your beautiful teeth and I love it that you like mine. Don't be silly, I shall never ever beg you to desist when you kiss me, for yes oh my love, my whole body is yours, we walk side by side, have but one will. You tell me exquisite things about the way you want to love me. I love your virginity of body as of mind. Yes, it is rare indeed to be able to possess a virgin whom one has forearmed though without seeking to seduce her or intimidate her (which last is much more vile). We are already married, for the sacrament of marriage has as its true ministers the bride and groom whose union is founded on their will, whereas the priest's role is merely a witnessing and not an officiating one. All we lack is the witnessing, but our marriage is already real and indissoluble in terms of Catholic teaching because our two wills have consented to it. So now we may study and understand each other without discord. In any case our minds were made to be married. Yes, we shall love one another in the dark night, as likewise in the day whenever you wish it. And we shall love one another in the violent embrace that you have imagined, which has nothing to do with conjugal correction but is rather a sort of motionless violence of your devising, surely a delightful refinement of which neither I nor for that matter the Hindu erotologists ever conceived. I am glad to know that you love Racine and that you have played Athalie. When I was at school that play introduced me to lyricism. I love it very much. You must have been an amusing Athalie with her train but a good deal more beautiful than Athalie. I once saw the piece put on by the Sylvains at Champigny in the open air with rain falling; it was comical because of the continual interruptions occasioned by the downpours. I know the Sylvains slightly, they are great friends of Moréas, it is even said that Louise Sylvain knew Moréas in the biblical sense of the word but I think that is a slander because I saw them together and one did not get the feeling that there was anything like that between them. Sylvain's own acting is not much to my taste, especially his accent. As a matter of fact I like the acting of very few actors and actresses. Your mother

363

GUILLAUME APOLLINAIRE

was quite right to discourage you from entering the conservatory. I know not a few of those young ladies and should not like you to resemble them, foolish as they are for the most part.

You are a thousand times superior to all actresses, because in you beauty is not everything, for your intelligence is on a par with that wonderful beauty. I adore your total caress and I adore the voluptuous weight of your body and your scent intoxicates me. I take your mouth.

Gui

My love no letter from you today. It is chilly here. I have received the news that the poet Léo Larguier, my friend, corporal in charge of stretcher-bearers in the 415th combined battalion, has been wounded. I have sent him a little poem—

LE BRANCARDIER

Le sol est blanc, le soir l'azure.
Saigne la crucifixion
Tandis que saigne la blessure
Du soldat de promission.

Un chien jappait, l'obus miaule,
La lueur muette a jailli.
À savoir si la guerre est drôle?
Les masques n'ont pas tressailli.

Mais quel fou rire sous le masque,
Blancheur éternelle d'ici
Où la colombe porte un casque
Et l'acier s'envole aussi.

THE STRETCHER-BEARER

The ground is white, dusk turns it blue.
The crucifixion bleeds
As does the wound
Of this soldier of the promised land.

GUILLAUME APOLLINAIRE

A dog was yapping, shells yowl,
A silent flash has erupted.
How to say if war is funny?
Masks have not quivered.

But what mad laughter beneath the mask,
In the endless whiteness of this place
Where doves wear helmets
And steel takes wing.

By the way, my love, things intended for the printer should be written on one side of the paper only. I forgot to warn you about this. Pardon me.

I love you today, my darling, with the same extraordinary gentleness as yesterday. I want to kiss you forever on the mouth while caressing you divinely. I am sure that I shall never weary of caressing you any more than you will ever tire of those caresses. Apropos of Racine I have been told that I resemble his portraits. I have an engraving of him in which I can see a certain likeness, especially were I to wear a wig in the 18th-century manner.

My love, this evening I take you in the night, just as you were saying yesterday, we are curled up together in wintertime under the covers and as the wind blows we hold each other tight in the exquisite warmth of our bed.

Your beautiful hair covers us both. My arms are around you and yours clasp me with all their might to your breast, where my mouth tarries in infinitely sweet dalliance. So sweet a sweetness that it seems the blissful night will never end, then our bodies unite even more closely. My hands squeeze your charming hips, our intimate beings arouse each other with a tender fury until opening yourself wide like a split fig you welcome me and our fleeces come together as we unhurriedly perform the act of love, after which our caresses resume and then at last slumber closes our eyelids and we fall asleep in each other's arms. See how tender my love for you is tonight. In my fancy I tell you things so simple and so pretty that you linger for the pleasure of hearing them, we speak of your beauty, choosing this or that feature and dwelling on it so minutely and lovingly that the hours pass without our heeding their passage and these explorations continue thus in sweet lucidity until the darkness I mentioned above casts its thrall over our ecstasy.

You were saying yesterday that you did not want to have a child right away. That is very possible and it is you who shall decide whether you wish motherhood or not. It is not within our power to have a child, but it is almost within our power not to have one. In a word it is simply a matter of hydrotherapy. We shall see. In a matter like motherhood it is up to you to decide, for it is you who must bear the burden. In any event I fancy that being with child you will be as pretty as a picture; but I wonder, do you have the broad pelvis needed, do you think you are made for childbearing? the little I know of your waist and hips tells me Yes, but of course I do not really know anything. There are some women whose bodies are disfigured by motherhood, especially the breasts, others are unaffected by it. To judge by the number of children in your family, I tend to think that your mother weathered maternity admirably and that her daughter Madeleine will probably be favoured in the same way and I take your mouth endlessly.

Gui

GUILLAUME APOLLINAIRE

My darling little love, I am so happy to have received your letter of the 17th which took only six days to reach me. But tomorrow I shall have none. You know, my darling, you must not imagine that I am not pleased or grateful for the fact that you spoil me, for on the contrary I think you are sweet to do so. What I said the other day was badly put. Abt the scissors and knife I'll keep the best things amongst those you send and those I already have—I wish you would be less impatient though my love, and I also wish for many secrets from you because I must know my Madeleine better. That is the main reason. Many of the things you tell me are sweet and passionate but I need a great deal of information about your intimate life, your feelings your soul as much as your body. Granted, you do tell me many things, which is perfect. But I am so greedy for you, it is quite incredible how one may go mad over a beautiful Madeleine such as you. But I want you to be patient calm and wait for me with the dignity of an empress, without revealing the secrets of our love, without anyone even being able to guess at them. And that is indeed what you are doing, and why I adore your reserve and your pride.

Yes, you are right, your naturalness is our greatest refinement. And I love you to be natural. I adore you as you are and if I were over there I should carry you off today because today I feel I have the soul of a pirate. And the corsair that I am is as you say in the power of his beautiful captive that is you.

Everything you tell me about jealousy agrees with my own thinking and both of us, together, have a far too elevated intellectual task before us to waste time making each other jealous.

The joys of the flesh shall be ours because our mystical and intellectual union is so complete that it is vital not just to us but to the whole universe, offering the world as it does a many-faceted and grand and pure work in which you will have as large a part as I shall, being my wife and having so broad a perspective—

In any case we simply cannot contemplate something so ridiculous. If ever I were to be jealous of you, I should be unhappy for a time and then it would be over and the end would be a frightful one unworthy of both you and me. We are too aware for that ever to happen, do not even speak of it again.

You have clearly understood that the more frequently you offer yourself to me the more passionately I shall love you. You are beginning to be well acquainted with your husband and I congratulate you on that, my dear wife. I kiss the red roses of your breasts and your mouth my love. I adore the flamboyant-tree that is just like your lips, send me a petal if you still have any.

I shall love you as the flower of the pomegranate, the flower of the peach or of the datura. I shall love you in every one of your bloomings oh my flower. Yes you are my poetry, I adore you my most beautiful poem. And if I were rich I should devote myself entirely to loving you. Yes I am on fire with love and this ardour is infinitely sweet to me because it rages in you too and because my will is the master of the immense flame of our love.

Please tell me the story, my dear Scheherazade, of this young woman who is about thirty. Is she settled in Oran and what does she want? Be careful not to attach yourself to her too readily. My hair

GUILLAUME APOLLINAIRE

when it is fairly long gets curly. I adore your hand running through my hair, I know how much I shall love that gesture. And I love your ardour, the way you tremble like a lioness. You are a beautiful trembling mare waiting for your horseman.

I adore your rapture and I take you gently, gently, invading you with a slow voluptuousness that grows imperceptibly. I adore you. I love you infinitely and I want you to be very calm even should this require that your letters be less passionate, for I want your nervous system to wait patiently for me my dearest wife. My pretty Madeleine. I take your mouth endlessly. You are my gracious guide along an adorable path, I adore you.

Gui

Love of mine, let me place a little note here as much for me as for you. In my last instalment of 'La Vie anecdotique' I evoked the German word *Rittergut*, adding that it means I believe a manor carrying with it the title of knight, in simple terms a noble estate which does not hold villeins. It was Baron de Stein who obtained this entitlement from Frederick William when he abolished serfdom.

As for what I was telling you yesterday about the frequency with which we should complete the act of love, it will be up to you to govern our habits, bearing in mind the need to husband our strength so that we may continue to love each for a long time, even into old age, without fatigue. A proper practice is excellent and healthy, abuse is to be feared and blunts the pleasure.

Our lack of water which you mentioned yesterday makes itself felt for the most part with respect to the washing of clothes. In any case I always draw enough to wash myself thoroughly and our unmounted driver does the laundry once a week without fail.

This is our life, we rise whenever we want unless we are bombarding or a shouted 'To your posts!' gets us up quick sharp, because we sleep fully clothed. For myself I turn out even without a call because I have duties at 7 a.m. When on day duty I distribute water, otherwise I breakfast immediately, black coffee and a cold meal of bread and either gruyère or jam. Then I strip to the waist and wash in a basin that I have had since the beginning, an enamelled zinc basin

371

GUILLAUME APOLLINAIRE

that hangs from the caisson when we are on the move so there isn't much it hasn't seen. I am still using your bar of soap, I wash my chest my neck my armpits my hands with the soap then rinse off after a change of water. After that I wash my hair and rinse it, then my face, and then everything that belongs to you in the marital sense. Then I get dressed and then we fire or read until soup at ½ past 10, then we wait for the post. Naturally this does not cover firing which can happen any time day or night and last as long as it lasts. In principle we eat again at ½ past 4 and take coffee once more, after which I write till 10 o'clock or if there is water I take an outdoor shower, brush my teeth and go to bed about eleven o'clock. One night out of two one does not sleep because of guard duty, which does not apply to me but to my men, but sleep is impossible anyway. In the daytime I often meet Berthier sgt. of Piece 2, which is not brought out much, or with Defreney sgt of Piece 1, he sleeps in a tiny hole where he can barely stretch out. A month and a ½ ago we shared a trench dugout with Berthier, we used to write there, he did photography, all of which has stopped since the offensive. I have a folding table that I made and one little bench and a bed that is not too bad. But I shan't be able to take the bed along and I am afraid that gradually with all the changes there will be fewer and fewer boards to be had. The bed is made of planks,[1] the bottom of wire netting, the nails are made from bits of steel wire, on the wire netting is straw and on top of the straw a sack and on the sack is an isolating sheet that I found near Rheims and my tent canvas folded in two in which I sleep with a horse blanket and my coat over my feet, and at the foot of my bed in front of the door is my table.[2]

1 See p. 267.

2 See p. 268.

My love I have just received your letters of the 18th and 19th. Yes my love be calm and patient when you do not receive any letter from me. My love I adore you. I take your mouth endlessly, and I love

372

your breasts that are as hard as bombshells my darling love. No, my love, you have not yet told me about your legs and I would like a long letter too about your hips. I adore your breasts they are so beautiful. They impress themselves on my flesh. And I caress you again in the special way that you can imagine. I eat you my love and your fleece that I adore gives me a real sapper's beard. I love that smile of yours that started everything off. For me too m'love everything that is not you is of no interest. I love the idea that everything in you Madeleine is desire, the same is true of me. Why yes, you are certainly very fond of me, my grand love, my beautiful enraptured one, my adorable evanescent creature, my voluptuous Ariel. Your flesh contracts because my touch is still unknown to you, and perhaps too because that is your way.

Speak to me at length about the amphora handles of your hips my love and tell me too how the pink and black mouth of your intimate being is positioned, is it set low looking down at the ground or higher up like a vertical split on the front of your body? And tell me what poets are your favourites, not counting me of course, I who am your love who worships you, and tell me if you love to eat and if you have a good appetite and what side you sleep on. And then tell me again that you love me, I who adore you. I take your mouth.

CLASSE 17

Boyaux et rumeur du canon
Sur cette mer aux blanches vagues
Fou stoïque comme Zénon
Pilote du cœur tu zigzagues

Petites forêts de sapins
La nichée attend la becquée
Pointe-t-il des nez de lapins
Comme l'euphorbe verruquée

GUILLAUME APOLLINAIRE

Ainsi que l'euphorbe d'ici
Le soleil à peine boutonne
Je l'adore comme un Parsi
Ce tout petit soleil d'automne

Un fantassin presqu'un enfant
Beau comme le jour qui s'écoule
Beau comme mon cœur triomphant
Disait en mettant sa cagoule

Tandis que nous n'y sommes pas
Que de filles deviennent belles
Voici l'hiver et pas à pas
Leur beauté s'éloignera d'elles

Ô Lueurs soudaines des tirs
Cette beauté que j'imagine
Faute d'avoir des souvenirs
Tire de vous son origine

Car elle n'est rien que l'ardeur
De la bataille violente
Et de la terrible lueur
Il s'est fait une muse ardente

CLASS OF '17

Trenches and rumbling cannon fire
Upon this white-waved sea
As mad and Stoic as Zeno
Helmsman of the heart you zigzag

Little pine woods
Nestlings waiting to be fed
Do rabbits' noses poke out
Like warty spurge

And like the spurge hereabouts
The sun is barely more than a bud
I adore it like a Parsee
That tiny little sun of autumn

An infantryman almost a child
Beautiful as the day running out
Beautiful as my jubilant heart
Said as he donned his smoke-helmet

While we are not there
So many girls become beautiful
Here comes winter and little by little
Their beauty will abandon them

Oh sudden flashes of cannon fire
This beauty that I imagine
For want of memories
Must have in you its source

For it is simply the ardour
Of violent battle
And he made that awful flashing
Into his ardent muse

My love I take your mouth and I take all of you.

Gui

27 October 1915

My love no letter from you today. Listen to me from afar my darling
little Madeleine, my beautiful one, my pure enamoured Madeleine,
the song I sing you is the song of my love, I sing it to you on the
battle front and I bequeath you my helmet my smoke-helmet my
sabre my spurs my revolver and my artilleryman's log. Listen
Madelon, let me tell you how much I love you. Let the whistling
bombshells declare that they mean to kill me alongside my gun,
they shall never succeed because you love me my darling. Over on
the other side the Boche gunners aim them, shouting loudly in
German. Shout on, bombardiers of the Kaiser, you won't be talking
forever. Dream of getting to Asia, you are not there yet. I am alone
in my trench dugout, come to me my love, my Madeleine, let your
dream and mine carry you here oh my African beauty. My
Madeleine's heart is blue, my Madeleine's adorable breasts harden
as she dreams of my kisses. I adore you my Madeleine. Today was a
truly cold day it was fine but very cold I have the strong impression
it will freeze tonight. Despite the prospect of winter we feel alright
here because it is interesting and because after all we can hardly
complain, we have not been spotted. We cannot know what the
future holds, but for the minute we are fine, the lack of water
notwithstanding. Apropos of which, though I told you yesterday
that we were managing, getting to drink is a problem, for we have
scarcely anything except for broth coffee and wine, all in small
quantities of course, and it would be so pleasant to have water, fine

376

spring water as cool as my darling Madeleine. But that is our sole real deprivation, along with the impossibility of taking a stroll away from the battery. The French army has nothing to complain about. It is well clad and well supplied.

My love I love you today all in blue, I love your blue heart and your hair so black that it too is blue, and the blue veins that run up and down your body as though on a beautiful map and I also love you in white like your skin and your clear-eyed gaze and your fine teeth and in red also like your lips and the tips of your breasts and also in green like the hope of seeing you again and also in yellow like the sun we love and also in black like your fleeces. I adore you, my very dearest, tell me about your beautiful teeth my love those teeth that love to bite and also about the exact colour of your eyes whose heavy-lidded yet candid gaze so transfixed me that I could not see them clearly.

377

Today I received a note from a horticulturist who asks me for a poem in exchange for whatever I might want from the plant world after the war. I enclose his letter and we can take him up on his offer if need be.

My love please describe your bedroom and your bed. As for me and my men we sleep in a hole covered by 2 layers of chalk slabs and corrugated iron—here is a diagram of our hole.[1]

1 See p. 269.

This drawing makes the dugout seem larger than it is, between the beds there is not really a space as wide as one of the beds.

To the right of the gun is the kitchen where we eat.

I sleep as we all do with my head towards the skylight.

At night before going to sleep we now often take tea, which I like very much and which is a good way of drinking some water.

GUILLAUME APOLLINAIRE

My darling I adore you for consenting to be docile, to be my love, to let yourself be adored, for to comply with my fantasy, to be my slave and to obey me is to be more and more mine. My caress my love envelops all of you very gently with the very lightest of touches and my mouth attaches itself like a sucker to the divine place where your desires are concentrated. My caress is soft but more and more insistent until the moment when you call upon me for the closest embrace, and I imagine wilder days when you straddle me and present to my view the adorable spectacle of your hips descending towards my mouth and placing upon it the delicious entrance of the 8th door and as my hands caress your bosom's delectable fruits your bold mouth caresses the tree of knowledge of good and evil, which are one and the same thing when one does so with our idea of duty in mind or under the sway of that redemptive notion, and now our passionate tongues inflame our desires to the point of an exquisite madness. With our mouths we devour each other with a marvellous ardour. I am sending you herewith the complete poem of which the two last poems I sent you were merely fragments.

378

I adore you my beautiful darling panther and I devour you. I worship your naked body, as beautiful as the most beautiful of poems, I savour your tongue and the adorable pink flesh of your secret lips and now I take you violently like a woodcutter planting his felling axe in the majestic oak. I take your mouth.

Gui

CHANT DE L'HORIZON EN CHAMPAGNE

Voici le tétin rose de l'euphorbe verruquée
Voici les nez des soldats invisibles
Moi l'horizon invisible je chante
Que les civils et les femmes écoutent ces chansons
Et voici d'abord la cantilène du brancardier blessé

Le sol est blanc la nuit l'azure

Saigne la crucifixion

Tandis que saigne la blessure

Du soldat de Promission

Un chien jappait l'obus miaule

La lueur muette a jailli

À savoir si la guerre est drôle

Les masques n'ont pas tressailli

Mais quel fou rire sous le masque

Blancheur éternelle d'ici

Où la colombe porte un casque

Et l'acier s'envole aussi

Je suis seul sur le champ de bataille

Je suis la tranchée blanche le bois vert et roux

L'obus miaule

Je te tuerai

Animez-vous fantassins à passepoil jaune

Les grands artilleurs roux comme des taupes

Bleu de roi comme les golfes méditerranéens

Veloutés de toutes les nuances de velours

Ou mauves encore ou bleus comme les autres

Ou déteints

Venez le pot en tête

Debout fusée éclairante

Danse grenadier en agitant tes pommes de pin

Alidades des triangles de visée pointez-vous sur les lueurs

Creusez des trous enfants de 20 ans creusez des trous

Sculptez les profondeurs

Envolez-vous essaims des avions blonds ainsi que les avettes

Moi l'horizon je fais la roue comme un grand Paon

Écoutez renaître les oracles qui avaient cessé

Le grand Pan est ressuscité

GUILLAUME APOLLINAIRE

Champagne viril qui émoustille la Champagne

Hommes faits jeunes gens

Caméléons des autos-canons

Et vous classe 17

Craquements des arrivées ou bien floraison blanches dans les cieux

J'étais content pourtant ça brûlait la paupière

Les officiers captifs voulaient cacher leurs noms

Œil du Breton blessé couché sur la civière

Et qui criait aux morts aux sapins aux canons

Priez pour moi Bon Dieu je suis le Pauvre Pierre

   Boyaux et rumeur du canon

   Sur cette mer aux blanches vagues

   Fou stoïque comme Zénon

   Pilote du cœur tu zigzagues

   Petites forêts de sapins

   La nichée attend la becquée

   Pointe-t-il des nez de lapins

   Comme l'euphorbe verruquée

   Ainsi que l'euphorbe d'ici

   Le soleil à peine boutonne

   Je l'adore comme un Parsi

   Ce tout petit soleil d'automne

   Un fantassin presqu'un enfant

   Beau comme le jour qui s'écoule

   Beau comme mon cœur triomphant

   Disait en mettant sa cagoule

   Tandis que nous n'y sommes pas

   Que de filles deviennent belles

   Voici l'hiver et pas à pas

   Leur beauté s'éloignera d'elles

Ô Lueurs soudaines des tirs
Cette beauté que j'imagine
Faute d'avoir des souvenirs
Tire de vous son origine

Car elle n'est rien que l'ardeur
De la bataille violente
Et de la terrible lueur
Il s'est fait une muse ardente

Il regarde longtemps l'horizon
Couteaux, tonneaux d'eau
Des lanternes allumées se sont croisées
Moi l'horizon je combattrai pour la victoire

Je suis l'invisible qui ne peut disparaître
Je suis comme l'onde
Allons ouvrez les écluses que je me précipite et renverse tout

SONG OF THE HORIZON IN CHAMPAGNE

Here is the rosy nipple of the warty spurge
Here are the noses of invisible soldiers
And as for me I sing of the invisible horizon
Let civilians let women hear these songs
And here first is the ballad of the wounded stretcher-bearer

The ground is white night turns it blue
The crucifixion bleeds
As does the wound
Of this soldier of the Promised Land

A dog was yapping shells yowl
A silent flash has erupted
How to say if war is funny
Masks have not quivered

GUILLAUME APOLLINAIRE

But what mad laughter beneath the mask
In the endless whiteness of this place
Where doves wear helmets
And steel takes wing

I am alone on the field of battle
I am the white trench the green and russet woods
A shell yowls
  I am going to kill you
Bestir yourselves infantrymen with your yellow braid
Tall redheaded gunners like moles
Royal blue like the bays of the Mediterranean
Velvety in every shade of velvet
Or maybe mauve or blue like the others
Or washed out
Come with your tin hats on
Get ready signal flare
Dance grenadier and flourish your pine cones
Sighting-triangle alidads aim at the flashes
Dig your holes 20-year-old boys dig your holes
Sculpt the depths
Fly off pale aeroplanes like swarms of bees
I the horizon spread my tail like a great Peacock
Listen to the oracles long silent now reviving
Great Pan is reborn
Manly champagne exhilarates Champagne
Grown men young lads
Chameleons of the motorized cannon
And you Class of '17
Crack of shells landing or else white blossoms in the sky
I was happy even though it burnt my eyelids
Captured officers wanted to conceal their names
Eye of the wounded Breton lying on the stretcher

Crying out to the dead the pines the guns
God in Heaven pray for me I am Poor Peter

Trenches and rumbling cannon fire
Upon this white-waved sea
As mad and Stoic as Zeno
Helmsman of the heart you zigzag

Little pine woods
Nestlings waiting to be fed
Do rabbits' noses poke out
Like warty spurge

And like the spurge hereabouts
The sun is barely more than a bud
I adore it like a Parsee
That tiny little sun of autumn

An infantryman almost a child
Beautiful as the day running out
Beautiful as my jubilant heart
Said as he donned his smoke-helmet

While we are not there
So many girls become beautiful
Here comes winter and little by little
Their beauty will abandon them

Oh sudden flashes of cannon fire
This beauty that I imagine
For want of memories
Must have its source in you

For it is simply the ardour
Of violent battle
And he made that awful flashing
Into his ardent muse

GUILLAUME APOLLINAIRE

He watches the horizon for a long time
Knives, water casks
Lighted lamps crisscrossed
I the horizon shall fight for victory

I am invisible I cannot disappear
I am like a wave
Come on open the floodgates let me surge through and overturn everything

My love, I sent you the rings and bracelet two days ago. These two engagement rings fallen from the heavens are made to your size and mine respectively and you should send me mine back after kissing it, it is the larger one. As for your exam, talk it over with your mother to see what needs to be done and the best way to proceed. I adore you for not making me jealous. But my faith in you is strong enough to guarantee that you will do what you have to do and what your mother wants you to do. In short do what is best. Of course we shall work together in the future but until I arrive consult your mother. The wrestling you describe is indeed divine and I adore the idea. You are my adorable Venus. But this is not conjugal correction, which is correction not wrestling. Yes I want you to be panting after the wrestling oh my voluptuous feline. Yes, I devour you, yes I take you deeply and arouse the wildest pleasure in you. By the way my love there are 9 doors not ten.

Eyes 1 and 2

Mouth 3

Ears 4 and 5

Nostrils 6 and 7

The grotto in the forest 8

The well in the valley between the hills 9

GUILLAUME APOLLINAIRE

The master of sacrifice will knock at the 9th door only at moments of great and delightful madness or when you ask.

That's right, you have it exactly, you shall belong to me to an extraordinary degree and in ways that we cannot yet put down on paper.

You have imagined your tongue's exquisite caress of the me that belongs to you and tautens passionately for you. You have apprehended the exquisite caress, so mysterious, of our two voracious mouths.

I adore my kiss on you and I feel it infinitely.

I adore the tips of your breasts and the ardent red of the vertical mouth that your letter helps me picture. I adore your hips your round and adorable hips. I impatiently await the kiss of your breasts and I impatiently but also patiently await the glorious day when your beautiful pure body shall belong to me in its virginity.

I do not want you to be afraid of me any longer, I who adore you. And your caresses are exquisite oh dearest director of our exquisite games. I want you my love so to arrange your life, so to order it that you may live in me while at the same time doing your work and also preparing for that exam if you must take it.

At all events my love be brave.

Those foolish Greeks banished beauty from their lives, rejecting the island of Cyprus the birthplace of Aphrodite goddess of beauty. Venus will never forgive them this insult. When shall I reach my own island of Cyprus where my adorable Venus is waiting for me?

Calm yourself my love, be patient, love me very much but do not get agitated.

386

Nourish your fine beauty for me who will worship it without any possibility of barriers existing between your beauty and me, just as none can exist between our two minds.

You have not told me about your new student, the elegant and sharp-witted lady.

My love I take into my mouth all the red roses of your delectable body. I love you I adore you and I take you endlessly.

Gui

My love, I adore you, it is beyond belief, it is mad, how much pleasure I got from your letters of the 21st and 22nd. How beautiful your
body is, love, I adore it, I am driven mad by it, and how beautiful are
your letters that render your body divine and provide me with a
marvellous divinity to worship. I thank you my love for saying that I
make you happy and I wish only to make you happier still. I quite
understand my love that you find it amusing to teach that young
woman the history of literature, which is indeed a highly diverting
subject. And yes, my love, I also love your rebellions but only in
order to quell them by force and sensuality. My love I kiss your
sensitive feet I adore the caress of your long legs your silky fleece
against mine. Yes, love, I want you to tell me every time you feel an
urge and I shall tell you when the same thing happens to me. Yes,
my mouth will also take the forecourt and your mouth will take me
likewise. Your woman's promptings will be the more fully answered
for it. Yes I eat you, I eat the divine seashell. Yes, we are inventing
one and the same love and all my urges belong entirely to you. I
adore your precious liberty with respect to me. My darling I adore
you and I am so affected by your letters that I no longer know what
to say except that I adore you, I adore you. Your beauty-letter drives
me quite out of my mind. I have opened every door of my body and
you have entered me as triumphantly, as cavalierly as a queen of
Spain. I adore your tall slender body, I adore your sensual eyes and
your electric body. I adore your ablutions that we shall perform

388

together, I adore your whiteness and I adore the opened pomegranate of your forecourt—what a beautiful analogy of yours my love—I adore the curve of your shoulders and the fine down at the nape of your neck, I adore your harmonious arms moving your hands in accordance with a delightful snake charmer's chiromancy. I adore the voluptuous dance of your arms with their sure gestures. I adore your mysterious armpit where the scorpions of our ardour nestle. I adore every one of your beauty spots and I shall pay homage to them meticulously every day my love and nibble your exquisite flesh. I adore the musky perfume of your armpits my Madeleine with their sweet and sensual scent. I adore your little round breasts hard and taut each with its tip standing up like an exquisite manhood I adore those erectile nipples and the range of variations induced in them by your sensations just as the chameleon's emotions affect its colour. I dedicate my heart to the brown hairs of your right breast and the delicate, almost imperceptible reddening of your left breast owing to a suffusion of blood. I adore the skin of your bosom and I cover your bacchante's flanks and legs with caresses. Feel how my vigour shakes those flanks, your pleas that I desist will be in vain, and before entering you I will place my manhood like a red carnation in the pretty valley between your breasts. I will clasp your waist in the way you say, your waist so round in my fingers, and I will bend you in every direction and then I will push you forward the better to display your magnificent fleshy dimpled behind and take you thus bent over after the fashion of a stallion mounting a mare. I will take you with a wild violence as I caress your breasts and hips and my belly slaps up against your great exquisitely white bottom. I adore your pure belly, your exquisite navel. I kiss the beauty spot on your arse. I separate the twin sisters, so plump and white, that kiss each other when you walk, love, and my mouth lingers in distraction at the most secret part of your body. I adore your thigh, I adore your

389

seashell, and I want to stay there all my life long, my love, exploring that isosceles triangle. I open your thighs wide to receive the love of my me and the love of my tongue as it melts into you, dallying longest way up high at the dwelling-place of a very excited little hermit whose essence will well into my mouth which loves you so. I adore the mauve veins of your right thigh. I adore your knees and calves and as I have told you already I shall visit every single beauty spot with my mouth, that devotee of your beauty. I adore your big toe which lords it over the other toes and likewise I adore your pink nails. My tongue wanders between your toes all your toes for the longest time, voluptuously. I adore you my love your song sings the masterpiece that is the universe and I prostrate my mind and my body before your beauty which I propose to assail with all the force of my desire for you. I feel your body, I adore you, I feel everything, as witness this letter, which is a symbolic foreshadowing of our wedding night. Three years ago I imagined an art or science of marks, an enormously subtle affair: there are extraordinary and endlessly artful marks on the stones of Gavrinis in Ireland;[1] the system of bertillonage takes individual traits for its own science of marks; writing also partakes of that subtle art and your letter my love is replete in this regard, for it is an ardent poem bearing the marks of your beauty and of our love, it is exquisite. You are mine in the most marvellous way, I adore you. I adore your flesh, your tears of ecstasy, your magnificent panther's laugh. I am happy, I wrap my arms about your flanks, I squeeze you tight, I take the pomegranate in my mouth and inhale the scent of your body. I put my manhood in your adorable mouth, feel me hardening at the touch of your tongue and if that tongue is too persistent a geyser will spout upon your face into your hair or inside your mouth which will welcome it as the very essence of your Gui whom you adore then I take you and

1 Apollinaire is mistaken: Gavrinis is an island in the Gulf of Morbihan.

our tongues and our eyes cannot part company and I likewise adore the great shudders that follow upon your pleasure. I adore you.

Along with the book I am sending you a Boche knife, a trench weapon manufactured in Solingen where the best German knives are made, our infantrymen too now have a knife. I am also sending you the buckle of a Bavarian belt bearing the motto *In Treue fest*, in faith unshakeable, to which nothing really needs adding, I adore you, tomorrow I'll send you a Bavarian helmet whose spike I am going to detach, the round-headed pins are used to secure it, the round heads go on the outside and you divide the pins on the inside of the helmet and fold the two parts down onto the black plate. There is also a cloth cover for the helmet, in this case bearing the number 19, the number of the regiment. I am also going to send you a Boche canteen made of aluminium. Denise has written me a very sweet letter, I shall reply to her. I adore you, I take your mouth and all of you.

Gui

My love, no letter, but what a delightful and very very sweet parcel, you are spoiling me. I immediately bit into the very place where you had sunk your teeth, what an intoxicating kind of kiss. I perfumed myself with the excellent eau de cologne; and I tasted the alcohol (a dozen first-rate bottles—multi-barrelled!). The knitted jersey is welcome, as are the socks, but you are overgenerous, love, where am I going to put all these things, it will be fine this time, or rather not altogether fine, because I am afraid I shall have to send you back the toilet bag. I'll keep the toothpaste, scissors, penknife and safety pins but shall return the bag with the mirror, comb, hairbrush and tooth-brush. I have no room for these things my love. I have a broken comb and a toothbrush with a replaceable brush. So save the other things for when I come home they will be useful then. My broken comb does for me here and should I come to need a toothbrush you can send this one back again.

The tobacco is very very good, not too strong, the nougat exquisite and how nice of you to have thought of sweets. You are so kind to have sewn the toilet bag, but rather than have it get filthy here where I have no need of it I would much rather you kept it for me. You spoil me too much. I adore you and I kiss your seashell for a very long time, I drink your soul in. My love we are working hard today. Believe me, I love you. The day is sad, but I am thinking of your precious beauty which is my sunshine; last night I was even sadder on account of the fog. But such sad moods are passing, they come with the first mists of winter.

L'hiver revient mon âme est triste

Mon cœur ne sait rien exprimer

Peut-être bien que rien n'existe

Hiver de tout hiver d'aimer

Où la peine seule résiste

Et pourquoi donc mon cœur bat-il

Par la tristesse qu'il endure?

Toi qui m'attends ô cœur gentil

Ne sais-tu pas que je m'azure

Pour te rejoindre plus subtil

Je suis le bleu soldat d'un rêve

Pense à moi mais perds la raison

Vois-tu le songe qui s'achève

Se confondre avec l'horizon

Chaque fois que ton œil se lève

Ô toi que j'aime éperdument

À qui je pense dès l'aurore

Et tout le jour je vais t'aimant

Et quand vient le soir je t'adore

Au fond du bois d'où nous tirons sur l'Allemand

Winter is returning my soul is sad

My heart can express nothing

Very possibly nothing exists

Winter of all winters of love

Which suffering alone resists

So why does my heart keep beating

As it endures such sorrow?

GUILLAUME APOLLINAIRE

You who await me oh sweetheart
Don't you know I donned the blue
To rejoin you as a keener man

I am the blue soldier of a dream
Think of me but abandon reason
Do you see the dream fading
Merging with the horizon
Every time your eyes look up

Oh you whom I love madly
Whom I think of from daybreak
And keep on loving all day long
And worship as night falls
Deep in this wood whence we fire on the German

394

I love you my darling and this evening I shall write at length.
Tomorrow morning I'll send you the helmet with the spike removed,
I have told you how to put this back on. Your brothers will do it. I
am also sending you a Boche canteen made of aluminium.

I am anxious for you to start wearing the chain on your wrist and to
send me back the engagement ring. I take your hips endlessly. I take
you deeply and passionately, mouth to mouth and eyes wide open.

Your Gui

Love, the letter of yesterday that would have borne the above date and left here today could not be sent. I never wrote it for an important reason. Change. This one that was supposed to go off tomorrow the 4th will not go until the day after tomorrow the 5th for the same reason. But I'll write you again tomorrow and the 2 letters will leave together. So you will be only one short. Ah! Madeleine, what mud, what mud, you simply cannot imagine the mud, you would have to be here and see for yourself how it can have the consistency of putty, or whipped cream, or sometimes of floor polish, slippery in an extraordinary way. You would have to see the teams lose their footing and get up under the whips of the drivers or break their traces when the fall is too violent. My horse has slipped three times, and fallen after one of those slips, fortunately I was able to get him up. Riding in such conditions on slick tracks chock-a-block with troops on foot and mounted is no picnic. And I should have hated to be rolling in the mud myself, but after he fell to his knees a touch of my spurs taught my good horse (who is no longer limping) that he must walk in the mud as he does elsewhere.

Hold fast, horses, do not slip. Soon we arrived at our new battery wagon line, which is not far from our positions of yesterday (and we shall see our new ones only tomorrow), I was thrilled to receive your letter of the 27th. I'll reply soon.

GUILLAUME APOLLINAIRE

Forgive me my love for ever having supposed that anything sent by you might not be useful to me. I shall return nothing and the toilet bag is safely packed away. What is more, during this rainy spell the alcohol has been very helpful indeed. The tobacco is excellent, you know, my love, truly wonderful, and the file is also a good idea for my nails.

So I shan't be able to deal with your Mama's ring for the next few days. You know that I don't want her to be jealous of me, because I am really fond of my Madeleine's little Mama. Tell her she must not be jealous, because we shall love her both of us. I am very happy that her idea about Beauvais has now become one that I share. Yes, the green and blue which were ever my favourite colours will become even more precious to me if they are the colours of my lady and what is more they will put me in mind of the eyes of my love. Tell your Mama that I am very grateful to her for dictating my verses to you. Does she like them? No, the fact is I have not received the packet of tobacco you mention. But since it is prohibited do not send any more, it would be idiotic to have a court case over something so trivial. The tooth with the lost filling does not hurt because it had been well looked after. It is not damaged. Tell me about your own beautiful teeth. You must stop being jealous my love because it is agreed that you shall no longer be jealous. You must no longer be jealous because you know full well that there is never any reason for it and that you can trust me completely. I really wish I could see the beautiful landscape visible from your Mama's bedroom window.

Why yes, love, I shall most often be on top of you, but sometimes it is you who will be on top of me, sometimes we shall be on our sides, sometimes you will turn over and your bottom will be up in the air, sometimes lying on your side you will offer me your voluptuous nether parts, all ways of arranging my triumphant arrival at the forecourt. Sometimes with you laying on your belly I shall spread apart your delicate behind and pass through the 9th door, or else as we look into each other's eyes I shall raise your delicate legs and pass through the ninth door by that route, and myriad variations ad infinitum.

Yes, my letters are always happy now my love and I adore you.

I want you also my love to describe your forecourt, for there are many different kinds, some are situated low down and face the ground, others high up, intruding upon the belly, some lie in a hollow, others on a downy eminence called the mount or mound of Venus, some are closed tight, others half-open, some have thin lips others long ones. Some lips are dark, others pale, the inside of yours is the colour of a pomegranate you tell me. The little organ at the top known as the clitoris can hardly be felt in some, in others is the size of a pea, and in yet others resembles a very tiny finger poking out slightly from its hiding-place; there are other varieties too, each corresponding to a particular temperament. Some may be discerned under the fleece, while a thick fleece may conceal the entire forecourt. Your behind too I should like to know about, whether it is rounded and prominent relative to your thighs or is it a mere swelling or broadening out of the back and hips?

I also spoke to you of me and of my sceptre the day before yesterday. It belongs to the [*illegible*] Aryan family and is highly eroticized. Which means that the pleasure it can elicit is much greater than that known to the Arabs, for instance, who damage their women without giving them any pleasure and who in any case do not know how to vary pleasure. I am so formed as to promote the greatest joy in you as an intelligent woman whose beauty is bound to be preserved for a very long time for all that we are bound to partake to the most

GUILLAUME APOLLINAIRE

fantastic degree of the pleasures of love, since we are both so admirably suited for them. My love many a time when we possess each other, as a way of perfecting the pleasure of our mouths or to enhance the most penetrating and exquisite of caresses you will offer me some delicacy a sweet or a piece of fruit that I may seek out in the depths of the seashell with a skilful tongue quivering with voluptuousness. Does this refinement appeal to you?

You cannot imagine oh my love how happy I am to know that you are a great walker. I am so fond of walking and since I have promised myself that after the war it will be my only physical exercise we'll be taking short outings or excursions together on foot. If we are rich we shall also go for runs in the car now and then, but most often we'll go walking. I do not care much for the bicycle, which is cumbersome and diminishes sexual vigour. Meanwhile you do not ride horseback and in any case I'll have had quite enough of riding by the end of the war and plan to have no more to do with that most noble pursuit.

You never told me, my love, whether your hair is long and how far it falls down your back.

Since you tell me about your sensations let me tell you about mine. When I read your letters, which are so sensual, an exquisite thrill runs through my whole body before taking up residence in the same place as with you but in me that place is very different, for it swells grows longer stands up straight, prances about bares its head and stretches out in your honour and direction, the attraction that it feels for your haunches is incredible but understandable in view of the fact that the two doors of love are in a sense their dependencies, my groin has an amazing appetite for you and for your buttocks and my sceptre also feels a deep longing for your armpits and mouth, and my mouth likewise longs for your three mouths and the tips of your breasts. My tongue too for your feet and my teeth for your flesh, my hands yearn for your breasts and your hair, your neck, your arms and your thighs and your waist, my feet wish for your back your belly your fleece, my belly wishes for your feet, my nose for your three patches of fur, my arms for all of you, my legs for your mouths and my eyes for all of you.

I am so happy, Madelon, that you are not the nervous type. That is quite wonderful, for since I myself am nervous I needed a wife who was not, who was my slave and my wits, and my calm and all of me, and you are more than all of me.

So I adore you my love, I undress you devoutly and place my distracted mouth upon a forecourt half-open and eager, I present my frightfully tense and swollen manhood to the redness of your mouth. Your lips anoint and caress it your tongue torments it and once the pomegranate has released its exquisite liquor into my mouth I plunge my dagger inside you, it slides the more easily for having been moistened by your loving saliva, and as madness overtakes us I shoot my vital juice into the innermost parts of you and we faint away, only to come back to ourselves even more in love, more in love than ever with each other, oh Madeleine take my kisses with your two mouths, and then too with your third, more secret one. I adore you.

Gui

My love, here we are, removed to a place very close by—no further away than the wagon line, same vicinity, same sector. We are about to start building new huts.

My love I got your letter of the 28th and 29th. When you write me and allude to something in my letters please do say what it is, when you refer to such and such a poem, secret or not, enclosed in a letter of mine you should give the first line or somehow let me know which poem you mean, or if you evoke a particular caress say which one. Do not fear repetition, we are far apart and if we are clearly to understand each other we should not be afraid of repeating ourselves; moreover repetition is an effect of style that is not to be feared. Classical authors whether Greek Latin or French were not afraid of it. We need to be precise. Meanwhile tell me more about yourself my darling—as I have said and let me say it again there is nothing suspect about repetitions, on the contrary.* We now know what our new positions are, but I am not permitted to tell you. We have to dig another hole (*trou*) and construct shelters (*abris*).[1] You too my love give me great joy, oh my sweet darling. And yes, our love will always be new. By now you must know just how Pasiphaë had knowledge of the bull, there is an engraved stone in some museum or other depicting the imaginary details of this legend. Pasiphaë appears bent forward offering her rump to the bull, which has its forehooves planted on the Cretan's back as its brute beast's

---

* This morning, sleeping in the open air, I was the first awake, and I shouted out 'Madeleine!' The echo that came back was 'I love you!'

1 Apollinaire is here seeking to convey to Madeleine that he is at Trou-Bricot, in the Somme-Tourbe sector.

male organ passes between her legs in search of the furnace. I have not yet had the time to make the napkin-rings and most likely shan't have any very soon, but remind me when you get this letter.

My word you are a true poet my love and I adore you. My repetitiveness ought not to shock you, my love, we are not writing literature here. You are right to make the young ones work hard. Tell me what they are going to do when they grow up. Do urge Denise to work hard at her painting. For me too, my love, the lovers' embrace is the important thing. For me too, ever since we began getting ready for that embrace everything that is not the two of us has disappeared, even war itself no longer exists. Consider your power and speak to me more and more of yourself so as to keep me in a state of perpetual ecstasy. I adore your description of how you rise in the morning. I adore the way your breasts press forward. I too have an admiration at once Greek and devotional for your body. Yes indeed, your body is beauty eternal. It is true my love that all the great passions are as nothing alongside ours and that we are marvellously alike. Yes, I take you on my knees my love and for a long while, for the embrace may also be performed in that way. Nectar was the drink of the gods of Olympus, but it was hydromel that the Northern gods favoured and I truly love hydromel. I have had it only once. It was delicious; they drink it in Poland and that is where I drank some. Yes, my love, I eat your mouth the red fruit of our love and your entire body and I shall cause you to die of love only to revive you by means of yet more love. Yes, we shall have nights of mad love in which our embrace will never end.

You ask that I talk to you after love's ecstasy and you are afraid that sadness might preside over that moment. *Post coitum animal triste*, says a Latin proverb. After coitus the animal becomes sad (coitus being the scientific name for the human act of love). For my part,

GUILLAUME APOLLINAIRE

however, I have never experienced such sadness, which is said to be characteristic of men and not of women. I repeat, though, that I have never felt it, but why are you afraid of sadness between us, my love? When I do feel sad, which happens suddenly sometimes, it never comes from ecstasy, after which in any case your caresses will soon bring me renewed joy. In fact you possess the cure for my infrequent, sudden and short-lived moments of sadness. No, no, my love, I am not scolding you. There is no reason to scold you because you ask things that it is perfectly natural to ask.

There is one thing: I have the bad habit of reading in bed, if only just one page, before I go to sleep, but of course if you don't like this you shall rid me of the practice with the greatest of ease! I kiss you my darling, I kiss you very hard and hold you tight nestled against me. I do not clearly recall the expression in the eyes of the person in my vision of this morning, which did not last long; but it was surely you coming to tell me that you would be mine, oh my love, oh my most beautiful love!

I adore you love and I take all of you. I don't know how I managed to write you today, and this letter is certainly messy enough for you to see that I wrote it under difficult circumstances. But I adore you, and that should suffice surely for you to forgive me, my darling little love, I kiss your breasts your mouth and all of you my love. I kiss all of you m'love and clasp your waist. I stroke your lovely hair and take your mouth.

Gui

402

My little love no letter from you today. I wonder have you now read my letter of yesterday and grasped the meanings of the words I underlined. Today we decorated our colonel, parade under arms with trumpets. I was serrefile to the 2nd Section. Sabres were drawn for the first time since the war began! A fine spectacle I must say. The sounding of cavalry trumpets has something more poetic more distant more celestial than the bugle call. Leaves are once more being granted but say nothing yet, there's no question of mine for the time being, I'll let you know as soon as it becomes a possibility. I love you, my very dearest love. I enclose a word from a friend of mine who is one of the best of today's poets. With an arm amputated![1]

I love you, I think of your dear beauty.

1 Blaise Cendrars.

2 Another 'Secret Poem', undated and out of order, is also described by Apollinaire as the seventh; see Addenda, p. 608.

LE SEPTIÈME POÈME SECRET[2]

Une grande ardeur en moi
Une grande mollesse ardente en toi
Tu ouvres délicieusement toutes les portes
Je me déguise et je t'emprunte des moustaches et la barbe
Ta toison
Je m'arme de la langue et je creuse un délicieux sentier
        Dans la forêt vierge
Madeleine est une jeune bergère
        Qui paît le blanc troupeau des brebis de son corps

GUILLAUME APOLLINAIRE

Madeleine est une jeune bergère d'une merveilleuse beauté

Ses seins sont d'adorables proues

Deux vaisseaux cuirassés qui serons mon escadre

Ma langue est le mineur qui fouille

Dans la mine de houille

    Ta toison

J'adore tes lèvres rouges

      Gondoles de parade

Qui larguent leurs amarres tressées comme tes cheveux noirs

      Tes cheveux

Tes cheveux qui sont le crépuscule de toutes les beautés

Et il ne demeure que la tienne

Naviguons sur tes yeux de sinople

Il s'y jette les fleuves des veines bleues de ta chair si noble

J'adore la source divine qui sourd

      Sous

      Ta toison

Ma langue sens ma langue

Elle te préparera à l'étreinte profonde

Le soc de la charrue creusera le sillon

Je t'adore mon amour

Entends chanter Ô Madeleine pâmée

     Entends chanter et rechanter

      Le rossignol caché

Le froid revient le froid terrible

      Sous les toiles tentes

Et je t'écris mon poème que je chante en l'écrivant

Et je t'écris couché par terre

     Le froid revient, le froid sans feu

     Car on n'a pas de bois

Je t'adore mon amour, je suis heureux par toi

Et je prends tous les trésors

De ton corps

Dans une immense caresse

Qui fait surgir dans l'hiver une liesse

De tout printemps

Le Lys la Rose

Sous ma caresse

SEVENTH SECRET POEM

A great ardour in me

A great ardent luxuriation in you

You open all your doors delectably

I am in disguise borrowing moustache and beard from you

Your fleece

Armed with my tongue I clear a delectable path

Through the virgin forest

Madeleine is a young shepherdess

Grazing the white flock of ewes of her body

Madeleine is a young shepherdess of splendid beauty

Her breasts are adorable prows

Two ironclad vessels that will be my squadron

My tongue is the miner delving

In the coal pit

Your fleece

I adore your red lips

Ceremonial gondolas

Casting off their moorings plaited like your dark hair

Your hair

Your hair that is the nightfall of all beauties

And only yours remains

Let us steer by your sinople eyes

Fed by the rivers of the blue veins of your so noble flesh

I adore the divine spring that trickles

Beneath

Your fleece

405

GUILLAUME APOLLINAIRE

My tongue feel my tongue
Preparing you for the deepest of embraces
The share ploughing the furrow
I adore you my love
Listen to the song oh Madeleine enraptured
        Listen to the song the repeated song
            Of the hidden nightingale
The cold is back the terrible cold
            Under the canvas
And I write your poem and sing it as I write
And I write lying on the ground
        The cold is back, and no fire
        For we have no wood
I adore you my love, I am happy thanks to you
And I take all the treasures
Of your body
With an immense caress
That amidst this winter draws forth the joy
        Of every spring
        The Lily the Rose
            Beneath my caress

                Gui

My love, still no letter from you today, that makes two days now, did you understand what I underlined in my letter of yesterday [*sic*], *trou* etc.? The censorship suppressed a portion of my latest 'Vie anecdo-tique'. I'll send you the *Mercure* tomorrow. I am expecting a long letter from you at least. Leaves have been reinstated, I think that in a few days I should be able to give you a rough probable date. Where we are there are thousands of rats, it is frightening. I really want the leave to come through this time. My darling Madelon, I adore you with all my heart. I picture you in a more and more familiar way. Today it is your lips that I imagine most of all your ravishing red lips and I have such a strong desire for the smells of your body that I could almost faint just thinking of them. You are the incense-burner of all the sweetest fragrances. I fancy I detect the vanilla'd scent of your whole body, that dark white woman's body with breasts so round.

Oh my darling your buttocks are the white bulls of hecatombs wherein you shall ever be the willing victim.

Today my love I nibble each of your ears in turn and slip my tongue behind and within them in a kiss that will cause your delectable breasts to swell. I dream too of the exquisite vale that cleaves your adorable behind.

I have had no letter from you for two days, and I wonder why.

GUILLAUME APOLLINAIRE

I think **endlessly** too of your feet, my mouth will offer them divine caresses and quiet their pain.

And I take you today just as you imagine, which is to say I upon you, breast to breast, all of me in you and then after the most delightful of struggles I take you once more, still perturbed by your own formidable voluptuousness and I take you upon me, with one arm around your exquisite waist while with my other hand I play with your quivering bottom. Your grey-green eyes look at me voluptuously. You have the most beautiful gaze imaginable and also the most unusual. I now remember the expression you wore on the train and how you were already absolutely certain about what was to transpire between us, oh Madelon darling my ever so sweet possession.

408   What I find most striking is how tall you are. I had not noticed that.

And your hands, tell me about your hands which must surely be heavenly.

Tell me, Love, apropos of my leave, does Lamur have its own station or is Lamur simply part of Oran? Should I give Lamur as my destination when on leave or should I say Oran? My thought is that I shall probably be able to come for Christmas.

Have I already pointed out to you that 'Lamur' is ever so close to 'L'Amour', so what could be more natural than that one get there by setting sail at Port-Vendres? But must I absolutely embark at Port-Vendres, after all you yourself my love once took ship at Marseilles, so please get the information and let me have it. I take your mouth and drink your saliva which I adore.

Gui

You are quite right to have made up your mind my love and I approve of what you have done for Marthe. The story about little Liliane is indeed not trivial. I have known her father Sadia Lévy for a good while, twelve years or so. We both used to write for *La Grande France*. The first book I had to talk or rather write about was *XI Journées en force* (11 Days of Brute Force) by Sadia Lévy and Robert Randau. After that, Sadia Lévy having moved to Paris, we became friendly. Not so with Randau whom I met at Lévy's later. Sadia Lévy came several times to my place and I visited him on occasion at his home in Montrouge. He is a belated follower of Villiers de l'Isle-Adam and he would have been a great talent had not that passion shackled his genius. But Sadia Lévy writes only with difficulty. He has written one good novel, *Rabbin*, and another rather curious one, never published as a book, which is the novel of his impotence. This work was fortunate enough to be imitated as *Un Uomo finito* (*The Failure*) by Giuseppe [Giovanni] Papini, one of Italy's finest authors today, and in this form it has met with great success. Lévy is a proud man yet very modest. He once began a magnificent translation of the Psalms but mistakenly abandoned it. He is a redheaded and priestly Jew. Being exceedingly honest, he was hopeless at business and relied on his savings, the entirety of which were eaten up and swindled from him in the most cynical manner by his best friend, who in order to achieve this at leisure spent several years stoking

Lévy's mania or rather his exclusive passion for the aforesaid author of *Cruel Tales*.

I was very fond of Sadia Lévy but we were never comrades in the way I and some others were, others who were not married as he was. His wife Rachel was good-hearted like him and she had a buxom and rather remarkable Jewish beauty, but unfortunately she was deaf. Their young daughter when I used to see her was the epitome of a pretty little Jewish girl. In the wake of the confidence trick of which they were the innocent victims the Lévys were obliged to return to Algeria, though I did not know that they went to Oran. They must be depending financially on Sadia's brother unless after all Sadia has gone into business or begun working. The fact is that for several years now he has not contributed to any of the reviews nor have I had any news of him.

Sadia Lévy is a decent fellow to the best of my knowledge. And should the opportunity present itself you might certainly remember me most sincerely and warmly to the family. Like you, my love, I never feel so well as I do in the sun, and thanks to the sun, but of course you are my sun.

How I adore the milky sensation you get from my caress and how I adore your naked body stretched out at my feet curling like a snake and I stroke all of you enveloping you little by little with a satin of voluptuousness that eventually reaches into your very heart. Yes, I shall always hunger for you my love, my hunger for you is immense, my fine, my adorable Madelon. I adore that shiver of yours just beneath the skin . . . I adore your mouth the well of our kisses. How I love our smiles as passion passes! I give you my smile and yours is surely mine. We smile at each other continually and even our seriousness will be a luminous smile. Oh my beautiful rider, I adore you. I feel the firmness of your breasts against my chest, and I likewise place myself upon you my fine steed and if you like you may cross your legs over my back to make our embrace deeper, tighter, wilder and more passionate. I am glad to hear that you no longer have to go home late at night.

The story of the old Arab I found very amusing, oh my white Madeleine of the grey-green eyes. I await with calm impatience the arrival of the engagement ring that will have touched every part of your body and that you will have worn for several days.

Tell me too my love about your bedtimes, and in great detail.

Perhaps after all it is not so easy to draw the outline of your breast on the basis of its shadow. . . .

Oh dearest perfection I nibble your entire body beginning with the toes the calves the belly I explore the pink conch of the belly button with my tongue, the gulley between the breasts, the sweet tips of the breasts, your exquisite neck the ears your mouth and I nibble at the forecourt and lying full length upon you I separate the exquisite lips of the darling wound so that as voluptuous feelings arise in you from my back-and-forth motion you respond with lascivious movements of the hips until the moment when our mouths joined together drink each other in and our eyes exchange our two souls. I adore the shudders that run through your whole body and the ever more passionate ardour that animates us and leads us at last to release streams of voluptuous nectar upon your body and what happy languor then follows upon our revels while my mouth, still alert, rejoins yours endlessly oh my Madelon.

Gui

GUILLAUME APOLLINAIRE

My love,

I adore you, we are still so poorly dug in here that I still cannot work
as I should like. There are millions of mice here. Mice have always
prospered on battlefields, just as they did during the long wars
recounted in the mediaeval legends of France, Germany and
especially Poland—legends in which they stand for the Norman
invaders: an old king is pictured besieged in his castle, often on an
island, besieged by the mice representing the Normans—a symbol
obviously based on reality, for war-ravaged lands are always infested
by mice. They gobble up everything in a frenzy, even chocolate, and
any number of soldier's service records have been devoured by rats
or mice.

Every night the mice begin their dance and I rather fancy their
nocturnal ruckus and squealing are at the root of the notion of a
Witches' Sabbath. They eat the bread, leave their droppings everywhere (mice, I mean—not witches). These animals are the bane of
the Front. Around here the gunners call them little pretties, no
doubt in hopes of conciliating them, rather as the ancient Greeks
called the Furies the Eumenides as though describing them as
friendly might somehow appease them. I have had no letter from
you today, my love, so the day has been far from gay. I hope that
tomorrow I shall get several letters. I dreamt for a good portion of
the night of your firm flesh, of the red roses of your breasts and your
mouth, of your fleece, of your intimate being of your adorable

thighs of your eyes of your pretty, saucy little nose that I love so much and of your ears that you have still not told me about. My love, this evening I caress you in an infinitely sweet way. My tongue runs ever so lightly up and down your spine and I nibble at the darling curls of your armpits, I become intoxicated by the smell of your body and like a prince charming I push aside the branches of the triangular virgin forest where in a coral-doored palace my sleeping beauty slumbers and when I enter armed with the arrow of love everything awakes, your nerves, your flesh, your breasts palpitate, your lower belly contracts and churns, your eyes flood your mouth seeks mine and even your hair becomes sensitive. I invade you so very slowly that you faint quite away. The dates were delicious my love. At present I am using your toothpaste which is said to be very good. Usually I use peroxide in tins for travellers, this is supposed to be the best product although it is not yet widely known to the public, but what you sent is good too. I packed 2 tins of peroxide when I left for the Front and had just finished the 1st when yours arrived. So I can now save my second tin intact.

LE 9ᵉ POÈME SECRET

J'adore ta toison qui est le parfait triangle
De la divinité
Je suis le bûcheron de l'unique forêt vierge
Ô mon Eldorado
Je suis le seul poisson de ton océan voluptueux
Toi ma belle sirène
Je suis l'alpiniste de tes montagnes neigeuses
Ô mon alpe très blanche
Je suis l'archer divin de ta bouche si belle
Ô mon très cher carquois
Et je suis le haleur de tes cheveux nocturnes
Ô beau navire sur le canal de mes baisers

GUILLAUME APOLLINAIRE

Et les lys de tes bras m'appellent par des signes
Ô mon jardin d'été
Les fruits de ta poitrine mûrissent pour moi leur douceur
Ô mon verger parfumé
Et je te dresse ô Madeleine ô ma beauté sur le monde
Comme la torche de toute lumière

THE 9th SECRET POEM

I adore your fleece the perfect triangle
Of the deity
I am the woodcutter in the sole virgin forest
Oh my Eldorado
I am the only fish in your voluptuous ocean
Oh my beautiful siren
I am the climber on your snowy mountains
Oh my Alp so white
I am the divine archer of your beautiful mouth
Oh my darling quiver
And I am the hauler of your night-time hair
Oh my fine barge on the canal of my kisses
And the lilies of your arms beckon me
Oh my summer garden
The sweet fruits of your breasts ripen for me
Oh my fragrant orchard
And I set you oh Madeleine oh my beauty above the world
Like the beacon of all light

Gui

My darling I neglected to mention the dear blue ribbons, they are my glory and your colours, green and blue, the green of your envelopes and the blue of your ribbons. With my mouth upon yours I faint away.

Gui

I am very concerned about all those transports sunk in the Mediterranean. The confounded Boches seem able to do as they please in our sea. Everything you tell me about this bothers me. Why yes love I shall adore you as a dove but just as much as a panther. I drink you in again and again, I devour you again and again. You are my adorable blue love. I adore your teeth and I adore your grey-green eyes which are those of a little Minerva, solid and wise and strong, sea-green eyes, eyes like a sun-filled meadow. And I adore your gums so red and I love your laugh and your smile that reveal them. I hear your nips at my ear and I feel them too. I feel those nips and the caress of your tongue upon my intimate being which is the lord of your voluptuousness and I take you passionately. I kiss your tooth the one that is a little chipped. It is perfectly natural that you should wish for me to spill your blood, for it will testify to your virginity. But my love, you should desire everything imaginable from me, be it correction or my detours to the 9th door. You will enjoy this last too. My tongue will play a part—and will yours perhaps do likewise? Do not be afraid of me, but be passionately mine. I adore you. We shall possess one another madly. All of me, every bit of me is yours my darling slave. I adore your haunches weighing down on my mouth. I feel your kiss upon me just as intensely as mine upon you. I am so happy my love that you are not the least bit upset. You have told me nothing of the social standing of your student. Who is this woman? Does she normally live in Oran? Is she married? I approve of the

GUILLAUME APOLLINAIRE

way you are with her. To come back to the Lévys, I am well acquainted with Sadia Lévy; we were colleagues for a long while as contributors to the little magazines, but never intimate friends. Moreover, I should warn you as a precaution against gossip that the Lévys know Marie L., whom they frequently saw with me and indeed even more often than me, for they would attend her at-homes, which I never did. Marie even painted a joint portrait of the three of them, father mother and little girl on a single canvas, which I do believe was bought by a Boche. Which said, I do not suppose they are much given to gossiping; Madame Sadia Lévy always struck me as a very good woman, albeit a little deaf. Theirs was a good marriage. Sadia Lévy, however, is somewhat too strict and priest-like. He is cut out to live like a Levite and in my view he understands very little about the world around him. He is a littérateur far removed from real life and very blinkered. His artistic tastes are obsolete. But I believe him to be an honest man. It seems to me my love that this war is going badly. All the same, the present Minister is an improvement and the Minister of War is finally someone to be reckoned with. I hope that there is still time enough for him to display the genius that I do believe he has, based on what I know of him. I liked the description you give of your bed, sweetheart. A fine bed, clearly. Like you I love very big beds. This one shall be a magnificent battlefield for us. Tell me of your hands too my love.

LE 10ᵉ POÈME SECRET

Mon amour est à genoux les jambes écartées
Sa tête est enfouie dans les coussins
La chevelure noire de mon amour s'étend autour d'elle comme mille serpents sortant
* de leur nid.*
Mon amour cambre la taille et hausse sa croupe autant qu'il lui est possible
Si bien que le maître voit entre les cuisses

La touffe de la forêt sur la coupole bombée qui couronne la sape que je veux prendre

Les abeilles y logent et le miel le plus doux s'y échauffe

La croupe étend sa blancheur polaire et apparaît dans toute sa splendeur

Et ma bouche aujourd'hui veut une autre sape qui s'ouvre petite et noire

Dans la longue et profonde tranchée

       Qui sépare les deux montagnes de ta croupe

Ma langue s'y attarde longtemps déplissant les replis secrets

Et tu t'étales complaisamment ravie de l'hommage inouï de cette caresse unique et
    jamais faite à d'autres, caresse unique, rare et délicieuse

Puis t'ayant sentie ô mon esclave, bien rassurée bien mienne

J'approche le sapeur de la petite sape

      Il entre doucement et n'entre que la tête et ta tête se rehausse pour que ta
      bouche cherche ma bouche

Ma main droite caresse tes seins et la gauche va éveiller la volupté au fond de la forêt
    mystérieuse

Tandis que le sapeur va et vient dans l'antre le plus secret et que tes fesses de cristal
    frappent en cadence sur mon ventre

Jusqu'au moment où la mine bien creusée

Je l'inonde tandis que tu t'évanouis en mordant ma langue et en inondant ma main
    gauche

THE 10th SECRET POEM

My love is on her knees with her legs apart

Her head is buried in cushions

The dark hair of my love spreads about her like a thousand snakes coming
    out of their nest.

My love bows her back and raises her rear as high as she can

So high that between her thighs the master can see

The tuft of the forest on the dome surmounting the sap I so much wish to
    enter

Where bees dwell and the sweetest honey is warming up

But the polar whiteness of your rear appears in all its splendour

And today my mouth seeks another sap opening up so small and dark

GUILLAUME APOLLINAIRE

In the long deep trench

      That runs between the two hills of your behind

There my tongue tarries long smoothing out secret folds

And you stretch out in complaisant delight at this unique caress, never

   bestowed on another, unique, rare and delicious

Then feeling oh my slave that you are fully reassured and fully mine

I bring the sapper to the little sap

      It enters gently and intrudes only its head and your head rises up

       so that your mouth can seek mine

My right hand strokes your breasts while the left steals deep into the myste-

   rious forest to arouse voluptuous feelings

The sapper comes and goes in the most secret of redoubts and your crystal

   buttocks count cadence on my belly

Until with the mine well excavated

I flood it as you faint away nibbling my tongue and inundating my left hand

It is your birthday today my love and it is also the first day of snow here. Everything that was not white, and God knows there is plenty of it in this land of chalk horribly ravaged by more than a year of war, has suddenly turned white and simply everything is now as white as your exquisite body. I have worked out how much longer it may take before I go on leave: roughly 4 more months, or slightly less, maybe it will happen even sooner but that is far from certain in view of the dearth of leave in our region. In some regions soldiers are already getting their 2nd leave. Winter is with us now, hard and not made easier by the ban on woodcutting imposed by the powers-that-be. It is curious how bureaucratic this war can be, as though it could run like clockwork. Still, one gets the vague feeling that a tiny glimmer of hope for peace is beginning to take shape in the limbo of the fate of nations. A peace that I am starting to yearn for with every ounce of my being. Meanwhile your love makes up for everything and consoles me for everything. I love you in blue almost white my love, I love you in winter and I want to be with you in a lovely warm bed and feel the whole lissome body of the delightful big girl that you are up against mine. I would warm my hands in your marvellous fur and your breath would enfold me in the warmth that I adore. Today I looked at my pictures of you. The last one, which pleased me so much, has almost completely faded. The lads cannot be doing a good job of tinting. This has happened too with the very first photo. My love I love you forever in blue I caress your

GUILLAUME APOLLINAIRE

Whiteness, I pluck your roses ardently and I breathe in the fragrance of your legs those lilies of my desire.

I devour you with tenderness this evening and so much sweetness eventually makes me greedy and I want to devour, truly devour all of you who are mine.

My big, my little darling Madelon how delightfully I love you. Tell me about your nails my love, about your neck and your nostrils and also your ears and tell me too about the little hermit whose existence you were unaware of and likewise about your tongue of which you have never spoken, your adorable tongue from which I anticipate thousands of caresses and which already gives me a divine sensation.

I adore my darling Madelon and I take your mouth with incredible fervour and press your whole exquisite and consenting body to mine. I feel the adorable litheness of your waist and our mouths play with each other in the most heavenly way like two bugles sounding the call to love.

Gui

420

My love, today I got yours of the 7th and now understand what
you were telling me yesterday about Sidi Ferruch and the English.
Dismal weather here. I want you to drink me in. I think of your
beauty my darling and hide my eyes in the violent odour of your
thick and delightfully dark fleece. It is true my love there is but one
painful thing for us and that is our separation. I am your king oh
my enslaved little queen. I take infinite delight in your shudders my
love. Yesterday I sent you the latest *Mercure* along with another
Bavarian belt buckle.

421

I am so happy that the engagement rings succeeded triumphantly
in making the sea crossings and that we are both now wearing our
rings. I never take mine off, I sleep and wash with it on. Yes, my
love, we shall wrap ourselves round one another and bring every
conceivable part of our bodies together.

The story of the lady musician is amusing.—And you must kiss
Pierre for having come to your defence. But he must beware of
fostering grudges.

Yes, love, I adore the fact that you like my me in every door of your
body. I adore you love and I take you onto me my mouth devouring
yours, my fine flower planted in the garden of your forecourt and a
single finger gently tapping at the 9th door. Electric tremors con-
vulse your body but I clasp you so tightly that you can hardly move.

GUILLAUME APOLLINAIRE

My love I adore you.

About Sadia Lévy, he is no doubt a highly intelligent person from a sacerdotal Jewish standpoint but may perhaps be foolish as seen in another light.

Oh how I long to love you my love far away from this horrible mud in which we are living, far away from this frigid half-melted snow.

I am very glad that you have received everything I sent you. At the same time I am a little concerned about what you write my love. I am worried because I cannot get a clear view of things from here and I can't help wondering how the defence of ports such as Oran is being ensured.

I adore you I take your mouth endlessly, deeply, I adore you.

Gui

My love, we are now definitely in position. With no regrets, because we are well out of that horrible artillery wagon line where we were freezing and sleeping in water. The fact is that at the time of our attack,[1] because we advanced too rapidly and because we were expecting to push much further forward, the wagon line had left behind everything except strictly regulation gear and thereafter it was devilishly difficult to find any kind of equipment. On top of that you have to picture the rain and snow falling on all those poor men with nothing but tent canvas to protect them. As for me I was in an old shack that resembled nothing so much as the cribs they set up in churches at Christmastime.

Finally last night we decamped in the darkness, in the snow, across the shell holes and the Boche trenches, and then suddenly the landscape changed, there were tall trees stripped bare often blasted it is true, but truly big trees, and on to the famous location, a steep-sided depression full of saps, our gun positions, and 200 metres away from our guns our shelters, constructed by the Boches, including my new digs (one of my men sleeps in our kitchen). This shelter is fine and I like it, in fact these are the most pleasant quarters I have had up to now. And all fixed up ready for use. Except of course for a table and chair. There was a big table, but to have my own I made myself a combination table-cum-bench. I sit astride it and can write perfectly like that and it is not at all awkward.[2]

1 At Tahure (the toponym is crossed out on the manuscript).

2 See p. 270.

423

GUILLAUME APOLLINAIRE

Surrounding our shelters is a large German cemetery almost all of whose graves date from February; I plan to copy down the inscriptions. There is a whole art to these tombs, the marble plaques and so on, one is put in mind of a stage set for *Hamlet*. Nearby there is also a small French artillerymen's cemetery; the fact is fighting has been fierce here. In September an entire Boche field-defence system was captured here and our men took a German colonel by surprise in the dugout which is now our telephone post. The colonel refused to surrender and they killed him and those with him when they broke in, and only when the fighting was over did it emerge that he was a Boche colonel who had two pretty women with him.

And that my love is about all I can tell you today about this curious and picturesque area, it is a bit like the Vosges. There are still a good many rifles lying about and piles of debris.

I am happy alone in my bed in the corner and I am making myself a separate alcove by hanging up a sheet of canvas. I think of you endlessly, my very dearest love. I am afraid they won't keep us here very long. It is rough to be moving continually in the depths of winter or nearly winter.

CHEVAUX DE FRISE

Pendant le blanc et nocturne novembre
Alors que les arbres déchiquetés par l'artillerie
Vieillissaient encore sous la neige
Et semblaient à peine des chevaux de frise
Entourés de vagues de fils de fer
Mon cœur renaissait comme un arbre au printemps
Un arbre fruitier sur lequel s'épanouissent les fleurs de l'Amour

Pendant le blanc et nocturne novembre
Tandis que chantaient épouvantablement les obus

Et que les fleurs mortes de la terre[2] exhalaient leurs mortelles odeurs
Moi je décrivais tous les jours mon amour à Madeleine

La neige met de pâles fleurs sur les arbres
       Et toisonne d'hermine les chevaux de frise
        Que l'on voit partout
          Abandonnés et sinistres chevaux muets
Non chevaux barbes mais barbelés
       Et je les anime tout soudain
        En troupeau de jolis chevaux pie
Et ils vont vers toi comme de blanches vagues
       Sur la Méditeranée
       Et t'apportent mon amour

Roselys ô panthère ô colombes étoile bleue
      Ô Madeleine
Je t'aime avec délices
Si je songe à tes yeux je songe aux sources fraîches
Si je pense à ta bouche les roses m'apparaissent
Si je songe à tes seins le Paraclet descend
        Ô double colombe de ta poitrine
Et vient délier ma langue de poète
      Pour te redire: je t'aime

Ton visage est un bouquet de fleurs
       Aujourd'hui je te vois non Panthère
       Mais Toutefleur
Et je te respire Ô Ma Toutefleur
Tous les lys montent en toi comme des cantiques d'amour et d'allégresse
Et ces chants qui s'envolent vers toi
      M'emportent à ton côté
Dans ton bel Orient où les lys
Se changent en palmiers qui de leurs belles mains
Me font signe de venir
La fusée s'épanouit fleur nocturne quand il fait noir

GUILLAUME APOLLINAIRE

Et elle retombe comme une pluie de larmes amoureuses
De larmes heureuses que la joie fait couler
Et je t'aime comme tu m'aimes
Madeleine

CHEVAUX-DE-FRISE

During white nocturnal November
As the trees ravaged by artillery fire
Continued to grow old beneath the snow
And looked almost like chevaux-de-frise
Surrounded by billowing barbed wire
My heart came back to life like a tree in springtime
A fruit tree blooming with the flowers of Love

During white nocturnal November
As shells sang their fearsome song
And the earth's[3] dead flowers gave off their deadly odour
I spent every day describing my love to Madeleine

The snow puts pale flowers on the trees
              And a woolly ermine trim on the chevaux-de-frise
                    That you see everywhere
                          Abandoned, sinister, silent horses
Not Barb horses but barbed horses
                    And all of a sudden I bring them to life
                          As a herd of handsome piebalds
Setting off for you like white waves
                    On the Mediterranean
              To bring you my love

Rose-lily oh panther oh doves blue star
              Oh Madeleine
I love you such delight
When I think of your eyes I think of cool springs
When I think of your mouth I see roses

3 The word 'terre' (earth) is a speculative reading only: the manuscript is unclear.

When I think of your breasts the Paraclete descends

        Oh twin doves of your bosom

And loosens my poet's tongue

        To tell you once more: I love you

Your face is a bouquet of flowers

        I see you now not as Panther

        But as Allflower

And inhale you Oh My Allflower

All lilies rise in you like hymns of love and gaiety

And these songs as they fly over to you

        Bring me to your side

In your beautiful East where lilies

Are changed into palm trees whose beautiful hands

Signal me to come

The flare blossoms a nocturnal flower in the darkness

        And rains down to earth as tears of love

Happy tears shed from joy

        And I love you as you love me

        Madeleine

My darling little love I adore you, and I should like to prove it to you in carnal fashion in my little alcove. I should like to feel your sweet weight upon me, a mass of fragrant rose petals. I should like to love you today fully dressed just as you are in the photo Anne sent, to ravage you, in a word to get under your skirts, and to love you like a cavalryman whose boot and saddle leaves him no time for niceties, to love you standing up and in the open air. I embrace you amorously and as with an anxious finger I explore the forecourt you yourself take hold of the fine flower and push it down as best you can towards the door and then we twist and turn standing and en-twined like a wreathed column. My Allflower, I take your mouth.

        Gui

GUILLAUME APOLLINAIRE

My adored love, today I got your exquisite letters of the 11th and
12th. I am exhilarated, filled with boundless joy. I now have a precious description of your forecourt. I'll make the rings and napkin-
rings as soon as I have time. I adore your marvellous eyes your
panther's eyes your fairy's eyes. I adore everything you tell me about
our love and I adore your voluptuous flanks straining towards my
infinitely hardened desire and I also adore entering the ninth door
as you like me to while looking into your eyes. I offer my lyrical
salute, oh dearest Madelon, to the Tessala Mountains. My love I kiss
and nibble your fleece and your mount of Venus. I adore your white,
closed lips and I part them passionately. It is the entire forecourt my
love that I call the 8th door. I adore you my love for having made this
admirably pure effort. You are my exquisite and headily fragrant lily.
I lick the blood-red depths of the forecourt. Yes it is a vertical tongue
that so far as I can tell from this distance is the instrument of your
pleasure. Ecstatically I lick the mucous membrane inside you just as I
do the mucous membrane of your mouth. I adore your bottom which
is so beautifully made, I slap it and I open it voluptuously and I kiss
it with passion; why yes we shall do a great deal of walking.

I am so happy that you like refinements involving sweets and I direct
my tongue to the very depths of the forecourt and I am thrilled to
know that you are searching for fruit whose smell approximates the
smell of that place. I adore stuffed dates my love and above all those

that are stuffed into your fleece and so let us create this exquisite
caress together. Your whole body will belong to my manhood darling
and I adore the rare and exquisite caress of your feet. An exquisite
caress invented by you my love, and one that you will bestow upon
me. I tremble with love to think of it and of your mouth, your
breasts, your hair caressing my manhood. We have had these ideas
at the same time: I wrote you about them only a few days ago. I
adore the fact that you my love just like me are a great walker and
we shall go walking on the flat as you prefer and in the woods and I
shall take you in the open air if possible and how charming it will be
to picnic and make love the two of us al fresco in the forest. Truly
delightful. Like you I am not smitten by the bicycle, which obliges
one to follow the road and is clumsy. Your hair is wonderful and I
must confess I dared not imagine such a marvel. I adore your bottom, which that hair must soon entirely cover, and I am also in love
with your hair my love. Yes, I will tell you if I am irritable and I
have no doubt my love that you will have no trouble calming me
down. I am concerned at what you tell me about the Sud-Oranais.—
Certainly I shall cure you of woolly thinking, but in fact there is no
such thing in your head. You are my marvellously lucid Madeleine
you think and enunciate with great clarity. I adore the fact that you
like to repeat yourself. Yes, I shall indeed enter the furnace after the
fashion of the Bull. Your sisters are very pretty my love but you shine
incomparably above them oh my peerless Madeleine. I adore the
red tints in your thick fleece and I love you as much when you are at
your darkest as any other way. I adore you always. I adore your
thinking of our fleeces as entangled and I adore the colour of your
skin, your warm colouring, and I take you onto my knee astride me
your breast pressed against mine or I picture you lifting your own
dress and offering me your exquisite behind and backing up to sit
on my lap and impale yourself. The only hydromel I am familiar

GUILLAUME APOLLINAIRE

with is made with honey but those that you describe must be exquisite. Yes we shall read the same book side by side, exquisite Madeleine, you are perfection. But I fancy we shan't be reading much we two. Thank you for the information you sent. If there are any changes let me know. Yes, Blaise Cendrars is married to a very charming woman, and he has a nipper. I adore you my love and plunge deep into you. Yes I shall compose that poem about our embraces. I adore the virgin forest and I adore your hair which falls all the way to your bottom and I adore your bottom. You are a sweet little pigeon my love. I have an intoxicating idea: you offer me your forecourt, open and held up high, and I fill you up with champagne and then get drunk from this very special liquor. Would you like for me to become inebriated by drinking from you and for our mouths to come together voraciously? Ah how I adore you. Today I wrote a melancholic little poem in the Boche cemetery. I am sending it to you but remember that the melancholy is strictly poetic and does not involve you and me in its sadness even if it has to do with our kisses and even if I was thinking as I wrote it of the wounded poet returning home to his wife.

EN SILENCE[1]

Et leurs visages étaient pâles
Et leurs sanglots s'étaient brisés . . .

Après la neige aux blancs pétales
Comme tes mains sur mes baisers
Tombaient les feuilles automnales

IN SILENCE

And their faces were pale
And they were wracked by sobs . . .

1 Earlier title (crossed out in the manuscript): 'Sous la Neige' ('Under the Snow').

After the snow's white petals
Like your hands on my kisses
Autumn's leaves began to fall

I adore you my love and I take your mouth with a madness that you cannot possibly conceive of my adored one.

Gui

My love, I got no letter from you today but was not expecting one.
Today I was sent a clipping from *La Renaissance*. I have not read the
item to which this is a response. Willy, who is too kind, found it
charming but I have no doubt that it must have contained some
treachery along the lines of the comment that follows Willy's letter—
the wretched man or woman who wrote this twaddle has not the
slightest inkling that had there been a little more Cubism, by which
I mean modern ideas, in we know where, the war might now be over
and we should be toasting victory. But I adore you and the rest does
not matter to me. I take you, all of you my darling, profoundly, and
my manhood taps playfully at the door of your forecourt. Today my
love I have had an especially erotic idea, the idea of a concert played
on your body. My darling you will help me discover the full range of
your sensations and then by delicately touching the various parts of
your body with my fingers tongue and lips I shall play divine sym-
phonies which you will experience in your depths and which will
culminate in the supreme embrace. My mouth will nibble at the tip
of your breast and then my right hand will slide gently all the way
down your spine to the beginning of the cleft my tongue will tickle
the soles of your goddess's feet, my mouth will go and draw the
liquor from the delicious organ of the forecourt while my spider-like
fingers on your flanks and hips sweetly excite your electrified
nerves. Then I shall take you wildly with you upon me our mouths
conjoined your forecourt filled by my manhood and my right

middle-finger teasing the ninth door. In this way I shall occupy three doorways to your sensuality and you will be filled by me my love and we shall gaze unwaveringly into each other's eyes. Yes, if you like my love, in winter we shall powerfully perfume our bed with a scent as close as possible to your own natural one and draw the covers completely over ourselves even over our heads until we are intoxicated by it and then we shall embrace one another wildly in that rarefied atmosphere.

I am living oh my love in the Shakespearian setting of a hypogaeum in the middle of a cemetery and near this ghastly dwelling-place this morning an exploding shell unearthed a Boche whose tibia is now protruding from the tatters of his earth-covered winding-sheet. The cemetery lies on a hillside but one cannot go up to the top of the hill because one would be exposed to view there. Did I tell you about the Boche colonel killed here along with 2 women who were with him? Well, today we came across the ladies' reticules. In one I found a German military postcard, and very mucky as it is I am sending it to you for its curiosity value. Have I told you that according to an inscription my dugout used to be known as *Lustige Mühle*, 'The Joyful Mill'? And have I told you that I have been reading the letters of one Jela Nuller, a young whore from Wiesbaden writing to her lover who forgot the letters here or who died here, letters where before her signature she writes *das hübschtes Püppchen*—the prettiest little dolly! The big event this morning was the discovery of two Russian soldiers whose garb identified them as German prisoners—the Boches had sent them out between the lines to set up networks of barbed-wire entanglements and position caltrops and chevaux-de-frise. But they managed to escape through the horrendous barbed wire, with the Boches firing at them but missing. They were not even spotted as they crossed through our lines (can you beat that!) and

433

GUILLAUME APOLLINAIRE

were stopped only at the third line, near the artillery. They had not a word of either French or German, I was asked to speak to them but I don't know Russian. One of them was named Kars, he is from Petrovsk. Kars is a Jewish name. They had left with blankets, ration bread (Pumpernickel) and a Greek missal—an in-quarto popular edition published recently in Constantinople and entitled Μεγα— I don't remember the next word exactly, something like Ευχολογιον— it contained psalms followed by doxology all according to the Greek persuasion. The men were much photographed bowing repeatedly after the Jewish fashion, then they were taken off to Division to be interrogated. It often happens here and in Italy that Russian prison-ers put to work by the Boches escape and make their way across the lines to their Allies.

I take your mouth unendingly.

434

Gui

My love, enclosed is a Boche letter, a woman named Rosa writing to her husband, you will see from it that the Germans want peace, she complains that cognac costs 4 marks the litre, etc. etc., also a military map rather torn and very battered but it will divert you. The owners are probably dead. No letter from you today my love. Tell me whether the crossing is free for soldiers on leave and whether there are special boats reserved for this kind of transport. Get me the best information you can. The cemetery is bounded by an attractive birchwood railing, the entrance is also made of birch and very pretty and on the chapel there is an inscription in tree branches, *Sei getreu bis in den Tod* (keep faith unto death), the graves are well made, with birch crosses, broken pillars, art-nouveau-style inscriptions on sign boards, a non-commissioned officers' corner which is a well-maintained bed of beautiful roses with small labels identifying the varieties, notably a 'Dijon Glory'; one of the N.C.O.'s was named Bismarck, also there are a number of officers' graves one of which containing several individuals has a great marble plaque broken around the edges with finely executed inscriptions, an Iron Cross that once adorned it having already been torn off. As I say, my Boche dugout is called *Lustige Mühle* (Joyful Mill), there is also a *Villa Hiddek*, a *Villa Beaulieu* bearing this design , a *Villa Schweizertal* (i.e., Swiss Valley) and one with the charming name *Café Sprind* and the following inscription in Gothic lettering:

435

GUILLAUME APOLLINAIRE

Dieser Unterstand ist von der
Gruppe Malinowski aufgebaut
Und wind auch von ihr bewohnt
1 gruppe 2 Zug
2/39

Which means: This shelter constructed by the Malinowski Group is also occupied by it, 1st Group, etc. My love I adore you and today I kissed your hair.

LE 11e POÈME SECRET

Sur tout toi, sur ton corps ton intelligence ta raison
J'ai fait déjà de beaux poèmes
Et j'en veux faire moi habitant des bois en ce temps de guerre
J'en veux faire sur cette jolie petite cagnat si bien aménagée au fond de la forêt vierge
Cette petite cagnat que tu m'as préparée dans la forêt vierge
Ô palais plus beau que celui de Rosemonde le Louvre et l'Escurial
C'est là que j'entrerai pour faire ma plus belle œuvre
Je serai Dieu lui-même et y ferai s'il plaît à Dieu, un homme plusieurs hommes même,
*   une femme plusieurs femmes même comme fit Dieu lui-même*
Ô petit palais caché de Madeleine
Tu es belle mon amour et tu es une artiste sublime toi qui as élevé pour moi le plus
*   beau palais du monde*
Madeleine, mon architecte adoré
Je jetterai un pont entre toi et moi un pont de chair dure comme le fer un pont mer-
*   veilleusement suspendu*
Toi Architecte, moi Pontife et Créateur d'Humanité
Je t'adore Architecte et toi adore le bâtisseur du pont
Sur lequel comme sur celui d'Avignon tout le monde dansera en rond
Nous-mêmes ô Madeleine nos enfants aussi et aussi nos petits-enfants
*   Jusqu'à la fin des siècles*

THE 11th SECRET POEM

On all of you, your body your intelligence your reason

I have already written fine poems

And now I want to write another as a forest dweller in this time of war

I want to write one about a pretty little dugout beautifully fixed up deep in
   virgin forest

The little dugout that you have readied for me in the virgin forest

Oh palace finer than Rosamund's than the Louvre than the Escorial

That is where I shall go to create my finest work of all

I shall be God himself and God willing make a man or even several men, a
   woman or even several women, just as God himself did

Oh little hidden palace of Madeleine's

You are beautiful my love and a sublime artist for building me the most
   beautiful palace in the world

Madeleine, my architect that I adore

I shall build a bridge between you and me a bridge of flesh as hard as iron a
   bridge marvellously suspended

You the Architect, I the Pontiff and Creator of Humanity

I adore you Architect and may you adore the builder of that bridge

On which as at Avignon everyone will dance in a ring

We ourselves oh Madeleine likewise our children and likewise our
   grandchildren
     Till the end of time

Madeleine I take your mouth endlessly.

                                                              Gui

GUILLAUME APOLLINAIRE

22 Nov. 1915

My love, today I received your letters of the 13th and 14th. It is just
a local name, not even on the maps, but now this '*Trou*' is famous,
much mentioned in communiqués of the 25th, 26th and 27th of
September. We took an entire staff headquarters, to the left of our
old position. My love how I adore our ear caresses and I adore your
feet as they clench and as I caress them for the longest time with my
fingers mouth teeth tongue and manhood. Yes I do indeed believe
that every part of your body has a soul. But no dearest you will not
be ashamed of your sensuality you will be proud of it and you will
thrust boldly with your hips as required will you not my love. I now
have all the information abt my leave. But tell me, since those on
leave must take the same boat back, is there a lapse of 6 days
between arrival and re-embarkation considering that the day of
arrival does not count? In which class do soldiers (N.C.O.'s) on leave
travel? My love, the photo of you in Moorish costume with Jean I
found delightful. As a child you truly were an adorable little
Mooress. I gather that you had a birthday party and a very good
time. Yes, you guessed right, your legs are around my waist, and my
love I feel you all of you tight against me. Your bedtime is at once
the most voluptuous and the most chaste tableau imaginable, I
adore it. Your description is exquisite. You must be very pretty too in
your nightdress and pulling it up I take you savagely. Eau de
cologne on your forecourt has the same effect as it does on my
manhood, and especially under my [*illegible*]. Its scent is very very

438

strong. Before washing yourself in cold water my love you should do a few exercises to get your blood circulating and then slap yourself with an open hand to bring the blood to the surface of the skin.

Love, speak to me a little of yourself and tell me all about your beautiful body.

We are under heavy bombardment at present but we are well protected in our Boche shelters, though our artillery pieces are not. All day long shells whistle and explode and the shrapnel goes bounding everywhere.

My love I take you passionately, be a little panther-like after you get this letter. It is when you are the panther that I can invent things to enhance our love, and I love you madly supremely.

EXERCICE

Vers un village de l'arrière
S'en allaient quatre bombardiers
Ils étaient couverts de poussière
Depuis la tête jusqu'aux pieds

Ils regardaient la vaste plaine
En parlant entre eux du passé
Et ne se retournaient qu'à peine
Quand un obus avait toussé

Tous quatre de la classe seize
Parlaient d'antan non d'avenir
Ainsi se prolongeait l'ascèse
Qui les exerçait à mourir

GUILLAUME APOLLINAIRE

EXERCISE

Towards a village in the rear
Four bombardiers were setting off
Covered with dust
From head to toe

They looked at the vast plain
And chatted about the past
Barely turning their heads
At the cough of a bursting shell

All four from the class of sixteen
Spoke of the old days not of days to come
So prolonging the ascetic life
That was training them to die

440

I take your mouth frantically and your darling tongue.

Gui

My darling love, I have gone two days without writing you. I have
been called upon to become an officer and cannot refuse. Or rather
I could have, but considering that I volunteered a refusal would have
suggested reservations on my part that I do not in fact entertain.
What is more I was tired of being an N.C.O., and far above all else is
the fact that my own special victory is you and that a love such as
ours demands a great sacrifice. You are the most beautiful thing in
the world, you are my everything, and I adore you my Madelon.
This love of ours grows unceasingly, I do not know how that can be,
but so it is. Each day brings us closer together. So here I am, an infantry officer, and it has happened so quickly. No one could believe
it. In that hole where I was living I had just discovered another
graveyard (which I shall tell you about) when my second lieutenant's
commission was delivered to me from main headquarters, and
immediately thereafter I was issued the 400-franc field outfitting
allowance and I left in search of my regiment. It took me two whole
days to find it. The colonel received me in the most charming manner and granted me leave to visit Châlons, where I'll be going
shortly to get kitted out. I will try to wire you my new address from
there. The commanding officer a charming man invited me to dinner last night. And I spent the evening with the Lt. Commander of
6th Company my direct superior and the second l[t] who is my fellow-
officer. We shall be messing together the 3 of us. My messmates are
very nice especially the lieutenant, a Parisian and actually the

GUILLAUME APOLLINAIRE

nephew of our general. 6th Company performed particularly well during the September attacks and was the 1st to enter Tahure, where it took many prisoners. So far as I can tell from my 1st night here, the life of infantry officers is extremely dangerous. Officers sleep on the ground. True, our uniforms keep us warm. But an N.C.O. in the artillery lives far more comfortably than a superior officer in the infantry. The attitude is very different too, and I very much savour the far more gallant spirit of the infantry officers.

I am continuing this letter from Châlons itself, where I have come to fit myself out. I go back this evening. I arrived by car but shall leave by train.—I fancy that my transfer to the infantry may bring my leave forward somewhat. I shall reply tomorrow to your delightful letters, I adore you.

Your Gui

Here is my address:

Second Lieutenant, 96th Infantry
    6th Company
        Sector 139.

I have finished the ring for your Mama. My last piece of work in the Arty—shall send it the day after tomorrow.

Gui

My love, couldn't write you yesterday didn't have the time. Today is
a sewing day, a day of packing my new kit into my officer's uniform
case—we go to the front line on the 28th the day after tomorrow.
The toilet set you sent me now has its place in my case. I forgot to
tell you that the bananas arrived on the 23rd, they were exquisite,
just right, indeed the best I have ever eaten and so good that as I ate
them I fancied that their savour, their wonderful soft ripeness was a
foretaste of your exquisite forecourt which is my paradise. I owe
you replies to letters of the 15th, 16th and 17th—three marvellous
letters. It is amazing how well you write my darling and how ably
you contrive to speak of everything with such tact and with such an
admirable feeling for sensuality and for me. I adore you. Your perfection is supreme and I thank you my love for knowing how to love
me so adorably and exactly as I love for you to love me, and I, my
love, do I love you well too? Just as you would wish to be loved? Ah,
but I desire you madly, the little photos are lovely. You are beautiful
in the most marvellous way. Your crossed legs show me the contours
of your thighs and hips the length of your trunk the roundness of
your behind of honey and light. Have I not spoken to you Madelon
of the absolute perfection of your forecourt, so neatly closed that it
in no way mars the perfection of your beautiful body and your fleece
in which I glory, merely thinking of it throws me into an uproar.—
The notion of my smoking you is entertaining, but I prefer to keep
you real and by no means wish to emulate Ixion who engaged in an

443

imaginary embrace with a phantom cloud resembling Juno. So for now I shall keep the two photos and should I need to inhale something of you wait until I can breathe in your scent and the delectable aroma rising from your body when making love has heated us up. Your progress *in us* is exquisite my love. You are my exquisite slave and I love you that way, when your flesh is entirely mine and I can cruelly awaken a fearsome voluptuousness in you. Yes, my love, we shall look closely at our beautiful panther the better to understand her, oh my exquisite fairy who is also my Allflower. I adore the charming image of your divine nakedness dispelling vapours before me, the one who adores you. Yes everything you say makes much very much sense and you say it divinely, you are not just my Madelon for you are also my favourite author and I passionately read and re-read your letters. I am sorry for that unfortunate woman in a marriage without love.— The fact is that few beings are destined to love each other and even fewer happen upon one other as you and I so miraculously did. That unhappy woman will probably be unhappy all her life long, especially judging by what you say of her character. If she is at all sensitive she will go from disappointment to disappointment, from lover to lover, experiencing no pleasure but merely a demeaning shame at having succumbed to vice—and barred utterly from the admirable and free joys of that virtue for which everything is permissible. Love, what you tell me of your modesty shows me just how well you have understood me and how well acquainted you are with virtue and how nobly such virtue resides in you and enables you to enhance your life and your voluptuousness with respect to the two of us in complete freedom. My darling, I am proud of your modesty concerning everything that is not us. I adore you. I likewise am passionately, madly, wildly yours. Yes I can clearly see the little chain on your beautiful arm in the photo and I also sense the exquisite palpitation of your bosom. Yes I

444

suckle delightfully at your breasts and my mouth runs over all [*illegible*] your fleece up to the 9th door. The story of the belly button I found very amusing. Do not be ashamed of this my darling love. It was with a deep voluptuousness that I received you secret caress my love.—I adore you, I adore your tongue and I lick your vertical mouth passionately just before our deep union. You are going to like being on top of me as well as my being on top of you. I adore the movements of your rear and I am after all rather happy that Moorish dancing taught you them without your even realizing it. You ask which position of my Madelon I like most, well, all of them naturally, but this evening I picture you asleep next to me with your backside turned to me and me entering you gently and you awaking in a state of great arousal, my love how I adore you. But you must not get frightened love, we shall be reasonable but we shall give each pleasure in the profoundest way, for my male reserves are very great as without a doubt your exquisite female reserves are too. I adore the delightful story of the Moorish dance. My love I caress your artful belly, your agile hips, your subtle and delectable bottom, and I press my mouth to your fragrant forecourt for the longest time then fill it with my flesh hardened by the mad desire I feel for you.

445

Gui

28 Nov. 1915

My love, today I got your two letters of the 18th and the 19th. I adore you, you are my love. But I cannot imagine where my love you got the idea that my navel protrudes. You are mistaken. It is perfectly inward-turning my love, just like yours. I adore your hair my love and the very white parting that divides it. I adore your admirable shoulders and the nape of your neck, my exquisite Madelon. I adore your breasts, I love it that you have no salt cellars and I adore your round waist, I adore it infinitely, and I draw it to me. I adore your pelvis, I love it that you are plump and firm everywhere, I adore your buttocks which get as hard as living wood when you flex your muscles. I adore your feet my love. I love them infinitely, I kiss them, I shall be a devoted worshipper of your feet my Madelon. I adore your caresses at my 9th door and [*everything*?] you invent by way of heavenly caresses. I adore the way you slither beneath me when I am on my knees. I love your ears and your long adorable hands I adore you. I wrap your arms about my neck and put my arms about your waist. I listen to what you whisper in my ear. I adore your whims. Yes, Jean is lucky to be able to go and see his wife. You are right love, we shall not leave each other's side once we are married. You are as sweet as anything to be so stoical about pain, my love, for my part I am very scared at the dentist's. I adore it too when I think of us sleeping back to back and my waking you up with kisses, my love, and my mouth's caress at your eighth door belongs to you too, for I have never wanted to bestow it upon any other and your beauty alone directs my mouth to your forecourt and you are the only woman who has ever caused me to desire this kind of caress, for such a desire presupposes passionate love. You are my all my Madeleine. I adore the new smell that you have discovered emanating from yourself. You are, my love, a unique cassolette. I adore the mantle of voluptuousness in which you envelop me. My darling, I kiss your heels that are chapped by the cold. I kiss you all of you my love. I forgot to tell you about Châlons my love—a gloomy town full of shirkers in outlandish garb. And I have to tell you my love that the infantry is truly the worthiest arm of our forces. The others—home cooking, all that—but the infantry, my word!!! It's another world. Tomorrow night I go to the front line for nine days. May your love protect me. I think I told you that it was my Company that took Tahure Hill by itself. I adore you my darling love, you are all the beauty and grace in the world, I take your mouth.

Gui

447

GUILLAUME APOLLINAIRE

My love, I could not write you yesterday we had too much to do. At 2 p.m., review by the Major with speech. For the 1st time I took cmd of my section. At a ¼ past 6 in the evening we set off, the ground was frozen, our men slipping and falling like flies, I don't know how I managed not to break a leg or sprain an ankle. All I had were my riding boots with no hobnails and it was only by a miracle that I got here. It was fantastic in the night. We went by the '*trou*' where I was before, then on and on across the pale ravaged plain with the white veins of the trenches, we went down one communication trench after another and from time to time a trench would run out and we would proceed in the open moving as fast as possible. Bullets whistled around us, then we found ourselves in the endless zigzagging trenches that lead to the front line. Here we are to remain for 9 days. All section leaders like me are present. In case of attack our sole orders are to die rather than fall back. We are under bombardment from the terrifying 105's. I am in my dugout. I have had a brazier lit. The only one we are able to fuel, we are so short of coal. I am 6 hours out of 24 on guard in the trench. My dugout is solid. I let the men of my section come in to warm up by turns when they are not on watch in the fire-bays. Since these are new lines they are still disorganized. No barbed wire. I shall have it set up by night and extend the communication trenches and make dugouts for men who have none. This is war, really and truly. I am writing crouched down, using my knee; this is going to go on for 9 days. From the depths of

448

my dugout I can see the lookout man in the bay directly across from me. He has a grand listening-post. In short, there it is, trench life in all its splendour. I was on duty last night from 2 to 4, I am back on again from noon to 2 p.m. I have received yours of the 20th. Please thank your mother for her very great kindness. The agenda you propose is splendid. It is my agenda too, and I say so from the heart. With a mad passion, my love, I have drunk every drop of the liquor you offer me from your secret spring, and I take your mouth until you beg for mercy! I also received your letter of the 21st. I so hope that my leave will be announced soon. I adore sucking the milk of my love, oh my love you are divine. I adore the fleeting touch of your hands. I adore your elbows, your arms. I adore your secret scents. I adore your knowledge of the art of fruit-growing. In this frightful and desolate trench I await your voluptuousness-letter.

I forgot to tell you my love that in Châlons I ate with the Lt in command of the short-155 battery evoked in the famous song 'Pont de Minaucourt' that I published in the *Mercure*.[1] His name is Lt Daurver and he is at present in cmd of the 10th Bat of the 116th Heavy Artillery Rgt. At that time it was known as the 5th Bat of the 6th Foot Artillery Rgt and we called it D Battery after the commanding officer's initial. The part-author of the song was the cook of the Arty Lt in question (a great gourmand and a connoisseur of wine), this cook being the only staff member of the short-155 battery left with the Lt at the time of action of the song. His name was Loiseau but they forgot to mention it. Such are the anecdotes of wartime! I take your mouth.

Gui

1 See 'La Vie anecdotique', *Mercure de France*, 1 August 1915.

GUILLAUME APOLLINAIRE

My love, our 2nd day on the front line has begun. It is quiet. For the moment there is only rifle and artillery fire. Our trench is enfiladed and bullets whistle through continually. I am having more excavation done to counter this risk which threatens the lives of good men. At certain times on a rather regular basis we are bombarded by 105 shells and a few 77 time shells from a gun that must be very close. But still, for the moment we are not being attacked by any of the weapons which are the most terrible of all but which are rarely spoken of:

'*Youyous*', ululations, so called because of the plaintive sound they used to make as they approached, a sound that the Boches have now managed to suppress. So we no longer hear them coming, and since they started painting them sky-blue we don't see them coming either.

'*Boîtes à merde*', shit cans, resembling beds or giant trunks that come in at a height of 60 or so metres and then drop steeply, destroying 200 metres of trench along with whatever is in there.

'*Seaux à charbon*', coal scuttles, on account of their shape: a kind of bomb stuffed with all manner of scrap metal. A horrible device.

'*Marie-Louise*', the largest of all, a shell that flies very high and produces terrifying results.

450

As for us, all we have are our little bags of hand grenades.

Whilst we are on watch the reserve section prepares barbed-wire coils, chevaux-de-frise and trebuchets to bolster our accessory defences.

It is all very strange, and truly horrifying. No more so, however, than trench life itself. The infantrymen sleep anywhere, in snatches, under the rain, on the ground. They like to dig niches for themselves some 40 cm high by 1 m 80 long, like cots up against the side of the trench; in this way, once screened off by tent canvas, they have hideaways where they feel at ease.

My adored love, no letters from you today, indeed no letter from anyone since my post has not yet been forwarded. I forgot to tell you that the day before yesterday I sent you two parcels via our field train. One of them contains two catalogues from the Delaunay show in 1913 or 1914. One copy is mine, please keep it for me. The second bears my dedication to you. In it you can read a poem of mine that is one of my own favourites, 'Windows'. In any case this fine edition of the poem is one of the rarest of my works, and I am happy to think you will have it my love. The second parcel contains my spurs which I no longer need and which you can keep for me, my artilleryman's smoke-helmet which should amuse you, my kepi-cover which I have rediscovered and which campaigned on the kepi you already have, and a little box holding the last ring I made as an artilleryman (here on the front line we have no time for that!). It is for your Mama, I think it needs a little silver polish. The papers in the box are also to be saved. They include my pass for Châlons and receipts for purchases I made there. I'll try to find out when my leave is and I'll let you let you know the moment I do. I so hope it will be soon. As an officer I travel first-class. I think from what I have

451

heard though I am not quite sure that the passage is not free but will cost perhaps a quarter of the full rate. My love we shall sleep as little as possible so as to spend as much time as we can together. You are my precious love. I take all of you in the profoundest way. I am longing for a letter from you today. If anything were to happen to me you would be informed, because I have given your name as a person to be notified. I gave you and my mother. But I am very confident, even certain, that nothing will happen to me even if we mount an assault on that awful hill (remember what I underlined in that Italian newspaper).

9 days without washing, lying on the bare earth, not so much as straw for bedding, in a place rife with vermin, and not a drop of water save that used by the Vermorel sprayer to moisten masks with hyposulphite of soda in case of a gas attack. We have placed weathervanes on the parapets to ascertain the direction of the wind and I have given a 75 shell casing to one of my lookouts so that he can strike it like a gong as soon as he spots gas wending its way towards us. The chalk trench is very weak and often collapses, so we are forever reinforcing it with sandbags. The 6-hour watch rotation is very annoying but absolutely necessary, for otherwise the men would fall asleep in the firing-bays from their enormous fatigue. Even as one who sleeps very little, I have only to lie down on the ground like the poor lads under my command and I fall asleep instantly.

It is amazing what one can put up with. There is barely any coal, but naturally officers continue to receive their regulation ration. So I have brought my two sergeants in to sleep with me and men who are cold can come in to warm up 4 at a time. And my fire serves to heat their soup. They are very grateful the poor wretches. I have 2 wonderful sergeants who have been in the field from the beginning:

Jean Jean-Marie from Toulouse, 33 years old, Croix de Guerre, in line for promotion to warrant officer, energetic, a grouser and griper but a first-rate fellow.

And Varroqueaux (from the Aisne, his village is occupied, 20 years old), bold as a lion.

The corporals are not so impressive, but the sergeants know how to lead them.

My love I take your mouth, I adore you. You are my darling Madelon and it is with passion that my mouth seizes upon your delectable forecourt.

Gui

453

My love, I have still received no letter from you or from anyone. Sad, so sad. Our sector is defending the Tree—the most famous tree of the moment. If you have been following the communiqués you will guess which one I mean. In short we are just beyond the place where we were with the battery. If you know where, I am happy, but if not I'm afraid I may not be more precise. Part of the parapet of my trench is built of dead bodies . . . Ugh! My command post is a trench dugout with ogival vaulting. My love I adore you. I slept for an hour this afternoon when I was off duty. Ah! How different an infantryman's life is to a gunner's! The artillery are barely fighting a war. They are living an idyll in comparison with the naked and thoroughly lethal drama of war on the front line. Ah, my love, how truly I shall have won you! You know that I have been assigned to the active forces now. I wonder to what I owe that honour. But enough said! I shall obviously be going over the top any day now. Not a shadow of a doubt!! And I even have a very good idea where we'll be going! In the meantime I am organizing my section's defence. Which is not a piece of cake when all you hear is the song of shells and projectiles, the *vroom* of exploding minnies, the *zizz* of falling shrapnel, the *plick* of bullets striking a parapet. It is half-past 7 as I write you this evening and tomorrow I shall resume this letter which will leave tomorrow evening and bears tomorrow's date.

My love I resume my letter, it is now 4 p.m. on the 1st. Not provisioned yesterday.—Among the curiosities of trench life are the

1 See p. 271.

anti-shrapnel traverses constructed in the trench and called elephants on account of their shape.[1] There are also weathervanes to tell the wind direction in case we are attacked by asphyxiating gas. My own dugout or cave has a sign marked 'Ville Sainte Anne'. If we have less to do I shall try to make those napkin-rings in the next few days; after that I suspect that I shan't be making many more things of that kind, for now I am an officer I won't be getting much free time at all. Did I tell you that before leaving my old battery's position at Trou-Bricot I visited another cemetery, much more beautiful than the one I described to you. Very well-carved crosses, eagles, inscriptions of a general nature. Here is one in old German taken perhaps from the *Nibelungen*: 'Liewer düd as slaw' (rather dead than a slave); another: 'Kein Schönrer Tod ist auf der Welt als Wer vor 'm Feind erschlagen' (There is no more beautiful death in the world than to be struck down before the enemy). And on each tombstone the name was preceded by the formula 'den Heldentod starb': (so-and-so) died the death of the Heroes. Life here is far more mysterious, and far more in thrall to fate than in the artillery, where you took cover when minnies began bursting. Here on the contrary when a shell explodes everyone rushes out and no matter if you are killed or wounded. The language of the infantrymen is not crude. Such poor brave soldiers! Their dream is a good wound (loss of an arm, say). Yet they are truly loyal fellows—obviously, for they have had to go over the top several times. Then there is the mystery of trenches enfiladed, whether by mechanical rifle, pompom or machine-gun, and the mysteries of the coils of barbed wire, the listening posts, the saps, the sounds you hear, the unlikely denominations of the various points on the secret map. My darling, I love you, washing amounts to splashing on a little of the eau de cologne you sent, I am smoking the cigarettes which arrived safely (6 packets in a box of figs). And I am wearing the nice jersey you sent me.

GUILLAUME APOLLINAIRE

My love, I washed those parts of me that are yours alone with your eau de cologne. You are my most precious little thing. I love you in a marvellously triumphant way my sweetest darling. My love has grown even more, which I had thought impossible. I am hoping for a letter this evening. Here in the trenches the chaplain has a part to play . . . Oh, the post is about to go, I take your mouth.

Gui

1 The correct date is 1 December 1915; see the opening sentence of Apollinaire's next letter, dated '2 December in the evening'.

My love, this letter will leave tomorrow 3 December, I am writing you this evening of the 2nd at 7 o'clock, as we await provisions that are not arriving. The men have had nothing hot to eat and nothing to drink all day.—And we have to work incessantly. Ah! the infantryman's lot is hard, much harder than anyone knows. Simply no comparison with the artillery. Gunners are gay, foul-mouthed, undisciplined. Here the odd sideways remark is as gay as people get, they are serious, never coarse, and highly disciplined. From the listening-post I have been looking at the corpses in the barbed wire. Love, I am writing to you now though I was already writing to you some 2 hours ago now, but in order to post your letter I had to break off. I was just going to tell you about our Rgt chaplain, a private, he is a monk from Parkminster Charterhouse near Partridge Green in England. I chatted for a good while with this Carthusian while I was on duty. He is a great consoling force for the men. . . . My love, during the two hours since I wrote to you last we have had a gas-alert drill, a harmless exercise that I must say I much prefer to the real thing. At present the Boches are sending 105's in groups of 4, they make a very rapid *pop-pop-boom* sound so powerful that your heart jumps at every thunderous report. It jumps not from fear or some other emotion, for after 15 months of war such reactions are non-existent, but rather because the displacement of air shakes everything. Yet another curious phenomenon: nearly the full length of my trench is being enfiladed by a Boche mechanical rifle blasting

GUILLAUME APOLLINAIRE

off every minute. The bullets come right up to the entrance to my dugout, and the regularity of the fire lends a mechanical sonority to the atmosphere, but even this does not figure among the greatest mysteries of this place. Did I tell you that we are three officers here in my C^{oy}, 1 l^t serving as a captain and 2 2nd l^{ts} who are section leaders, the other 2 section leaders of the C^{oy} being the warrant officer and the quartermaster sergeant. We three officers live and mess together, we have a former cook from the Hôtel de Paris in Monte-Carlo to prepare our food. As you must imagine this is not half bad. What we are a little short of is fruit. Our president of the mess 2nd Lt Ferrier gets excellent fish from home and our own l^t obtains all kinds of first-rate delicacies. The meat we have as a rule is exquisite. I have never eaten such good meat. But today and perhaps tomorrow no water no bread no coal. We shall therefore have hardly anything except dry sausage and chocolate without bread or drink.

I am trying to keep free of vermin but I don't know if I shall succeed, in any case when I go on leave I shall smear myself thoroughly with mercurial ointment to kill all the lice I feel sure I'll be getting very soon—even the Colonel has them! And thus well smeared I shall come all the way to Oran where I have no idea how I shall dress (I'll buy everything in Marseilles). The moment I arrive I'll be obliged to bathe and change and you my love should find out how to obtain a hot oven to disinfect my uniform, linen etc. on the very day of my arrival.—We have no head lice just body and pubic lice. Infantry officers are more soldierly than their opposite numbers in the artillery who are after all engineers, and they are far more elegantly turned out, but just the same they are crawling with bugs. The fact of the matter is that no writer could ever describe the sheer strangeness and horror of trench life.

But enough of this cold white contemplative war in these excessively white trenches. I love you my exquisite Madelon, I love you in a way at once childish and manly and both suit the feelings of my heart perfectly. I caress you divinely even as I offer my breast as a rampart for the whole nation. Today I thought with a mad ardour of your mouth so well formed and your breasts so exquisitely beautiful.

I thought of your long hands that you have described to me and of your long waist. My love how I love you! My mouth travels gently over your whole body and I graze in an adorable meadow, you know which one I mean. My mouth bestows on you all those special caresses that you love oh my love oh my Madelon.

Here in the trenches despite the endless work time passes rather slowly. We talk only of the war, the Boches so close, the daily toll of dead or wounded. The country will never conceive sufficient admiration for the simple infantrymen gloriously dying in droves. Oh what an unreal solitude, so to speak, inhabits the space between the Boche trench and the French. What a truly odd thing it is.

I am exhausted I take your mouth and give you my tongue oh my dearest darling slave.

Gui

2 December[1] in the evening   **1** 1915.

I got the date wrong yesterday, my love, it was the 1st. Today no letter yet, no newspapers, no supplies. The officers are still alright because our cook makes do, but not so the poor men! They are admirable in their simple heroism. I fancy supplies will arrive only overnight about 4 a.m. I have had the Pioneers set up a board for me to write on. Trench collapses are continual, the men no longer sleep, they work all the time. Life in the trenches in winter has something so simple about it that it gives you an idea of what the life of prehistoric troglodytes must have been like. In fact we really are troglodytes.

I have two pleasant companions here, one of whom is my superior, the lieu[t] serving as captain in command of the company and one of my two sergeants. The former is distinguished and an agreeable talker with a fair knowledge of artistic and literary matters and the latter is a simple man, extremely cunning, adroit, sharp, decent and a fine leader of men. You get a sense here of what authority is and what it can do when it is at once gentle and firm. I have my two sergeants sleeping with me and I have also invited in a young lad from the class of '15, he is innocent and upstanding and I am teaching him to read because he does not know how.

My sergeant Jean-Marie is a very good man. Admittedly he is a first-class grumbler but you feel you can trust him even if he moans all the time. And what an entertaining fellow he is! My love the

460

anti-shrapnel elephants are crumbling more and more at their base, which merely enhances their elephant-like appearance.

My love, amidst this mysterious metallic horror, mute but not silent on account of the horrible whistling whining and loud bursting sounds of the engines of war, our love is the sole star, a fragrant angel floating high above the black or yellow smoke of the exploding bombs.

It smiles, that love, deep in the saps where it listens anxiously, it mounts vigil over firing-bays that have been spotted and are traversed at regular intervals by enemy fire and it hovers over the whole ineffable mystery of the front lines whose white horror suggests some lunar landscape. There is a terrifying monotony about life from which water even non-potable water has disappeared. Oh pure trenches like lilies flowering within the earth instead of opening to the sky. It is the earth itself that is in flower. To husband the very little coal that I dispose of I have had a heating pan made from an old canteen with holes punched in it. We hang it from a wire.

Write me about love, be my panther to get back into the swing of our dear love.

Just think how deprived we are in the trenches of everything that attaches one to the universe, one is nothing more than a breast proffered to the enemy.

Like a rampart of living flesh.

How clear it now becomes that fighting in the artillery is pure pleasure, a country outing, an adventure scarcely riskier than mountain-climbing. Out here the commitment is more solemn, more desolate. Life is unadorned even by vegetation, for we are down below ground.

461

GUILLAUME APOLLINAIRE

Tonight I end my fourth day on the front lines. Today we killed a Boche who had ventured over the parapet into the mysterious hexahedrons,[2] chevaux-de-frise and coils of barbed wire.

I am acutely aware now of the sheer horror of this secret war without strategy but replete with stratagems that are terrifying and atrocious.

My love I think of your exquisite body with its divine fleece and I take your mouth and your tongue a thousand times over.

Gui

[2] Defensive devices similar to chevaux-de-frise.

My love, at long last I have received your two precious letters of the
23 and 24 Nov. Judging by your letter of the 23rd I think you have
written me a voluptuousness-letter dated the 22nd, which I seem not
to have received. Since I always acknowledge receipt of your letters
it should be an easy matter for you to see whether I ever mentioned
getting it or whether I am right in thinking it has gone astray. If so,
please, please promise me you will reproduce it for me. Your 2 letters have transfigured this trench for me, I adore you. I have submit-
ted my request for leave. The Colonel had asked whether I had any
family in Oran and whether I was legally domiciled there. I replied
that I planned to go there to visit the family of my fiancée who is a
teacher at the local girls' lycée, as the mayor of Oran would confirm
should he be asked. I hope that he will because it is the truth. In
which case I think my leave will not be long in coming through. I
want nothing more than that the war should end as quickly as you
predict but for the moment I cannot see it. Today I begin my 5th day
in this trench. It is all mud and continual collapses against which we
have to struggle day and night like Sisyphus with his rock. I adore
you my love, and your love is my consolation for everything. Yes, I
feel your caresses, I feel my Madeleine's supple body against me, I
hold you tightly to me, we are but one, I sense your sweet warmth
penetrating me and the sweetness of your limbs entangling themselves with mine and the smell of your body makes my head swim.
For me too the voluptuous feelings coming from you are one with
mine, thanks to that caress which is the most ardent and deepest of
all. I adore your flanks bending backwards and your belly and breasts

463

GUILLAUME APOLLINAIRE

thrusting towards my kiss. I take you, my love, with a superhuman violence. I am madly greedy for you Madelon and I devour you. I adore your nails, delicate porcelain. I love my little chameleon of a Madeleine. I adore her pointed fingernails and her rounded toenails. I adore your neck and its warm hue. I shall bite madly at that round and pliant neck. I shall feast upon your little curls my exquisite love. I shall release them from your low chignon. I shall lick your voluptuous nostrils throbbing like a live sparrow in the hand.

My love what you tell me about the little hermit thrills me wildly. I love him, hard as he was at that moment. It was certainly him, you found him my dearest love. I adore your tongue, your beautiful tongue. Yes I am madly in love with your breasts and I eat them. I offer my hard manhood to your mouth. Then I penetrate you deeply. The mad caress that you have invented is exquisite. Yes, love, we have the same nature. I love the little meal that you envision. Thank you love for everything you say I may take during my leave. I eat you. Everything in me thrills when I think of you. Yes love I am beginning to feel our embrace from afar, you begin to make me feel it thanks to all the sensual artistry you put into your letter. Yes you are my Allflower and I adore you, I adore you, and I take your bottom and I kiss it with all my strength and with all my gentle and insistent voluptuousness. I take you in my arms, love, and impale you while standing, with your legs wrapped around my middle and your arms around my neck and my hands support your marvellous behind and slap it and open it and one finger makes its way in to stroke its secret door, the goal is to enter as many of your doors as possible, and my mouth is affixed to yours, I adore you madly, I love you, I want you madly. Your fleece is the only vegetation that I can recall in this place where there is no vegetation. I take your mouth and then the hard little hermit also offers himself to my frantic mouth.

Gui

My love, this morning 2 masses were held in the fire-bay across the trench from my dugout. This is the 1ˢᵗ time that a complete mass has been celebrated on the front line. It has already been done in the support trenches but not yet on the very front line. At noon a visit from the Colonel. He understood my very straightforward explanation and told me I would be 3rd in line to go on leave—there are two officers ahead of me—which means that it should be in the first days of January. Sooner than when I was in the Arty. He told me to remember him to the Boulevard Séguin, for he is an old colonial! So this time my leave is at last really taking shape! My love! This is my seventh day in these trenches.

465

Without having experienced the wretchedness of life here oneself no one could imagine it. Love I adore you, yet how very odd it is that since your two letters arrived everything seems fine to me. It is quite extraordinary how you have transformed this grim life. I may lead my section over the top tonight. . . . My love, I adore you with all my heart, my darling Love, my beloved Madeleine.

The corpse has been removed. So much the better, we were getting too familiar with it. The men had taken to hanging their haversacks from its feet, which stuck out like coat pegs. For part of the night I was looking at the photo sent by Anne in which, you tell me, you challenge me to a duel of voluptuousness. You are exquisite, you are the eighth wonder of the world. I adore you and everything I now

GUILLAUME APOLLINAIRE

know of the forecourt makes me quake. No letters from you last night, maybe today.

Your lovely promise turns my head. I shall be your marble during my leave. All the doors will belong to me, you say. What a doorman I shall be then while on leave!

I adore you I kiss your breasts, my lips and your forecourt intersect, my tongue slides in delightfully and I adore the hermit hardening from your voluptuous feelings.

Love how I love you and I write supremely hardened by love.

I love you and I take your mouth, your tongue and I devour your breasts.

Gui

466

I have now my love experienced the indescribable joy of receiving your letter of the 22nd, the voluptuousness-letter. I was so afraid it was lost. Not only is it true, it is also a masterpiece in itself. You are my love and truly a very superior intelligence. I am proud of you Madeleine and I adore you. And this voluptuous dream of yours is so exquisite and so far-reaching that it carries voluptuousness to triumphant heights. I adore your desire and the spiritual voluptuousness that we both feel so acutely. I too am yours even in my most secret thoughts and I am the sole master you the sole slave which comes to the same thing. Voluptuousness thrills every atom of my being. I adore your hair which covers me caresses me perfumes me.

I love your eyes which love my eyes and the sight of my body. I adore the silky caress of your eyelashes and eyelids and likewise the mysterious caress of your closed eyes.

I adore your ears that want to hear me.

I adore your nose that thrills voluptuously at my smell.

I adore your mouth the seat of your most sensitive voluptuous feelings. My mouth yearns divinely for your lips. I adore your mouth upon every part of me. Your vampire's mouth that desires my spit my sweat my blood. I will go further, oh my exquisite Madeleine, and say that my mouth desires your [*illegible*] of love and [*illegible*]. That I love you madly and I love your teeth and your tongue.

GUILLAUME APOLLINAIRE

467

I adore your hands those exquisite flowers, those palms of my oasis. I adore your intimate caresses.

I adore, oh how I adore and desire your divinely beautiful breasts, I eat and caress them gently and suck them very gently and very little so as not to alter their shape. Their form is so delicate my love you must preserve it by making sure never to stretch them, by washing them in cold water and by raising your arms above your head. Your breasts are adorable and together you and I will tend them passionately. You are my beauty my love and I adore you.

I adore your belly and your rump (tell me at length about your posterior and the 9th door, which you have not yet done). I adore the way they tremble and I adore the exquisite forecourt which you have written to me about comparing it to a seashell, the most beautiful the most lyrical of phrases, my adored one, and the most accurate too. I adore the contractions of the forecourt which are women's rarest gift, and few possess it. You do, oh my unique love. I adore your 9th door my love. I adore your admirable fleece. I adore you all of you, you are exquisite and my mouth travels all over you.

This morning I heard some Boches talking to each other.

It is agreed, I shall await your dear daily letters without getting impatient—at least insofar as that is possible for me. My leave is coming darling. I love you, it is extraordinary, my dearest love. I shan't be writing you any more really long letters, unless I can find some more envelopes, until we are relieved. The others are in my mess-box and because of the bad weather we are being resupplied hardly at all and then only at the price of great fatigue and hardship. I take all your doors my love. I am mad over you, I adore you, I take your tongue and your exquisite breasts. I clasp you madly against me.

Gui

Enclosed my love you will find a portrait of the 2 Russians I told you about who came to my then battery, they were intercepted in the first place by my present C^{oy} which is where I was given the enclosed photo of them.

LA TRANCHÉE

Je suis la blanche tranchée au corps creux et blanc

Et j'habite toute la terre dévastée

Viens avec moi jeune dans mon sexe qui est tout mon corps

Viens avec moi pénètre-moi pour que je sois heureuse de volupté sanglante

Je guérirai tes peines, tes soucis, tes désirs ta mélancolie

Avec la chanson fine et nette des balles et l'orchestre d'artillerie

Vois comme je suis blanche, plus blanche que les corps les plus blancs

Couche-toi dans mon sein comme sur un ventre bien-aimé

Je veux te donner un amour sans second, sans sommeil, sans paroles

J'ai tant aimé de jeunes gens

Je les aime comme les aime Morgane

En son castel sans retour

Au haut du mont Gibel

Qui est l'Etna dont s'éloignent vite nos soldats destinés à la Serbie

Je les ai aimés et ils sont morts et je n'aime que les vivants

*Allons viens dans mon sexe plus long que le plus long serpent, long comme tous les
    corps des morts mis l'un devant l'autre*

Viens écoute les chants métalliques que je chante bouche blanche que je suis

*Viens ceux qui m'aiment sont là armés de fusils de crapouillots de bombes de grenades
    et ils jouent silencieusement*

GUILLAUME APOLLINAIRE

THE TRENCH

I am the white trench with the hollow white body

And I inhabit all this devastated land

Come with me young man into my sex that is my entire body

Come with me penetrate me make me delight in bloody voluptuousness

I shall minister to your hurts your troubles your desires your melancholy

With the fine clear song of bullets and an orchestra of artillery

Look how white I am whiter than the whitest of bodies

Lie down in my bosom as though on a beloved belly

I want to give you a love that is peerless, sleepless, wordless

I have loved so many young men

Loved them as Morgan le Fay loves them

In her keep whence none return

High on Mount Gibel

Which is the Etna from which our soldiers hasten off for Serbia

I loved them and they are dead and I love only the living

So come, come into my sex longer than the longest snake, long as the bodies
    of all the dead laid head to toe

Come hear the metallic songs I sing white mouth that I am

Come, those who love me are here, armed with rifles with mortars with
    bombs with grenades and all playing silently

My love I had no letter from you today. I adore you. I begin to
wonder whether letters for you or me have gone astray. But I think
not. I take your mouth.

LE . . . POÈME SECRET

Voilà de quoi est fait le chant symphonique de l'amour qui bruit dans la conque de
    Vénus
Il y a le chant de l'amour de jadis
Le bruit des baisers éperdus des amants illustres
Les cris d'amour des mortelles violées par les dieux

470

*Les virilités des héros fabuleux érigées comme des cierges vont et viennent comme une
    rumeur obscène*

*Il y a aussi les cris de folie des bacchantes folles d'amour pour avoir mangé l'hippo-
    mane sécrété par la vulve des juments en chaleur*

Les cris d'amour des félins dans les jongles

La rumeur sourde des sèves montant dans les plantes tropicales

Le fracas des marées

*Le tonnerre des artilleries où la forme obscène des canons accomplit le terrible amour
    des peuples*

Les vagues de la mer où naît la vie et la beauté

*Et le chant victorieux que les premiers rayons du soleil faisaient chanter à Memnon
    l'immobile*

Il y a le cri des Sabines au moment de l'enlèvement

Le chant nuptial de la Sulamite

       Je suis belle mais noire

Et le hurlement précieux de Jason

Quand il trouva la toison

*Et le mortel chant du cygne quand son duvet se pressait entre les cuisses bleuâtres de
    Léda*

Il y a le chant de tout l'amour du monde

Il y a entre tes cuisses adorées

       Madeleine

*La rumeur de tout l'amour comme le chant sacré de la mer bruit tout entier dans le
    coquillage*

THE . . . SECRET POEM

This is what the symphonic song of love heard in the conch shell of Venus is
    made of

There is the song of the love of times gone by

The sound of the wild kisses of famous lovers

The love-cries of mortal women raped by gods

The male members of fabled heroes erect as church candles come and go
    like obscene murmurs

GUILLAUME APOLLINAIRE

There are also the demented cries of Bacchantes mad with love from eating
the hippomanes secreted in the vulvas of mares in heat
The love-cries of felines in the jungle
The dull sound of sap rising in tropical plants
The racket of the tides
The thunder of artillery batteries' obscenely shaped cannons enacting the
terrible love of peoples
The waves of the sea birthplace of life and beauty
And the song of victory that the first rays of sunshine caused Memnon the
unmoving to sing
There is the cry of the Sabines at the moment of their ravishment
The wedding song of the Sulamite
I am black but beautiful
And Jason's priceless cry
At finding the Fleece

And the swan's mortal song as its down snuggled between Leda's blue-tinged
thighs
There is the song of all the love in the world
And between your beloved thighs
Madeleine
May be heard the murmur of all love just as the sacred song of the entire
ocean resounds in the seashell

Gui

Instead of 9 days we shall be spending 10 or 11 or even more on the front lines. Today we underwent a terrible bombardment reports of which will no doubt reach you via the newspapers. At this moment it is still going on, everyone on the look-out in the fire-bays, some with bayonets fixed. Naturally there is no post today, not even the news-papers.

I love you my darling and my desire for you is boundless. I pictured you all day long while distractedly watching fearsome cigar-shaped bombs coming in.

What pests those Boches are! And speaking of pests, I am letting my beard grow because there is no way of shaving regularly under these conditions. I imagine my whiskers beginning to curl (though I am not certain they will, never having grown a beard) and getting entangled with your magnificent fleece. I adore you my love. And I run my nascent beard over every part of your body; I think of your beauty spots. I was thinking, love, since you are so supple, that when I take the 9th door from in front you might wrap your legs about my neck and your agile and clever feet could caress me. Would you like that my love?

My exquisite love, in front of me is the little photo sent by Anne and my manhood is as hard as wood before your gaze challenging me to feel voluptuous. As I see you in this little portrait and in the one with you in your peignoir which heightens my desire thanks to the

GUILLAUME APOLLINAIRE

charm of your sweet expression and the intimations of your nakedness, you embody all the beauties of the Universe. I feel that you are
shameless like Leda, wise like Helen, passionate like Sappho, well-
bred like Heloise, charming like Agnès Sorel, and ardent like
Catherine of Russia.

I also desire my love to see you naked before me tonight, crouching
but presenting your regal hind parts for me to slap. You are my
exquisite slave and I inflame your hemispheres with the rough caress
of stinging blows from a switch. You are my thing, my passionate
slave and your forecourt opens and closes with desire until at last I
bring my me to it to calm our burning desires. Love, you are mine, I
clasp you to me passionately, I move back and forth madly inside
your forecourt and the movements of your compliant loins are just
as wild as mine.

How beautiful you are in these two photos my beloved and how I
love you. Every day now brings me closer to my longed-for leave. I
take you with all my strength. I wrap my arms about your waist and I
take your mouth.

Gui

My love I have received your dear letters of 30 Nov. (2 letters) and
1st Dec. My love, of course you are worthy of my love—but I detest
this war as much as you do. I have given the particulars of my transfer to the Infantry in a letter to your mother. No need to repeat
them here. Do not be distressed my love, perhaps after all I need to
be wounded so as to be worthy of you and pure for you.

If ever I am taken prisoner or go missing, wait for me. If I should
die I leave you everything and this letter vouches for that and
should be treated as my will. I think of you all the time and it
seems to me, indeed I am quite sure that the thought of you protects
me my love and I promise you *I shall not volunteer for any dangerous
mission*. All the same there is no denying that danger is ever-present
and extraordinarily grave. Our regiment according to the quartermaster sergeants has chewed up 28,000 men and 90 officers since
September. Still, it was best that I join the Infantry as an officer for
there are undoubtedly still N.C.O.'s in the Arty who will transfer to
the Infant. and possibly not become officers right away. In any case,
I was assigned to the Infant. on a temporary basis as an officer on
active duty, which is unusual, as witness a senior sergeant in the 9th
in the same situation as me albeit a much younger man (at 22) who
was assigned to the reserve line and is thus in a regiment that goes
into action less often than ours. A further consideration is that a
lucky wound could end this war for me and get me to safety. I adore

475

GUILLAUME APOLLINAIRE

you Madeleine. You are my strong woman. I do not believe any serious accident will befall me and you don't believe so either. This is our 10th day in the trenches and I think we shall be relieved tonight. I love you, my Madelon. My love what you say of your desire to be impregnated is so beautiful that I want to worship you from my knees. I kiss your reddened eyes. Poor humanity that we are! I adore your feet. I adore your passion for our voluptuousness and the doughty thrusting of your loins. Why no, you were not ugly as a child, on the contrary you were extremely delicate and pretty. I just love my darling Mooress with her red lips and deep fiery eyes. You are my beloved panther. What you tell me of the Mediterranean is very worrying indeed and I only hope they do not forbid me to go there on leave—you are my sole victory, my darling Madeleine. I so wish I could calm your trembling with sweet caresses. I feel your throes, my love, I take you in my arms. I squeeze you tightly, I say you are my Madelon and how happy our love makes me. I adore your serpentine kiss. My mouth and my manhood take your exquisite forecourt. I adore your sensitive and electrifying skin, I adore your belly against mine and the play of our tongues. I love your soul and body whole and entire. I adore your hips breaking the steels of your corset. I grasp your hips and your breasts and I place my manhood in the white forecourt formed by your breasts pressing together. I adore your hair pulled forward so that my mouth may more easily kiss the nape of your neck. I adore running my hands through your hair. I adore our infinite sensuousness. Oh love we had the same idea at the same time because in my letter of yesterday which you will find in the one envelope with this one you will see how I caress you in that exquisite fashion on the softest part of your thighs, so sweet to the touch with their fine-grained skin, and how my tongue seeks out the adored forecourt between your spread legs and causes you to lose your senses. I shall reconquer you every

476

single day, love, and our embrace shall be ever new. I am the worshipper and tamer of my darling panther. Love I take you ardently, my adored love I possess your body madly. Yesterday love and the day before the artill. fire was terrifying, especially that of the Boche artill. They did what we did in Sep. but against a very small sector. The fire went over our heads but we got nothing here. Had the bombardment been intended for us we should have been done for. That is what is terrible in this war and the men have not slept in 2 days. They fall asleep in the fire-bays and I am obliged to shake them awake and threaten them with court-martial to get them moving. The fact is they are fine lads, loyal and as brave as can be. But they eat badly not to say not at all and many a day it's rice which they hate. The infantryman's life is no picnic. Even for an officer it is scarcely bearable and then there are all the risks. But I have faith in us my love, faith in you in our future and I adore you madly magnificently. You are my Madeleine. I take your mouth.

Gui

10 December 1915

My adored love,

Yesterday about four o'clock an action was unleashed, it was at once fantastic and frightening. No theatrical performance could ever give an idea of the fearful bombardment that suddenly turns the whole sky crimson, the shells whistling through the air like racing cars on a track, the shattering sound of bombs and aerial-torpedo bursts, and the mindless fire dominated by the chatter of machine-guns close by. At last things calmed down, no harm done to the Company, it was close but not directed at us. In the evening we were relieved and I stayed behind to inform the new company arriving on the front line about the organization of duties. The night was quiet and I left at 9 in the morning and arrived here at 2 in the afternoon. How horrible the mud is in those horrible communication trenches. I got your adorable letters of the 2nd and 3rd. Love, you truly are my love. So I am at rest now, a rest that is a far cry from restful and that may end at any instant, in a dugout with the rain coming in. The mud is endless. I adore your 2 letters. I am writing you as much as I can. The first officer ahead of me went on leave today.

I adore you plump just as you are. Yesterday I was demoralized and could see no ways out of my present situation other than horrible ones. Today I have recovered my good sense. I am happy that you love me as you do, you are my beloved wife, my exquisite virgin. Today I received the book of a complete madman and I shall forward it to you tomorrow. You are my queen. I think of your exquisite caresses, I love your thick hair. I think of nothing save our love, everything in me reaches towards you my love, your words are sweetness to my heart my body and my soul my Madeleine. I caress you in every way you wish.

Yes, it will be a marvellous concert that I play upon your senses and one that will amaze you more each day. You shall forbid me, and such is my wish, whatever does not perforce add to your happiness. That happiness must be the only consideration and I expect you to remind me of it continually my love. My beautiful Madeleine, my most noble Madeleine. I love your thick hair and eyes that are so long when they are closed and I love their smoky quality. I adore your breasts those exquisite fruits of my desire, your adorable breasts, and I caress you in all the ways that you like. Yes, I do believe that my glance will exercise an exquisite power over you my love and I adore your shudder when I look deep into your forecourt and you faint away without my even touching you until my embrace brings you to a wild wakefulness before annihilating us in an exquisitely languorous love. Yes you are right nudity should be the rule at home; we shall reserve clothed embraces for outings. But still, I want you at times in peignoir or nightdress for the sake of variation. The sensation of having your skirt pulled up will doubtless seem outlandish to you but do we not seek every kind of sensation my Love? Certainly the only true caresses are executed naked, but as attached as you may be to them we shall revert to clothed ones unless we are far out in the country. I adore our love and your marvellous consent thereto my love, my love. I hope you have now received my letters. My love, my love. I adore the artery in your forecourt pulsating alongside my manhood with its own throbbing vein.

I do adore your modesty regarding your person, but please look at your body for me and tell me about it. I adore your belly and your

479

thighs and I too just like you take pride in your virginity. I feel sure
that novels can have no virtue for us inasmuch as we are living such
a marvellous and beautiful novel of our own.

Oh yes, a day or two ago in a letter which you have not yet received
(it was yesterday I think) I expressed the thought that the paradisia-
cal perfection of our love might well demand a sacrifice of my blood.
I accept that sacrifice Madeleine and I love you passionately and if
so we shall adore each other more and more and more. My darling
wife. I adore my liana. I love you, I give you my sap, my mouth takes
the breasts that it adores. I picture you slipping into bed and tremble as I imagine your supple body twisting and turning voluptuously
in my embrace. I adore that calm voluptuousness of yours which you
tell me about and our fleeces come together in an exquisite way, one
against the other. So you wish for a new caress my love. I shall take
you as the bull took Pasiphaë and do so with a mirror alongside us
to reflect the image of our union, would you like that, love? And just
before I shall chastise you with odoriferous roses. I kiss your mouth
madly exquisitely.

Your Gui

My love, today I am sending you that remarkably daft book I received. I am mentioned in it in connexion with my account of the burial of Walt Whitman which aroused a terrific controversy all over the world. In the same parcel is a wallet made by the leatherworker in my old battery, a ring with a Boche button that I have been wearing up to now but can no longer wear in case I should be taken prisoner and a chased gold ring which is my signet and which please to keep for me, you can wear it yourself, it is yours as much as mine.

We leave for battle shortly, you must have heard from the communiqués about the trench captured by the Boches a few days ago, well it was not us that lost it but we are the ones who must get it back—

Yesterday I got the magnificent parcel of tobacco cigars and cigarettes. Thank you my love, but now that I am an officer you need not worry about sending me tobacco, we have plenty as officers and of fine quality too, and cigarettes.

I wish with all my heart that this leave of mine would arrive, and I cannot say how much I wish we were back from this operation. What is more my men are exhausted from 11 days in the trenches.

My love, I adore you. I think only of you, your divine body is my sun. I think of your lips, of all your lips my love, I think of your exquisite passion and of your beauty.

I love you but here comes the post orderly. I'll write tomorrow.

Gui

GUILLAUME APOLLINAIRE

My love that I adore, 3 letters from you, that of the 29 Nov., which
was delayed, and those of the 4th and 5th. Yesterday I went over to
7th C^{oy} as the replacement for the officer who went on leave, but you
need not change my address, this is for a few days only. I adore you.
We were in reserve. Result nil. Everyone is tired. But the brass are
furious, they never come to see what is happening in the trenches.
Couldn't write you last night. Slept or rather didn't sleep on the
ground. . . . I adore you. I now have all the particulars about my
leave. The likelihood is that as an officer travelling 1st class I shall
get onto the first boat leaving. So if you are not there when we dock
and I fail to get advance notice to you (which I will do as best I can)
I shall take a car whatever time it is and have myself driven to the
girls' school in Lamur. If it is night-time I shall knock at your door
and call your name. I fear that between now and then this business
of a trench not retaken, though it was not us that lost it, is going to
cause us a great deal of misery. What the infantry suffers is beyond
all imagining, especially at this time and in this foul region. The
other arms by comparison are not even at war.—I adore you. The
thought of you bucks me up. Yesterday when we were a hair's-
breadth away from going into action I had not a moment of sadness
and God knows there were plenty of fine and brave men who were
stricken. The Lt-Comm^{dr} of my C^{oy}, son of the Captain Deloncle who
was skipper of *La Bourgogne* and perished when you were still a child
in a shipwreck that caused quite a stir, entrusted me with several

482

tasks to be carried out should anything befall him. But I was not sad my love, I was thinking of you. Your hair is glorious, love, say nothing against it. I adore you and I take your mouth madly. I adore what you have to say about our embraces. Let me remind you that I have asked you several times already to emphasize your hinder parts and 9th door, with which I am still poorly acquainted. I enter your forecourt and plunge into the depths of you. I adore the shape of that forecourt. Mad with love my mouth drinks in the divine liquor that you distil. How I like it oh my love when your sensations become so manifest! And now mad pleasure overwhelms me as I think of you! Marvellous! I adore your tangled hair my prettiest one! I adore your reddish parts [*illegible*] some parts of your secret fleece. I adore the scent of your hair. I adore your fluttering eyelashes. You are my slave darling. Bourget's view is mistaken with respect to the very very greatest artists. Racine, Goethe, even Hugo, Gauthier and many others were very happy thanks to women.

483

My solitude is solitude with you, indeed I do not like solitude, I like to share it with someone and that someone is you. I adore you, I undress you, I take you madly, madly: yes, love, the 1st entrance into the 9th door will be a little painful. My love I love you with a wild tenderness and I take your mouth.

Gui

My love, I had no letter from you yesterday, but I did receive 3 [*the day before*] yesterday. Please send me each week in an envelope separate from your letters a little writing paper and a few envelopes so I can write you because we cannot stock up and nor can we lumber ourselves down. The officer's box is a myth, we see it when we are at rest but we are never at rest. I am longing for my leave to come through. My love I adore you, you are my everything, you are me, myself. How I love the fact that you understand what belongs to the physical and what to the moral realms. You are my Madeleine my quite perfect Madeleine. You cannot possibly imagine how weary we are in this dugout with the rain coming down!! My love you are beautiful and you are perfect, you are pretty and vivacious you are strong and delicate you are frank and subtle. I adore you my love. Did I tell you that the Colonel asked that you remember him to the Boulevard Séguin? Yesterday I posted the parcel whose contents I described to you earlier. I forgot to say that I was also sending you back the little compass that you had sent me. I want to keep it because you gave it to me, but it does not work and is thus an encumbrance. So save it for me. I have one on my map holder my love. The tragic, awful, nameless horror of the hellish hand-to-hand fighting in the trenches in the communication trenches in the shell-holes merely strengthens the voluptuousness of my love for you, for me you are far more than the Promised Land could ever have been for the Israelites. This morning I thought for a long time before rising of your body with its fleece, I pictured your legs spread apart and the exquisite redness of the forecourt gaping open with desire. The sharp points of your breasts imparted an unparalleled ardour to my mouth. I love you too with your head buried in cushions pulling in your flanks and raising your rump like a mare in heat inciting a stallion. I kissed every one of your beauty spots as my manhood hard as steel moved back and forth within an exquisite sanctum lubricated by the sticky sap of your desire. My love I also took you on top of me and to excite your ardour still more birched your superbly trembling bottom and the better to enjoy the movements of your hips placed a mirror at the foot of the bed to reflect your loins and my manhood that fine column of flesh disappearing and reappearing according as your buttocks fell back or rose upwards. If only you knew how much I desire you at this moment.

Tell me my love whether the breadth of your hips is greater or less than that of your shoulders. Kiss your feet for me my love. My love I adore you. I feel your mouth at my 9th door as your tongue digs a fiery well there. Then I penetrate deep within you and as we embrace your finger fills your Gui's 9th door as he takes your mouth and tongue in the most exquisite way.

Gui

Envelopes are the most important thing for you to send, but not in any quantity.

GUILLAUME APOLLINAIRE

486

My love, I would like my leave to coincide with your holidays, but it doesn't matter in the end because I am sure you will manage to be with me all the time. I have your letter of the 6th my love with its full account of your trip to Nice last year, and the story of the weapon, the jewels and the headwaiter. My love, I adore you, I love you with all my soul and all my body. I can only tell you once again how your entrance into that compartment was like a thunderbolt for me and how you noticed that. I instantly adored your passionate face, your magnificent thick hair and your svelte body so replete with delicious promise. I immediately imagined your fleeces. I succumbed to a mad admiration for your eyelashes, and the pure bow of your mouth, your wonderful glance and your voice sealed this marvellous capture of my heart, which was yours in the twinkling of an eye. Do you remember the force which caused me to address you and you to reply? Do you remember how to save you embarrassment I made use of a passenger there with us in the carriage who by chance had attended the Stanislas College in Cannes and was thus a fellow-pupil of my brother's? Seeing your slightly ruffled good manners I included him vaguely in our conversation so that you could not duck the obligation to exchange a few pleasantries with the other travellers in your compartment. And soon I felt that you had fallen a little under my spell but were surprised at it, and my heart was beating very fast when we swapped addresses, you wrote yours yourself in my notebook and I felt as though we were exchanging our very souls oh my love. I adore your love, which is that of a little wild beast in the jungle. I adore it that you surrender yourself so completely, even to the unforeseeable. My love I adore the little heart that beats so strongly in your forecourt. I fear we shall be going back to trenches tomorrow or the day after tomorrow, which stinks. My love, would you copy out a poem of mine in free verse— naturally not the cry 'To Italy' nor 'Song of the Horizon in Champagne', but another, or two even, but in free verse, and send them to me or directly to Mr Ardengo Soffici in Poggio a Caiano, near Florence (Italy).

I adore you my love, you are my beauty, my paradise, I take you violently, madly, I desire you as no woman has ever been desired you are my adored love, I take your mouth.

Gui 487

16 Dec. 1915

My love, I have received your letters of the 7th and 8th. I adore you.
I too am dying with impatience to be by your side. We go forward
again tomorrow. Obviously everything Jean says is very likely, I have
known it for a long time but never speak to you of it. After all only
idiots worry about that sort of thing. It doesn't bear contemplating.
But store up your courage my love. Yes, I too have heard talk of the
4-day stint, but in point of fact it appears that last winter those 4
days lasted for as long as 25 days. We ourselves were supposed to
stay for 9 days and we ended up spending 11 and in my own case 12
nights. Now we are going back. I adore it that you stretch like a very
beautiful panther, I adore you as a snake and I adore the length of
your muscular arms and legs.—For our part this war diminishes us,
makes us fat and softens our muscles, for curiously it is not the
muscles that get exercised in this war but rather patience and the
nervous system, all the rest softens up the better to survive while the
will gets very strong. My love when you speak to me of voluptuousness tell me also about your body that I adore. I am also mad with
impatience to be your husband. Yes if you like we shall set aside
[*illegible*] for days of great voluptuousness. What you say about my
poem 'Windows' is quite true and I only wish you had read all the
poems from that time, which are scattered in reviews. You had a
premonition of that poem in one of your old letters, as I pointed
out to you at the time. Delaunay's prismatic painting which he calls
simultaneism is a continuation of impressionism, he is a rather

488

vulgar artist. I am happy to know that your Mama likes the ring.—
Yes, we shall do whatever you like during my leave. Yes, my men are
fond of me because I am cheerful and do not go to ground in my
dugout but instead go and see them, buoy them up, see if they have
enough to eat. Apparently my passage is free too. Agreed as to the
wire. My love I take your forecourt madly. Won't you just as madly
describe your rump for me my love? We shall never separate my
love because you are my little slave full of authority and sense, and
because we adore each other and love our duty. Love, I take your
ninth door and after a few ins and outs invade your forecourt and
plunge deep and long into you until we faint away.

Gui

489

My love, the Colonel has had me informed that I should be ready to go on leave on the 23rd.—Tonight we are off to the front line again. No letters from you yesterday.—Yesterday was reconnaissance, terrific mud, shelling. I am exhausted at the prospect of going up there tonight.

My love, I was thinking of you all night long. You are my exquisite love and I adore everything you think about our love. As soon as I can I'll wire you in Lamur. In theory this letter should reach you on Christmas Day. I shall be on the way by then, but first and foremost let me send you my warmest kisses for Christmas. Am getting all the information I can concerning the steps I need to take to make my leave as long as possible. I think I am going to arrive just as your own leave begins oh my beloved.

I think of your beauty, of your dear plump beauty. I think of your fleece, of the 9 adorable doors of your body, and of the exquisite pink and white opening of your mouth.

I think of your downy flesh, of your great door. You are deliciously graceful my love.

My love, a pale ray of sunshine is playing on a few pale reeds. It is a long time since I last saw sunshine. But the mud is unimaginably thick.

490

My love, I await the 23rd with such impatience, still 6 days away! And you my love? I shall have your answer in Lamur.

When you receive this letter you should not write me any more, my love, but I'll keep you abreast of my whole journey by telegram. I adore you, I kiss you passionately, my soul. I take your mouth, our tongues play divinely and our hands caress our bodies. I kiss your long hair and I adore you, darling love, my beautiful, divine Madeleine, my very own Madeleine.

Gui

491

My love, I could not write you yesterday. I had not a minute to myself. I have received your adorable little letter of the 13th. My little chicken promises me another voluptuousness-letter which may perchance arrive today. My love, when you get this letter please reply to me care of poste restante in Marseilles, or rather keep writing to me here until you get a wire informing you that I have really left, because until we actually depart you can never be quite sure. I am now back on the front line. I told you in my letter of the 18th how I had been on reconnaissance the day before and that we would be going back to trenches that night. I duly left with 7th Cᵒʸ, the lᵗ who had been in command of it for 13 months having gone on a machine-gunners' training course. I am replacing the lᵗ now on leave after whom I am supposed to take mine and 1 new capᵗⁿ has arrived. We are 2 officers. My captain comes to us from the African chasseurs, from Morocco, so that as green an infantryman as I am myself I am still more au courant than he, who is even greener. We left by night, under moonlight, and the ghastly mud of the day before had dried. Since I had reconnoitred, I was at the head of the column. Because I feared mud in the communication trenches we proceeded in the open. At the edge of a wood I spotted cannon without cover but draped with sacking, and I thought of my old gun. It was odd. Then I heard voices whispering: 'Maybe it's Kostro's Cᵒʸ?' (that was the abbreviation of my name used by the N.C.O.'s in my battery, the men for their part never managed to get my name exactly right and would mangle it either as 'Kostro l'exquis'—Kostro the exquisite—or as 'Cointreau-Whisky', depending on whether they were Picards or Flemings). I heard the voices quickly turned my head halted the C^oy on the spot and among the trees discerned two old comrades, the battery warrant-officer a fellow named Benoît who is a tobacconist in Carcassonne and Horb the chief of the 3rd piece a farmer from the Aisne, they knew me right away and their visible emotion affected me, the more so since these are usually very dour people especially Horb. The battery has advanced considerably and is now close to the second lines in a very dangerous area and the guns have no cover. I chatted for a couple of minutes with my former comrades and had enough time to learn things that upset me events whose full details I shall probably never know, for I was able to exchange but a few words with them and who knows when we shall meet again. The fact is, anyway, that almost all my gun crew have been slaughtered or wounded. My master gun layer Louis Déportère from Lille has been killed. He was a lad superior (in terms of his spirit not his education) to his social station as a worker, he looked like the young Beethoven of the portraits, a pure high brow, very sweet, very determined very serious. A quite remarkable gun layer, 1st prize in marksmanship. I had found him protectors in the shape of Gaston Picard (editor of the *Bulletin des Écrivains*) and his wife whom I do not know. Déportère was recently married and had left a pregnant wife behind in Lille. He was never able to get news from her or from any member of his family. 10 days ago I got a note from Gaston Picard telling me that Déportère was happy because he had at last had news of his wife and of a baby girl born since the out-break of war. . . .

I don't remember the other losses, I was too upset, except that my telephone orderly Montélimart was wounded. . . .

GUILLAUME APOLLINAIRE

It is your love, Madeleine, that has protected me. Had I remained with my battery I would surely have been wounded at the least, those most at risk being the gun layer and the chief of piece.

All this news was imparted in a few moments then off we went again. The relief was effected splendidly, I had reconnoitred the sector, which is slightly to the right of where we were before and more dangerous. I was worn out yesterday. Our predecessors did nothing, everything is yet to be done. I spent the night getting barbed-wire coils prepared and deployed, constructing new fire-bays and positioning new chevaux-de-frise. But there is still much work to be done; those Boche pigs let us have a few bursts and demolished our trench. No serious harm done though. But we are badly positioned and there is moonlight. Extremely dangerous for work purposes. Yesterday morning the Colonel came by and told me once again that I would get off as soon as the officer now on leave returns and very likely that would be the 23rd. Here I am in command of the 2nd section, my dugout is small but not bad and—*a good omen!*—there is a little communication trench off to the side named 'Paget Trench'— very close to Pagès, and when shall I be able well and truly to en- filade you my little Pagès Trench!! My dugout is called 'Madeleine's Forecourt', it was I who carved the words in the chalk at the entrance, which is very low on account of the 50-centimetre bombs; on the 1st level as you go down is my bag and it is there that my servant Crapouillot, the jolliest little soldier imaginable, a Croix de Guerre for taking ten prisoners single-handed at Tahure Hill and distinguishing himself at Hill 196, is at present busy sewing a button on my tunic; on the second level down (each step being 80 cm deep by 90 cm high) is my brazier, lit because it is freezing and at night Private Labin a native of Touraine and a woodworker, who has fitted the place up for me, sleeps here. Hanging on the right-hand prop is

494

the Draeger apparatus which officers now use to deal with gas. It is all ready and filled with hyposulphite. On the third level is my table on which I am writing this to you (sitting on the 2nd). It is on this 3rd level that Crapouillot sleeps each night while on the 4th is my wire-netting bed (a system I imported from the artillery into the infantry, where one normally sleeps on the ground). Meanwhile my love what is happening is that the Boches are busy but our artillery is harassing them. For my part I am waiting for my leave I adore you. I adore your very special voluptuousness. I take your mouth and your tongue. My left hand strokes your breasts and my right excites the little hermit who at first contracts but then moistens abundantly under my finger's prolonged exquisite caress to which you abandon yourself, you are my exquisite flower and my manhood stands up in your honour my exquisite queen.

Gui

495

P.S. Inscription on my dugout wall: Auque Segula bugler 122nd Inf. 3rd C^{oy} 2nd section: Give me naked women give me booze on demand.

My love I adore you.

Gui!!

22 December 1915

My love, I live in anxious anticipation. Snow fell for part of yesterday and overnight. Christmas weather with the pines and the
snow—even the Christmas trees. No letter from you or anyone. I
adore you my love, yesterday I looked at the drawing of your
exquisite nipple oh my adorable Madeleine. Looking at your
photographs made my head swim. . . .

496

My little one, some fantastic news: the l^t who was on leave whom I
am replacing in 7th C^{oy} has just got to the communication trench.

So I hope to be leaving today or tomorrow.

I adore you. I hardly know what I am writing. I am bowled over to
think that this leave is in the offing at last, at long last.

My love, I adore you madly, I love you. I'll close now will write
tomorrow, I think I shall be on my way by then.

I draw your mouth and all your body to me.

Gui

1 Telegram. The originals of this and the
following telegram are now lost; the
text here is that given in the first edition of this book, *Tendre comme le
souvenir* (1952).

25 December 1915[1]

Marseilles—Taking next mail-boat.

Gui

497

GUILLAUME APOLLINAIRE

10 January 1916[1]   **1** Telegram.

Marseilles—Arrived safely—Kisses.

Gui

My love, I adore you.—I simply cannot thank you enough—you your kind Mama and the whole family for the delightful leave that you vouchsafed me and you love are my love. The crossing was good, the troop comm^dr was that captain with the fierce moustache whom we saw at the Continental and who amused your Mama so much, almost everyone was seasick, even Monsieur Six who was unable to make a single pun. There were just 5 of us who did not get sick. During the night in rolling seas the torpedo-boat had to abandon us—But in the end all went well. I catch my train in an hour.

I am happy to love you my darling. You are my delight and I love you.

I shall write you at greater length tomorrow,

My mouth on your mouth and our tongues my exquisite darling play divinely with each other.

Gui

. . . I am tired.

Keep writing to the same address Sector 139.

GUILLAUME APOLLINAIRE

Épernay, 12 January 1916[1]

1 On headed notepaper of Hôtel de la Cloche.

My love, I was able to stay in Paris only until noon yesterday. Since then I have been searching for my regiment. I now know where they are at rest and will be joining them shortly. A tiring journey. Fine weather. In Paris lunched with Mama, told her of our engagement to which she has no objection.—I adore you my darling love. I caress you tenderly and I love the way your arm rests on mine. Could not go by the *Mercure* to talk about a new book of verse but shall do so by correspondence. Odd how the light even in Marseilles is dimmer than in Algeria. The moustachioed old captain was insufferable on the boat: just because I was polite to an ugly and horrifyingly thin woman from Oran who was seasick he made jokes implying that I had made advances to the poor lady. I was obliged to tell him that I was engaged to be married and that his baseless insinuations offended me. He is an architect employed by the Drôme départe-ment and spent several months with the brother of my Colonel, to whom therefore I am the bearer of some news.

We also had on board General Lyautey's aide-de-camp and a *goumier* lieutenant with whom I had lunch in Marseilles (just fish at the Hôtel des Phocéens). I took a couchette on the train and slept well; I was with a grocer who lives in Paris at 128 rue de la Roquette and is named Lequoy, a man who seemed to me remarkably well informed about political and military matters, perhaps merely because he has good sense but if so then he has a great deal of it.

500

Talking to this fellow makes one more optimistic. I have just had lunch in Épernay it is 2 p.m. and at 2.17 I catch a train that will take me not very far from here near to the place where my company is billeted. This morning I travelled back from Châlons with an officer who was going 'on leave for the 4th time'. It is a fine day, I am thinking of you my love, I adore you, I am thinking about our reunion, about your beauty, your sweetness, your imagination that I love, your look that I adore, your tremors of excitement, about the whole of you my dear very very dear love, my Madelon that I adore. I take your mouth.

Kiss your dear Mama and the little ones for me.

Gui.

501

15 January 1916

My love, we are at rest at Damery near Épernay and I have just
arrived to take up my duties as commander of the same C^oy,
although I am being dressed down from all sides, by the Comm^dr,
by the Colonel. Yesterday even by the General, who demanded to be
informed why the sentry on some road or other had no lamp. In
short for the time being I haven't a moment of rest, reports after
reports. I am swamped. Fortunately I was a quartermaster sergeant
and consequently know, if not much, at least enough to balance the
Company's books. At this precise moment I have to make a report
on why my Company was wearing helmets yesterday while the
neighbouring C^oy was in kepis. Yesterday I witnessed a medical scene
that Molière would have known how to turn to good use. In a word
this so-called rest, however entertaining it may be, almost makes one
miss the front lines for their peace and quiet. Out there at least it is
only the Boches that bother you, whereas here not only is the
prospect of the Boches ever-present, you also have all the aggrava-
tions of barracks life. . . . I am writing your letter in several instal-
ments, love.—I have just received your letter of the 9th my beloved
and I was bowled over by it—I don't know how to explain it to you—
better that I not explain—I adore you, that's all—we adore each
other.—I was not able to take care of my book in Paris, but keep
on copying my love, I'll handle things by correspondence. I have
received all your letters from just before my leave. I have read them
and shall reply gradually, I enclose a view of Damery. How long we

502

shall be staying here I don't know.—Adrienne Lecouvreur did something here, possibly she was born here.

The local priest is a well-educated and sensitive man.

But the most splendid thing here is the battalion chief, my commanding officer who is truly a splendid man, courageous, discriminating, well-bred, a true gentleman. I like him very much even though he is giving me what-for at the moment. And in the whole universe what I love most is you, my beloved little darling Madelon.

Oh, little Madelon, I have just been informed that all leaves for Algeria have been cancelled. How lucky I was!! I don't suppose this decision is final, but still, such a policy would certainly have delayed my leave!!

Kiss your Mama and all the family for me oh my precious love. I am   503
thinking of your beauty, your sweetness. I love you my pretty
Madeleine, I adore you. I am going to send you a parcel of books
and some other things, I have found my watch and since I don't
need two I am sending Pierrot's back to you.

I adore you. I take your mouth.

Gui

My adored one, I love you.

My beloved, I adore you.

Gui

I have come across a parcel of dates, still good, and two parcels of mandarin oranges, of which I was able to eat only half of one.

504

My love today I received your delicious letters of the 9th and 10th. You were right to be nice to your headmistress. You are my delicious wife. I am going to see abt marriage by proxy. Try to find out to what extent leaves to Algeria have been discontinued. I adore you my love and your letters have put me in a dismal mood yesterday and today. I warm your hands my love, I love you. Yes the sea was awful, or so they said, for my part I didn't notice it for thinking of Oran—in my mind I was still in Oran—and I didn't get seasick.

Tell Denise that she is very sweet.

Muster up all your courage my love. My love, my love, I adore you. The story about your mother shook me. Who is this man. . . . But when all is said and done I don't care, we adore each other.

I spoke today to the Colonel about machine-guns, because they are forming new machine-gunner units and I did not understand why I was not included. He was very kind about it; in fact he is a good commanding officer, indeed good in every sense, and he said he had considered me but wanted to get me used to the life of the ordinary infantryman. All the same, I would sooner this did not last too long.

I think that the day after tomorrow my C^oy Comm^dr will be coming back and if so I'll be having a somewhat quieter life for a while.

I adore you and take your mouth my love.

Gui

GUILLAUME APOLLINAIRE

18 January 1916

My love, the photos are superb, all of them, send me another set, Louise has done wonderful work. I obviously wish with all my heart for her to photograph you again my charming creature. Please kiss your Mama warmly for me my love, your Mama is wonderful.

I'll see all these Arab festivals after the war.—Whatever you think should be done—so long as you are in agreement with your Mama— shall indeed be done. In any case do not for the moment leave your Mama, and put off learning Spanish. Which said, it seems to me that working at a gentle pace on your Latin and Greek would perhaps not be a bad idea, but you have a better sense of that than I and so does your Mama. My love, you know better than to ask whether I agree with you and whether I prefer kisses to letters!!! Your kisses my darling little slave are my joy! I adore your gracefulness my love. The little ones are so sweet. And Marthe turns out to be a sister as kind as she is sharp-witted.

Émile who has an ear for languages should certainly take advantage of his surroundings and apply himself seriously to Arabic and Span- ish *as they are actually spoken*, for this is something that would serve him admirably well later on. And as for you my love you ought to speak a little English, with an Englishwoman perhaps. It seems to me that the French Universities' longstanding irrelevance has not been remedied and that they still teach only vague elements of diction and syntax but never living languages. It is deplorable, and not the only thing that is deplorable. My darling love, I take your tongue, I adore you and I take your mouth.

Gui

My love, I wonder whether we might not go to the Orient one of these days. Alas for the moment it is all marching and manoeuvres.—I have had no letter from you today my love. I have sent the parcel of books, a canvas bucket of no use to me here—some black puttees, we have to have blue ones now, Émile and Pierre can share them, a few letters, etc. (a few draft manuscripts that may come in useful later).

508

I am thinking of how exquisitely graceful you are my adored love and I am a little bit sad to be so far from you my love.

Today I had a visit from a corporal in the 81ˢᵗ weighed down by ghastly kit and wearing a monocle. It was my friend Gabriel Boissy, poor fellow, his monocle created a real stir, he must be the only corporal with a monocle in the entire French army.

He struck me as much aged.

I am thinking of your gracefulness my darling amidst all those Moorish and Spanish women.

I think of our evening at Mers el Kébir and I am a little sad.

Love, I cannot write properly today. I am weary. I am beginning to be impatient for winter to be over.

My love, I adore you and I take your mouth passionately, madly.

Your Gui

20 January 1916

My love, I told you that the lieu[t] who is the C[oy] Comm[dr] has returned, but he is suffering from albuminuria and excused from service, so I have to carry on in charge. Today was a route march for the Rgt. Our battalion took the lead and my C[oy] was at the head of the battalion. Can you picture your Gui at the head of the whole regiment on a war footing with machine-guns and everything else! I was indescribably thrilled, on horseback of course but with a horrible mean jade of a mount frightened by the motor-car engines. Tomorrow, skeleton exercises, meaning strategy, and then in 2 days we leave for full army manoeuvres. What fun, don't you think?

Today, love, your 2 letters of the 13th and 14th. Yes, I did think from the look on the face of the Comm[dr] of the *Sidi-Brahim* as it left Oran that something was up, he didn't seem very confident.

I can feel your arms around my neck and I adore you my darling.

Your stories tickled me and I treasure them.

My sweetheart I adore you. M[lle] Glotz is quite fine, so your woman friend made a big mistake.

I have to go to bed now because tomorrow morning we have trials of some kind.

I'll have to be off very early.

509

GUILLAUME APOLLINAIRE

I adore you.

I take your mouth.

                                                        Gui

My love, I adore you, today 7th C^{oy} to which I was detached earlier delivered several letters from you and the 2 ever so sweet letters from your Mama, please thank her and tell her that I kiss her as a son.

We leave tomorrow for a training camp and manoeuvres. It is no picnic and I don't have a moment to write.

I adore you. I am tired of all this fuss and palaver.

I am beginning to be truly stupefied by all the work.

Today I got a letter from a friend who had long been declared unfit for service but not long ago became a Zouave and is now at the Front. Equivalent more or less to the lot of a simple private.

I adore you my adored darling. Keep me up to date with all your doings my love. I had no letter from you either today or yesterday. I posted you another parcel yesterday.

The beret is no longer required, only the *bonnet de police* forage cap (and helmet). So the parcel contains my beret along with books I have not had time to read, also the album of the battle of Champagne. I'll explain this to you later but you will recognize Le Mesnil-lès-Hurlus Perthes Tahure Le Trou-Bricot Hill 193 York Trench Hamburg Trench etc. etc., all locations that I will tell you about later.

GUILLAUME APOLLINAIRE

In my pocket I am carrying around a novel published by *La Feuille Littéraire*[1] but have not had the time to read anything.

I take your mouth madly my adored one. I kiss you.

Gui

[1] A periodical publication offering well-known works in affordable format.—Tr.

1 As a way of conveying his whereabouts to Madeleine, Apollinaire had agreed with her during his leave that he would use a code: the first letters of each line of any letter headed by the words 'Aux Armées' (With the Armed Forces) would, if read in order, furnish his location. Thus in this case the initial letters of each line constituted the sentence 'I am at Ville-en-Tardenois'.

With the Armed Forces, 22 January 1916[1]

My love

I adore you my darling love and I am writing almost immediately following our arrival at our new billets. We have had a very long march.

It drizzled, and we were on the march for six hours.

In the end the men found their board hutments with paliasses laid on 'green beds'—well named, for they consist in hurdles of small green tree-branches.

We officers are lodged in the large village nearby. The house where I am is splendid, and the interior is exquisite except for the fact that my room is frankly no good, very small and low-ceilinged, with just a paliasse for my servant. No way to get washed (but that can be remedied), apples and pears heaped in a corner and a superb red eiderdown. Do not imagine that I'll be uncomfortable here. We have slept in worse conditions. Once I lay my hands on a basin and a towel everything will be fine.

We shall be on manoeuvres and then go back to the lines. I have continued as C^{oy} commander during this change of station. But I made the march on foot to get used to that (and held up well), we were the rear company.

Jean-Marie is insufferable when we are at rest.

GUILLAUME APOLLINAIRE

He went ahead with the advance billeting party which he abandoned along the way and the Colonel found him lunching at leisure on a chicken. Since he was the worse for drink the Battalion Comm^{dr} instructed me to give him an 8-day detention. I don't believe things will go any further because he is a marvellous soldier.

There you have it my love, a little of my daily life. I adore you my darling, I think of you continually, I think of your breasts, your gracefulness, I adore you.

Write and tell me what you are doing at your lycée, kiss your sweet Mama and the little ones, and don't forget to say hello to our photographer Louise.

I adore you and madly I take your mouth your mouth your tongue.

Your Gui

Tell Marthe not to torment you just because I am not there to stop her.

My love, I am very far behind—I did not write you yesterday—and I could not have, what with the manoeuvres, full army manoeuvres, in other words the most deadly dull thing in the world, as if war were not sufficient we have to have manoeuvres; ah well! just so long as it all leads to Victory, we may as well enjoy giving ourselves over to this gruelling sport. But love, first and foremost your letter of the 18th (the latest). You are a good judge of Anatole France, a very good one in fact, his novels are badly organized and their various parts lack a logical sequence. A comparison of his *Les Dieux ont soif* (The Gods Are Thirsty) with Dumas *père*'s *Le Chevalier de Maison-Rouge* (The Knight of Maison-Rouge), which have almost the same plot, is a case in point, because Dumas's superiority as a storyteller is instantly apparent. I adore you my love and I'll write you a better letter as soon as I can—I don't have the time at present. Get plenty of sleep my darling and as for your feet massage them gently from toe to instep for 2 minutes each at night—and apply the Philopode ointment, and I was forgetting stand on tiptoe ten times every morning it will do you good.

I also have your letter of the 17th, don't force yourself to eat fish.

I also have your letter of the 15th with your pretty poem. I adore you.

I also have your letter of the 16th; don't send me your copies of my poems until I ask you.

GUILLAUME APOLLINAIRE

Tomorrow my love we carry on just like today and I am weary. I think of your exquisite delicacy.

But at the minute I am seriously overworked and beginning almost to miss the trenches.

I do hope I shall have an hour or two free so that I may write you.

At the moment Santa Cruz Mountain must be at the acme of its floral display. My love, I adore you. I take your delightful breasts and kiss them passionately.

I am going to bed now. Remember what I told you about my letters headed 'With the Armed Forces'. I take your mouth madly.

Your Gui

516

My darling love, I adore you. Today I got your letter of the 19th. No there is no mental separation from you but it is true that I have so little time to write to you at the moment my exquisite love, and this creates a feeling of separation for me. Today however we came back earlier and I have more time to devote to you, so I am calmer, it is as though you had come closer to me my Madelon. It is even the 1st time since I left Oran that I have had a minute for you. I have resumed command of my section and I am learning about the manoeuvres as I go. Because there is a big difference between artillery manoeuvres and infantry ones.

The village where we are billeted has an exquisite church the Stations of the Cross there are quite interesting but it is above all the church itself that is beautiful. A curious feature of the place is that each house has access to a spring (not a well but a real spring). It runs through the cellars and the local people keep it very clean.

My love I shall take care of our marriage just as soon as I have time to take care of anything, which should I think be in about ten days. Do not send me the poems now I haven't the time to deal with them and I don't want to carry them around with me much before their publication has been decided upon. I haven't even had the time to write to the *Mercure*. I adore you my love. As for the 2 or 3 secret poems you mention my love do not be alarmed because your name will never appear in them. You know that they are for you and that is enough. The others we shall print up just for us.

Gui

GUILLAUME APOLLINAIRE

My love your letters of the 20th and the 21st have arrived. Today it was the same old routine. I am getting used to it and feel less weary.

Do not speak of tuberculosis, my love, we shall neither of us have tuberculosis.

I am very happy to know that leaves for Algeria have been suspended only temporarily. But those at home who are waiting for visits should nevertheless continue to use the newspapers to press for the rapid restoration of these leaves and especially for officers since there are always berths for them on both outbound and inbound vessels.

At the moment the men are getting their knuckles rapped for not always complying with the obligation we are under to refrain from revealing billet locations.

It sometimes happens even that correspondents in their replies repeat such place-names to indicate that they have understood them and thus compromise the soldiers to whom they are writing.

Apparently even some officers have not always respected these directives (which I for my part feel are necessary) and have received reprimands in consequence.

It is up to the families at home never to ask their soldiers where they are. They are at the Front. I believe it suffices to say so and that no further details are required.

The story about your priest's proof of the existence of God is excellent and I am going to tell it in the *Mercure*.

My darling love, I love you infinitely.

As for Montenegro, I am not the least bit surprised. I thought I had already spoken to you about this. I certainly spoke to my fellow officers in the Company as soon as I joined the 96th. It is astounding how poorly acquainted the higher-ups seem to be with the tortuous politics of the Balkan nations, even those which are our allies.

My love kiss your Mama for me and the little ones too. Let me know when leaves are reinstated. I really want them to be. Meanwhile what does the headmistress of your school have to say? I take your mouth madly.

Gui   519

My love, I have had no letter from you today. It is mild and damp here. The ground is waterlogged. Walking across ploughed land is taxing. Hares abound. You see them covering the doe. When they bolt across the fallow fields they seem to be cocking a snook at us. As for the partridges they drill in covies in the fields and do not disband even when we approach them but merely wheel by fours in quick time.

I am tired today. I think I shall sleep really well tonight.

For news I have hardly any save to say that winter has not been too bad up to now.

I spoke earlier of Corporal Gabriel Boissy whom I discovered in a neighbouring regiment. I felt enormous sympathy towards him thinking that he was in a section. In point of fact he is simply an archivist in his regiment's combat train.

I adore you my love your exquisite look never leaves me.

I love you infinitely my dear little wife and I take your mouth.

Gui

My love,

I adore you. I am to get a 48-hour leave because while I was on leave in Algeria quite a few of my things were lost including my overcoat. Today we were presented to a big general and were supposed to wear overcoat or greatcoat. I had to go in a jacket. And my Colonel told me to go and get re-equipped. So I shall write you the day after tomorrow, in all likelihood from Paris. Today, though, is rest. I have done my 'Vie anecdotique' instalment and am writing to you from our mess.

521

I have had no letter from you today. I expect one tomorrow. This 'Vie anecdotique' deals with Oran.

I adore you my love, you know it.

I am hoping for a letter from you tomorrow.

I think it has been 2 days now since I heard from you.

I kiss you, I take your darling mouth and I drink deeply of your exquisite gaze.

Your Gui

My love, all of a sudden I am in receipt of an envelope containing writing paper and envelopes and 3 letters from you, your adorable letters of the 22nd, 23rd and 24th of January.

Marie Laurencin's watercolour is a very pretty sketch after Goya. It is very delicate, even in its execution.

The Jean story is odd but don't work yourself up about this there may turn out to be nothing to it.

Enjoy yourself and if this girl from Haton's is not prone to misbehaviour and it amuses you I don't see the harm in your seeing her. Yes, tell young Louise the photographer that she got very passable likenesses of us and I hope her shyness about me will disappear before I come back again. Tell me about Jean's poem. I haven't had the time to write a single verse since I got back; it is astonishing how little time I have.

I have had manuals on machine-guns delivered to me but haven't been able to look at them, not so much as a glance.

Last evening I met someone from my old battery who told me that Berthier was going to go to Fontainebleau. I have received another charming and very flattering letter from my former captain (who has gone into the 9th).

My love I adore you, you are as sweet as anything. Do not get too fat. There is no need to put on weight. I like you just as you are. I want you to quiet your emotions and let there be a little less chameleon in my panther.

I told you I haven't been reading. Well, before we are served in the mess, in the 2 or 3 minutes just before dinner I did manage to read one remarkable work from the handful of *Feuilles Littéraires* that I brought back with me from Oran, namely *Le Coeur du Poète* (The Heart of the Poet) by Henri Delatouche (who was Marceline Desbor-ders-Valmore's lover and André Chénier's 1st publisher). The 1st part of the work, which treats of the life of M. J. Chénier, is 1st-rate.

I always carry a *Feuille Littéraire* in my pocket so as to have something to read whenever we make a halt.

My love, I forgot to mention the botargo which was awful, really not very good at all even for me, and I love fish.

On the other hand the candied pumpkin peel was delicious.

I still have cigarettes. I think the best are the gold-tipped Job's that you prepared for me.

Another thing is that I want to begin a long poem on the war. I'll try and get started on the train.

My love you are my delight do not be impatient now.

Be calm, pretty and sweet.

My love, I adore you. I have to close now because we are about to have dinner. I shall write you at length tomorrow and I expect in the form of a long poem that will become the first song of my new collection.

I love you, I take your mouth madly, my dearest darling little wife. Wait for me with me.

Your Gui

GUILLAUME APOLLINAIRE

My love, I left on the evening of the 30th and ever since then have not had a minute to write you because I couldn't get into my house having lost my keys and not having had a chance to get new ones made. I had a new outfit made for me—very smart. I learnt many things but was not able to write to you about them. I never stopped thinking of you. I took care of my naturalization papers and shall get to our marriage once I know exactly what the procedure involves. I did not like Paris at all during those two days. I have your adorable letters of the 24th, 26th, 27th. The story of Denise's dalliance got my attention. My love I adore you. I'll send you the *Mercure*—I picked it up when I went by.

PARIS

J'ai vu Paris dans l'ombre

Hypogée où l'on riait trop

Paris une grande améthyste

Ces soldats belges en troupe

Vieilles femmes habillées en Perrette

Après le pot au lait

L'officier-pilote raconte ses exploits

J'ai entendu la berloque

Mais quel sourire celui de celui qui eut sursis d'appel illimité

Ombre de la statue de Shakespeare sur le boulevard Haussmann

Laideur des costumes civils des hommes qui ne sont pas partis

Les peintres travaillent
Mon cœur t'adore

PARIS

I saw Paris in shadow

A hypogeum with too much laughing

Paris a great amethyst

Those Belgian soldiers trooping by

Old women dressed like Perrette

After she spilt her milk

An aviation officer recounting his exploits

I heard the dismiss sounding

But what a smile on the faces of those with unlimited deferment

Shadow of Shakespeare's statue on Boulevard Haussmann

Ugliness of the civilian dress of men who did not go

The painters are at work

My heart adores you

Today a march and we are now somewhere else. I adore you my love, I have just arrived, a delightful little place. It has rained all day, we are soaking but the light is not too dreary and I am not tired. I came through a village in ruins which was almost picturesque despite its ruinous state. The inhabitants were going about their business and for a moment you felt very far away from the war.

I am looking forward to getting Louise's photos, especially the one where I have my arm around your waist.

I am writing to you from the mess while waiting for my servant to finish reconnoitring my room.

Anyway, I adore you my very dearest love and I take your mouth. I hope I shall be able to write at length tomorrow.

Gui

GUILLAUME APOLLINAIRE

My love, I am replying to your letters of the 28th, 29th, 30th and 31st of January. Thank goodness that leaves have been reinstated. Curious that Jean should be in the 38th. The stories of the various teachers I found very amusing. The clandestine conversations are also hilarious and so is the story of Mlle Adeline. As for your priest's tales, they are indeed inappropriate and for the sake of your peace of mind you would be well advised not to get involved with him at all; this man could take against you and make difficulties for you. The little place where we are billeted is pretty and there is a splendid view. My only fear is that we shan't be here very long. I am lodging with old people who have sons and sons-in-law at the war so they are all very kind. I have the finest room in the house. Everything is spick and span. As servant I no longer have Crapouillot but a sharp little fellow from Lyons nicknamed Fleur de Nave (Blockhead).

I adore you my love; while in Paris I happened to read an article in *The Times* by the best English military critic, Colonel Repington, dealing with English conscription. According to him this conscription is liable to produce fewer men than announced—far fewer even. It is extraordinary that the English seem not yet to have grasped the importance of high troop levels.

For my part I have very little to tell you about my life here—merely how impatient I am to see you again my darling love. Have you received the copies of my poem from Italy? And my parcels? You don't mention them. I wish the war was less bureaucratic. But what can you do? In Paris I saw a few friends who were dodging military service in aeroplane factories. Frankly, I ask you! These are people with 150 or 200 thousand francs a year of private income. Some workers, I must say! Apart from that Paris is a veritable hive of painting and sculpture. Cubist naturally. They sell whatever they want at mad prices. The German dealers are said to be back in business and selling the works of young French painters in America. As for Paris School painters they are 'mobilized' as camouflagers, something I may not explain to you just now because it comes under the heading of military matters. Anyway all this is quite extraordinary and in Paris the war is a curiously gentle affair, the Zeppelins notwithstanding. I have a new outfit, complete with what you call godets, but blue, because khaki is reserved for our armed forces in the Orient. We should have adopted it for all our fighting forces or even better dressed the whole army in motley, which is the least conspicuous garb.

I think that my *Poète assassiné* will be out soon, if and when the gentlemen at the printers see fit, for it is entirely up to them now.

I adore you my love and I kiss your eyes. You don't mention Jean's poem.

I take your mouth.

Gui

My love I have your letter of the 30th. First of all let me ask you please to send me the small manuscript notebook containing a short course on hippology and a compendium concerned with topography. I forgot to mention the botargo which is a most disagreeable thing and I quite understand your distaste for this preserve. I trust you'll say hullo to Louise for me and ask her to take some more photos. It was in this vicinity that champagne was born 2 centuries ago, so the champagne here is good and we drink it. I have been obliged for the first time to discipline someone, it cost me dearly but it was necessary. I think it is going to rain, and if we get back early I shall try to write a poem. It is amazing how little one is able to do one's own work in the infantry! Remember how many poems I wrote in the Arty, and in the infantry I have possibly not written a single one—but no, I'm wrong, I think there was a little one on Paris in one of my recent letters.

LE VIGNERON CHAMPENOIS

Le Régiment arrive au cantonnement
La châsse de Sainte Hélène s'endort dans la lumière parfumée
Un prêtre a le casque en tête
La bouteille champenoise est-elle ou non une artillerie
Les ceps de vigne comme l'hermine sur un écu
Et le bouchon gonflé est mon obus qui cède
Bonjour soldats

Je les ai vus passer et repasser en courant

Bonjour soldats bouteilles champenoises où le sang fermente

Vous resterez quelques jours et vous remonterez en ligne

Échelonnés ainsi sont mes ceps de vigne

J'envoie mon vin partout comme des soldats qui savent mourir

J'envoie mes bouteilles partout comme les obus d'une charmante artillerie

La nuit est blonde ô vin blond

Un vigneron chantait courbé dans sa vigne

Un vigneron sans bouche au fond de l'horizon

Un vigneron qui était lui-même la bouteille vivante

Un vigneron qui sait ce qu'est la guerre

Un vigneron champenois qui est un artilleur

C'est aussi le soir et l'on joue à la mouche

Puis les soldats s'en iront là-haut

Où l'artillerie débouche ses bouteilles de champagne

Allons Adieu messieurs tâchez de revenir

Mais nul ne sait ce qui peut advenir

THE CHAMPAGNE WINEGROWER

The Regiment arrives at its billets

The shrine of Saint Helen is falling asleep in the perfumed light

A priest is wearing a helmet

Is the champagne bottle an artillery piece or not

Vine-plants like ermines on a coat of arms

And the swollen cork my shell about to be released

Hullo soldiers

I saw them running back and forth

Hullo soldiers champagne bottles where blood ferments

You will stay a few days and then go back up to the front

In serried ranks just like my vines

I send my wine everywhere like soldiers who know how to die

I send my bottles everywhere like charming artillery shells

The night is fair oh my fair wine

GUILLAUME APOLLINAIRE

A winegrower sang bent over his vines
A winegrower with no mouth far away on the horizon
A winegrower who was himself the living bottle
A winegrower who knows what war is
A winegrower from Champagne who is in the artillery
Now it is evening and they are playing blackjack
Soon the soldiers will be going back up there
Where the artillery uncork their bottles of champagne
So be it Goodbye gentlemen try to come back
But no one knows what may befall

My love, I take your darling mouth. Off to exercises now.

Gui

530

My dear love, I received no letter from you yesterday but perhaps I shall still get one today—I am writing to you in the morning as I shan't be able to find the time this afternoon. About the parcel my thought was that you were expecting it earlier than it could arrive. The fact is that it was sent via rail. I think I may even have sent you 2 parcels. But you can refer to my letters to see whether there was 1 or 2. At all events am going to send you another in a day or two with the *Mercure* and a bedcover that has become an encumbrance.

531

At the moment it is freezing every morning and rains during the day. In Paris I met my friend Max Jacob who foresees a 30-year war, a fantastical idea, and predicts that 1916 will be far bloodier than 1915. Saw an old granny yesterday who forecasts a 5-year war. As for me, I feel that by all appearances it will not last till next winter, yet deep down I also have the sense that we shall be at war until the winter after that, until 1918 or the end of 1917.

That is about all, if I have the time today I'll try to write a poem.

I adore you my darling Madeleine write me pleasant things because one gets a bit fed up with having so little time to oneself and it's not the way it was in the Arty. I take your mouth.

Gui

GUILLAUME APOLLINAIRE

My love, I have your 2 letters of 2 Feb. I love the story of little Abora Giazo's blotting paper. Why yes my love, all my poems should be copied except for most of the secret poems, which is why I marked certain ones. As for the 'Cry to Italy' and all such poems which must obviously be copied, I did not mark them. The precious poem so far as I recall is not to be copied and as to the 2 other poems sent to Italy I cannot see what could be added to them. Your tale about the 3 days of suspension for the girl who was exchanging love letters with the pupil at the boys' lycée I thought priceless, and so long as the boy's suspension coincides with the girl's they will be perfectly well able to proceed with their epistolary heart-to-heart. They must be delighted with this punishment. As for the little girl who wrote to the old man I view it as more serious and I am not enthusiastic about such lopsided matches. But my love let me assure you I don't care in the least if you do not know something. So, poor Marthe was punished unjustly, but knowing how well grounded she is I fancy it has not affected her unduly for she takes a rather philosophical view of things. Yesterday the decision was communicated that leaves will be re-instituted with certain conditions and that as of now some leaves may be granted in exceptional cases, but the fact remains that leaves have not yet been restored and one has to wonder what the said conditions might be!

Tell me in a letter all about that teacher in your school who was asked to make a confession in England and disappointed the

English by failing to do so. I can no longer recall the story, but fancy something might be made of it.

My love it is snowing. I did not go on exercises this morning but perhaps we'll do so this afternoon. I am coughing a little, but for me coughs tend to be nervous and soon pass. It is even snowing quite hard.

I adore you and take your mouth.

Gui

My very dearest love no letter from you today. I adore you, but do not be surprised or worried by the brevity (in every respect) of my letters, we really and truly have no time, it's incredible.

In the Arty I could write as I wished. In the trenches things were less epicurean of course but you could still write your letter, now it is simply impossible never have the time. Today I had C^oy day duty. Tomorrow the C^oy itself is on full-day duty at the Rgt., and the day after on part-day Battalion duty. Tomorrow skeleton manoeuvres, there is always something. This afternoon I had thought I would have free time but bang! a briefing about gas. I am writing you by night, the first time for ages because since we have been at rest I have been sleeping much better on account of the fatigue, so as I [told] you yesterday, despite the snow and exercises in the snow, damp feet coughing and sneezing I am doing well. Changed servants again: Thibaut nickname Fleur de Nave having played a practical joke (not on me) I now have a devilishly big man named Roux, a very fine fellow, not so intelligent as his predecessor but more loyal.

My little love, for the moment do not expect very much of a romantic sort in my letters. I adore you, but have neither the leisure nor the words to express it. But you know that I love you, come on, I know you do, my darling sweet love. I think the war is about to grow extremely violent, but perhaps then come to an end. Am writing a poem, 'Cotton Wool in the Ears' but have only just started it, today during the briefing. Shall try and finish it tomorrow.

Sending you a photo, me in my helmet. What of Louise's photos? And my parcels, have they arrived? tell me my very dearest love.

I adore you and I love you and I take you ardently my Madelon.

Your Gui

GUILLAUME APOLLINAIRE

11 Feb. 1916

My love I adore you and meanwhile I'm sending you the long poem that I have finished at last and am going to send to Paris. (I am sending you the draft version.)

I adore you my pretty sweetheart, no letter from you today, still wanting to know have you received the parcels, am about to send another one.—I adore you, but today I'm tired from the poem. Have a bad cold, which is why I could stay inside writing the poem.

536

Now I am tired. But I love you completely my darling and embrace you and kiss you on the mouth.

Gui

Guillaume Apollinaire   DU COTON DANS LES OREILLES[1]

1 See reproductions on pp. 270–77.

Tant d'explosifs sur le point VIF!

Les points d'impacts dans mon âme toujours en guerre
Ton troupeau féroce crache du feu
Écris un mot si tu l'oses

OMEGAPHONE

Et ceux qui revinrent de mort
Ne s'attendaient qu'à la pareille
Et tout ce qui venait du Nord
Allait obscurcir le soleil
Mais que voulez-vous c'est son sort
          Allô la truie

C'est quand sonnera le réveil

	T	
	r	allO
Courage	a	caverne-abrI
Ivresse	la	amouR
Vie	la	FrancE[2]
	RF	
POPUL	O	AVENIR
ALL	O	SOUVENIR
ALLO ALL	O	LA TRUIE
ALLO ALL	O	LA TRUIE

2 Read clockwise, the initial or terminal letters of these words spell out the word VICTOIRE.—Tr.

La sentinelle au long regard
La sentinelle au long regard
Et la cagnat s'appleait

LES CÉNOBITES TRANQUILLES

La sentinelle au long regard
La sentinelle au long regard
Allô la truie

Tant et tant de coquelicots
D'où tant de sang a-t-il coulé
Qu'est-ce qu'il se met dans le coco
Bon sang de bois il s'est soûlé
Et sans pinard et sans tacot
Avec de l'eau
Allô la truie

Le silence des photographes
Mitrailleuses des cinémas
Tout l'échelon là-bas piaffe
Fleurs de feu des lueurs-frimas
Puisque le canon avait soif

GUILLAUME APOLLINAIRE

Allô

         la truie

Et les trajectoires cabrées

Trébuchements des soleils-nains

SUR TANT de chansons déchirées

Il a l'Étoile du Benin

Mais du singe en boîtes carrées

Crois-tu qu'il y

         aura la guerre

         Allô la truie

Ah! s'il vous plaît

Ami l'Anglais

Ah! qu'il est laid

Ton frère, ton frère ton frère de lait

Et je mangeais du pain de Gênes

En respirant leurs gaz lacrymogènes

         Mets du coton dans tes oreilles

         D'siré

Puis ce fut cette fleur sans nom

À peine un souffle un sovenir

Quand s'en allèrent les canons

Au tour des roues heure à courir

La baleine a d'autres fanons

(Éclatements qui nous fanons)

         Mais mets du coton dans tes oreilles

Évidemment les fanions des signaleurs

Allô la truie

LETTERS TO MADELEINE

(Mettes du coton dans vos oreilles
Et chacun se souvient d'une joue rose
Parce que même les airs entraînants
Ont quelque chose qui étreint le cœur
Lorsqu'on les entend à la guerre)

Allô la truie

Mettez du coton dans vos oreilles
Ne prenez pas les feuillées
Pour autre chose qu'elles ne sont

Comme faisaient pas mal d'auteurs
       avant
la guerre

mettez du coton dans vos oreilles
Ce fut bien quand sonna le réveil

Et	*la*	*et*	*la*	
puis	*pluie*	*d'*	*nuit*	
regardez	*si*	*au*	*la*	
tomber	*douce*	*tres*	*pluie*	
la	*la*	*souvenirs*	*tout*	
pluie	*pluie*	*qui*	*cela*	*la*
	si	*se*	*c'*	*pluie*
	tendre	*ressemblent*	*est*	*si*
	la	*Madeleine*	*une*	*douce*
	pluie	*reviennent*	*crême*	*ô*
	si	*sur*	*au*	*Madeleine*
	douce	*l'eau*	*chocolat*	*la*
		précieuse		*pluie*
		ô		*si*
		pluie		*douce*
		si		
		douce		

GUILLAUME APOLLINAIRE

Les longsboyaux où tu chemines

Adieu cagnats d'artilleurs

Tu retrouveras

La tranchée en première ligne
Les éléphants des pare-éclats
Une girouette maligne
Et le regard des guetteurs las
Qui veillent le silence insigne

> *Ne vois-tu rien venir*
>> *au*
>> *Pé*
>> *ris*
>> *co*
>> *pe*
> *La balle qui froisse le silence*
> *Les projectiles d'artillerie qui glissent*
> *Comme un fleuve aérien*

Ne mettez plus de coton dans les oreilles

Ça ne vaut plus la peine

Guillaume Apollinaire   COTTON WOOL IN YOUR EARS

So many explosives coming to LIFE!

 Impact points on my soul ever at war
Your fierce herd spits fire
Write a word if you dare

OMEGAPHONE

And those who came back from death
Expected nothing but more of the same

And everything that came from the North
Would block out the sun
But what can you do it's one's fate
        Come in the sow

A matter of when reveille will sound

              T
              r   come in

Courage   a   trench dugout

Drunkenness   la   love

Life   la   France

              RF[3]

PLEBS   FUTURE

COME IN COME IN   MEMORY

COME IN COME IN   THE SOW

COME IN COME IN   THE SOW

        The sentry with the lingering eye
The sentry with the lingering eye

And the dugout was called

            The Quiet Cenobites[4]

The sentry with the lingering eye
The sentry with the lingering eye
        Come in the sow

So many many poppies
Where could so much blood have come from
Whatever has got into his noodle
Strewth! he has got drunk
Without a drop of red without a dram
        Just water
           Come in the sow

3 République Française.—Tr.

4 By virtue of an untranslatable pun, the French words here, 'Les cénobites tranquilles' may be heard as 'Laissez nos bites tranquilles', 'Leave our pricks alone'.—Tr.

541

GUILLAUME APOLLINAIRE

Silence of the photographers
Machine-guns of the cinemas
Back there the whole wagon line is fidgeting
Flowers of fire frosted flashes
Because the canon was thirsty

      Come in
           the sow

And the bucking trajectories
And the toppling dwarf suns
To SO MANY ragged tunes

He has the Star of Benin
But eats bully beef from square tins

Do you think there
                will be a war

      Come in the sow
Ah! I beg your pardon
My friend the Englishman
Ah! how ugly he is
Your brother, your brother your foster brother

And I was eating *pain de Gênes*
As I breathed in their tear gas
            Put cotton wool in your ears
            D'siré my man

Then came that nameless flower
Hardly a breath hardly a memory
When the guns departed
Rolling away with an hour to spare
The whale is changing its baleen

(Explosions and we too are fading)

LETTERS TO MADELEINE

but put cotton wool in your ears

Obviously just the signallers' flags
               Come in the sow

(Here the military band plays something
And everyone remembers a pink cheek
For even stirring airs
Have something heart-stopping
When you hear them in the thick of war)

               Come in the sow

Please put cotton wool in your ears
Do not take the latrines
For anything other than what they are

As not a few authors did
          before
the war

put cotton wool in your ears

it was a good thing when reveille sounded

543

GUILLAUME APOLLINAIRE

And	the	and	at	
then	rain	other	night	
listen	so	memories	the	
to	gentle	which	rain	
the	the	are	and	the
rain	rain	much	all	rain
falling	so	alike	that	so
	tender	Madeleine	is	gentle
	the	return	a	oh
	rain	with	*crème*	Madeleine
	so	the	*au*	the
	gentle	precious	*chocolat*	rain
		water		so
		oh		gentle
		rain		
		so		
		gentle		

You make your way down long communication trenches

Goodbye artillerymen's shelters

You are going to rediscover

The front-line trench
The anti-shrapnel elephants
A malicious weathervane
And the expression of the weary lookouts
Keeping watch over a startling silence

LETTERS TO MADELEINE

Don't you see anything coming

through

the

pe

ris

co

pe

A bullet ruffling the silence

Artillery shells sliding along

Like an aerial river

Put no more cotton wool in your ears

There is no point in it now

GUILLAUME APOLLINAIRE

My love, I adore you, I have received heaps of letters from you, with Jean's verse, and the parcel with the tobacco cigarettes and jersey, the photos have arrived too, you are my love but I have too bad a headache to reply to the letters in detail, will do so tomorrow, will read Jean's poem later.

As to the tobacco, my love, the kind you got is too dear, I used to buy the kind at 1 fr 75 and it was quite acceptable. About the photos there are some people here who say that they have not been toned so ask Louise Décor I know nothing about this sort of thing. My love, I adore you. They read our letters so much now that I can no longer risk pouring out my heart to you as I used to. But the feelings are there my exquisite love my pretty Madelon and as soon as they come back to me naturally you'll know it. My love I am disorientated at the moment by this perilous infantryman's life. But I adore you my sweet. I do not want you to be getting any ideas to the contrary. I am sending you a short new poem, I am going to write more for you as well and the long one of yesterday is for you my exquisite love.

I am sorry to see that the weather is bad in Oran, here it is freezing on top of the snow—I have a bit of influenza and a headache. I knew that the soldiers in Salonica could cable, one would indeed be too long without news of them were they unable to use the telegraph.

But I adore you my sweet love all your school stories are greatly amusing but it is you my love that I love more than anything, I think of your look my sweetheart and so yearn to see it once more. I think that leaves for Algeria have been restored and I am so happy about that my love.

In any case I think that for officers there should be no difficulty and that our leaves will not be held up.

My little love, I think of your sweet look and your laugh, tomorrow I'll have something to say about your Moorish-bath story, which seems almost to have come from the *Thousand and One Nights* or from Casanova.

What a wonderful storyteller you are my sweet love!

I love you, come, I don't have to say it to you for you to know it and I do have to say it so that my words may caress you.

I adore you my love. I take your mouth.

Gui

1 See p. 280.

AUSSI BIEN QUE LES CIGALES[1]

gens du midi GENS DU MIDI VOUS N'AVEZ DONC PAS REGARDÉ LES CIGALES QUE VOUS

NE SAVEZ PAS CREUSER? QUE VOUS NE SAVEZ PAS VOUS ÉCLAIRER NI VOIR? *QUE VOUS* manque-t-il donc Pour voir aussi bien que les cigales?

Mais vous savez encore boire comme les cigales ô gens du Midi gens du soleil gens qui devriez savoir creuser et voir aussi bien pour le moins aussi bien que les cigales eh! quoi! vous savez boire et ne savez plus pisser aussi utilement que les cigales

CREUSEZ VOYEZ BUVEZ PISSEZ *aussi bien que les cigales*

GUILLAUME APOLLINAIRE

Allons enfants de la patrie le jour de gloire sera celui où vous saurez creuser pour
bien sortir au soleil

gens du midi il faut creuser voir boire pisser aussi bien que les cigales pour avoir le
droit de chanter comme elles

La joie adorable
      de la paix solaire

AS WELL AS CICADAS

people of the South PEOPLE OF THE SOUTH SO YOU HAVEN'T
   OBSERVED THE CICADAS AND SO

YOU DON'T KNOW HOW TO DIG? SO YOU DON'T KNOW HOW TO
   LIGHT YOUR WAY OR SEE? *WHAT ARE YOU short of then in order to see*
   as well as cicadas?

But you know how to drink like cicadas oh people of the South people of the
   sun people who ought to know how to dig and see as well at least as well
   as cicadas? what is it? you know how to drink yet no longer know how to
   piss as usefully as cicadas

DIG SEE DRINK PISS *as well as the cicadas*

arise children of the fatherland the day of glory will be the day you learn to dig all the
way out into the sunshine

people of the South you must dig see drink piss as well as cicadas to have the right to
sing like them

lovely joy
      of solar peace

                        Guillaume Apollinaire

13 February 1916

My adored love so let me reply to your letters of the 3rd, 4th, 5th, 6th Feb., received yesterday. Today I had no letter from you. I read Jean's verse, full of talent, generosity and rich poetic vigour, full of truth also. First though, the story of Denise is bothersome but hardly the end of the world! True, it suggests a failure of supervision. This girl has done this just 2 or 3 times in all and she has no seriously evil intent.

549

The Turkish baths you describe are not as I envision them, perhaps you should go to those on Avenue Gambetta (at least I think they are on Gambetta), I am talking about the brand new ones near the cliffs, it seems to me that they correspond more closely to my picture than the ones you mention. In any case, the powder for untangling the hair is a very good idea, I am sure you know all about it.

The Prailles, you say? Do you mean the blonde girl at Haton's?

The story about the eye amused me, not least because you will find a similar tale entitled 'L'Oeil bleu' in my book *Le Poète assassiné* which is in press at the moment. The tale itself first appeared in *Le Matin* in 1911.

But no, leave the photo's background white, that is the best thing and also the simplest. The highest good taste is the natural order, and above all *what is*.

GUILLAUME APOLLINAIRE

I want you to be stronger my love, and not torment yourself with figments of your imagination and the like.

Sent you another parcel yesterday with a bedcover that I didn't need.

Sleeping bags are too bulky, my love, I could not take one into a trench, it could only be of use to me while in reserve behind the front lines. They are simply too voluminous for the trenches and in any case simply not customary there, we sleep in our shoes and for barely an hour at a stretch—A sleeping bag is a good and practical thing in the artillery and indeed very useful when in reserve. Leave your headmistress be, what can it matter to you whether or not she is trustworthy.

I have never read anything by Farrère so I can hardly say anything about him, but what you say about Mme de Sévigné seems to me to have the ring of good sense.

Have you yes or no received my parcel(s)?

In there in fact, and apropos, was a copy of *Les Plus Belles Pages de Saint-Simon* (Finest Pages of Saint-Simon). The story of the skinned cats is very pleasing, I fancy it is also very old, but I can't remember where it comes from, is it perhaps from [Étienne] Tabourot des Accords? Your priest is an extraordinary man, a cleric of the old school, just the kind I like. Such priests are very useful and primary-school teachers ought to be patterned after them but sad to say they are usually patterned after the impoverished clergyman type.

My Madelon do not be nervous love, you know I love you, you know I adore you. Be nice about this, be calm. I kiss you everywhere my treasure, your feet your hands your mouth your eyes your brow your hair, please do not get impatient. Be calm, do not overwhelm me with these bouts of impatience which are not a good thing.

At present I am in a state of great moral chastity, not that I have made any kind of vow, it must have been brought on by all these manoeuvres, by the fact that we are never alone and have so very little time to ourselves. I am thinking of you my darling and it is your smile more than anything else that appears to my mind's eye, your fresh smile. I still have influenza you know. I am not smoking. I am better than yesterday though and expect that tomorrow or the next day will be the end of it.

I so much want to see the back of this war at last. But I am afraid it is not yet time to be hoping for that.

I kiss you my darling and take your mouth for the longest time.

Gui

GUILLAUME APOLLINAIRE

It is astonishing that on the 9th F. you should have received nothing from me since the 29th Jan. I take it, my dear love, that you have had some news from me by now.

But I do love you my little Madelon, put your mind at rest. Look here, just as soon as I have more free time more quiet than I do now with this cold and all these exercises, I'll write you long letters as I used to when I was a gunner. You are my darling love, do not be alarmed, above all do not be alarmed, be calm, I beg you. You are my pretty one, you know you are. I adore you, be kind, be a darling.

I kiss you with all my might my exquisite little love. Be calm, be nice. My dearest love, I'll move heaven and earth to write you long letters. Today I received the new outfit that I had made in Paris.

I am enclosing the bill to give you an idea of Paris prices.

My love, you are calmer now, the sight of those high figures has quieted you down a little, say it has, my Madelon. Say it is true my darling.

Anyway my Madeleine do please be less anxious, less sensitive. I really want to know whether or not you have received the parcels. After all it is truly extraordinary that they should not have arrived! I hope that the weather has turned fine again in Algeria, here the snow has stopped but we have had storms. I have lost my voice as

552

well, my sweet, I take care of myself as best I can, there is a very kind medical officer here who is doing everything he can to get me better and I hope that in 2 or 3 days this will be over. I have not been smoking during this time so the tobacco is still intact and I shan't smoke it until I am quite better.

I kiss you all over my very dearest little Madelon and I stroke you for the longest time so that you are no longer heavy-hearted.

Your Gui

I write you, my Love, from Épernay, where I am spending half a day. It is raining. The weather is horribly dismal. We are to leave Hautvillers in 2 or 3 days (Sunday 20th). There is a good chance we shall be going over towards Soissons (to Fismes). They say it is bad there, what is more I think the whole Northern Front is bad now. In any case we are a flying division and it is no coincidence that they let us stay at rest for two months.

554

Have you been paying attention to the 1st letter of each line whenever a letter of mine is headed 'With the Armed Services'? From now on you should look at both the 1st and the last letters of each line up to the end of the paragraph. I am very hoarse and have quite lost my voice. I adore you my darling little Madelon, write me long letters and always tell me everything.

As for the machine-guns there is no movement. I fancy a good deal of water will go under the bridge before I get there. Same thg on other fronts. I'll write you again this evening.—I adore you and I kiss you everywhere. Put no place-names in your letters. Everything is being read at the moment. But when you have understood just tell me so.

Gui

My love, I am writing from a hamlet. I did not have the time to write yesterday, and shall perhaps be obliged to interrupt this letter if duty calls.

I have to reply to yours of the 7th, 11th, 12th, 13th. The story of the pupil who took the ether did indeed strike me as comical.

I hope your cold is better now. I myself still have a bad cold.

555

André Theuriet has written some very appealing things and I for my part find him superior to Bazin. Furthermore Theuriet is a poet whose portrayals of nature are quite keen. There is something in him of the English novel with cottages, tea, etc.

I love your love, my darling my darling, the photos of you I had in my pocket (one taken in Narbonne and the one when you were 18) are stuck together and hopelessly damaged . . . I am rather tired at present. It rains all the time; the damp, the cold, the prospect of sleeping on the ground once again, none of this is very inviting, but there it is and I daresay in 2 or 3 days I'll be used to it.

I am in a hamlet, as I said, and billeted with solid country people. I am writing in their living-room.

On the mantlepiece, above a fireplace where the bubbling family pot dangles from its chimney-hook, on the mantle, I say, stands a small earthenware pot with metallic glints that I believe is English and of Second Empire vintage.

GUILLAUME APOLLINAIRE

There is also a Louis-Philippe half-poster bed with copper fittings, as well as a country clock like the ones you see in Arab cafés, but the copper pendulum is not decorated while the face has chased and cut-out copper with flower-spray motifs and the motto *Hora Fugit* (time flies), and the ceiling has visible beams with flitches of bacon hanging from them and there are huge old-fashioned linen cupboards.

On the outside of the house, verdigrised by Bordeaux mixture like all the houses in this region, there are climbing vines.

There are no copper utensils. Indeed for some years now in France the old pots and pans have been replaced by enamelled ones. We ate in a household poorer than the one where I am staying.

We were invited to try the local brown honey which has a taste of balm. I may be mistaken but I think that is what it is.

Today I am in a state of deep melancholy. The clock says a quarter to 5, a blank, cold time of day.

I am thinking of the sea so blue and the purple mountains of Oran.

Night is about to fall but without those colours of dusk that lend such a magical charm to Mediterranean shores when night prepares to scatter its violets over the Africa where you are falling asleep my sweet darling.

I take you gently in my arms and caress you as you gaze at me with tenderness.

Your Gui

My very dearest love,

I have some letters from you. I adore you my little Madelon.

It is cold here, it has been snowing all day long.

This evening I took a little stroll, saw some pretty balconies, a pretty house with a mansard roof, and earlier on I walked across ploughed land.

The countryside here is rich, with lots of pleasant views. But of course the war is still on.

The local people, and there are still a few, are used to it. We are too for that matter.

I have started reading something quite out of date and truly hilarious: *Les Chasses du fameux tueur de lions Gérard* (Hunts of Gérard the Famous Lion Killer). In those days there must have been lions on the prowl near Lamur!

I have also read a newspaper that showed me the foul way in which the Boches must be working on public opinion. I consider this paper, which is called *Le Journal du Peuple*, to be an abomination— and what a mass of vile things you learn from it!! I was disgusted.

My goodness, I'm inclined to think that abolishing the press would have been more intelligent than censoring it, moreover the excessive number of shirkers is what has allowed this disgraceful state of

GUILLAUME APOLLINAIRE

mind, which is certainly deliberately maintained and as it were stoked, to arise in the first place.

On the one hand you have an excessive and reactionary exceptionalism attempting to get a stranglehold on patriotic sentiment while on the other hand the bourgeois papers peddle humbug in the apparent belief that our soldiers are stupid enough to believe it. These two extremes have together fostered an unhealthy attitude which has made headway and which ought to be quickly squelched by whatever means and in any case completely suppressed.

It is impossible to overstate the harm done us by all the flattery lavished on the neutral parties.

Cordial but inflexible—that is the posture our governments ought to assume towards the neutral nations.

Jean must be doing alright in Salonica.

Has he written you since he got there?

How are the little ones getting on?

I take you gently in my arms, my love, and I cradle you, I love you.

Your Gui

558

1 In accordance with the code agreed upon by the fiancés, this letter indicates that Apollinaire is at Fismes.

My very dear love,

I'm quite done up after 3 days of marching. Rest is over.

Are we going to be in a good sector? I have cured my influenza with rum and am fine now. In great fettle.

During all this time, my love, couldn't write you. It was as though we did not exist, like gypsies. I would read your letters but had neither time nor strength to reply. I slept in the most unlikely little places. I fancy I even did write you along the way but I am not sure of it. The fact is that all this while I have been in a dream. I feel as if I have been dragging my feet down muddy main roads forever. Like an automat with no real thoughts of my own. I forget names. If you want to get an idea of what I mean read Alfred de Vigny's *Servitude et Grandeur militaires* (*The Military Necessity*). What a magnificent work! What a book! How extraordinary that I had never read this, perhaps the greatest masterpiece of nineteenth-century French literature. I am reading it now bit by bit before going to sleep and it is destroying the admiration (moderate in any case) that I felt for Villiers de l'Isle-Adam, who is merely an epigone of Vigny's. But my word, what a marvellous storyteller Vigny is, one who thinks and one who knows. To think that the historic scene of the Pope and Napoleon is here and only here. To think that every single line of this book is a wonderful lesson. How I regret that I never soaked myself in this

GUILLAUME APOLLINAIRE

marvellous creation before the war. I would have been so much better acquainted with it than I am.

As for you my love please calm down, do not write me about how worried you are. Be nice. Write me about literary or other matters that are liable to elevate our thoughts.

But no, my love, *Le Poète assassiné* is not a terrifying book; it is a collection like *The Heresiarch* but with more humorous things in it than *The Heresiarch*. It takes its title from its first story, which is longer in any case than those in *The Heresiarch* and of a new kind, being an attempt to write a lyrical story such as I had already tried to do with 'Que Vlo-ve?' and 'The Poets' Napkin', but in this case I sought even greater lyricism and added an element of satire. I am forgetting things so quickly at the moment that I have no recollection at all of the poems on 'Paris' and 'The Winegrower' which you mention.

560

The story about the Prailles I found entertaining but I do not like Maupassant as much as is customary. I do not know why exactly, but that is how I feel. He is a vigorous storyteller but to my mind his tone is the bourgeois tone of nineteenth-century journalistic short stories, which I do not like at all even though I acknowledge their merits.

Do not worry about leave at present because I shan't be getting any for the time being.

I can no longer recall the story of the station-master's wife.

On another subject, my dear Madelon, your jealousy is not nice. I forbid you to be jealous.

This morning I saw a fine Louis XIII doorway not sentimental in the least, to the left a half-nude mythological woman with a tunic covering her from just beneath the breasts to mid-leg and to the other side a Louis XIII figure dressed after the fashion of Corneille's *Liar*.

Yesterday in another little backwater an otherwise not very interesting church had an appealing sculpture set into the wall.

I think I shall soon have time to write you very long letters and to write at length for myself too.

I take your mouth.

Gui

561

25 Feb. 1916

My love,

I have received the cigarettes and the notebook.

Leaves for Algeria have been restored.

I do not have the time to write at length my darling little love.

I will do so as soon as I can.

Snow, I have a cold, but don't worry above all don't you worry.

The war is indeed becoming violent. Perhaps, who knows, these are its death throes.

From now on I'll send you cards or envelopes bearing the sector postmark with a view to making a collection. So keep them. You should keep the whole envelope or card.

I adore you.

Your Gui

My love, a walk in the snow. I have got your letters of the 19th and
the 20th—the story of the open-minded lady and her maid is amusing. Apropos of which, do you know what the expression *'en bataille'*,
which you used to describe the lady's nose, actually means? It refers
in the cavalry to battle formation; in the infantry the equivalent is
'en ligne', in line. The opposite is 'in column'. Cavalrymen used to
wear their two-pointed hats *en bataille*, broadside on, whereas
generals wore theirs *en colonne*, fore-and-after. You are as pretty as
anything my love and your letter is very very sweet. I am going to
close now because I am tired and must get to bed. Tomorrow I don't
know where we shall go. Maybe to a good place. I kiss you my
darling. I kiss you tenderly. I don't want Marthe pulling your hair.
It is beyond me how a girl as quick-witted as she and so elegantly
coquettish could take pleasure in twisting her nose this way and that,
pulling your hair and all that sort of thing.

When I come on leave I'll show her what for—and it won't have to
do with her face either!

I kiss you passionately. Louise is really sweet to take such pretty
photos.

I take your mouth.

Gui

563

GUILLAUME APOLLINAIRE

28 Feb. 1916[1]   **1** Military postcard.

My love, in great haste I want to inform you of our change in postal sector. It is now *Sector 130* (one hundred and thirty).

I'll write you a long letter tomorrow I hope.

Your very own Gui

564

1 Military postcard.

6 March 1916[1]

My love

do not worry. I have not had the time to write. As soon as I do I will. I have received your precious letters. Keep on writing to me and do not worry.

It is cold. We have snow, I no longer have influenza. I am very well in fact but have absolutely no time.

Kisses.

565

Your Gui

You should put Sector 139 again now.

My love, I have been marching so much that I have not been able to
write. Sent a card a few days ago. That is all. I got your exquisite letters. I saw the royal city [of Rheims] and its cathedral and I collected
some fragments of stained glass. I lived through 2 days of the
strange life of a town under bombardment. I visited the cathedral
with the guardian M. Huart the architect and M. Gulden an Englishman who owns the Heidsieck trademark. I lunched at the Lion d'Or
across the way. The cathedral's interior has suffered little whereas
all the woodwork outside has burnt. A single 77 shell has left a hole
in the vault a very little hole that one can barely see near a pillar.
Inside some Louis XIV panelling was burnt (by a fire not by
shelling), uncovering statuary that sadly was itself severely damaged
by the fire; the rose window that was so beautiful was likewise
destroyed by the flames but the choir stained-glass windows, known
as the St Louis windows (1227) are almost unharmed along with the
ecclesia remensis. Otherwise I have nothing to tell you about our
billets indeed I am not allowed to describe them but I did see that
little church. We are off once more tomorrow on the roads near the
Front and this wandering life tends to make you feel detached from
everything.

Today (this morning) I wrote some short poems for painters. It has
been a long time since I wrote anything.

566

POÈMES PR PEINTURES

I

2 lacs nègres

    Entre une forêt

        Et une chemise qui sèche

II

Bouche ouverte sur un Harmonium

    C'était une voix faite d'yeux

        Tandis qu'il traîne de petites gens

III

Une petite vieille au nez pointu

    J'admire la bouillotte d'émail bleu

        Une femme qui a une gorge épatante

IV

Un monsieur qui se rase près de la fenêtre

    Il est en bras de chemise

        Et il chante un petit air qu'il ne sait pas très bien

Ça [fait] tout un opéra

POEMS FOR PAINTINGS

I

2 nigger-brown lakes

    Between a forest

        And a shirt drying

II

Mouth open over a Harmonium

    It was a voice made of eyes

        With plain folks loitering around

GUILLAUME APOLLINAIRE

III

A little old lady with a pointed nose

    I admire the blue-enamelled kettle

        A woman with a splendid bosom

IV

A gent shaving near the window

    In his shirt sleeves

        And singing a little tune that he does not know very well

This [makes for] quite an opera

INSCRIPTION À BRODER SUR UN COUSSIN

(avec d'autres ornements)

Je suis la discrète balance
De ce que pèse ta beauté

568

INSCRIPTION TO BE EMBROIDERED ON A CUSHION

(with other decorations)

I am the discreet scale
That weighs your beauty in the balance

INSCRIPTIONS PR DES GRAVURES

I

Vous qui m'écoutez Belle
Bien que je sois bien loin

II

Comme un grave empereur
Qui saurait l'avenir

III

Une créole à la Havane
Créée par Dieu l'amour la damne

Allô la Destinée
Comment envoyer des baisers

INSCRIPTIONS FOR PRINTS

I

You who are listening to me Beauty
Though I am so far away

II

Like a solemn emperor
Who could foresee the future

III

A Creole woman in Havana
Created by God damned by love

IV

Hullo Destiny
How do you send kisses

My dear love, we had spoken with your mother about the D.E.S.,
which sounds like 'la Déesse' ('the Goddess'), and we could not
find out what this barbaric abbreviation meant; well, it stands for
Direction des Étapes et Services [Directorate of Stages and Services]!

I adore you my love and must close now and pack my trunk.

I love you my love.

Gui

GUILLAUME APOLLINAIRE

11 March 1916

My love, I have received your brothers' charming journals and your own sweet letter. I adore you and am thinking of you, my darling, we are now part of a corps in which 6-day leaves for officers are restricted to 8 days all travel delays included no matter how far the distance. So I am hoping that we shall get out of this corps as soon as possible. Anyway between now and my leave we shall see, I'm not up to that yet. A little poem:

570

L'AVENIR

Soulevons la paille
Regardons la neige
Écrivons des lettres
Attendons des ordres

Fumons la pipe
En songeant à l'amour
Les deux tours sont là
Regardons la rose

La fontaine n'a pas tari
Pas plus que l'or de la paille ne s'est terni
Regardons l'abeille
Et ne songeons pas à l'avenir

Regardons nos mains
Qui sont la neige
La rose et l'abeille
Ainsi que l'avenir

THE FUTURE

Let's lift up the straw

Look at the snow

Write letters

Wait for orders

Smoke a pipe

Thinking of love

The two towers are there

Look at the rose

The spring has not tarried

Any more than the straw's gold has tarnished

Let's look at the bee

And not think of the future

Look at our hands

Which are the snow

The rose and the bee

And the future too

My love I adore you and that is all I have to say to you for I have very little to tell you today we are in an exhausting state of waiting.

Yesterday I was chatting with a very intelligent priest who had the soundest things to tell me about this war. Good sense has taken refuge in the brains of women and old clerics.

I am suffering from almost insurmountable sleepiness but I wonder shall I have the time to sleep. The snow spreads over everything, you would think it was a Christmas night.

I kiss you completely my darling, my rose.

Your Gui

GUILLAUME APOLLINAIRE

My love, I had no letter from you yesterday, today I do not know
yet. We are at a place that I may not tell you the name of but its
nickname is the chamber pot of France, rather as Lucca in Italy was
formerly known as the urinal of the clouds. Apropos of such things
tell Pierre that his newspaper's title *Peter* is a little too bizarre and
would be acceptable only for a paper of the Artillery at the Front.
Everyone cannot be expected to know that Peter is the Boche
translation of his name Pierre. The idea of giving a paper a personal
forename is rather amusing. I can think of only one precedent, and
that never got beyond the proposal stage. Before he launched his
paper *Excelsior* Pierre Lafitte when casting about for a title decided
on Edgard or Edmond, I forget which now. But in short the idea
seemed so strange that the name of *Excelsior* was the eventual
choice. I am writing to you at a round table spread with a round
oilcloth bearing a naive reproduction of the Louvre's mediocre
painting of Rouget de Lisle singing the *Marseillaise* at the home of
Dietrich, Mayor of Strasbourg; circling the picture are the score and
all the words of the *Marseillaise*.

I don't know whether there are mail-boats leaving for Algeria at the
moment, I do hope so my love and I do so want to see this war come
to an end.

It is very irritating not to be able to give the names of villages. When
I was telling you about Rheims I forgot to mention one of the things

that most struck me in that now deserted city. On the utterly deserted Place d'Erlon, into which such shell-pocked streets as the Rue de l'Arquebuse lead—on that main Place d'Erlon, I say, stood a dozen hackney cabs stoically awaiting improbable custom; those cabmen still sporting their traditional white top-hats must be living on love alone.

In a little place we have now left our mess boasted 4 very amusing Louis-Philippish prints recounting the progress of a young man lost to the billiard-table. 1st scene: He arrives in Paris and begins living it up 2nd He plays billiards cheats and is exposed hence dishonoured 3rd He becomes a thief more precisely a burglar 4th Condemned to penal servitude and waiting on the dock he is pointed out by a father to his children as a bad example.

I adore you my love, my sweet Madelon and I take your mouth.   573

Gui

My dear love,

I have just received two letters from you. We are going to the front line shortly. I write you in great haste. In helmets but don't know quite what we are going to be doing. In any case I leave everything I own to you and this should be treated as my will if need be.

But I hope that for the moment nothing will happen. I adore you. The weather is very fine.

I want you to be brave now and always.

Your Gui

Kostrowitzky 2ⁿᵈ Lᵗ 96ᵗʰ Infantry 6ᵗʰ Cᵒʸ
With the Armed Services 14 March 1916.
Sector 139

1 Military postcard.

15-3-16[1]

My love,

Have not slept all night.

No description possible. It is unimaginable. But the weather is fine. I think of you. We are sleeping completely in the open. This morning saw a sweet little squirrel climbing climbing.

I am tired and gay at once. My mouth is full of sand. I don't know whether we shall get any post tonight. I hope so.

Your Gui

575

GUILLAUME APOLLINAIRE

18 March 1916[1]

1 Military postcard, in barely legible pencil.

My love, I was wounded yesterday when a fragment of a 150 shell went through my helmet and into my head. It turns out the helmet saved my life. I am wonderfully well cared for and it seems it won't be serious. I'll write when I can.

Your Gui

Ambulance 1/55 Sector 34

576

My love, I am not doing badly though I still have that splinter in my head which it was impossible to remove.

I adore you, my love, but am too tired to write.

I had better not.

I adore you.

Gui   577

Amb. 1/55
Sector 34

GUILLAUME APOLLINAIRE

21-3-16

My love,

I am to be operated on this morning.

Here is my new address:

2nd Lt G. de K.—wounded

Hôtel Dieu
Château-Thierry
(Aisne)

My love

For the moment everything is fine and on the basis of X-rays there is no need to repeat the operation performed at the Ambulance at 2 a.m. on the 18th.—I do not know yet whether I shall be removed to the rear, head injuries heal quickly.

I was wounded just above the right temple and I was very lucky.

I am tired.

I adore you my love and take your mouth.

Gui

GUILLAUME APOLLINAIRE

My love, I am doing better and will leave Château-Thierry tomorrow. If I am invalided out no doubt I'll get sick leave otherwise I shall have my leave in the ordinary way in which case I'll come and see you. It tires me to write. I adore you my Madelon.

Gui

580

My love,

Since my temperature had not come down last evening I shan't be evacuated today but probably Tuesday.

I adore you my sweetheart and I can't wait to get your letters I have had none since I was wounded.

Today I am doing better but we shall see what happens this evening because one's temperature goes up in the evening.

I adore you.

Gui.

GUILLAUME APOLLINAIRE

Château-Thierry, 27 March 1916[1]

All well will be evacuated tomorrow Paris will wire address.—I love you.

Gui

[1] Telegram. The originals of this and the telegrams below dated 12, 19 and 26 April, and 2 and 11 May, are now lost; the texts here are those given in the first edition of this book, *Tendre comme le souvenir* (1952).

582

28-3-16

My love,

I am not doing badly, my wound needs to close up, but don't worry any more. I'll be evacuated to Paris today and they will finish my treatment there.

I adore you.

Gui

No more letters from you since the 16th.

583

My love,[1] I am rather tired from the journey and shan't write much. I am very comfortable here at the Val de Grâce in Paris. I adore you hope to see you soon. My wound is doing well it is already almost gone. Head wounds heal fast. I adore you.

1 Postmarked 30-3-16.

Gui

Here is my address:

584

> *2nd Lt G. de K.*
> *1st Wounded*
> *Hôpital du Val de Grâce*
> *Paris*

My love,

I am not supposed to write or read much.

I am at the Hôpital du Val de Grâce (1st Wounded). I am going to wire you the address to reassure you but haven't done so yet because it is likely that I'll be going to the Italian Government Hospital at 41 Quai d'Orsay in a very few days and I'll wire you as soon as I do.

The weather is glorious and I am doing better, but tire easily.

I adore you and kiss you.

Gui

GUILLAUME APOLLINAIRE

6-4-16

My love

I am a great deal better. But it still tires me to write.

Which is why you must not be cross with me my darling.

It was fine here for the 1ˢᵗ few days after my arrival now the weather is foul, nice weather for Zeppelins. My wound is closing up little by little, good progress.

In fact I doubt whether I'll be having a long convalescence. I was wounded at Bois-des-Buttes by Berry-au-Bac, a really vile spot.

It is several days now since I heard from you.

Write soon.

Kiss the whole family for me.

I adore you.

Your Gui

12 April 1916

Paris[1]

1 Telegram.

At Italian Government Hospital 41 Quai d'Orsay parcel received—I love you.

Gui

587

GUILLAUME APOLLINAIRE

My love,

Your letters are reaching me regularly now, but obviously a whole bundle of letters that were supposed to be delivered has been lost.

I am going out just a little, which means I am doing better, but it will be some time still before my wound closes.

I have left the Val de Grâce for the It. Govt. Hospital where we are much more comfortable. Indeed there are only a few of us here. The medical orderly is my friend Serge Jastrebzoff, who is truly big-hearted, and we are cared for by the Ambassador's wife Mme Tittoni, a charming lady rather like your Mama. I don't think I wrote you that I was in Rheims. I was wounded at Bois-des-Buttes to the west of Choléra and Berry-au-Bac.

Your letters are exquisite my darling.

I believe you mentioned relatives of yours in Brittany, at Quimper I think. My friend Max Jacob who is also from Quimper spoke of them to me.

Send me the poems for the book which I think will be published by the *Mercure*.

I'll write you a longer letter tomorrow because I am tired.

I love you.

                                                                Gui

588

19 April 1916

1 Telegram.

Paris[1]

Do not undertake journey now.

Gui

589

26 April 1916

Paris[1]   **1** Telegram.

Send copied poems do not worry but I am not allowed to write yet
shall dictate letter tomorrow. I love you.

Gui

590

1 1 May 1916.

My darling love.[1]

I am not allowed to write at the moment nor go out, I was doing well my wound is almost healed up. I adore your exquisite letters but you must not be alarmed. I have been forbidden to go out because I have had a few incidents such as fainting fits and trouble with my left side, especially the left hand. But they think it will amount to nothing. So don't worry. I'll try to obtain postcards and send you a few words each day but I have no one to hand to get them.

The Italian ambassador's wife who looks after me is an exquisitely kind lady but I dare not ask her to write for me.

I am tired so please don't send me wires, they make me too emotional.

Wait for my news and do not be distressed my sweetheart.

I kiss you.

Gui

591

2 May 1916

Paris[1]   **1** Telegram.

Poems received. Letters to follow.

Gui

592

11 May 1916

1 Telegram.   *Paris*[1]

Operation performed excellent results am as well as possible.

Gui

593

Because I love you[1]

1 May 1916. [See p. 281.]

594

1 Letter discovered recently, written on headed notepaper of the Italian Government Hospital on the Quai d'Orsay (Bibliothèque Historique de la Ville de Paris, Adéma Donation).

11 July 1916[1]

My love,

I go out for walks but not allowed to write it is too tiring.

Gui

595

GUILLAUME APOLLINAIRE

26 August 1916

My dear Madeleine,

Above all do not come, it would be too emotional for me.

Do not write me sad letters either, particularly not, they terrify me.

I am going to write you each week. You do the same, because the arrival of any letter scares me. I cannot see anyone I know. I write neither to my brother nor to Mama and I have not seen Mama since the 15th of April. She is upset by this but I can't help it. I have become very emotional and I expect to settle down only very gradually.

Send me my notes, my artilleryman's log, because there is a good chance I shall be sent back to the Artillery, my gold signet ring which I can now wear again and the ring with the round Boche button.

I am going to sort some things out to pass the time and submit the poems if I can polish them up and if not send them anyway to the *Mercure* with a view to a book.

I am disgusted by Paris—so very little attention is paid here to the war that it throws me into despair.

I feel it will go on for another three years. Very, very distressing.

Don't send me anybody, visits from strangers frighten me. Monsieur Gui is I am sure very nice but it upsets me too much when I don't know the person.

I fancy however that I can work a bit. Going to try. But everything seems to me to have been thrown into doubt by this disaster, so long drawn out. All the good positions have been taken by the shirkers and there is very little on offer for those who went to fight.

I kiss you a thousand times.

Gui

597

16 Sep. 1916

My little Madelon,

I have been doing rather poorly recently on account of the coming of autumn. I get many many dizzy spells and have grown very irritable. I have received the parcel for which I thank you. It does not contain the notes I requested; I did not mean Artillery notes but notes taken while I was an artilleryman. They are the observations of gunners that I took down and would like to make use of. I should also like my map and Dupont's letters which I want to show to his family who are collecting them, for he was killed by 17 shell fragments at Douaumont. I should also like you to send the 2 watercolours by M[arie] L[aurencin], which I want to return since some people back from Spain attribute feelings to her that I cannot accept and so prefer to return them. Also the 2nd copy of *Case d'Armons* that you have and that I would like to present to Mme Tittoni as a token of appreciation, and then the books of mine that you have especially a work on the folklore of the Marne and a directory of the Marne and Aisne departments which I need to write articles. My regiment has reaped hell and honours both. I think there is precious little left of it. But its flag has been decorated. My comrades-in-arms are almost all dead. I dare not even write the Colonel to ask him for details. He was wounded himself so I have heard.

My friend Berthier's brother was killed a few days after being promoted to second lieutenant.

All of which is rather macabre and in view of such ghastly considerations I don't know what else to say.

I kiss you,

Gui

GUILLAUME APOLLINAIRE

I am very tired[1] after the great effort of writing a preface to a catalogue of paintings.[2] The weather is grey and bad. Everything safely received. The Soffici book was not there. But I daresay I forgot to mention it in my letter.

A thousand kisses. I'll write in 2 or 3 days.

Gui

600

1 Postmarked 9-10-16. Picture postcard discovered recently. The illustration, signed Bisca, shows a little boy in infantry uniform standing on the edge of a cliff; the caption reads: '. . . *di qui non passa*'. Military post, stamped at the Italian Government Hospital, where Apollinaire was being treated. (Bibliothèque Historique de la Ville de Paris, Adéma Donation).

2 Catalogue of the Derain show at the Paul Guillaume Gallery (15–21 October 1916).

1 23 November 1916. Letter added in the second pocketbook edition of the present work (Paris: Gallimard Folio, 2006). —Tr.

My dear little Madeleine.[1]

I am tired and there are so few friendships for me in Paris at this moment that it distresses me.

Selfishness reigns. I am much better but still have bad dizzy spells and my left arm is useless.

I am not the man I used to be from any standpoint and were I to follow my instincts I should become a priest or a monk. I am so detached from my own book which has just come out that I cannot even remember if I had a copy sent to you. If not, let me know. I'll have it sent at once.

I kiss you a thousand times.

Gui

601

Four Undated Poems and an Undated Postcard

The four 'secret poems' presented below are grouped without date or classification at the end of the sheaf of correspondence now in the Manuscripts Department of the Bibliothèque Nationale de France. The 'Fourth Secret Poem' was sent with the letter to Madeleine of 17 October 1915 and the 'Seventh' with that of 6 November 1915. Apollinaire clearly made a mistake in his numbering of these poems, however, for there is a second 'Seventh Secret Poem' (see below) among these stray undated poems. At all events it is very likely that all four of the poems that follow were composed between mid-October and early November 1915.

1.

LE CINQUIÈME POÈME SECRET[1]

1 See pp. 282 and 283.

Je te baise sur la bouche goulûment

Nous faisons du bruit avec nos bouches

Notre amour fait de nous un seul être bisexuel

Et nos bouches sont deux battaries qui se répondent

Échevelée et vierge la chevelure épanouie

Tu te prosternes devant moi

Tu adores mon sexe dressé comme la borne du chemin que tu dois suivre

Puis debout cambrée tu m'offres tes seins

Tu offres aussi tes beaux flancs mûrs comme les fruits d'Éden

Tu hurles comme font dans le rut nocturne les chattes en chaleur

Et alors je me précipte sur toi comme une musique soudaine et merveilleuse

Comme les obus quand ils arrivent

Et nous sommes un, bisexués

Fleurs d'une même tige

Nous

À qui il ne faudra qu'un lit et plus tard qu'un seul sépulcre

Et par nous le plaisir désertera le vice pour fleurir en vertus

Tes mamelles sont les alcancies parfumées que lançaient les Maures de Grenade dans leurs fêtes

Et notre hymen est un accouplement éternel

Ta chevelure est la tente où je veux m'abriter

Tes jambes sont l'arc de triomphe où je passerai vainqueur

Le poème de tes jambes j'adore ton

genou et

ta cuisse

ainsi je veux symboliser aujourd'hui ton plaisir, et mon désir mon adorée Madeleine

Je t'aime

Et voici mon cœur que je t'envoie

Phèdre Poppée

Vierge Ange

GUILLAUME APOLLINAIRE

603

Vénus

voici le Bateau de Port-Vendres

je t'aime je t'aime je t'aime je t'aime je t'aime je t'aime

une bougie qui coule tendrement

image imparfaite de l'oiseau parfait

mon cheval qui attend que TU l'enfourches

Roselys

L'oiseau
Bleu comme ton cœur bleu
L'oiseau Madeleine

TOI—MOI

Tes genoux devant moi
Pieds de Madelon
Et de Gui
Mad Gui Gui Mad
Dans leur lit

Et le lys en rose
Madeleine Gui

Le sphinx secret de notre amour

Et voici le cercle parfait de notre amour

Gui aime Madeleine aime
Grâce Union Immortalité Adoration Ivresse Maternité Éternité Mysticité Amour Di-
    vinité Élan Lumière Émerveillement Immensité Nature Élévation Atachment Île
    Môle Espoir

Je t'adore et je prends ta bouche et toutes les roses
En une éternelle caresse close

Gui

THE FIFTH SECRET POEM

I kiss you gluttonously on the mouth

We make noise with our mouths

Our love turns us into a single bisexual being

And our mouths are two batteries exchanging fire

Dishevelled virgin hair spread out

You prostrate yourself before me

You worship my member upright as a milestone on the road you must follow

Then standing arching your back you offer me your breasts

Offer too your beautiful flanks ripe as the fruits of Eden

You shriek as cats in heat do at night-time rut

And I fall upon you like a sudden wonderful burst of music

Like shells when they come in

And we are one, bisexual

Flowers with a single stem

We

Who need but one bed and later but one tomb

And through us pleasure will desert vice and flower in virtues

Your breasts are the perfumed *alcancías* that the Moors of Granada used to
    throw in their fiestas

And our hymen is an eternal coupling

Your hair is the tent where I want to shelter

Your legs are the triumphal arch through which I shall pass victorious

The poem of your legs I adore your

knee and

your thigh

so today I want to symbolize your pleasure, and my desire my beloved
    Madeleine

I love you

And here is my heart that I send you

Phaedra Poppaea

Virgin Angel

Venus
here is the Port-Vendres Boat
I love you I love you I love you I love you I love you I love you

a candle dripping tenderly

imperfect image of the perfect bird

my horse waiting for YOU to straddle him

another imperfect image of your perfect breast

Rose-Lily

The bird
Blue like your blue heart
The bird Madeleine

YOU—ME

Your knees before me
Feet of Madelon
And of Gui
MAD—GUI—GUI—MAD
In their bed

And the lily in the rose
Madeleine—Gui

The secret sphinx of our love

And here is the perfect circle of our love

Gui loves Madeleine loves Gui loves . . .
Grace Union Immortality Adoration Drunkenness Maternity Eternity
    Mysticity Love Divinity Élan Light Awe Immensity Nature Elevation
    Attachment Island Harbour Hope

I adore you and I take your mouth and all the roses
In a never-ending private caress

                                                        Gui

2.

LE 6ᵉ POÈME SECRET[1]

1 See p. 284. This poem and the following one, 'The 7th Secret Poem', are written on a single sheet of paper.

Ton corps est ma faune ô ma belle panthère

Le ouistiti charmant et sauvage ô petit singe noir grimpé le long de ton bras jusqu'à
    l'aisselle

Ils sont deux, chacun dans leur arbre au creux de l'aisselle

Petites bêtes charmantes

    ET CES PAONS DE TA CHEVELURE

Rouant LA NUIT d'amour

    Mais les hirondelles des yeux d'hiver tes cils

    Jolis chevaux dans la plaine tes sourcils

    Cygnes tes beaux yeux aux neiges éternelles

Mais ce nœud de serpents se love à ton nombril

    Colombes de tes seins qui palpitent pour moi

Belles mules attelées à tes hanches tes fesses adorées

Et l'ourson qui dérobe un rayon de miel entre tes cuisses

    Il y a là aussi un coquillage marin

Les trompes d'éléphants sacrés que sont tes jambes

Les oreilles hippocampes roses dans un océan de délices

Ton ventre est une raie qui glisse dans le sable marin de la mer aphrodisiaque

Les plis du coude écureuils sautillant sur des branches de corail

Hermines de tes mains si douces sur mon cœur

J'entends bêler les brebis rouges du bout des seins

    Et la taupe qui dort entre tes fesses

Abeilles de ton nez qui palpite narines

Lèvres lévriers rouges qui courez après le tigre rose de la langue

    La luette cactoès sur le perchoir

Et ce vol de mouettes ô dents sur la Méditerranée parfumée de la bouche

    Le petit renard malin tapi tout en haut de tes lèvres secrètes

    Ô Pieds ô gazelles

Papillons ongles des doigts

    Lucioles ongles des orteils

Yeux oursins des lumières profondes

607

GUILLAUME APOLLINAIRE

Et tes flancs semblables aux lionnes

Cernes aigles planant sur ma royale ardeur

       Chèvres tes doigts

       Porcelets vers les orteils

Ton corps est ma faune ô ma belle panthère

       Et parmi cette faune je suis l'homme

          Et tu es la femme

       Et notre union est Dieu ô mon amour

THE 6ᵗʰ SECRET POEM

Your body is my fauna oh my beautiful panther

The charming wild marmoset oh little black monkey who has climbed all the
    way up your arm to the armpit

There are two, each in its own tree deep in an armpit

Charming little beasts

       AND THOSE PEACOCKS YOUR HAIR

Thrashing THE NIGHT of love

       But oh the swallows of winter eyes your lashes

       Pretty horses on the plain your eyebrows

       Swans your beautiful arms with their eternal snow

But oh the nest of snakes curled up at your navel

       Doves your breasts trembling for me

Splendid she-mules hitched to your hips your adorable buttocks

And the bear cub stealing a trickle of honey from between your thighs

       There is a seashell there too

Those holy elephants' trunks your legs

Your ears pink sea-horses in an ocean of delights

Your belly a ray-fish slipping into the sea sand of an aphrodisiac ocean

The bends of your elbows squirrels hopping on branches of coral

Ermines your hands so soft upon my heart

I hear the bleating of red ewes the tips of your breasts

       And the mole asleep between your buttocks

Bees your quivering nose your nostrils

Lips red greyhounds chasing the pink tiger of your tongue

       Uvula a cockatoo on its perch

And oh your teeth a flight of gulls over the fragrant Mediterranean of your

    mouth

       Cunning little fox crouched high atop your secret lips

       Oh Feet oh gazelles

Butterflies the fingernails

         Fireflies the toenails

Eyes sea-urchins lights of the depths

And your flanks like lionesses

Shadows beneath your eyes eagles gliding over my royal ardour

       Goats your fingers

       Pink piglets the toes

Your body is my fauna oh my beautiful panther

       And amidst that fauna I am the man

       And you are the woman   609

       And our union is God oh my love

GUILLAUME APOLLINAIRE

3.

LE 7ᵉ POÈME SECRET

Nombril de mon amour calice de tubéreuse

Nuit tendre et parfumée où

      Il me semblait que tes hanches s'en allaient devant moi

Comme un vaisseau superbe qui tangue au long des côtes barbaresques

Il me semblait que je te prenais comme l'étalon prend la jument

Nous frémissions l'un l'autre d'amour et du suprême désir

Fesses joufflues comme les têtes ailées des jeunes anges soufflant de toutes leurs forces

    qui ornent la lourde et riche architecture jésuite

Don de la vie furieuse douceur

      Quand tu prononçais des mots sans suite

Tes mamelles bondissaient comme des cavales attelées à un char triomphal

Ô mon char

Et je triomphais

      Exquise apothéose

Où s'unissent les joies de nos destinées

Et maintenant nous conversons avec animation les mains unies et nous regardant

    avec amour

      Nous sommes du même avis et ne nous lassons pas de nous entendre

Nos bouches s'unissent parfois avec des clartés d'extase

Et dans l'ombre nous parlons encore et nous nous caressons

Tandis que de ton nombril fleuri monte la grisante odeur des tubéreuses.

610

THE 7ᵗʰ SECRET POEM

Navel of my love the calyx of a polyanthus

Tender perfumed night when

    It seemed to me your hips ran ahead of me

Like a proud vessel pitching its way by Barbary coasts

It seemed to me I took you as the stallion takes the mare

We shuddered the one and the other from love from supreme desire

Buttocks chubby-cheeked as those winged heads of young angels puffing

    with all their might that adorn the Jesuits' heavy rich architecture

Gift of life wild sweetness
        As you uttered disconnected words
Your breasts leapt like mares hitched to a victory chariot
Oh chariot of mine
And I the victor
        Exquisite apotheosis
Uniting the joys of our two destinies
And now we talk animatedly holding hands and gazing at each other with
    love
        We are of one mind and never tire of being in agreement
Our mouths come together from time to time in ecstatic revelation
And in the dark we go on talking and caressing one another
While from your flowering navel comes the heady scent of polyanthus.

611

GUILLAUME APOLLINAIRE

4.

LE HUITIÈME POÈME SECRET[1]

J'ai rêvé que ta beauté arrivait jusqu'à moi

C'était un jour divin où tu étais précieuse

*Tu m'attends en lisant l'*Astrée

Tu suis d'un œil distrait la touchante histoire du bien disant Sylvandre

De l'inconstant Stylas [Hylas] *et du Parfait Amant Céladon*

Et tu te plais à te reconnaître la bergère au bon renom

Et tu me vois arriver dans un nuage de poussière

Je suis monté sur un cheval trois balsanes et liste en tête

Et suivi d'un laquais

Tu m'attends mais cependant tu es étonnée

    Tu crois au prodige de l'Enchanteur Merlin

        Que j'ai chanté

    Ou du sage Druide Adamas

Ou bien encore d'Armide mais tu souris

Et tu souris tandis que tombe ton éventail

Et tu me dis vous car une Précieuse ne tutoye pas

    'Vous m'allez faire un impromptu

    En souvenir du triomphe que vous allez remporter

    Et pour qu'êtes assuré

        Que nul feu n'est plus vif

    Que celui dont je brûle pour vous

        Et que nul Amant ne fut plus ardemment aimé'

Et je réponds

    'Roselys voilà qui sent sa passionnée?'

Et je déclame un impromptu

    'Deux monts de neige ont su tenter mon escalade

        Les voici tous deux devant moi

    Entre deux monts encor je vais battre l'estrade

        Ils sont tout blancs derrière toi

    Mais d'un mont noir je veux faire enfin la conquête

        Et mon cœur est bien situé

612

1 Undated postcard. Poem written, assuming Apollinaire's numbering is correct, around 8 November 1915; the notepaper's letterhead reads: 'Women's Union of France / Corps / Division / Brigade / Regiment / Squad.'

Je monterai dix fois dans la forêt, au faîte

Où baye bouche d'un muet' . . .

Et nous contraignons nos âmes sous le joug de l'Amour

À Tendre-sur-Inclination

THE EIGHTH SECRET POEM

I dreamt your beauty came right here to me

One glorious day with you in precious mood

You are waiting for me reading *Astrée*

Following with distracted gaze the touching story of the well-spoken
    Sylvandre

Fickle Stylas [Hylas] and perfect lover Céladon

And you are happy to recognize yourself in the shepherdess of good repute

And you see me arrive in a cloud of dust

I am riding a horse with three white-stockinged feet and a list on its nose

Attended by a lackey

You were expecting me yet are astonished

    You believe in the miracle of Merlin the Enchanter

        Of which I have sung

    Or of the wise Druid Adamas

Or again of Armide but you smile

And you smile as your fan drops

And you address me as 'vous' because a *précieuse* does not use the familiar
    form

    'Would you offer me an impromptu

    In memory of the victory that you are going to win

    And to reassure yourself

        That no flame is fiercer

    Than that with which I burn for you

        And that no Lover was ever more ardently loved'

And I reply

    'Roselily are you feeling your passionate side?'

And I declaim impromptu

'Two snowy hills have dared me to climb them
         There they are the two of them before me
Between two other hills too I shall reconnoitre
         They are all white behind you
But it is a black hill that I would conquer at the last
         And my heart is well set to do so
I shall go up ten times through the forest, to the summit
         Where a dumb man's mouth gapes open' . . .
And we shackle our souls to the yoke of Love
         At Tender-upon-Inclination

614

I love you, my Madelon

Gui

[1] Hand-made postcard, probably sent in late December 1915. The picture shows five black cats around a fruit tree and the caption is:

Autour d'un arbre dansons chantons en choeur
Que Noël nous apporte une année de bonheur
Around a tree let's dance and sing together
May Christmas bring us a year of happiness

GUILLAUME APOLLINAIRE